Java Event Handling

Grant Palmer

Prentice Hall PTR
Upper Saddle River, NJ 07458
www.phptr.com

ISBN 0-13-041802-1

Cataloging-in-Publication Data available.

Palmer, Grant.
   Java event handling/Grant Palmer.
     p. cm.
   Includes bibliographical references and index.
   ISBN 0-13-041802-1
     1. Java (Computer program language) I. Title.
   QA76.73.J38 P33 2001
     005.13'3--dc21   2001024942

Editorial/Production Supervision: *Jan H. Schwartz*
Acquisitions Editor: *Karen McLean*
Marketing Manager: *Dan DePasquale*
Manufacturing Manager: *Alexis R. Heydt*
Buyer: *Maura Zaldivar*
Cover Design Director: *Jerry Votta*
Cover Design: *Anthony Gemmellaro*
Art Director: *Gail Cocker-Bogusz*
Series Interior Design: *Meg VanArsdale*
Editorial Assistant: *Rick Winkler*
Compositor: *Laurel Road Publishing Services*

© 2002 Prentice Hall PTR
Prentice-Hall, Inc.
Upper Saddle River, NJ 07458

Prentice Hall books are widely used by corporations and government agencies for training, marketing, and resale.

The publisher offers discounts on this book when ordered in bulk quantities.
For more information, contact Corporate Sales Department, phone: 800-382-3419;
fax: 201-236-7141; e-mail: corpsales@prenhall.com
or write: Prentice Hall PTR, Corporate Sales Department, One Lake Street, Upper Saddle River, NJ 07458

All rights reserved. No part of this book may be reproduced, in any form or by any means, without permission in writing from the publisher.

All product names mentioned herein are the trademarks or registered trademarks of their respective owners.

Printed in the United States of America
10 9 8 7 6 5 4 3 2 1

ISBN 0-13-041802-1

Pearson Education LTD.
Pearson Education Australia PTY, Limited
Pearson Education Singapore, Pte. Ltd.
Pearson Education North Asia Ltd.
Pearson Education Canada, Ltd.
Pearson Educacíon de Mexico, S.A. de C.V.
Pearson Education–Japan
Pearson Education Malaysia Pte. Ltd.
Pearson Education, Upper Saddle River, New Jersey

Contents

Acknowledgments   xiii

Introduction   xv
    A Roadmap for this Book   xv
    A Note on the Code Examples   xvii
    What This Book is Not   xvii

About the Author   xix

Part I The Basics

Chapter 1 An Introduction to Java Events   3
    What Is an Event?   3
    Local Versus Distributed Events   4
    The Evolution of Java Event Handling   5
    The Java Event Model   6
        The Java 1.0 Event Model   6
        The Java 1.1 Event Model   9

Chapter 2 The Java Event Life Cycle 15

Event Life Cycle Methods 17

Basic Event Life Cycle Methods from the Component Class 17

Event Processing Methods 18

Methods to Fire Events 20

Deprecated Methods from the Component Class 20

Event Life Cycle Methods Defined in the Component Subclasses 20

Chapter 3 Event Classes 23

Event and Support Class Hierarchy 23

Low-Level Versus High-Level Event Types 25

A Description of the Event Classes in the J2SE 25

The EventObject Class 25

The AWTEvent Class 26

Low-Level Event Classes Defined in the java.awt.event Package 26

High-Level Event Classes Defined in the java.awt.event Package 27

Special Event Classes Defined in the java.awt.event Package 28

Low-Level Event Classes Defined in the javax.swing.event Package 28

High-Level Event Classes Defined in the javax.swing.event Package 29

High-Level Event Interfaces Defined in the javax.swing.event Package 31

Event Support Classes Defined in the javax.swing.event Package 31

Event and Support Classes Defined in the java.beans Package 31

Event Classes Defined in the javax.swing.text.html Package 32

Event Support Classes Defined in the javax.swing.undo Package 32

Other Event Classes Defined in the J2SE 33

User-Generated Events 33

User-Defined Events 36

Chapter 4 Event Listeners 37

A Brief Review of Interfaces 38

Event Listener Interfaces in the J2SE 38

EventListener Interface 39

Listener Interfaces Contained in the java.awt.event Package   39

Listener Interfaces Contained in the javax.swing.event Package   41

Listener Interfaces Contained in the java.beans Package   42

Other Listener Interfaces Defined in the J2SE   43

Event Listener Objects   43

Creating an Event Listener   44

Method 1: Have a GUI Component Serve as the Event Listener   44

Method 2: Implement the Event Listener as a Separate Class   46

Method 3: Implement the Event Listener as an Inner Class   47

Method 4: Implement the Event Listener as an Anonymous Inner Class   49

Listener Adapter Classes   50

Listener Adapter Classes Contained in the java.awt.event Package   53

Listener Adapter Classes Contained in the javax.swing.event Package   54

User-Defined Event Listener Interfaces   54

Connecting an Event Source to an Event Listener   55

Disconnecting an Event Source from an Event Listener   56

The getListeners() Method   59

Event Listener Manager Classes   60

AWTEventMulticaster Class   60

EventListenerList Class   61

CHAPTER 5 EVENT HANDLING ODDS AND ENDS   63

Determining the Event Source   63

Consuming Events   67

Event Consumption Methods   68

The Event Queue   70

EventQueue Class   71

The Event-Dispatching Thread   75

Running Code in the Event-Dispatching Thread   75

Part II A Java Event Reference

Chapter 6 Event Classes and Interfaces   79

ActionEvent Class   80

ActiveEvent Interface   86

AdjustmentEvent Class   92

AncestorEvent Class   98

AWTEvent Class   103

CaretEvent Class   106

ChangeEvent Class   110

ComponentEvent Class   114

ContainerEvent Class   118

DocumentEvent Interface   124

DocumentEvent.ElementChange Interface   127

DocumentEvent.EventType Class   128

EventObject Class   129

FocusEvent Class   131

HierarchyEvent Class   136

HTMLFrameHyperlinkEvent Class   142

HyperlinkEvent Class   149

HyperlinkEvent.EventType Class   155

InputEvent Class   156

InputMethodEvent Class   159

InternalFrameEvent Class   163

InvocationEvent Class   168

ItemEvent Class   174

KeyEvent Class   179

ListDataEvent Class   186

ListSelectionEvent Class   192

MenuDragMouseEvent Class   196

MenuEvent Class   202

MenuKeyEvent Class   205

MouseEvent Class   212

PaintEvent Class   218

PopupMenuEvent Class   219

PropertyChangeEvent Class   223

TableColumnModelEvent Class   230

TableModelEvent Class   234

TextEvent Class   239

TreeExpansionEvent Class   243

TreeModelEvent Class   248

TreeSelectionEvent Class   253

UndoableEditEvent Class   258

WindowEvent Class   263

Other Event Classes in the J2SE   267

Chapter 7 Event Support Classes   269

PropertyChangeSupport Class   270

SwingPropertyChangeSupport Class   272

UndoableEditSupport Class   276

VetoableChangeSupport Class   284

Chapter 8 Event Listener Interfaces   295

ActionListener Interface   296

AdjustmentListener Interface   298

AncestorListener Interface   299

AWTEventListener Interface   301

CaretListener Interface 304

CellEditorListener Interface 306

ChangeListener Interface 310

ComponentListener Interface 312

ContainerListener Interface 316

DocumentListener Interface 318

EventListener Interface 320

FocusListener Interface 320

HierarchyBoundsListener Interface 322

HierarchyListener Interface 326

HyperlinkListener Interface 331

InputMethodListener Interface 332

InternalFrameListener Interface 334

ItemListener Interface 337

KeyListener Interface 339

ListDataListener Interface 342

ListSelectionListener Interface 344

MenuDragMouseListener Interface 346

MenuKeyListener Interface 348

MenuListener Interface 349

MouseInputListener Interface 351

MouseListener Interface 356

MouseMotionListener Interface 360

PopupMenuListener Interface 363

PropertyChangeListener Interface 365

TableColumnModelListener Interface 367

TableModelListener Interface 369

TextListener Interface 371

TreeExpansionListener Interface   372

TreeModelListener Interface   376

TreeSelectionListener Interface   378

TreeWillExpandListener Interface   380

UndoableEditListener Interface   382

VetoableChangeListener Interface   383

WindowListener Interface   385

Other Listener Interfaces in the J2SE   389

Chapter 9 Listener Adapter Classes   391

ComponentAdapter Class   391

ContainerAdapter Class   393

FocusAdapter Class   397

HierarchyBoundsAdapter Class   400

InternalFrameAdapter Class   402

KeyAdapter Class   407

MouseAdapter Class   409

MouseInputAdapter Class   411

MouseMotionAdapter Class   415

WindowAdapter Class   417

Chapter 10 Event Life Cycle Methods   421

AbstractAction Class Methods   422

AbstractButton Class Methods   422

AbstractCellEditor Class Methods   423

AbstractListModel Class Methods   423

Button Class Methods   423

Checkbox Class Methods   424

CheckboxMenuItem Class Methods   424

Choice Class Methods   425

Component Class Methods   425

Container Class Methods   430

DefaultBoundedRangeModel Class Methods   430

DefaultButtonModel Class Methods   431

DefaultListCellRenderer Class Methods   431

DefaultListSelectionModel Class Methods   432

DefaultSingleSelectionModel Class Methods   432

JApplet Class Methods   433

JComboBox Class Methods   433

JComponent Class Methods   433

JDialog Class Methods   435

JEditorPane Class Methods   436

JFrame Class Methods   436

JInternalFrame Class Methods   437

JList Class Methods   437

JMenu Class Methods   437

JMenuBar Class Methods   438

JMenuItem Class Methods   438

JPopupMenu Class Methods   440

JProgressBar Class Methods   441

JScrollBar Class Methods   441

JSlider Class Methods   441

JTabbedPane Class Methods   441

JTextArea Class Methods   442

JTextField Class Methods   442

JTree Class Methods 442

JViewport Class Methods 443

List Class Methods 443

MenuComponent Class Methods 444

MenuItem Class Methods 444

PropertyChangeSupport Class Methods 445

Scrollbar Class Methods 446

SwingPropertyChangeSupport Class Methods 446

TextComponent Class Methods 446

TextField Class Methods 447

Timer Class Methods 447

VetoableChangeSupport Class Methods 447

Window Class Methods 448

Part III Advanced Topics

Chapter 11 Event Listener Manager Classes 451

AWTEventMulticaster Class 451

EventListenerList Class 461

Chapter 12 User-Defined Event Classes and Event Listeners 471

Creating a User-Defined EventListener 472

Creating a User-Defined Event Class 473

Defining a Component that Supports a User-Defined Event 475

Putting it All Together 477

Chapter 13 Putting It All Together 483
Stagnation Point Heating Rate Program 483

A Java Document Editor 497

Chapter 14 Distributed Events 513
Distributed Event Model 514

Remote Event Classes 516

    RemoteEvent Class 516

    RemoteDiscoveryEvent Class 518

    RenewalFailureEvent Class 521

    ServiceEvent Class 523

Remote Event Listener Interfaces 526

    Remote Interface 526

    RemoteEventListener Interface 527

Remote Event Listener Support Classes 528

    EventRegistration Class 528

Appendix Java GUI Components and the Events They Generate 541

Index 577

Acknowledgments

There is a conventional wisdom that says it is very difficult to get published. If this is true, then I was very fortunate to have contacted Mark Taub, the senior editor at Prentice Hall. You would expect a person in such a high position at such a big company to be unapproachable, but I found the complete opposite to be true. Mark was very courteous and receptive towards an idea for a Java book from a relatively unknown author such as myself. I am grateful for the chance that Mark gave me to bring my idea for a Java event handling book to fruition.

I would like to thank Karen McLean, the senior managing editor at Pearson PTG Interactive. Karen was always there to guide me through the process of writing this book. Karen is a highly effective manager. She kept this project running smoothly yet, at the same time, gave me the creative control to fashion the book as I had envisioned it. I would also like to acknowledge Jan Schwartz and Carol Lallier, members of the production team at Prentice Hall PTR, for correcting my sometimes fractured syntax, catching small, but important typos that everyone else had missed, and generally polishing the rough edges off of the book.

This would not be the book that it is without the expert technical help of Marc Loy and W. Keith Edwards. Marc was the main technical reviewer for the book. His excellent suggestions for improvement and keen eye for errors drastically improved the quality of this book. He is also rare among technical reviewers in that he didn't mind (or didn't seem to mind) my contacting him directly with questions about the material covered in the book. Keith was similarly gracious when it came to helping me with the remote event handling section of the book. Keith was kind enough to let me use a remote event handling example from the second edition of his excellent book *Core Jini*.

Finally, I would like to acknowledge the sacrifices my family made for this book. My sons, Jackson and Zachary, had to deal with my shooshing them out of my office for the four months it took me to write the book. My wife Lisa had to put up with a tired and cranky husband during that time as well. The support she gives me in my writing endeavors is a credit to her and to the love we have for each other.

INTRODUCTION

Welcome to the interesting world of Java events. What is an event? Events are Java's messengers, traveling from an event source to a final destination, carrying information about something that has taken place. Events are what allow graphical user interfaces (GUIs) to do what they are supposed to do. Events are central to the concept of implementing bound and constrained properties in a Java Bean. Events are also important in distributed applications such as those using Jini or JavaSpaces technologies.

Java event handling is an important subject but, unfortunately, most Java reference books don't do a good job of covering it. There is so much in the wide world of Java to write about that general reference books tend to devote only a few dozen pages to events and event handling. The material also tends to be interspersed throughout the book. This book, however, is the complete reference on Java event handling. It is the only book on the market that focuses entirely on Java event handling. It is a definitive work on the subject, including not only a complete technical reference on the event classes and interfaces but also a detailed look at the Java event model itself.

A ROADMAP FOR THIS BOOK

The book is divided into three parts. Part 1 goes over the basics of Java event handling. It starts with a definition of what an event is and what it does. A history and description of the Java event model is presented. The Java event life cycle is described, telling what happens to an event from the time it is generated to when it reaches its final destination. The concept of an event listener is introduced. Finally, Part 1 covers some useful topics, such as the event queue and the event dispatching thread, that are basic to Java event handling.

Part 2 of the book is a complete technical reference for the event classes and interfaces contained in the Java Platform 2 Standard Edition (J2SE), from ActionEvent to WindowListener and everything in between. The information provided for each class or interface includes the syntax, the package it belongs to, the class or interface hierarchy, when it was introduced to the Java API, and the constructors, fields, and methods the class or interface defines. Each section is completely self-contained to provide "one-stop-shopping" for all information about a given class or interface, including a description of the fields and methods inherited from other classes or interfaces. Part 2 should answer all of your questions about what a class or interface can do and how to use it.

Parts 1 and 2 of this book will give you a solid understanding of Java event handling. The elements covered in Parts 1 and 2 are the things you will use in most of your programming work. In Part 3, we delve into some more advanced topics. These advanced topics are things you may not use very often, but they can be very powerful (and fun) to work with and can be used to customize the event handling aspects of a given code. The event listener manager classes are detailed. These classes are normally used by the system but can be accessed by the programmer to create new event classes and/or event-generating objects. The process for creating user-defined event classes and interfaces is described.

Part 3 also demonstrates how we can take everything we have learned and develop a couple of "real-world" GUI applications. We will have to make programming design decisions on how to implement the event handling sections of our code. The final section of Part 3 discusses the concept of a distributed event. Up to this point, the book has dealt with local events. These are events generated by an application running on a single machine using a single Java Virtual Machine (JVM). Distributed or Web-based applications might run on multiple platforms using multiple JVMs. Java provides a framework for the generation, transmission, and processing of events generated by a remote source.

The book also includes a handy appendix that lists the event-generating objects provided by the J2SE API. The list details the events each object can generate and how it generates them. The list not only includes all of the GUI components and containers, but also details the event-generating capabilities of the various models, documents, and other event-generating objects. For instance, if you want to know if a JTextField object can generate a TextEvent, the appendix will tell you.

A Note on the Code Examples

Like any programming language, the best way to learn Java is by example, and this book supplies a lot of them. They are written as complete standalone applications. There are no code fragment examples, as these can be misleading and not show the whole picture. Most of the examples, particularly the ones in Parts 1 and 2 of the book, are intentionally simple, straightforward programs. They are easy to follow and are intended to demonstrate one or two key elements of an aspect of Java event handling without a lot of extra code to clutter things up.

The examples are all compiled and run in a similar fashion. For instance, to create the byte code for the SimpleExample.java, program you would type

```
javac SimpleExample.java
```

To run the example, you would then type

```
java SimpleExample
```

You are encouraged to try the examples out. Most of them are short enough so that you can type them in yourself if you want to, or you can access the examples by copying them from the CD-ROM included with this book.

You are also encouraged to play around with the examples. Change some things and see what happens. Just as you can't learn how to swim without getting your feet wet, you can't really gain an understanding of Java event handling, or Java in general for that matter, without writing or modifying some code.

With the exception of the remote event example in Part 3, all of the examples in this book use the J2SE API. You should have Java Development Kit (JDK) version 1.3, as many of the examples use classes and methods that were introduced in version 1.3. The Java Software Development Kit, which includes everything you will need for most of the examples, can be downloaded from the Sun Web site at *http://java.sun.com*. The remote event handling example also requires that you install Jini on your system. For more details on this, see Part 3 of this book.

What This Book is Not

Now that we have spoken about what the book is, let's talk briefly about what it is not. This book is not a beginning tutorial on Java and does assume some (although not a lot) of Java experience. You should be familiar with basic object-oriented principles, such as classes, inheritance, constructors, and so on. You should know about the different types of access, what they mean, and how to use them. You should know what the "this" keyword means and about inner and anonymous inner classes. Beyond this, it is probably useful to have at least an elementary understanding of the classes and interfaces contained in the core Java packages.

This book is also not a reference on AWT or Swing GUI components. These components are used in every example, but they are pretty much presented and used without explanation. Most of the examples use the GUI components in a simple, straightforward manner. If you have some prior experience with the GUI component classes, it should be clear what is being done and why. If anything looks confusing to you, consult a good Swing or AWT reference for illumination.

About the Author

Grant Palmer has been a scientific programmer at the NASA Ames Research Center since 1985. In the mid-1990s, it became clear to him that his programming skills were becoming seriously outdated. He was doing most of his work in FORTRAN while the world around him was moving more and more to object-oriented programming languages such as C++ and a new language called Java. Grant took his first forays into the Java world in the winter of 1996 and has been hooked ever since. What he likes most about Java is its versatility. He can write a GUI front-end to a scientific program and turn the whole thing into a Web-based application, using one programming language.

Grant lives in Chandler, Arizona, with his wife Lisa and two boys, Jackson and Zachary. When he's not taking care of the boys, he enjoys swimming and indulging in the occasional futile attempt at playing golf.

PART I

THE BASICS

This section of the book describes some fundamental aspects about Java events. It is written for beginning programmers who are unfamiliar with the concept of events and event handling. That said, there are sections in Part I that will benefit more experienced programmers. The sections on user-generated events, the various ways to implement an event listener, and the event queue are examples that come to mind.

This section, and the book as a whole, doesn't assume the reader knows anything about Java events or event handling, but does assume a certain familiarity with the basics of Java programming. The reader should know about basic class structure, inheritance, constructors, importing packages, declaring variables, overriding class methods, and so on. Other concepts commonly used in the examples are the "this" keyword, inner classes, and the implementation of interface methods within a class.

This book is also not intended to be an AWT or Swing reference. The examples provided in this book are generally simple, stand-alone programs that show the basics of every Java event type, every listener, and the various support and life cycle methods. The event handling processes are well commented, but the GUI aspects of each example, the components and containers that make up the interface, are usually presented without explanation. If anything seems unfamiliar or odd about the way the examples are constructed or about how the GUI components are used, consult a good AWT or Swing reference for (hopefully) an explanation of what is going on.

Since actually writing and running Java code is the best way to learn the language and to get a feel for how things work, the reader is encouraged to either type in or download the examples and to try them out on your own machine. Feel free to experiment with the examples by changing things around to see what happens. One thing about Java event handling is that there are usually several ways to do things. By playing around with the examples, you can discover what your preferences are and what works best for you and your programs.

One final note on the examples is that you will notice as you go through the book that some of the examples use AWT GUI components and some use Swing GUI components. Most of the examples use Swing components because they are more powerful and have more potential for creating effective applications than their AWT counterparts. Many of the events contained in the javax.swing.event package are only generated by Swing components. Sometimes however, it is appropriate to use the AWT classes. For instance, the example in the "MouseEvent Class" section in Chapter 6, "Event Classes and Interfaces," uses a Canvas object to implement a simple doodle pad. Since Canvas is an AWT component and since it is bad programming practice to mix and match AWT and Swing components, that whole example is done using AWT components. Similarly, the discussion of event consumption later in Part I is really only relevant for events generated by AWT components, so the example in that section also uses that type of component.

Now that the preliminaries are over, let's talk about Java events.

An Introduction to Java Events

In this chapter, we will go over the most basic elements of Java event handling, starting with a description of what a Java event is and what an event does. Next we will discuss the two basic types of events, local and distributed events. A brief history of Java event handling is presented along with the two basic local event models. The final element of this chapter is a simple example that demonstrates the key elements of Java event handling.

What Is an Event?

Any book on Java event handling should first address the basic question, What is an event? A formal definition of an event is that it is an object that represents a change in the abstract state of another object. An event is itself an abstract occurrence. It is not directly observable outside of the object that generated the event.

But what does this definition really mean? Let's look at the example of a graphical user interface (GUI) with various buttons, menus, combo boxes, and so on. When you interact with the GUI, you expect that something will happen. For instance, if a Quit menu item is selected, the expected outcome of that action is that the application will terminate. A mechanism must exist that tells the program when the Quit menu item has been selected. In Java, this mechanism is an event. When the Quit menu item is selected, an event is generated and sent to another piece of code called an *event listener*. The event listener contains code to process the event. In the case of a Quit menu item, the listener might contain the `System.exit(0)` command.

Almost every activity that is performed around a GUI will generate an event. Moving the mouse cursor across an empty frame will generate mouse events. Resizing a window will generate a container event. When a user navigates his or her way around a typical program, a veritable torrent of events will be generated. Fortunately, the Java event model lets you pick and choose which events you will process.

Events are not restricted to GUI components. The Java Beans component framework provides for events that are generated when a property associated with the component changes. The property might be the value of a primitive variable, a change in an object associated with Bean, or anything that is declared as an instance variable of the class or of any field that is inherited from a superclass. The ability to generate events even goes beyond GUI components and Java Beans. The Java application program interface (API) provides support and utility classes that make it possible to extend an event-generating capability to almost any user-defined class.

One way of thinking about events is that they are Java's messengers. They carry information from the source of the event, the GUI component or other object that was interacted with, to any interested event listeners. The information an event carries always includes a reference to the source of the event and may contain additional information to indicate the exact nature of the event.

An event is an object with similar characteristics to any other object contained in the Java API. It has a constructor, fields, and class methods. An event object can be passed as a parameter to a method. One difference from other objects is that events are usually generated automatically by the system and are passed automatically to the appropriate event handler. Much of the nuts and bolts of the event process are hidden from the programmer. However, it is possible to create a user-defined event to suit the special needs of a particular application.

LOCAL VERSUS DISTRIBUTED EVENTS

A local event is one generated by an application running on a single platform using a single Java Virtual Machine (JVM). The local event model is used by most GUI components in the Java API. It is also part of the Java Beans framework, meaning that classes that are not GUI components can also generate events. The GUI components will usually generate events automatically when certain interactions take place. The Java API provides the event listener interfaces and the tools needed to register event listeners to the components.

A distributed event is one that is generated from a remote source. The application that generates the event may be running on a different platform or using a different JVM, or both. Distributed events occur in network- or Web-based applications using the Jini or JavaSpaces technologies. The primary emphasis of this book is on local events, but a brief description of the distributed event model and its classes and interfaces is provided in Part III.

The Evolution of Java Event Handling

It is useful at this time to give a brief summary of the evolution of the Java programming language, focusing on the way events were implemented and handled.

Java 1.0 (1995). In development for years, first as a platform-independent language for consumer electronic devices and then as a way to create Internet applications, Java burst onto the public scene in 1995. It borrowed elements from both C and C++, and yet offered the promise of capabilities far beyond those languages. Once the developers began to work out how Java could be used to create Internet applications, they realized the need for a Java event model. The Java 1.0.2 event model provided a basic event handling functionality. This was a *containment* model. All event types were encapsulated in a single class, the Event class. All event objects were processed by a single method, `handleEvent()`, which was defined in the Component class. Because of this, only classes that were subclasses of Component could serve as event handlers. The event handling was passed up the component hierarchy. If the target component was not able to completely process the event, the event was passed up to the target component's container.

Java 1.1 (1997). The initial public release of Java was a revolution in programming, but the deficiencies and idiosyncrasies of Java 1.0.2 soon became apparent. The Java development team began working on Java 1.1 to fix some of its shortcomings and add some important additional functionality. Java 1.1 represented a second revolution in the Java language. With Java 1.1, the naming convention for methods began to become standardized with the "get-set-is" nomenclature. Important new features such as Remote Method Invocation (RMI), the Java Native Interface (JNI), and Java Database Connectivity

(JDBC) were added, as was the concept of a Java Bean. Most importantly, for the purposes of this book, the Java event model, the basic framework for how events are handled in the Java language, was completely reworked, moving from the Java 1.0.2 model to a delegation event model in which an event source generates the event and then "delegates" the handling of the event to another piece of code.

J2SE v1.2 (1999). The expression "J2SE v1.2" is shorthand for Java 2 Platform Standard Edition version 1.2. The change from Java 1.1 to J2SE v1.2 was more evolutionary than revolutionary. One of the big changes was the addition of the Swing packages. These were more powerful, more customizable GUI components and their associated support classes. The Java 1.1 event model was still the standard event handling model and remained more or less intact. The javax.swing.event package was introduced containing new event classes and event listener interfaces that provided the additional event handling capability required by the Swing GUI components.

J2SE v1.3 (2000). The J2SE version 1.3 was a refinement of the version 1.2 release. The emphasis was on improving the performance of the Java language. Some additional event classes and interfaces were added to the event packages, but the overall event model remained pretty much the same. Version 1.3 saw the introduction of the Robot class, which simulated mouse and keyboard events and is used for automated testing, self-running demos, and other applications that require control of the mouse and keyboard.

THE JAVA EVENT MODEL

The Java event model is really just a fancy name to describe the framework Java uses to generate and process events. The Java event model went through a revolutionary change between Java 1.0.2 and Java 1.1. This occurred in 1997. It is certainly hoped that by the time this book is published, developers are no longer using the Java 1.0.2 event model for new development. It is more likely that there might still be some legacy code that uses the 1.0.2 event model. For this reason and to give a complete history of Java event handling, both event models are described in the following sections.

The Java 1.0 Event Model

As its name implies, the Java 1.0 event model provided the methodology for processing events up to Java 1.0.2. The Java 1.1 event model with the release of Java 1.1 superseded this event model in 1997. Under the most recent Java release, Java 2 Platform Standard Edition version 1.3, most of the Java 1.0 event model has been deprecated. As such, the Java 1.0 event model should not be used for new code. A description of the Java 1.0 event model is provided here solely to give some historical context for the development of the Java event handling methodology.

Under the Java 1.0 event model, every type of event is encapsulated in a single class, the Event class, which is contained in the java.awt package. An Event object contains information about the type of event it represents, when the event was generated, where the event occurred, and what keys were pressed when the event was generated. A system-generated Event object will have one of the following event IDs:

public static int ACTION_EVENT
public static int KEY_ACTION
public static int KEY_ACTION_RELEASE
public static int KEY_PRESS
public static int KEY_RELEASE
public static int LIST_DESELECT
public static int LIST_SELECT
public static int MOUSE_DOWN
public static int MOUSE_DRAG
public static int MOUSE_ENTER
public static int MOUSE_EXIT
public static int MOUSE_MOVE
public static int MOUSE_UP
public static int SCROLL_ABSOLUTE
public static int SCROLL_BEGIN
public static int SCROLL_END
public static int SCROLL_LINE_DOWN
public static int SCROLL_LINE_UP
public static int SCROLL_LOCK
public static int SCROLL_PAGE_DOWN

public static int `SCROLL_PAGE_UP`
public static int `WINDOW_DEICONIFY`
public static int `WINDOW_DESTROY`
public static int `WINDOW_ICONIFY`
public static int `WINDOW_MOVED`

The event handling process under the Java 1.0 event model is performed by the following methods. The `deliverEvent()` method is used to determine the target for the event. The target is the component or container that is intended to process the event. This process begins at the outermost GUI layer and works inward. For instance, consider a frame that contains three buttons. When the user clicks one of the three buttons, the frame will call its `deliverEvent()` method. This method will match the location of the cursor when the mouse was pressed to the bounding areas of the Button objects. If a match is found, the corresponding button will call its `deliverEvent()` method. This operation is done automatically by the system. The user does not need to write any code to affect this process.

Once a target component has been identified, the appropriate type of event is sent to that component's `postEvent()` method. This method in turn sends the event to the `handleEvent()` method and waits for that method's return value. A return value of true indicates that the event has been completely processed. A return value of false will cause the `postEvent()` method to contact the target's container in hopes of completing the event handling.

The `handleEvent()` method calls an event handler method based on the type of event it is processing. For example, if an action event is sent to the `handleEvent()` method, the method will in turn call the `action()` method. The event handler method will return a value of true if the event was completely processed or false if it was not. The following is a list of event handler methods provided under the Java 1.0 event model. These methods are defined in the Component class.

public boolean `action(Event evt, Object obj)`
public boolean `gotFocus(Event evt, Object obj)`
public boolean `keyDown(Event evt, int key)`
public boolean `keyUp(Event evt, int key)`

```
public boolean lostFocus(Event evt, Object obj)
public boolean mouseDown(Event evt, int x, int y)
public boolean mouseDrag(Event evt, int x, int y)
public boolean mouseEnter(Event evt, int x, int y)
public boolean mouseExit(Event evt, int x, int y)
public boolean mouseMove(Event evt, int x, int y)
public boolean mouseUp(Event evt, int x, int y)
```

The system provides default implementations of the event handling methods. The default implementations do nothing and return the value false. If one or more of the methods is intended for use, it is overridden to provide the desired event-processing methodology. One drawback of the Java 1.0 event model is that because the event handler methods are defined in the Component class, only Component subclasses can override these methods. What this means is that the event handling must be performed by the GUI components themselves. It is very difficult under the Java 1.0 event model to decouple the event handling code from the GUI itself.

The Java 1.1 Event Model

Deficiencies of the Java 1.0 event model became readily apparent. It wasn't very efficient to have the system search for the target component every time an event was generated. Another problem was because the event handler methods were defined in the Component class, only subclasses of the Component class could implement event handling. Thus the event handling code was explicitly tied to the GUI code. This created inheritance problems. Instead of using one Button class for all Button objects, an application might have to create a Button subclass that would quit when pressed, another Button subclass that would open a file when pressed, and so on.

One of the significant changes from Java 1.0 to 1.1 was the way that events were handled. The Java 1.1 event model employs a concept called *delegation* and cleans up many of the deficiencies of the Java 1.0 event model. An event source generates the event and then "delegates" the event handling process to another piece of code. The event handling object can be completely separate from the GUI components themselves. Under this model, any class can serve as the event handler.

Instead of all events encapsulated in a single class, the Java 1.1 event model contains individual event classes encapsulating a particular type of event. For instance, the hierarchy for the events contained in the java.awt.event package is shown in Figure 1.1.

The EventObject and AWTEvent classes provide methods common to the individual event classes. The individual event classes define methods useful to that particular class. For instance, the KeyEvent class defines the

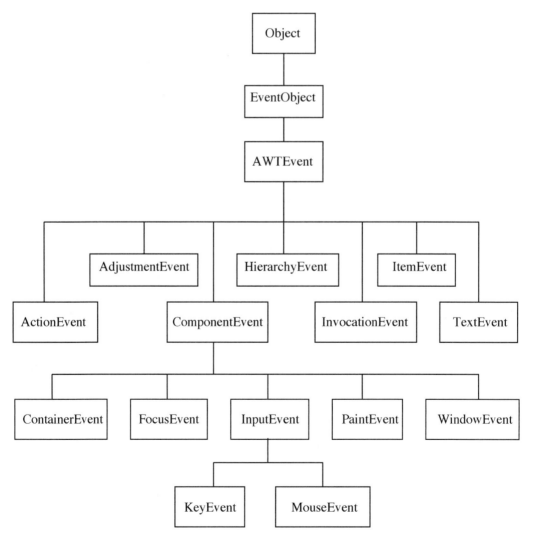

FIGURE 1.1 AWTEvent class hierarchy.

`getKeyChar()` method that returns the keyboard character that was pressed to generate the event.

Instead of the cumbersome `dispatchEvent()`-`postEvent()`-`handleEvent()` way of handling events, the Java 1.1 event model performs event handling using listener classes. Every event class has an associated listener interface that contains methods used to process the event. A listener class is a class that implements one or more listener interfaces and usually overrides one or more of the event handler methods defined in the interface. Any class can implement the listener interface. The interface can also be implemented as an anonymous class.

A GUI component sends the events it generates only to registered listener objects. Listeners that are not registered with the event source do not receive the event. Every object that can generate events maintains a list of listeners that are registered to receive events generated by the object. The object registers a listener by adding it to its listener list. This is done using one of the object's add-Listener methods, passing the method a reference to the Listener object as an argument. An object deregisters or disconnects from an event listener by removing the listener from its listener list. This is accomplished by calling one of the object's remove-Listener methods. The process of registering and disconnecting event listeners is explained in more detail in Chapter 4, "Event Listeners."

Under the Java 1.0 event model, the dispatching and processing of events was a linear process. An event was sent to a single target component. If the event handler method indicated that the event had not been completely processed, it could be sent to another component, but the system couldn't broadcast an event to multiple event listeners simultaneously. Under the Java 1.1 event model, events can be sent to any number of event handler objects. Any listener class that is registered with the source component will receive the event.

The Java 1.1 event model also allows the developer to examine the contents of the event queue by using the methods defined in the EventQueue class. It is also possible to execute a block of code from the event queue, using the event-dispatching thread. These topics will be explained in more detail in Chapter 5, "Event Handling Odds and Ends."

A SIMPLE EXAMPLE

Before examining further details of the Java 1.1 event model, let us look at a simple example that contains the basic elements of Java 1.1 event handling. The SimpleExample class represents a frame containing a single Button component. When the button is pressed, the system will generate an ActionEvent object corresponding to this action. It is intended to have the application terminate when this happens. Example 1.1 is the listing of the SimpleExample class.

EXAMPLE 1.1 THE SIMPLEEXAMPLE CLASS

```java
import java.awt.*;
import java.awt.event.ActionEvent;
import java.awt.event.ActionListener;

public class SimpleExample extends Frame implements ActionListener
{
   Button b;

   public SimpleExample()
   {
/*  A Button is created and registers an ActionListener. */

      b = new Button("quit");
      b.addActionListener(this);

      setLayout(new FlowLayout());
      add(b);

      setBounds(100, 100, 200, 200);
      setVisible(true);
   }

/* The SimpleExample class serves as the ActionListener and   */
/* provides an implementation of the actionPerformed()        */
/* method.  When the Button is pressed, an ActionEvent is     */
/* generated and sent to the actionPerformed() method which   */
/* calls the System.exit() method terminating the program.    */

   public void actionPerformed(ActionEvent ae)
   {
      System.exit(0);
   }

   public static void main(String args[])
   {
      SimpleExample se = new SimpleExample();
   }
}
```

Try out this example and notice that the program does indeed terminate when the button is pressed. This is accomplished using an ActionEvent that is sent to the `actionPerformed()` method of a registered ActionListener. Now let's look at the individual event processing aspects of this program.

Importing the event class and interface: The SimpleExample class needs access to the ActionEvent class and the ActionListener interface. These are both contained in the java.awt.event package. Access to these elements is achieved by the following two statements:

```
import java.awt.event.ActionEvent;
import java.awt.event.ActionListener;
```

As you probably know, import statements are placed at the top of the Java code. Often when dealing with a larger number of events and interfaces, it is more convenient to import the entire java.awt.event package. This is accomplished with the following syntax:

```
import java.awt.event.*;
```

Creating an ActionListener to process the event: An ActionEvent object is generated automatically by the system whenever the button is pressed. The event will go unnoticed, however, unless an ActionListener object is created and set up to be notified when the event occurs. An ActionListener object is any class that implements the ActionListener interface. Under the Java 1.1 event model, any class can serve as an ActionListener. In this case, the SimpleExample class itself is designated as the ActionListener using the following syntax:

```
public class SimpleExample extends Frame implements ActionListener
```

Registering an ActionListener with the Button: For an ActionListener to be notified when a particular component generates an event, the ActionListener must be added to the listener list maintained by the button. This is accomplished by having the button invoke the `addActionListener()` method, using the following syntax:

```
b.addActionListener(this);
```

The argument passed to the `addActionListener()` method is a reference to the ActionListener that the button is adding to its listener list. The `this` keyword indicates that the ActionListener object corresponds to the SimpleExample class itself.

Implementing the methods declared in the ActionListener interface: When a class implements the ActionListener interface, it must provide implementation of the methods declared in that interface. The ActionListener interface declares one method, `actionPerformed()`. Because the SimpleExample class implements the ActionListener interface, an implementation of the `actionPerformed()` method is included in the SimpleExample class. Remember that we wanted the application to terminate when the Quit button was pressed. The `actionPerformed()` method calls the static method `exit()` from the System class, which causes the program to terminate.

```
public void actionPerformed(ActionEvent ae)
{
   System.exit(0);
}
```

These four steps are all that is needed to create a functioning Quit button. The process described in this example, importing the event classes and interfaces, creating a Listener, registering the Listener, and implementing the methods declared in the Listener interface, is the basic process for handling events under the Java 1.1 event model. Now that we have looked at a simple example, let us look in more detail at some of the elements of the Java 1.1 event model.

THE JAVA EVENT LIFE CYCLE

Like a little minnow in the ocean, a Java event is born, travels about, and finally is consumed. All kidding aside, Figure 2.1 shows a schematic of the life cycle of a Java event. The event is initially created by an event source. The event source can be a GUI component, a Java Bean, or any other object that has an event-generating capability. In the case of a GUI component, the event source will either be a component peer (for Abstract Window Toolkit [AWT] GUI components) or the component itself (for Swing components).

After the event is generated, it is placed inside the system event queue. It is now under the control of the event dispatch thread. The event waits in the event queue until it is its "turn." The event is then taken off of the event queue and passed to the dispatchEvent() method of the component that generated it. The dispatchEvent() method calls the processEvent() method and passes the processEvent() method a reference to the event. At this point, the system checks to see if there is anywhere to send the event. If there are no registered listeners for this event type, or if no components have been enabled to receive this event type, the event is discarded.

If there is someplace to send the event, the processEvent() method calls an event-specific process method. An example of an event-specific process method would be the processMouseEvent() method defined in the Component class. The event-specific process method sends the method to all registered event listeners of the event type and to any components that have been enabled to receive the event.

Figure 2.1 shows the life cycle for events that are subclasses of the AWTEvent class. The dispatchEvent() and processEvent() methods take an AWTEvent object as an argument. However, many of the event classes contained in the javax.swing.event package are not subclasses of AWTEvent but instead inherit directly from the EventObject class. What is the life cycle process for these events? The objects that generate these events will also define a fireEvent() method that will send the event to any listeners

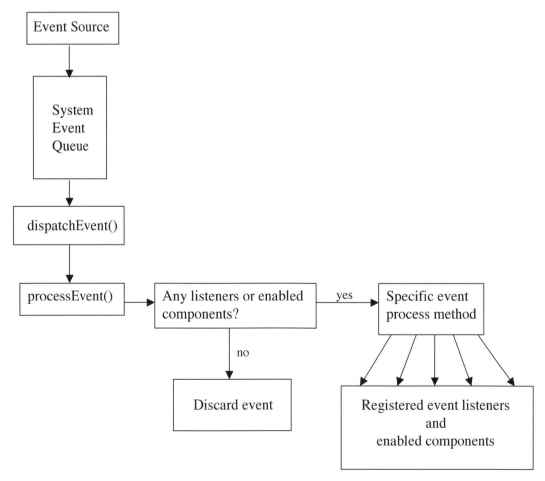

FIGURE 2.1 Java event life cycle.

of that type contained in the object's listener list. For instance, the JTree class defines a `fireTreeWillExpand()` method. When an attempt is made to expand or collapse a node of the JTree, this method is called to send a TreeExpansionEvent to any TreeWillExpandListener objects in the listener list of the event source.

EVENT LIFE CYCLE METHODS

The Java language provides methods for managing and enacting the life cycle of a Java event. These methods are defined in the Component class and its subclasses. Many of these methods, in particular the protected methods, are usually called only by the system. The user might override some of these methods if, for instance, user-defined event classes are being used.

Basic Event Life Cycle Methods from the Component Class

protected AWTEvent `coalesceEvents(AWTEvent oldEvent, AWTEvent newEvent)`
protected final void `disableEvents(long eventMask)`
public final void `dispatchEvent(AWTEvent event)`
protected final void `enableEvents(long eventMask)`

These methods provide the basic event handling functionality of dispatching, enabling, disabling, and coalescing events. Other than the `dispatchEvent()` method, the following methods have protected access.

`coalesceEvents()` attempts to combine an existing event on the event queue with a new event. The method either returns the coalesced event or returns null if the combination was not possible. This method is generally called by the system only and is used primarily to combine a series of sequential mouse or paint events into a single event.

`disableEvents()` prevents the event types corresponding to the specified event mask from being delivered to the invoking component. The event mask is a number identifying the event type.

`dispatchEvent()` dispatches the specified event by calling the invoking component's `processEvent()` method. This method is called automatically by the system and is sometimes used when creating user-defined components that generate events.

`enableEvents()` allows event types corresponding to the specified event mask to be delivered to the `processEvent()` method of the event source. Normally, events of a given type will be automatically enabled by the system when a listener for that event type is registered with the component. This method can be used to have events delivered to the invoking component's `processEvent()` method whether or not a listener has been registered.

Event Processing Methods

protected void `processEvent(AWTEvent event)`
protected void `processComponentEvent(ComponentEvent event)`
protected void `processFocusEvent(FocusEvent event)`
protected void `processHierarchyBoundsEvent(HierarchyEvent event)`
protected void `processHierarchyEvent(HierarchyEvent event)`
protected void `processInputMethodEvent(InputMethodEvent event)`
protected void `processKeyEvent(KeyEvent event)`
protected void `processMouseEvent(MouseEvent event)`
protected void `processMouseMotionEvent(MouseEvent event)`

These are the top level methods for processing AWTEvent objects when they are generated by an event source and sent through the `dispatchEvent()` method. The `processEvent()` method is the controller. It determines what type of event has been sent to it, and then sends it on to the appropriate specific event-processing method. The Component class defines specific event-processing methods for all of the low-level events contained in the java.awt.event package. The specific event-processing methods are often overridden by the individual component classes.

`processEvent()` is called by the `dispatchEvent()` method. It determines what type of event has been passed to it and calls the specific process method to deal with the event. If a user-defined event is being used, this method would be overridden to provide access to the process method for the user-defined event. See the section "User-Defined Events" in Chapter 3, "Event Classes," for more details.

`processComponentEvent()` is called when the `processEvent()` method is passed a ComponentEvent object as an argument. It dispatches the event to any registered ComponentListener objects or to any components that have been enabled to receive ComponentEvents.

`processFocusEvent()` is called when the `processEvent()` method is passed a FocusEvent object as an argument. It dispatches the event to any registered FocusListener objects or to any components that have been enabled to receive FocusEvents.

`processHierarchyBoundsEvent()` is called when the `processEvent()` method is passed a hierarchy bounds-type HierarchyEvent object as an argument. It dispatches the event to any registered HierarchyBoundsListener objects or to any components that have been enabled to receive HierarchyEvents.

`processHierarchyEvent()` is called when the `processEvent()` method is passed a HierarchyEvent object as an argument. It dispatches the event to any registered HierarchyListener objects or to any components that have been enabled to receive HierarchyEvents.

`processInputMethodEvent()` is called when the `processEvent()` method is passed an InputMethodEvent object as an argument. It dispatches the event to any registered InputMethodListener objects or to any components that have been enabled to receive InputMethodEvents.

`processKeyEvent()` is called when the `processEvent()` method is passed a KeyEvent object as an argument. It dispatches the event to any registered KeyListener objects or to any components that have been enabled to receive KeyEvents.

`processMouseEvent()` is called when the `processEvent()` method is passed a non-motion-oriented MouseEvent object as an argument. It dispatches the event to any registered MouseListener objects or to any components that have been enabled to receive non-motion-oriented MouseEvents.

`processMouseMotionEvent()` is called when the `processEvent()` method is passed a motion-oriented MouseEvent object as an argument. It dispatches the event to any registered MouseMotionListener objects or to any components that have been enabled to receive motion-oriented MouseEvents.

Methods to Fire Events

```
protected void firePropertyChange(String propertyName,
Object oldValue, Object newValue)
```

`firePropertyChange()` is used to fire a PropertyChangeEvent representing a change in the value of a bound property. The event is sent to any registered PropertyChangeListeners in the invoking component's listener list.

Deprecated Methods from the Component Class

```
public void deliverEvent(Event event)
```
```
public boolean handleEvent(Event event)
```
```
public boolean postEvent(Event event)
```

`deliverEvent()`, used in the Java 1.0.2 event model, is deprecated as of Java 1.1 and should not be used for new code. It has been replaced by the `dispatchEvent()` method.

`handleEvent()`, used in the Java 1.0.2 event model, is deprecated as of Java 1.1 and should not be used for new code. It has been replaced by the `processEvent()` method.

`postEvent()`, used in the Java 1.0.2 event model, is deprecated as of Java 1.1 and should not be used for new code. It has been replaced by the `dispatchEvent()` method.

Event Life Cycle Methods Defined in the Component Subclasses

The specific event process methods defined in the Component class (i.e., `processMouseEvent()`) are for low-level events, those that can be generated by any GUI component. The event process methods for high-level or semantic events are defined in each Component subclass that generates a high-level event. The classes will also override the `processEvent()` method from the Component class to send the semantic event to the semantic event process method. For instance, a Button object generates ActionEvent objects when the button is pressed. The Button class defines the following two event life cycle methods.

```
protected void processActionEvent(ActionEvent event)
protected void processEvent(AWTEvent event)
```

`processActionEvent()` is called when the `processEvent()` method is passed an ActionEvent object as an argument. It dispatches the event to any registered ActionListener objects or to any components that have been enabled to receive ActionEvents.

`processEvent()`. The `processEvent()` method defined in the Component class only processes low-level events. The Button class overrides the Component class method with a new version of `processEvent()` that can process ActionEvents generated by the Button. If the event is an ActionEvent, this method calls the `processActionEvent()` method. Otherwise, the Component class `processEvent()` method is called.

The other AWT and Swing classes define similar event-processing methods. The Container class, for instance, defines an overridden version of `processEvent()` and a method called `processContainerEvent()` that sends ContainerEvent objects to any registered listeners or enabled components. These classes also commonly define methods to fire the events they generate, meaning the events are sent to any event listeners of the appropriate type contained in the invoking component's listener list.

3

EVENT CLASSES

The event classes represent the events themselves. They are essentially packets of information that travel from the event source to any interested event listener object. Every event object will contain information about the source of the event. The event may also contain additional information, including the type of event, a value that was changed, any mouse buttons that were pressed during the event, and so on.

Events are usually generated by the system, but the event classes provide public constructors for creating event objects. These user-generated events can be dispatched using the event life cycle methods described in Chapter 2, "The Java Event Life Cycle." The event class framework can be used as the starting point for creating user-defined events. This topic is covered briefly in this section and discussed in more detail in Chapter 12, "User-Defined Event Classes and Event Listener."

EVENT AND SUPPORT CLASS HIERARCHY

The event and support class hierarchy is shown in Figure 3.1. The parent class of all Java event classes is the EventObject class that is contained in the java.util package. The superclass of the EventObject class is the Object class, which is the ultimate superclass of all Java classes. The AWTEvent class is a subclass of EventObject and is the parent class of all event classes in the java.awt.event package. The Swing event class hierarchy is a little less straightforward. Some of the event classes in the javax.swing.event package are subclasses of AWTEvent subclasses, some are subclassed directly from the AWTEvent class, and some are derived directly from the EventObject class.

The support classes are contained in the java.beans, javax.swing.undo, and javax.swing.event packages. They are used to facilitate the handling of UndoableEditEvent and PropertyChangeEvent objects. UndoableEditEvents are generated by Swing text components when an edit is performed that can be undone. PropertyChangeEvent objects are generated when an attempt is made to change a bound or constrained property. A property can be anything related to an object: its color, the font that is used, its enabled state, and so forth.

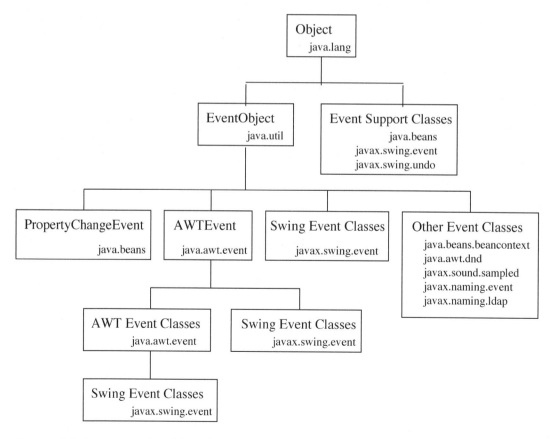

FIGURE 3.1 Java event class hierarchy.

The Other Event Classes box represents event types that are not covered in detail in this book. A brief description of these events is provided in Chapter 6, "Event Classes and Interfaces."

LOW-LEVEL VERSUS HIGH-LEVEL EVENT TYPES

Java events are divided into two main categories, low-level and high-level events. High-level events are also referred to as semantic events. Low-level events are those that can be generated by any component type. Examples of low-level events would be keyboard or mouse events. The methods to add or remove a low-level listener from the listener list maintained by a component (the `add-Listener()` and `remove-Listener()` methods) are defined in the Component and JComponent classes.

High-level, or semantic, events are component-specific events. A high-level event is generated only by a small subset of GUI components. For example, only components that implement the Adjustable interface, such as a Scrollbar or JScrollBar, can generate AdjustmentEvent objects. The methods to add or remove a high-level event listener from an event source's listener list are generally defined in the classes that generate the event. For instance, a Button can generate ActionEvent objects. The `addActionListener()` and `removeActionListener()` methods are defined in the Button class.

A DESCRIPTION OF THE EVENT CLASSES IN THE J2SE

The following is a brief description of the event classes contained in the java.util, java.awt, java.awt.event, javax.swing.event, javax.swing.text.html, and java.beans packages. A complete description of each event, the classes that generate them, and examples of how to process and apply the event can be found in Chapter 6. For a listing of every Java GUI component and the event types it generates, see Appendix 1.

The EventObject Class

The EventObject class is the parent class of all Java event classes. It is contained in the `java.util` package. Its superclass is the Object class. It has one constructor and defines two methods. The first is the `getSource()` method, which returns a reference to the object that generated the event. This method can be used to identify the event source. The second method implemented by the EventObject class is an overridden version of the `toString()` method, which returns a String representation of the EventObject.

The AWTEvent Class

This is the parent class of all the event classes in the java.awt.event package and some of the events in the javax.swing.event package. Its parent class is the EventObject class. It defines a series of field constants for selecting different event types. It also provides the `getID()` method, which returns an identification constant for the event. Other methods defined by the AWTEvent class are the `paramString()` method, which returns a String representing the state of the event, and a `toString()` method that overrides the version from the EventObject class.

Low-Level Event Classes Defined in the java.awt.event Package

The events contained in the java.awt.event package were originally designed to work with the java.awt GUI components, although many of these event types are also generated by the newer Swing GUI components. Generally speaking, these are the older event types. Many of them date from Java 1.1. The low-level events from the java.awt.event package are designed to be generated by any Component subclass.

Keep in mind that the descriptions of the event classes in this and subsequent sections are intentionally brief. A comprehensive description of these events can be found in Chapter 6.

public class `ComponentEvent` extends `AWTEvent`
public class `ContainerEvent` extends `ComponentEvent`
public class `FocusEvent` extends `ComponentEvent`
public class `HierarchyEvent` extends `AWTEvent`
public class `InputMethodEvent` extends `AWTEvent`
public class `KeyEvent` extends `InputEvent`
public class `MouseEvent` extends `InputEvent`
public class `WindowEvent` extends `ComponentEvent`

`ComponentEvent` is generated whenever a component is shown, hidden, moved, or resized. This is also the parent class for the ContainerEvent, FocusEvent, InputEvent, and WindowEvent classes.

`ContainerEvent` occurs when a component was added or removed from a container.

`FocusEvent` is generated whenever a component gains or loses keyboard focus. The component has focus when it is the current active component and is ready to receive input.

`HierarchyEvent` is generated by a component when some aspect of its component hierarchy changes. The hierarchy consists of a component's container, its container's container, and so on.

`InputMethodEvent` is generated when the text that is being composed by the input method changes.

`KeyEvent` is generated by the component that has focus when the user types on the keyboard.

`MouseEvent` occurs when the mouse does something over the bounding area of a component. This "something" the mouse can do includes entering, exiting, moving through, or being dragged through the bounding area. MouseEvents also occur if the mouse is pressed, released, or clicked (pressed and released) over the component.

`WindowEvent` indicates that a window has been activated, deactivated, iconified, deiconified, opened, or closed.

High-Level Event Classes Defined in the java.awt.event Package

There are four high-level events defined in the java.awt.event package. The ActionEvent, AdjustmentEvent, and ItemEvent classes represent events that can be generated by both AWT and Swing GUI components. TextEvents are only generated by AWT text components. The ActionEvent and ItemEvent classes are two of the most commonly generated high-level events.

| public class `ActionEvent` extends `AWTEvent` |
| public class `AdjustmentEvent` extends `AWTEvent` |
| public class `ItemEvent` extends `AWTEvent` |
| public class `TextEvent` extends `AWTEvent` |

`ActionEvent` is generated when a component-specific action has been performed on the specified components, for instance, when a button is pressed.

`AdjustmentEvent` is generated by an object that implements the Adjustable interface. These objects, for example, a JScrollBar, have a value that can be changed by manipulating the component's slider.

`ItemEvent` is generated by components that can be selected or deselected when the selected state of the item changes.

`TextEvent` is generated by AWT text components when the text they contain changes.

Special Event Classes Defined in the java.awt.event Package

```
public class InvocationEvent extends AWTEvent implements ActiveEvent
```

`InvocationEvent` is used to execute the `run()` method of a Runnable object on the AWT event-dispatcher thread. This can be useful as a way to avoid a deadlock situation in a multithreaded application.

Low-Level Event Classes Defined in the javax.swing.event Package

The introduction of the Swing classes in J2SE 1.2 greatly increased the capability of Java to produce sophisticated user interfaces. The GUI components contained in the javax.swing package utilized some of the event classes from the java.awt.event package, but their enhanced capabilities required new event classes to represent them. A new package was included in the J2SE, the javax.swing.event package, which contains many of these new event classes. Most of the events defined in the javax.swing.event package are high-level events. Many of them are generated only by one type of component. The javax.swing.event package does define one low-level event that can be generated by any JComponent subclass object.

As was noted in the discussion of the events in the java.awt.event package, the descriptions of the javax.swing.event classes in this section are brief. A complete description of these classes can be found in Chapter 6.

```
public class AncestorEvent extends AWTEvent
```

`AncestorEvent` indicates that a change has occurred to a component hierarchy. A component hierarchy consists of the component itself and any ancestors to the component.

High-Level Event Classes Defined in the javax.swing.event Package

The javax.swing.event package defines a large number of high-level event classes. The enhanced capability these event classes provide mirrors the enhanced capabilities of the Swing GUI components. While every event in the java.awt.event package was a subclass of the AWTEvent class, many of the events in the javax.swing.event package are not. These events are direct subclasses of the EventObject class.

`public abstract class CaretEvent extends EventObject`
`public class ChangeEvent extends EventObject`
`public class HyperlinkEvent extends EventObject`
`public class InternalFrameEvent extends AWTEvent`
`public class ListDataEvent extends EventObject`
`public class ListSelectionEvent extends EventObject`
`public class MenuDragMouseEvent extends MouseEvent`
`public class MenuEvent extends EventObject`
`public class MenuKeyEvent extends KeyEvent`
`public class PopupMenuEvent extends EventObject`
`public class TableColumnModelEvent extends EventObject`
`public class TableModelEvent extends EventObject`
`public class TreeExpansionEvent extends EventObject`
`public class TreeModelEvent extends EventObject`
`public class TreeSelectionEvent extends EventObject`
`public class UndoableEditEvent extends EventObject`

`CaretEvent` is generated by Swing text components when their caret position is changed. The caret is the cursor that appears inside the text area of the component.

`ChangeEvent` is generated by certain Swing components when a component property changes.

`HyperlinkEvent` is generated by JEditorPane components when the user interacts with a hyperlink inside the JEditorPane.

`InternalFrameEvent` indicates that the state of a JInternalFrame object has changed.

`ListDataEvent` is generated when a change is made to the contents of a list.

`ListSelectionEvent` indicates that a change has been made in the current selection of a list.

`MenuDragMouseEvent` is generated when the mouse is dragged into or out of a Swing menu component's display area. It is also generated if the mouse is dragged into a menu component's display area and then released.

`MenuEvent` is generated when a JMenu object has been selected, deselected, or removed from the screen.

`MenuKeyEvent` is generated whenever a Swing menu item receives a KeyEvent. This can be via an accelerator or mnemonic key, or it can happen if a keystroke is pressed when the menu item has been selected.

`PopupMenuEvent` is generated by a JPopupMenu object before the popup menu becomes visible, before it becomes invisible, or when it is canceled.

`TableColumnModelEvent` is generated when some aspect of a TableColumnModel has changed.

`TableModelEvent` is generated when some aspect of a TableModel has changed.

`TreeExpansionEvent` is generated by a JTree object whenever a path in the tree has been expanded or collapsed.

`TreeModelEvent` is generated when some aspect of a TreeModel has changed. Possible changes include inserting, removing, or altering a node in a tree or a change in the tree structure below a given node.

`TreeSelectionEvent` is generated whenever the currently selected node of a tree changes.

`UndoableEditEvent` is generated by components when an edit has been made that can be undone.

High-Level Event Interfaces Defined in the javax.swing.event Package

One of the event types defined in the javax.swing.event package is implemented as an interface instead of a class. This event describes changes to a Document.

```
public interface DocumentEvent
```

A `DocumentEvent` object is used to provide detailed information to a Document observer about how a Document has changed. Unlike the other Swing events, it is implemented in the API as an interface instead of a class.

Event Support Classes Defined in the javax.swing.event Package

The javax.swing.event package provides one event support class that makes it easier to implement bound properties in Swing components.

```
public final class SwingPropertyChangeSupport extends PropertyChangeSupport
```

`SwingPropertyChangeSupport` is a subclass of the PropertyChange Support class found in the java.beans package. The SwingPropertyChange Support class provides methods to add or remove a PropertyChangeListener as well as methods to fire PropertyChangeEvent objects.

Event and Support Classes Defined in the java.beans Package

A Java Bean is a reusable component that adheres to a standard design architecture. One of the elements of this architecture is that a Bean supports bound and constrained properties. A property is simply some characteristic or attribute that helps define the state or behavior of an object. The foreground color is an example of a property. A bound property is one that can be shared by more than one component. A constrained property is one that can limit the changes it will accept. The event and support classes for dealing with property changes are contained in the java.beans package.

```
public class PropertyChangeEvent extends EventObject
public class PropertyChangeSupport extends Object implements Serializable
public class VetoableChangeSupport extends Object implements Serializable
```

`PropertyChangeEvent` is generated whenever a Bean changes a bound or constrained property. A bound property is one that can be shared between multiple objects. A constrained property is one that has limits to the values it can have.

`PropertyChangeSupport` is a utility class that makes it easier for objects to support bound properties. It provides methods to add or remove a PropertyChangeListener object to an object's listener list, and the PropertyChangeSupport class provides methods to fire PropertyChangeEvents.

`VetoableChangeSupport` is a utility class that makes it easier for Java Beans to support constrained properties. It provides methods to add or remove a VetoableChangeListener object to an object's listener list, and the VetoableChangeSupport class provides methods to fire PropertyChangeEvent objects that represent an attempt to change a constrained property.

Event Classes Defined in the javax.swing.text.html Package

The javax.swing.text.html class defines one event that is used to process events that occur when a hyperlink inside an HTML frame is interacted with.

```
public class HTMLFrameHyperlinkEvent extends HyperlinkEvent
```

`HTMLFrameHyperlinkEvent` is generated by a JEditorPane object if a hyperlink inside an HTML frame is interacted with.

Event Support Classes Defined in the javax.swing.undo Package

The javax.swing.undo package provides an event support class that is used to implement an undoable edit capability.

```
public class UndoableEditSupport extends Object
```

`UndoableEditSupport` makes it easier to implement an undoable edit capability into a component. It provides methods to add or remove an UndoableEditListener and methods to post an undoable edit.

Other Event Classes Defined in the J2SE

There are some additional event classes defined in the J2SE. These are found in the java.beans.beancontext, java.awt.dnd, javax.sound.sampled, javax.naming.event, and javax.naming.ldap packages. These event classes are not described in detail in this book. They are listed in the following table, and a brief description of them is provided in Chapter 6.

public class `BeanContextEvent` extends `EventObject`
public class `BeanContextMembershipEvent` extends `BeanContextEvent`
public class `BeanContextServiceRevokedEvent` extends `BeanContextEvent`
public class `BeanContextServiceAvailableEvent` extends `BeanContextEvent`
public class `DragGestureEvent` extends `EventObject`
public class `DragSourceEvent` extends `EventObject`
public class `DragSourceDragEvent` extends `DragSourceEvent`
public class `DragSourceDropEvent` extends `DragSourceEvent`
public class `DropTargetEvent` extends `EventObject`
public class `DropTargetDragEvent` extends `DropTargetEvent`
public class `DropTargetDropEvent` extends `DropTargetEvent`
public class `LineEvent` extends `EventObject`
public class `NamingEvent` extends `EventObject`
public class `NamingExceptionEvent` extends `EventObject`
public class `UnsolicitedNotificationEvent` extends `EventObject`

USER-GENERATED EVENTS

The system will automatically generate the events listed in the previous sections when an appropriate manipulation occurs to a particular component. All of the system event classes have constructors, so it is possible to generate your own instances of the system event classes for your own purposes. For instance, you might want to generate an event when a certain computation is completed or when a timer has expired.

User-generated events are sent to any interested listeners using the event life cycle methods described in Chapter 2, "The Java Event Life Cycle." Two common ways to dispatch a user-generated event are by using the `dispatchEvent()` method from the Component class or by using one of the `fireEvent()` methods that are defined in many of the Component subclasses.

One word of caution: A user-generated event that is sent to a listener using the `dispatchEvent()` method bypasses the system event queue. Events that are sent to the system event queue are processed sequentially by the event-dispatching thread such that an event will not conflict with any other event on the event queue. If you bypass the system event queue, you no longer have this protection and you open the door to potential problems. You should proceed carefully (and have a good justification) when using user-generated events.

EXAMPLE

Example 3.1 shows how to create and dispatch a user-generated event. Two Button objects and a textfield are placed on a frame. The buttons add an ActionListener to their listener list. When either of the buttons is pressed, an ActionEvent object is generated and sent to the `actionPerformed()` method. The textfield is updated to indicate which button was pressed.

After a delay of five seconds, a user-generated ActionEvent is created with the first button designated as its source. This ActionEvent is sent off by having the first button invoke the `dispatchEvent()` method. The user-generated ActionEvent is sent to the ActionListener via the `processEvent()` method. When the `actionPerformed()` method receives this event, the first button is disabled. Here is the source code for this example.

EXAMPLE 3.1 CREATING AND DISPATCHING A USER-GENERATED EVENT

```
import java.awt.event.*;
import java.awt.*;

public class UserGenerated2 extends Frame
{
   Button b1, b2;
   TextField jtf;

   public UserGenerated2()
   {
/*   Two buttons and a textfield are created and placed on a frame   */
/*   The buttons register an ActionListener.                         */
```

```java
        b1 = new Button("b1");
        b1.addActionListener(new ButtonListener());

        b2 = new Button("b2");
        b2.addActionListener(new ButtonListener());

        jtf = new TextField(30);

        Panel p = new Panel();
        p.setLayout(new FlowLayout(FlowLayout.CENTER, 20, 20));
        p.add(b1);
        p.add(b2);

        add(p, BorderLayout.CENTER);
        add(jtf, BorderLayout.SOUTH);

        addWindowListener(new WinClosing());
        setBounds(100, 100, 200, 200);
        setVisible(true);

/*    After a delay of 5 seconds, an ActionEvent is instantiated and   */
/*    dispatched by the b1 button using the dispatchEvent() method.    */

        try
        {
           Thread.sleep(5000);
           ActionEvent ae =
new ActionEvent(b1,ActionEvent.ACTION_PERFORMED,"disable");
           b1.dispatchEvent(ae);
        }
        catch (InterruptedException ie) {}
    }

/*    The ActionListener is implemented as an inner class.  If the      */
/*    action command of the incoming event is "disable", the object    */
/*    that dispatched the event is disabled.  Otherwise, a message     */
/*    indicating which button was pressed is written in the textfield  */

    public class ButtonListener implements ActionListener
    {
       public void actionPerformed(ActionEvent ae)
       {
          if ( ae.getActionCommand().equals("disable") )
          {
             Button b = (Button)ae.getSource();
             b.setEnabled(false);
          }
          else
          {
             jtf.setText( ae.getActionCommand()+" was pressed");
          }
       }
    }
```

```
   public static void main(String args[])
   {
      UserGenerated2 ug = new UserGenerated2();
   }
}

/*   The WinClosing class is a WindowListener that terminates the   */
/*   program if the application window is closed.                   */

class WinClosing extends WindowAdapter
{
   public void windowClosing(WindowEvent we)
   {
      System.exit(0);
   }
}
```

Start this program and press the buttons. Whichever button is pressed is indicated in the textfield. After five seconds, the first button will become disabled. This is due to a user-generated ActionEvent.

User-Defined Events

There is nothing preventing a programmer from defining new event classes. For instance, a ColorEvent might be desirable when there is a change in the color of a component. A BorderEvent might be created if the border of a component is changed. User-defined event classes should be subclasses of the EventObject or AWTEvent classes. The user-defined event would then define whatever additional fields or methods are required to implement the desired functionality of the event. A more complete discussion of user-defined events and an example of how to create one are provided in Chapter 12.

Once you have written a user-defined event class, you will have to create a user-defined event listener interface that will declare the method or methods used to process the user-defined event. This is also described in more detail in Chapter 12.

4

EVENT LISTENERS

Under the Java 1.1 event model, the event source is only half of the event delegation equation. The torrents of events that a GUI application may generate don't do any good without an object that can receive and process the events. These event-receiving objects are called event listeners.

Java provides the framework for an event listener but leaves the implementation of that framework up to the programmer. It does this by implementing the event listeners as interfaces. These interfaces declare methods that will be called when the appropriate type of event is generated from an event source. An event listener class of a given type must implement the methods defined in the event listener, but what code is placed inside the event listener methods is left completely up to the developer. When an event of that type is generated by an event source, the event-dispatching thread will send the event to the appropriate event listener method.

This is a very powerful event handling process and is a central and crucial element of the Java 1.1 event model. It allows Java event handling to be both compact and completely expandable. For example, an ItemEvent can be generated by many different types of components and can represent many different types of user interactions. The methodology is compact because every ItemEvent can be processed by the same ItemEvent listener as long as the listener's `itemStateChanged()` method is written to process the desired

ItemEvent. The methodology is expandable because new components that generate ItemEvents can be added to the Java API without altering the structure of the ItemEvent listener.

A Brief Review of Interfaces

Java does not allow multiple inheritance. This means that a class can have only one superclass, which in turn can have only one superclass, and so on. This simplifies many aspects of Java programming, but can lead to problems. For instance, what if classes that have different inheritance hierarchies need to share some common behavior? One way to solve this problem is to place the shared behavior higher up the inheritance hierarchy in a location common to both classes. Another solution is to simply copy the functionality into both classes. Neither of these solutions is desirable, however, as they violate object-oriented programming principles of shared behavior and code reuse.

The acceptable solution to this problem is through the use of interfaces. An interface declares a set of methods and constants. There are no instance variables in an interface, and the methods declared in the interface are *stubs* (methods without bodies). A class can implement any number of interfaces. The implementation of the methods declared in the interface is left up to the class that implements the interface. In effect, the interface imposes a certain functionality upon a class, but provides the class the flexibility to determine how to implement that functionality. For instance, the ActionListener interface declares one method, `actionPerformed()`. Every class that implements the ActionListener interface must provide an `actionPerformed()` method. But what is inside the body of the `actionPerformed()` method can be different for every class. In one case, the `actionPerformed()` method might terminate the program. In another, the `actionPerformed()` method might change the background color, and so on.

Event Listener Interfaces in the J2SE

The EventListener interface, defined in the java.util package, is the parent interface for all event listener interfaces in the Java API. The EventListener interface declares no methods but is used as a marker to indicate that any subinterfaces of it are event listeners. Most listener interfaces are direct subinterfaces of EventListener, but some are subinterfaces of EventListener subinterfaces.

Most of the event listener interfaces contained in the J2SE are defined in the java.awt.event, javax.swing.event, and java.beans packages. These interfaces will be described briefly here and in more detail in Chapter 8, "Event Listener Interfaces." Event listener interfaces are also defined in the java.beans.beancontext, java.awt.dnd, javax.sound.sampled, javax.naming.event, and javax.naming.ldap packages. These interfaces are touched on briefly but are not covered in detail.

EventListener Interface

The EventListener interface is from the java.util package and is the parent of all listener interfaces. It declares no methods or constants but is used as a marker to indicate that any interface that extends EventListener is an event listener interface.

Listener Interfaces Contained in the java.awt.event Package

The listener interfaces defined in the java.awt.event pacakge are all direct subinterfaces of EventListener. They are used to receive and process the events found in the java.awt.event package. The following is a table and a short description of these interfaces. A complete description of these listener interfaces as well as examples on how they are used can be found in Chapter 8.

```
public interface ActionListener extends EventListener
public interface AdjustmentListener extends EventListener
public interface AWTEventListener extends EventListener
public interface ComponentListener extends EventListener
public interface ContainerListener extends EventListener
public interface FocusListener extends EventListener
public interface HierarchyBoundsListener extends EventListener
public interface HierarchyListener extends EventListener
public interface InputMethodListener extends EventListener
public interface ItemListener extends EventListener
```

```
public interface KeyListener extends EventListener
public interface MouseListener extends EventListener
public interface MouseMotionListener extends EventListener
public interface TextListener extends EventListener
public interface WindowListener extends EventListener
```

The names of these listener interfaces pretty much tell you what it is they do. The ActionListener interface declares a method for processing ActionEvents, The KeyListener interface declares methods for processing KeyEvents, and so on. There are two listener interfaces for dealing with MouseEvents and HierarchyEvents. There is also the AWTEventListener interface that is not tied to any specific AWTEvent. These listeners are described here in more detail.

`AWTEventListener` declares one method, `eventDispatched()`, which is used to passively monitor events being dispatched in the AWT. The method is called whenever an event is dispatched in the AWT.

`HierarchyBoundsListener` is one of two listener interfaces that receive and process HierarchyEvent objects. It declares two methods that are called if an ancestor in a registered component's hierarchy is moved or resized.

`HierarchyListener` declares methods for processing non-bounding-type HierarchyEvent objects. These can happen, for instance, if an ancestor is added or removed from the hierarchy or if the hierarchy is made visible or invisible.

`MouseListener` is one of two interfaces for responding to MouseEvents. The MouseListener interface declares methods for processing non-motion-oriented MouseEvents. These occur whenever the mouse is pressed, released, clicked (pressed and released), or enters or leaves the bounding area of a GUI component.

`MouseMotionListener` declares methods to process motion-oriented MouseEvent objects. These occur whenever the mouse moves or is dragged within the bounding area of a GUI component.

As a side note on WindowEvent objects, one of the idiosyncrasies of Java is that when the main window of an application is closed, the application does not automatically terminate. Before J2SE 1.3, the best way to ensure that the application would terminate when the main window was closed was to register the window with a WindowListener. The `windowClosing()` method defined in that interface is implemented to call the `System.exit()` method. For Swing containers running under J2SE 1.3, the application can be set to terminate upon window closing by using the `setDefaultCloseOperation()` method.

Listener Interfaces Contained in the javax.swing.event Package

The interfaces contained in the javax.swing.event package are used to receive and process the Swing event classes. With one exception, they are all direct subinterfaces of the EventListener interface. The following is a table and a brief description of each interface. A complete description of the javax.swing.event listener interfaces as well as examples on how to use them can be found in Chapter 8.

public interface `AncestorListener` extends `EventListener`
public interface `CaretListener` extends `EventListener`
public interface `CellEditorListener` extends `EventListener`
public interface `ChangeListener` extends `EventListener`
public interface `DocumentListener` extends `EventListener`
public interface `HyperlinkListener` extends `EventListener`
public interface `InternalFrameListener` extends `EventListener`
public interface `ListDataListener` extends `EventListener`
public interface `ListSelectionListener` extends `EventListener`
public interface `MenuDragMouseListener` extends `EventListener`
public interface `MenuKeyListener` extends `EventListener`
public interface `MenuListener` extends `EventListener`
public interface `MouseInputListener` extends `MouseListener, MouseMotionListener`
public interface `PopupMenuListener` extends `EventListener`
public interface `TableColumnModelListener` extends `EventListener`
public interface `TableModelListener` extends `EventListener`
public interface `TreeExpansionListener` extends `EventListener`
public interface `TreeModelListener` extends `EventListener`

```
public interface TreeSelectionListener extends EventListener
public interface TreeWillExpandListener extends EventListener
public interface UndoableEditListener extends EventListener
```

As with the java.awt.event package event listener interfaces, the javax.swing.event interface names generally indicate what the interfaces are intended to do. A DocumentListener declares methods to process DocumentEvents, a PopupMenuListener declares methods to process PopupMenuEvents, and so on. There are some exceptions. The CellEditorListener receives ChangeEvents generated by a CellEditor, for instance.

A CellEditorListener is used to process ChangeEvents generated by a CellEditor when an editing session is canceled or stopped. The HyperlinkListener serves a dual purpose. It is used to receive and process both HyperlinkEvents and HTMLFrameHyperlinkEvent objects. The TableColumnModelListener defines methods for receiving and processing every type of event a TableColumnModel can generate. These include TableColumnModelEvents, ChangeEvents, and ListSelectionEvents.

TreeExpansionEvents can be sent to either a TreeExpansionListener or a TreeWillExpandListener. The TreeExpansionListener is called after a JTree node has been expanded or collapsed. The TreeWillExpandListener is called when a JTree node is about to be expanded or collapsed, before the action has taken place.

Listener Interfaces Contained in the java.beans Package

The java.beans package provides the event listener interfaces that are used to implement bound and constrained properties. Recall that a bound property is one that is shared between multiple objects. A constrained property is one whose change can be restricted. As with the java.awt.event and javax.swing.event package listener interfaces, a complete description of the listener interfaces from the java.beans package can be found in Chapter 8.

```
public interface PropertyChangeListener extends EventListener
public interface VetoableChangeListener extends EventListener
```

`PropertyChangeListener` declares one method, `propertyChange()`, that is called when a PropertyChangeEvent object is fired from an event source. The PropertyChangeEvent might represent a change to a bound property or a proposed change to a constrained property.

`VetoableChangeListener` declares one method, `vetoableChange()`, that is called when an attempt is made to change a constrained property of an event source.

Other Listener Interfaces Defined in the J2SE

There are some additional listener interfaces defined in the J2SE beyond those found in the java.awt.event, javax.swing.event, and java.beans packages. These listener interfaces are not described in detail in this book. They are listed in the table below, and a brief description of them is provided in Chapter 8.

public interface `BeanContextMembershipListener` extends `EventListener`
public interface `BeanContextServiceRevokedListener` extends `EventListener`
public interface `BeanContextServicesListener` extends `EventListener`
public interface `ControllerEventListener` extends `EventListener`
public interface `DragGestureListener` extends `EventListener`
public interface `DragSourceListener` extends `EventListener`
public interface `DropTargetListener` extends `EventListener`
public interface `LineListener` extends `EventListener`
public interface `MetaEventListener` extends `EventListener`
public interface `NamespaceChangeListener` extends `NamingListener`
public interface `NamingListener` extends `EventListener`
public interface `ObjectChangeListener` extends `NamingListener`
public interface `UnsolicitedNotificationListener` extends `NamingListener`

EVENT LISTENER OBJECTS

An event listener class is one that implements one or more event listener interfaces. An event listener class provides implementations of the methods declared in the interfaces to suit the specific needs of an application. Any class can serve as an event listener, and there is more than one way to implement an event listener.

For an event listener to receive events generated from an event source, the event source must add the listener to its listener list. The event source does this by invoking an `addListener()` method. This process is also known as having the event source register the listener. Similarly, if you wish to disconnect the listener from the event source, the event source must remove the listener from its listener list. The event source does this by calling a `removeListener()` method. The process of connecting or disconnecting an event listener and event source is covered in more detail later in this chapter.

Creating an Event Listener

Because any class can serve as an event listener, there are several ways to implement an event listener. Remember that for a class to serve as an event listener class, all the class need do is implement the appropriate event listener interface and provide implementation for the event handling methods defined in the interface. Each of the different ways to create an event listener is more useful in some situations, less useful in others. Four ways to create an event listener are discussed in the following sections.

Method 1: Have a GUI Component Serve as the Event Listener

This is the situation that is most similar to the Java 1.0.2 event model, where event handling was always performed by a Component subclass. The component, oftentimes the container, implements the listener interface and provides implementation of the methods declared in the interface. This method has its advantages. Because the event handling code is contained within the GUI code, the event handling methods automatically have access to the private data members of the GUI. However, this method becomes awkward if a large number of GUI components are sending events to the same listener because logic must be built in to the event handler method to determine which event generated the event before applying the appropriate event processing.

EXAMPLE

Example 4.1 is very similar to the SimpleExample class described in Chapter 1, "An Introduction to Java Events." The container class serves as an ActionListener and implements the `actionPerformed()` method.

EXAMPLE 4.1 A GUI COMPONENT SERVES AS THE EVENT LISTENER

```java
import java.awt.*;
import java.awt.event.*;

public class TestListener extends Frame implements ActionListener
{
   private Button b;

   public TestListener()
   {
/* A Button is created and registers an ActionListener      */
/* Because the TestListener class itself is serving as the  */
/* ActionListener, the addActionListener() method is passed */
/* the "this" reference.                                    */

      b = new Button("quit");
      b.addActionListener(this);

      setLayout(new FlowLayout());
      add(b);

      setBounds(100, 100, 200, 200);
      setVisible(true);
   }

/* The TestListener class serves as the ActionListener and must */
/* provide an implementation of the actionPerformed method.     */

   public void actionPerformed(ActionEvent ae)
   {
      System.exit(0);
   }

   public static void main(String args[])
   {
      TestListener tl = new TestListener();
   }
}
```

In this example, a button is placed on a frame. The TestListener class serves as an ActionListener and implements the `actionPerformed()` method. The button adds the ActionListener to its listener list by invoking the `addActionListener()` method and passing the method the "this" reference. When the button is pressed, an ActionEvent is generated and sent to the `actionPerformed()` method where the program is terminated.

As a general note, there is no limit to the number of listener interfaces a class can implement. If the container is serving as the event listener, it is not uncommon for it to implement multiple event listeners.

Method 2: Implement the Event Listener as a Separate Class

One of the advantages of the Java 1.1 event model is that it allows the event handling to be performed separately from the GUI development. The event listener can be implemented as a separate class. This has the advantage of making the event handling code completely portable and is useful for situations where the event handler does not need access to the private data members of the GUI.

EXAMPLE

In Example 4.2, an ActionListener is implemented as a separate class. The QuitHandler class implements the ActionListener interface and overrides the `actionPerformed()` method.

EXAMPLE 4.2 EVENT LISTENER IMPLEMENTED AS A SEPARATE CLASS

```java
import java.awt.*;
import java.awt.event.*;

public class TestListener2 extends Frame
{
   private Button b;

   public TestListener2()
   {
/*  A Button is created and registers an ActionListener.       */
/*  The addActionListener() method is passed a reference to    */
/*  an ActionListener object.                                  */

      b = new Button("quit");
      b.addActionListener(new QuitHandler());

      setLayout(new FlowLayout());
      add(b);

      setBounds(100, 100, 200, 200);
      setVisible(true);
   }

   public static void main(String args[])
   {
      TestListener2 tl = new TestListener2();
   }
}

/*  The ActionListener is implemented as a separate class   */

class QuitHandler implements ActionListener
```

```
{
   public void actionPerformed(ActionEvent ae)
   {
      System.exit(0);
   }
}
```

This example is similar to the previous one, except that the event listener is implemented as a separate class. The frame no longer implements the ActionListener interface and no longer provides implementation of the `actionPerformed()` method. This is done in the QuitHandler class. The button adds the ActionListener to its listener list by invoking the `addActionListener()` method and passing the method a reference to a QuitHandler object.

Method 3: Implement the Event Listener as an Inner Class

This is a combination of methods 1 and 2. The event handling is performed by a separate class, but this class is written as an inner class. The advantage of this method is that the event handler has access to the private data members of the outer class and allows the event handling to be modularized. Every GUI component could conceivably have its own corresponding inner class to handle the events it generates.

EXAMPLE

In Example 4.3, the TestListener3 class is a frame that contains a button and a textfield. The TestListener3 class also defines an instance variable named `count`. The button registers an ActionListener that is implemented as an inner class. When the button is pressed, an ActionEvent is generated and sent to the `actionPerformed()` method defined in the ButtonHandler class. The count is incremented and the textfield is updated to display the current value of the count.

EXAMPLE 4.3 EVENT LISTENER IMPLEMENTED AS AN INNER CLASS

```
import java.awt.*;
import java.awt.event.*;

public class TestListener3 extends Frame
{
   private Button b;
   private TextField textField;
   private int count;
```

```java
   public TestListener3()
   {
/*   The count is initialized to be zero    */

      count = 0;

/*   A Button is created and placed on a Frame    */
/*   The Button registers an ActionListener       */

      b = new Button("Add");
      b.addActionListener(new ButtonHandler());

      textField = new TextField(20);
      textField.setEditable(false);
      textField.setText("count is "+count);

      setLayout(new FlowLayout());
      add(b);
      add(textField);

      addWindowListener(new WinAdapter());
      setBounds(100, 100, 200, 200);
      setVisible(true);
   }

/*   The ActionListener is implemented as an inner class,  */
/*   so the actionPerformed() method has access to the     */
/*   count variable.                                       */

   class ButtonHandler implements ActionListener
   {
      public void actionPerformed(ActionEvent ae)
      {
         ++count;
         textField.setText("count is "+count);
      }
   }

   public static void main(String args[])
   {
      TestListener3 tl = new TestListener3();
   }
}

/*   This makes sure the application terminates if the window is
closed    */

class WinAdapter extends WindowAdapter
{
   public void windowClosing(WindowEvent event)
   {
```

```
      System.exit(0);
   }
}
```

When you run this example, a button and a textfield appear on a frame. Press the button and notice how the count is updated in the textfield. This is possible because the `actionPerformed()` method has access to the count instance variable.

Method 4: Implement the Event Listener as an Anonymous Inner Class

The most compact way of implementing an event listener is by using an anonymous inner class. The code for the anonymous inner class is passed as an argument to the `addListener()` method. This is useful for simple event handlers, although it does tend to make the code somewhat more difficult to follow.

EXAMPLE

In Example 4.4, a button is placed on a frame. The code to process the events generated by the button is passed to the `addActionListener()` method as an anonymous inner class.

EXAMPLE 4.4 EVENT LISTENER IMPLEMENTED AS AN ANONYMOUS INNER CLASS

```
import java.awt.*;
import java.awt.event.*;

public class TestListener4 extends Frame
{
   private Button b;

   public TestListener4()
   {
/* A Button is created and registers an ActionListener.         */
/* The addActionListener() method is passed a reference to an   */
/* ActionListener object. The ActionListener is implemented     */
/* as an anonymous inner class.  The entire anonymous inner     */
/* class is passed as an argument to the addActionListener()    */
/* method.                                                      */

      b = new Button("quit");
      b.addActionListener(new ActionListener() {
         public void actionPerformed(ActionEvent ae)
         {
```

```
            System.exit(0);
        }
    });

    setLayout(new FlowLayout());
    add(b);

    setBounds(100, 100, 200, 200);
    setVisible(true);
    }

    public static void main(String args[])
    {
        TestListener4 tl = new TestListener4();
    }
}
```

The code inside the curved brackets of the `addActionListener()` syntax defines an anonymous inner class that implements the ActionListener interface. It provides an implementation of the `actionPerformed()` method. It is very compact and is well suited to simple operations such as terminating the program when the Quit button is pressed. But the code looks a little squirrelly, and it can take even experienced programmers a while to figure out what is going on here.

LISTENER ADAPTER CLASSES

An annoying aspect of interfaces is that a class that implements an interface must provide implementations for all methods declared in the interface. Oftentimes, a developer only needs to use some of the methods for a given application. Implementations of the other methods must be included even if they are written as stub methods (methods with an empty body).

To avoid this nuisance, the Java programming language provides event listener adapter classes for many of the listener interfaces that define more than one method. These adapter classes implement the corresponding listener interface and provide stubs for all of the methods declared in the interface. The developer then need only override the methods required for a given application.

EXAMPLE

As an example, let us look at the problem described previously—that of ensuring that an application terminates when its main window is closed. First, in

Example 4.5, let us look at the code required if a WindowListener is used that directly implements the WindowListener interface.

EXAMPLE 4.5 WINDOWLISTENER IMPLEMENTING WINDOWLISTENER INTERFACE

```
import java.awt.*;
import java.awt.event.*;

public class NoAdapter extends Frame
{
   private Label lbl;

   public NoAdapter()
   {
      lbl = new Label("No Adapters Here");

      setLayout(new FlowLayout());
      add(lbl);

      addWindowListener(new WinListener());
      setBounds(100, 100, 200, 200);
      setVisible(true);
   }

   public static void main(String args[])
   {
      NoAdapter na = new NoAdapter();
   }
}

/*   This is a WindowListener that implements the         */
/*   WindowListener interface directly.  Every method defined  */
/*   in the WindowListener interface must be implemented.      */
/*   In this case six of the seven methods are implemented     */
/*   as stub methods.                                          */

class WinListener implements WindowListener
{
   public void windowClosing(WindowEvent we)
   {
      System.exit(0);
   }

   public void windowActivated(WindowEvent we) {}
   public void windowClosed(WindowEvent we) {}
   public void windowDeactivated(WindowEvent we) {}
   public void windowDeiconified(WindowEvent we) {}
   public void windowIconified(WindowEvent we) {}
   public void windowOpened(WindowEvent we) {}
}
```

The WindowListener is defined as a separate class called WinListener that implements the WindowListener interface. We only really care about the `windowClosing()` method, but have to provide stubs for the other six methods defined in the interface.

Now, in Example 4.6, let's look at the code if an adapter class is used.

EXAMPLE 4.6 WINDOWLISTENER USING AN ADAPTER CLASS

```java
import java.awt.*;
import java.awt.event.*;

public class WithAdapter extends Frame
{
   private Label lbl;

   public WithAdapter()
   {
      lbl = new Label("Adapters are nice");

      setLayout(new FlowLayout());
      add(lbl);

      addWindowListener(new WinListener());
      setBounds(100, 100, 200, 200);
      setVisible(true);
   }

   public static void main(String args[])
   {
      WithAdapter na = new WithAdapter();
   }
}

/*   This WindowListener extends the WindowAdapter class   */
/*   The WindowAdapter class is a WindowListener that      */
/*   provides stub implementations for all the methods     */
/*   from the WindowListener interface.  The program       */
/*   only needs the windowClosing() method, so that is     */
/*   the only method that needs to be implemented in the   */
/*   WinListener class.                                    */

class WinListener extends WindowAdapter
{
   public void windowClosing(WindowEvent we)
   {
      System.exit(0);
   }
}
```

In this case, the WinListener class is written as a subclass of the WindowAdapter class. The WindowAdapter class implements the WindowListener interface and provides stubs for the seven methods declared in that interface. The WinListener class only needs to override the `windowClosing()` method. The other six methods are taken care of by the adapter class.

Listener Adapter Classes Contained in the java.awt.event Package

The following is a short description of the event listener adapter classes found in the java.awt.event package. There is an adapter class for every listener interface that declares more than one method, with the exception of the InputMethodListener interface. A complete description of these adapter classes as well as examples of how to use them can be found in Chapter 9, "Listener Adapter Classes."

public abstract class `ComponentAdapter` extends `Object` implements `ComponentListener`

public abstract class `ContainerAdapter` extends `Object` implements `ContainerListener`

public abstract class `FocusAdapter` extends `Object` implements `FocusListener`

public abstract class `HierarchyBoundsAdapter` extends `Object` implements `HierarchyBoundsListener`

public abstract class `KeyAdapter` extends `Object` implements `KeyListener`

public abstract class `MouseAdapter` extends `Object` implements `MouseListener`

public abstract class `MouseMotionAdapter` extends `Object` implements `MouseMotionListener`

public abstract class `WindowAdapter` extends `Object` implements `WindowListener`

Note that all of these adapter classes are abstract. This is because adapter classes are intended to be subclassed rather than used directly. They all provides stubs for the methods declared in their associated listener interface. The adapter classes are subclasses of Object and have access to the methods defined in the Object class.

Listener Adapter Classes Contained in the javax.swing.event Package

Unlike the java.awt.event package, where there is an adapter class for nearly every event listener that defines more than one method, the javax.swing.event package contains only two adapter classes. A short description of the two classes follows. As before, a complete description of these classes and examples of how to use them can be found in Chapter 9.

```
public abstract class InternalFrameAdapter extends Object
implements InternalFrameListener
public abstract class MouseInputAdapter extends Object implements
MouseInputListener
```

`InternalFrameAdapter` provides stubs for the seven methods declared in the InternalFrameListener interface.

`MouseInputAdapter` provides stubs for the methods used to process MouseEvents and is useful if you want to access both motion-oriented and non-motion-oriented MouseEvent processing methods.

User-Defined Event Listener Interfaces

It really is quite simple to create a user-defined listener interface. The user-defined interface will extend either the EventListener interface or one of the EventListener subinterfaces. The user-defined interface then declares whatever methods are desired. An example of how this is done is provided in Chapter 12, "User-Defined Event Classes and Event Listeners."

Once the user-defined listener interface has been created, a mechanism must be set up to add or remove a user-defined listener object from the listener list maintained by the event source component. This can be done using either the EventListenerList or AWTEventMulticaster classes. A description of these classes and an example of how to use them are provided in Chapter 11, "Event Listener Manager Classes."

Connecting an Event Source to an Event Listener

The delegation model used by the Java 1.1 event model is not complete without a mechanism for delivering the events from source to listener. The system must know where to send the events. The mechanism that is used is a listener list. Every event-generating object, whether system-defined or user-defined, maintains a list of associated event listeners. When the object generates a certain type of event, the listener list is checked to see if it contains any listeners of that type. If it does, the event is sent to those listeners. This process is performed automatically for system-generated events. For user-generated events, the list-checking code is incorporated into the method used to fire the event.

Adding a listener to the listener list of an event-generating object is quite easy. Java provides methods to add every built-in listener type. The methods to add low-level event listeners are provided in the Component, Container, and JComponent classes. For example, the Component class defines the following methods.

```
public void addComponentListener(ComponentListener listener)
public void addFocusListener(FocusListener listener)
public void addHierarchyBoundsListener(HierarchyBoundsListener listener)
public void addHierarchyListener(HierarchyListener listener)
public void addInputMethodListener(InputMethodListener listener)
public void addKeyListener(KeyListener listener)
public void addMouseListener(MouseListener listener)
public void addMouseMotionListener(MouseMotionListener listener)
public void addPropertyChangeListener(PropertyChangeListener listener)
```

A reference to the listener to be added is passed to the method as an argument. The process of an event-generating object adding a listener to its listener list is also referred to as having the object register an event listener. Note that it is the event source that invokes these methods. Therefore the proper terminology is that the event source registers an event listener.

Methods to add high-level event listeners to a listener list are generally defined in the classes of the objects that generate the event. For example, a JEditorPane object can generate HyperlinkEvents. The JEditorPane class defines the `addHyperlinkListener()` method to add a HyperlinkListener to the JEditorPane object's listener list.

There is no practical limit to the number of event listeners that can be added to an object's listener list. There are limits to the type of event listeners that can be added, and this varies from object to object, depending on the types of events the object can generate. For instance, a JButton can add a ComponentListener, a MouseListener, and 10 ActionListeners, but it cannot add a DocumentListener because a JButton does not generate DocumentEvents and does not have access to an `addDocumentListener()` method. An event will be sent to every listener of that type contained in the listener list. In the previous example, if the JButton generated an ActionEvent, it would be sent to all 10 ActionListeners in the JButton object's listener list.

See Example 4.7 in the next section, "Disconnecting an Event Source from an Event Listener."

Disconnecting an Event Source from an Event Listener

Just as there is a mechanism for adding event listeners to an object's listener list, there is a way to remove listeners as well. The process is identical. Java provides `remove()` methods for every type of event listener. The event-generating object invokes the method and passes it a reference to the listener it wants to remove from its listener list. The low-level event listener removal methods are contained in the Component, Container, and JComponent classes. For instance, the Component class defines the following methods.

```
public void removeComponentListener(ComponentListener listener)
public void removeFocusListener(FocusListener listener)
public void removeHierarchyBoundsListener(HierarchyBoundsListener listener)
public void removeHierarchyListener(HierarchyListener listener)
public void removeInputMethodListener(InputMethodListener listener)
```

```
public void removeKeyListener(KeyListener listener)
public void removeMouseListener(MouseListener listener)
public void removeMouseMotionListener(MouseMotionListener listener)
public void removePropertyChangeListener(PropertyChangeListener listener)
```

A listener that is removed from an object's listener list will no longer be notified when the object generates an event of that type. The process of removing a listener from a listener list is also referred to as disconnecting, or deregistering, the listener. As with the methods to add listeners, it is the event source that invokes the `remove()` methods.

Methods to remove high-level event listeners from a listener list are generally defined in the classes of the objects that generate the event. For example, a JMenu object can generate MenuEvents. The JMenu class defines the `removeMenuListener()` method to remove a MenuListener from the JMenu object's listener list.

EXAMPLE

Example 4.7 demonstrates how components add and remove listeners from their listener lists. A large yellow JPanel is placed in a JFrame. A JButton and a non-editable JTextField are placed at the bottom of the JFrame. The JPanel initially adds a MouseMotionListener to its listener list using the `addMouseMotionListener()` method. Whenever the mouse is moved or dragged inside the bounding area of the JPanel, a motion-oriented MouseEvent is generated and sent to the MouseMotionListener. If the mouse is moved within the bounding area of the JPanel, the `mouseMoved()` method is called and the current position of the mouse is printed inside the JTextField.

The JButton adds an ActionListener to its listener list using the `addActionListener()` method. When the JButton is pressed, an ActionEvent is generated and sent to the `actionPerformed()` method. Inside the `actionPerformed()` method, the JPanel removes the MouseMotionListener from its listener list using the `removeMouseMotionListener()` method. Motion-oriented MouseEvents generated by the JPanel are no longer sent to the MouseMotionListener.

EXAMPLE 4.7 HOW COMPONENTS ADD AND REMOVE LISTENERS

```
import javax.swing.*;
import java.awt.*;
import java.awt.event.*;
```

```java
public class AddRemoveListener extends JFrame
{
   private JPanel panel;
   private JTextField jtf;
   private JButton button;
   private MMListener mml;

   public AddRemoveListener()
   {
/*  A MouseMotionListener object is created  */

      mml = new MMListener();

/*  A JTextField, JPanel, and JButton are created and placed    */
/*  on a JFrame.  The JButton adds an ActionListener to its     */
/*  listener list.  The JPanel adds a MouseMotionListener to    */
/*  its listener list.                                          */

      jtf = new JTextField(30);
      jtf.setEditable(false);

      panel = new JPanel();
      panel.setBackground(Color.yellow);
      panel.addMouseMotionListener(mml);

      button = new JButton("Remove");
      button.setBorder(BorderFactory.createRaisedBevelBorder());
      button.setFont(new Font("Serif", Font.PLAIN, 14));
      button.addActionListener(new ButtonListener());

      JPanel p = new JPanel();
      p.add(jtf);
      p.add(button);
      getContentPane().add(panel, BorderLayout.CENTER);
      getContentPane().add(p, BorderLayout.SOUTH);

      setDefaultCloseOperation(JFrame.EXIT_ON_CLOSE);
      setBounds(100, 100, 600, 250);
      setVisible(true);
   }

/*  When the "remove" button is pressed, an ActionEvent is      */
/*  generated and sent to the actionPerformed() method.         */
/*  The JPanel removes the MouseMotionListener from its         */
/*  listener list. MouseEvents generated inside the JPanel      */
/*  are no longer sent to the MouseMotionListener               */

   class ButtonListener implements ActionListener
   {
      public void actionPerformed(ActionEvent ae)
      {
         panel.removeMouseMotionListener(mml);
         jtf.setText("");
```

```
            }
       }
       /* The MouseMotionListener is called whenever a motion-oriented */
       /* mouse event is generated.  This MouseMotionListener extends  */
       /* an adapter class.  Only the mouseMoved() method is overridden. */
       /* When a motion-oriented MouseEvent is generated, the current  */
       /* mouse position is printed in the textfield.                  */
       class MMListener extends MouseMotionAdapter
       {
          public void mouseMoved(MouseEvent me)
          {
             jtf.setText("Mouse at position "+me.getX()+",""+
                        me.getY());
          }
       }

       public static void main(String args[])
       {
          AddRemoveListener arl = new AddRemoveListener();
       }
}
```

Run this application and move the mouse around inside the yellow area of the frame. You will see the current position of the mouse updated in the textfield. Press the button. The textfield is cleared. Now if you move the mouse around inside the yellow area of the frame, nothing appears inside the textfield. The JPanel is still generating MouseEvent objects, but there is nothing to listen to them and process them.

The getListeners() Method

Java provides the getListeners() method to return an array containing every listener of the specified type contained in the listener list of the invoking object. The getListeners() method is defined in many classes, including the Component class. The method syntax is given below.

```
public EventListener[] getListeners(Class listenerType)
throws ClassCastException
```

If there are no registered listeners of the specified type, an empty array is returned. The method throws a ClassCastException if the argument passed to the method is not a recognized subclass of java.util.EventListener.

The return array can be cast to whatever type may be desired. For example, if you wanted to return an array of all ActionListeners in the listener list of an object named `blah`, you would use the syntax

```
ActionListener[] listeners =
(ActionListener[])(blah.getListeners(ActionListener.class));
```

EVENT LISTENER MANAGER CLASSES

The J2SE provides two classes that are used to manage event listener lists and for dispatching an event to the appropriate listener when one is generated. The AWTEventMulticaster class is used for managing AWT event listeners. It maintains a separate list for each listener type. The EventListenerList class can be used for any event type and maintains a single list for all listeners. Both the AWTEventMulticaster and EventListenerList classes can be used to create components that fire user-defined events.

AWTEventMulticaster Class

The AWTEventMulticaster class, defined in the java.awt package, is used to manage registered event listeners and to dispatch events that are subclasses of the AWTEvent class. What the AWTEventMulticaster does is maintain a linked list of event listeners. It can do this for every listener type defined in the java.awt package. Every time an event source updates its listener list, a new AWTEventMulticaster object is created containing the updated list. The AWTEventMulticaster object also has access to the methods defined in the event listeners. Whenever an event is generated, the AWTEventMulticaster sends the event to the appropriate method for every listener in the linked list.

This operation usually goes on in the background and is of no concern to the programmer. However, the AWTEventMulticaster class can be used to create new types of components. It can also be used to extend the event capabilities of existing GUI components. For instance, it is possible to define a new JLabel class such that this new JLabel object will generate an ItemEvent when the mouse is pressed over its bounding area. In other words, it is possible to define a JLabel object that can be selected. This is really more of an advanced topic and is covered in detail, including an example, in Chapter 11.

EventListenerList Class

Like the AWTEventMulticaster class, the EventListenerList class, defined in the javax.swing.event package, facilitates the addition and removal of event listeners from a listener list. Unlike the AWTEventMulticaster class, an EventListenerList can handle any type of event. An EventListenerList maintains a single list containing all of the listeners registered to a given object. The list is really a series of class description and listener object pairs. The Class objects let you determine the type of each listener.

The JComponent class defines an EventListenerList field named `listenerList`. This means that any subclass of JComponent has access to an EventListenerList that can be used to register event listeners to that component.

A detailed discussion of the workings and use of the EventListenerList class is an advanced topic that can be found in Chapter 11.

5

EVENT HANDLING ODDS AND ENDS

This chapter covers topics that are important in understanding Java event handling but that don't really fit in the previous chapters. The subjects described include how to determine the source of an event, event consumption, the event queue, and the event dispatching thread.

DETERMINING THE EVENT SOURCE

Oftentimes when processing an event, it is necessary to determine the event source. This is the case, for instance, when several components are registered to the same listener object. The Java language provides methods to determine the event source. All event classes are subclasses of the EventObject class defined in the java.util package. The EventObject class defines the following method:

```
public Object getSource()
```

which returns a reference to the object that generated the event. The return value is of type Object and is normally cast to whatever specific class type is desired.

EXAMPLE

In the program presented in Example 5.1, two JButton objects are placed on a JFrame. It is intended that whatever JButton is pressed will be disabled. Both JButton objects are registered to the same ActionListener class. When either JButton is pressed, an ActionEvent is generated and sent to the `actionPerformed()` method. The method uses the `getSource()` method to determine which JButton generated the event and disables that object.

EXAMPLE 5.1 USING THE GETSOURCE() METHOD

```
import javax.swing.*;
import java.awt.*;
import java.awt.event.*;

public class GetSource extends JFrame
{
    JButton button1, button2;

    public GetSource()
    {
/*  Two JButtons are created and placed on a JFrame.  The JButtons  */
/*  register an ActionListener.                                     */

        ButtonListener listener = new ButtonListener();

        button1 = new JButton("Button1");
        button1.setBorder(BorderFactory.createRaisedBevelBorder());
        button1.setFont(new Font("Serif", Font.PLAIN, 14));
        button1.addActionListener(listener);

        button2 = new JButton("Button2");
        button2.setBorder(BorderFactory.createRaisedBevelBorder());
        button2.setFont(new Font("Serif", Font.PLAIN, 14));
        button2.addActionListener(listener);

        JPanel p = new JPanel();
        p.add(button1);
        p.add(button2);
        setContentPane(p);

        setDefaultCloseOperation(JFrame.EXIT_ON_CLOSE);
        setBounds(100, 100, 200, 200);
        setVisible(true);
    }

/*  When either button is pressed, an ActionEvent is generated      */
/*  and the actionPerformed() method is called.  The getSource()    */
/*  method is used to determine the event source.  The return       */
/*  value of the getSource() method is of type Object.  It is       */
```

```
/* cast into type JButton. Whatever JButton was the source of  */
/* event is disabled.                                          */

   class ButtonListener implements ActionListener
   {
      public void actionPerformed(ActionEvent ae)
      {
         JButton b = (JButton)ae.getSource();
         b.setEnabled(false);
      }
   }

   public static void main(String args[])
   {
      GetSource gs = new GetSource();
   }
}
```

Run this example and press one of the two buttons. The button that was pressed will become disabled because the `getSource()` method identifies it as the source of the event.

Many of the event classes themselves have methods for identifying the source of the event. For example, all ActionEvent objects have a String called the action command associated with them. This action command can be used to identify the source of the ActionEvent. The ActionEvent class defines the `getActionCommand()` method, which returns the action command. As another example, the ItemEvent class defines the `getItem()` method, which returns an Object containing some component-specific information about the object that generated the event. The ItemEvent class also defines the `getItemSelectable()` method, which returns a reference to the ItemSelectable object that generated the event. This ItemSelectable object could directly access the `getSelectedObjects()` method without having to be cast to another object type.

Many of the other event classes define similar methods to return a more specific event-source type than the `getSource()` method.

EXAMPLE

In Example 5.2, a List that supports multiple selections is created and placed on a JFrame. The List object registers an ItemListener. When the selection of the list is changed by single-clicking a List element, an ItemEvent is generated and sent to the `itemStateChanged()` method of the ListListener class. The `getItemSelectable()` method is used to obtain a reference to the ItemSelectable object, in this case, the List, that generated the event. The return value from the ItemSelectable object is used to retrieve an array containing the selected elements of the list. The selected items are noted in a textfield placed at the bottom of the frame.

EXAMPLE 5.2 USING THE GETITEMSELECTABLE() METHOD

```java
import java.awt.event.*;
import java.awt.*;

public class GetSource2 extends Frame
{
   List list;
   TextField tf;

   public GetSource2()
   {
/*   List and Textfield objects are created and placed on     */
/*   a Frame.  The List registers an ItemListener.            */

      list = new List();
      list.add("Diamond");
      list.add("Sapphire");
      list.add("Emerald");
      list.add("Quartz");
      list.setMultipleMode(true);
      list.addItemListener(new ListListener());

      tf = new TextField(30);
      tf.setText("Selections: ");
      tf.setEditable(false);

      Panel p = new Panel();
      p.add(list);

      add(p, BorderLayout.CENTER);
      add(tf, BorderLayout.SOUTH);

      addWindowListener(new WinClosing());
      setBounds(100, 100, 400, 200);
      setVisible(true);
   }

/*   The ItemListener is implemented as an inner class.  The     */
/*   getItemSelectable() method is used to return a reference    */
/*   to the List object that generated the ItemEvent.            */

   public class ListListener implements ItemListener
   {
      public void itemStateChanged(ItemEvent ie)
      {
         Object[] selections =
```

```
                    ie.getItemSelectable().getSelectedObjects();
         String str = "Selections: ";
         for (int i=0; i<selections.length; ++i)
         {
            if ( i != 0 )
            {
               str = str.concat(", ");
            }
            str = str.concat(""+selections[i]);
         }

         tf.setText(str);
      }
   }

   public static void main(String args[])
   {
      GetSource2 gs2 = new GetSource2();
   }
}

/* The WinClosing class is a WindowListener that terminates the  */
/* program if the application window is closed.                   */

class WinClosing extends WindowAdapter
{
   public void windowClosing(WindowEvent we)
   {
      System.exit(0);
   }
}
```

Run this program and make a selection in the list. The textfield is updated to indicate the current selection. Now make multiple selections. The textfield lists all of the selected elements. When you deselect an item, the textfield display is updated to show that this has happened.

CONSUMING EVENTS

Before discussing the topic of event consumption, let us briefly review the difference between AWT and Swing GUI components. Every AWT GUI component has an associated peer. The peer is an implementation of the component in the native environment. It is the component peer, written in some native programming language that displays the component on the screen and responds to user input. Swing GUI components, on the other hand, are pure Java. A Swing component knows how to draw itself and can respond directly to user input.

This brings us to the topic of event consumption. When an AWT component generates an event that is a subclass of the InputEvent class, most notably KeyEvents and MouseEvents, the event is first delivered to the event source and any registered listeners before it is processed by the event source's component peer. If the event invokes the `consume()` method, it is designated to have been consumed. A consumed InputEvent is not delivered to the event source's component peer.

What does all this mean? Well, for example, let us say there is a TextField that has keyboard focus and has added a KeyListener to its listener list. If a keystroke is pressed, a KeyEvent is generated and sent to the `keyPressed()` method of the KeyListener. Normally, the character corresponding to the keystroke would appear inside the TextField. However, if the KeyEvent invokes the `consume()` method inside the `keyPressed()` method, the KeyEvent would not be delivered to the TextField object's component peer and the character corresponding to the keystroke would not appear inside the TextField.

Event consumption can therefore be used to limit the type of input to AWT components. If a TextField is intended to only contain numbers, event consumption can be used to prevent non-numeric characters from being entered. Note that this only works with AWT GUI components. Swing components have no component peers and therefore event consumption has no effect on them.

Event Consumption Methods

These methods are used to consume events or to determine if an event has been marked as being consumed. They are defined in the InputMethodEvent, InputEvent, and AWTEvent classes.

public void `consume()`

public boolean `isConsumed()`

`consume()` marks the invoking event as having been consumed.

`isConsumed()` returns true if the invoking event has been marked as being consumed.

EXAMPLE

In Example 5.3, event consumption is used to restrict the input into a TextField to alphabetic characters. A TextField registers a KeyListener and is placed on a Frame. When the TextField has focus and a keystroke is pressed, a KeyEvent is sent to the `keyPressed()` method of the KeyListener. The event is checked to see if it is an alphabetic character, the backspace, or the delete. If it is not, the event is marked as consumed and the character corresponding to the keystroke does not appear in the TextField.

EXAMPLE 5.3 EVENT CONSUMPTION

```
import java.awt.*;
import java.awt.event.*;

public class ConsumeDemo2 extends Frame
{
   private TextField tf;

   public ConsumeDemo2()
   {
/* A TextField is created and placed on a Frame.  The TextField   */
/* registers a KeyListener.                                        */

      tf = new TextField(15);
      tf.addKeyListener(new KeyHandler());

      Panel panel = new Panel();
      panel.add(tf);

      add(panel, BorderLayout.CENTER);

      addWindowListener(new WinAdapter());
      setBounds(100, 100, 500, 200);
      setVisible(true);
   }

/* The KeyListener is implemented as an inner class that extends   */
/* the KeyAdapter class.  When a key is pressed, the resulting     */
/* KeyEvent is sent to the keyPressed() method before it is sent   */
/* to the component peer of the TextField.  The keyPressed()       */
/* method tests the KeyEvent to see if it was due to an            */
/* alphabetic key, the delete key, or the backspace key.  If it    */
/* was not, the event is consumed and the keystroke does not       */
/* appear in the TextField.                                        */

   class KeyHandler extends KeyAdapter
   {
      public void keyPressed(KeyEvent event)
```

```
        {
           if ( event.getKeyCode() < KeyEvent.VK_A ||
              event.getKeyCode() > KeyEvent.VK_Z )
           {
              if ( event.getKeyCode() != KeyEvent.VK_DELETE )
              {
                 if (event.getKeyCode() != KeyEvent.VK_BACK_SPACE)
                 {
                    event.consume();
                 }
              }
           }
        }

        public static void main(String args[])
        {
           ConsumeDemo2 demo = new ConsumeDemo2();
        }
}

/* This makes sure the application terminates if the window is
closed    */

class WinAdapter extends WindowAdapter
{
   public void windowClosing(WindowEvent event)
   {
      System.exit(0);
   }
}
```

When you start the code, a blank textfield appears on your screen. Type some letters into the textField. Now try to type a number or some other non-alphabetic character. The character does not appear in the textfield because the event corresponding to the non-alphabetic keystroke has been consumed.

Note that this example would not work properly if Swing components (JTextField, JFrame, etc.) were used. Swing components do not have peers, so event consumption has no effect. Rewrite this example using Swing components and see what happens when a non-alphabetic keystroke is typed into the JTextField.

The Event Queue

The system event queue stores events after they have been generated, until they are dispatched by the `dispatchEvent()` method. Normally, the operations of the system event queue are transparent to the user. It does what it does in the background automatically. It is possible to look into and even manipulate the system event queue using the EventQueue class.

EventQueue Class

The EventQueue class encapsulates the Java event queue. It has a public constructor in the unlikely event a programmer would want to create an event queue object, but it is more common to use this class to access the system event queue. This is accomplished using the `getSystemEventQueue()` method defined in the Toolkit class.

Among the methods defined in the EventQueue class are `invokeAndWait()` and `invokeLater()`. These methods allow you to execute code from the event-dispatching thread. This can be useful in preventing a deadlock condition in a multithreaded application. See the section "ActiveEvent Interface" in Chapter 6, "Event Classes and Interfaces," for more details.

Syntax: public class EventQueue extends Object

Package: java.awt

Class hierarchy: Object—EventQueue

The EventQueue class is a subclass of Object. An EventQueue object has access to the methods defined in the Object classes.

Introduced: JDK 1.1

Constructors

public EventQueue()

The EventQueue class provides one public constructor in the unlikely event you would want to create an EventQueue object.

EventQueue Class Methods

protected void `dispatchEvent(AWTEvent event)`
public AWTEvent `getNextEvent()` throws InterruptedException
public static void `invokeAndWait(Runnable runnable)` throws InterruptedException, InvocationTargetException

public static void `invokeLater(Runnable runnable)`
public static boolean `isDispatchThread()`
public AWTEvent `peekEvent()`
public AWTEvent `peekEvent(int eventID)`
protected void `pop()` throws EmptyStackException
public void `postEvent(AWTEvent event)`
public void `push(EventQueue newEventQueue)`

`dispatchEvent()` dispatches an AWTEvent. If the event is an ActiveEvent, the event will invoke its `dispatch()` method. If the event is another type of AWTEvent and the event source was a Component or MenuComponent subclass, the event source will invoke its `dispatchEvent()` method.

`getNextEvent()` removes an event from the EventQueue and returns a reference to it.

`invokeAndWait()` executes the `run()` method from a Runnable object on the event-dispatching thread of the EventQueue. This takes place after all pending events have been processed. This method blocks until the `run()` method has been executed.

`invokeLater()` executes the `run()` method from a Runnable object on the event-dispatching thread of the EventQueue. This takes place after all pending events have been processed. This method returns immediately without waiting for the `run()` method to execute.

`isDispatchThread()` returns true if the current thread is the AWT event-dispatching thread.

`peekEvent()` returns a reference to the first event on the EventQueue without removing it. If an `eventID` parameter is provided, the return value will be the first event of this type.

`pop()` stops dispatching events from the current EventQueue. Any pending events are transferred to the previous EventQueue. If there isn't one, an EmptyStackException is thrown.

`postEvent()` places the specified event on the EventQueue.

`push()` replaces the current EventQueue with the one specified. Any pending events are transferred to the new EventQueue.

Methods Inherited from the java.lang.Object class

> public final Class getClass()

getClass() returns a Class object representing the runtime class of the invoking object. In this case, it would return an object representing the java.awt.EventQueue class.

The other methods inherited from the Object class, clone(), equals(), hashCode(), notify(), notifyAll(), and wait(), are generally not used in conjunction with EventQueue objects.

EXAMPLE

In Example 5.4, a button and textfield are placed on a frame. Whenever the button is pressed, an ActionEvent is generated and sent to the actionPerformed() method, which updates the textfield to indicate the action command of the event source.

A reference to the system event queue is used to post an ActionEvent onto the event queue. This event is processed just like any other ActionEvent generated by the button. This is usually the preferable way to dispatch a user-generated event rather than bypassing the event queue using the dispatchEvent() method, as was done in the user-generated events example in Chapter 3, "Event Classes." The event queue helps ensure that event dispatching and processing is done in a smooth manner. Swing components in particular rely on this to keep the component painting in sync with the component model.

EXAMPLE 5.4 MANIPULATING THE EVENTQUEUE

```
import java.awt.*;
import java.awt.event.*;

public class EventQueueExample extends Frame
   implements ActionListener
{
   Button b;
   TextField tf;

   public EventQueueExample()
   {
/*   A Button and TextField are created and placed on a Frame.    */
/*   The Button generates an ActionEvent whenever it is pressed.  */
```

```
   /*   The TextField is updated to indicate the action command of   */
   /*   the event source.                                             */

      b = new Button("Hello");
      b.addActionListener(this);

      tf = new TextField(30);
      tf.setEditable(false);

      Panel panel = new Panel();
      panel.add(b);
      add(panel, BorderLayout.CENTER);
      add(tf, BorderLayout.SOUTH);

   /*   A reference to the system event queue is retrieved using the  */
   /*   getSystemEventQueue() method.  The getToolKit() method        */
   /*   returns a reference to a ToolKit object.  The EventQueue      */
   /*   object posts an event onto the system event queue.            */

      EventQueue eq = getToolkit().getSystemEventQueue();
      eq.postEvent(new ActionEvent(b, ActionEvent.ACTION_PERFORMED,
"help"));

      addWindowListener(new WinListener());
      setBounds(100, 100, 300, 200);
      setVisible(true);
   }

   public void actionPerformed(ActionEvent ae)
   {
      tf.setText("action command is "+ae.getActionCommand());
   }

   public static void main(String args[])
   {
      EventQueueExample eqe = new EventQueueExample();
   }
}

class WinListener extends WindowAdapter
{
   public void windowClosing(WindowEvent we)
   {
      System.exit(0);
   }
}
```

When you run the program, you will notice that the initial entry in the textfield is "action command is help." This is because the ActionEvent posted onto the system event queue by the EventQueue object is processed first.

The Event-Dispatching Thread

All event handling code executes in a thread called the event-dispatching thread. It is the event-dispatching thread that calls any event listener methods. The event-dispatching thread processes each event sequentially. Every event handler finishes executing before the next event handler is called. One reason this is done is to keep the component model in sync with the component display and to block other activity on a component while an event is being processed. For instance, when a button is pressed it will appear to sink into its container display and its color will change. While the ActionEvent that is generated is being processed, the event-dispatching thread will block any other repainting or user interactions with the button. If the user keeps clicking the button during the event handling process, nothing will happen.

The `isDispatchThread()` method defined in the EventQueue class can be used to determine if the current active thread is the event-dispatching thread. Some operations, calling the `invokeAndWait()` and `invokeLater()` methods, for example, cannot be performed inside the event-dispatching thread.

Running Code in the Event-Dispatching Thread

Java allows a Runnable object to be placed on the system event queue. This is accomplished using the `invokeAndWait()` and `invokeLater()` methods defined in the EventQueue and SwingUtilities classes. The `run()` method of the Runnable object is then executed in the event-dispatching thread.

A special event type, InvocationEvent, is used in this process. The InvocationEvent class, defined in the java.awt package, implements the ActiveEvent interface. ActiveEvents are events that know how to dispatch themselves. When either the `invokeAndWait()` or `invokeLater()` method is called, the Runnable object passed to the methods as an argument is bundled into an InvocationEvent by the system and the InvocationEvent is placed on the event queue using the `postEvent()` method. The `run()`

method of the Runnable is executed after all other pending events on the event queue have been processed.

Executing code in the event-dispatching thread can be useful in preventing deadlocks in a multithreaded application. A deadlock occurs if there is a monitor conflict between two or more threads. If the code that is placed on the system event queue detects a monitor conflict, it will simply block until any other competing threads have finished.

EXAMPLE

See the example in the "ActiveEvent Interface" section of Chapter 6, where the `invokeAndWait()` method is used to prevent a deadlock condition.

PART

II

A JAVA EVENT REFERENCE

This section of the book provides a comprehensive reference to the event classes, interfaces, listener interfaces, support classes, and life cycle methods provided by the J2SE. You will find in Part II all the information you need to generate, manipulate, and process any Java event. Since the best way to learn how something works is to see it in action, dozens of clear, concise examples are provided.

Part II is intended to provide "one-stop shopping" for all the information on a given class or interface. The descriptions start with the constructors, fields, and methods defined in the class or interface. To minimize the need to flip back and forth through the book, each description also includes any inherited methods the class or interface can access. The examples in each section are all complete, standalone programs. You won't need to worry about modifying or attaching any previous example to get the one you are looking at to work.

In Chapter 6, "Event Classes and Interfaces," the classes and interfaces are detailed from ActionEvent to WindowEvent. Each section starts with a description of the event and what objects generate the event. The "vital statistics" are provided, including the event class or interface syntax, the package in which it can be found, the class or interface hierarchy, and when the event was introduced into the Java API. Next comes a description of the constructors, fields, and methods available to the event object. Finally, there is a clear, concise example illustrating how the event is used.

Several of the event types, `PropertyChangeEvents` and `UndoableEditEvents`, for instance, require a lot of support code to implement them into a Java program. This is the flip-side of the power and flexibility these event types offer a program developer. The creators of Java were thoughtful enough to provide event support classes for the `PropertyChangeEvent` and `Undoable-EditEvent` classes. The support classes, described in Chapter 7, "Event Support Classes," provide all the support methods you need to generate, receive, and process these events.

In Chapter 8, "Event Listener Interfaces," we go over the event listeners as the recipients of the messages carried by the Java events. They wait patiently in the background of your Java program for an event to be sent to them. Each section of Chapter 8 gives complete details for one of the event listener interfaces. First, the general characteristics of the listener are provided: what events it listens for, how a listener object of this type can be created, how a component can add or remove a listener of this type from its listener list, and so on. The listener interface syntax, package, and hierarchy are then given. The methods declared in the interface and any of its parent interfaces are described, along with methods that are used to add or remove a listener object from a listener list. Finally, an example is provided that demonstrates every aspect of using the event listener.

One of the drawbacks of defining the event listeners as interfaces is that when you create an event listener class, you have to provide an implementation of every method declared in the interface whether you need them for your program or not. In Chapter 9, "Listener Adapter Classes," we discuss the adapter classes provided for some of the listener interfaces contained in the Java API. They provide stubs (methods with no body) for every method declared in the corresponding listener interface. To use an adapter class, you write a subclass of the adapter class and override only the methods you need for your program.

Finally, in Chapter 10, "Event Life Cycle Methods," we discuss the event life cycle methods provided in the J2SE. These are the methods used to fire and process Java events. Most of the time, these methods are used by the system, but the programmer also has access to them. They can be used to modify the event-generating or event handling capabilities of an existing component, or they can be used to create new event-generating classes.

Event Classes
and Interfaces

The event classes encapsulate the various events supported by the Java programming language. Event objects are Java's messengers carrying information about what happened to any interested listeners. The event classes—and in one case, interface—define the structure of the events used by the Java programming language. Each event object type carries different information. All of them contain information about the source of the event. Many of the classes provide additional information about what interaction took place and what has changed because of it.

This section provides a detailed description of the event classes in the java.awt.event, javax.swing.event, and java.beans packages, as well as selected events from some of the other packages in the Java API. It also details the event superclasses found in the java.awt and java.util packages. The information provided for each class includes the class syntax, package, hierarchy, and when it was introduced into the Java language. The constructors, fields, and methods well as the fields and methods that are inherited from other classes, are described. Every class description also includes a clear, concise example showing how to apply the event type in a GUI application.

ActionEvent Class

An ActionEvent is a semantic (high-level) event that is generated when a component-specific action is performed on a GUI component. This is a fancy way of saying that ActionEvent objects are generated in different ways by different components. They are generated by

1. Button or JButton items when the button is pressed.
2. MenuItem or JMenuItem objects when the menu item is selected..
3. List objects when the list item is double-clicked.
4. TextField, JTextfield, or JPasswordField objects when the "Return" or "Enter" key is pressed.
5. JComboBox items when the user makes a selection.

Classes that implement the Action interface can also fire ActionEvents, as can Timer objects.

When an ActionEvent object is generated, it is sent to every registered ActionListener object. The ActionListener object provides an implementation of the `actionPerformed()` method that contains the code necessary to process the event.

Every ActionEvent object has an action command associated with it. The action command is a String that can be used to identify the component that generated the ActionEvent. Most components that generate action events set the action command to the component label by default. An ActionEvent object will also contain information about the event ID and the source of the event.

Syntax:	public class ActionEvent extends AWTEvent
Package:	java.awt.event
Class hierarchy:	Object—EventObject—AWTEvent—ActionEvent
	The ActionEvent class is part of the AWTEvent hierarchy. An ActionEvent object has access to the methods defined in the AWTEvent, EventObject, and Object classes.
Introduced:	JDK 1.1

Constructors

public ActionEvent(Object `source`, int `id`, String `actionCommand`)

public ActionEvent(Object `source`, int `id`, String `actionCommand`, int `modifiers`)

Most of the time, ActionEvents are generated by the system. The ActionEvent class provides two public constructors to create ActionEvent objects. The source is the object that generated the event. The `id` parameter identifies the ActionEvent type. With a system-generated ActionEvent, this will be the ACTION_PERFORMED field described below. The `actionCommand` is an identifying String that can be used to identify the component that generated the event. The `modifiers` parameter is used to indicate which modifier keys were pressed when the event was generated.

Constants

public static final int `ACTION_FIRST`
public static final int `ACTION_LAST`
public static final int `ACTION_PERFORMED`
public static final int `ALT_MASK`
public static final int `CTRL_MASK`
public static final int `META_MASK`
public static final int `SHIFT_MASK`

These fields are used to identify or modify an ActionEvent object. The `ACTION_FIRST` and `ACTION_LAST` fields indicate the range of IDs used for action events. In this case, there is only one ID, so `ACTION_PERFORMED`, `ACTION_FIRST`, and `ACTION_LAST` will be the same number. The numerical value of `ACTION_PERFORMED` is 1001.

An ActionEvent can be modified by pressing a control key (ALT, CTRL, META, or SHIFT) when the ActionEvent is generated. More than one modifier key can be pressed. The `ALT_MASK`, `CTRL_MASK`, `META_MASK`, and `SHIFT_MASK` constants are used to identify if a modifier key was pressed. The `getModifiers()` method can be used to determine if the desired control keys were pressed. If more than one modifier key was pressed, the `getModifiers()` method returns the integer sum of the modifier constants.

However, a system-generated ActionEvent object will have modifiers set only if it is appropriate to do so. For instance, the `CTRL_MASK` modifier will not be set if the CTRL key is held down when a button is pressed. The pressing of a button is an action that is not intended to be modified. The modifier will be set if the CTRL key is held down when a MenuItem is selected.

Fields

Beyond those constants described in the preceding section, the ActionEvent class does not define any additional fields. An ActionEvent object does have access to the fields defined in the AWTEvent and EventObject classes.

ActionEvent Class Methods

public String `getActionCommand()`
public int `getModifiers()`
public String `paramString()`

`getActionCommand()` returns the action command associated with the invoking ActionEvent object. This can be used to determine, for instance, which of a number of buttons generated the ActionEvent and was therefore pressed.

`getModifiers()` returns the integer sum of the value of any modifier constants associated with the invoking ActionEvent object. The modifier constants will be one or more of the following: ALT_MASK, CTRL_MASK, META_MASK, or SHIFT_MASK. If two or more modifier keys were pressed when the ActionEvent was generated, the return value will be the sum of the individual modifier constants. As was stated previously, a system-generated ActionEvent will have its modifier constants only if it is appropriate to do so. An ActionEvent will be generated if a button is pressed while the ALT key is held down. However, if this ActionEvent invokes the `getModifiers()` method, the return value will be zero.

`paramString()` overrides the method defined in the AWTEvent class and returns a parameter String that identifies the action event. This is generally used for event-logging and debugging purposes. When an ActionEvent object calls the `toString()` method, the return value of the `paramString()` method is incorporated in the return value of the `toString()` method.

Methods Inherited from the java.awt.AWTEvent Class

protected void `consume()`
protected void `finalize()` throws Throwable
public int `getID()`

| protected boolean `isConsumed()` |
| public String `toString()` |

An ActionEvent object has access to the methods defined in the AWTEvent class. For a description of these methods, see the section "AWTEvent Class" in this chapter.

Methods Inherited from the java.util.EventObject Class

| public Object `getSource()` |

`getSource()` returns a reference to the object that generated the invoking event. This method can be used to determine which component generated the invoking ActionEvent object.

Methods Inherited from the java.lang.Object Class

| public final Class `getClass()` |

`getClass()` returns a Class object representing the runtime class of the invoking object. In this case, it would return an object representing the java.awt.event.ActionEvent class.

The other methods inherited from the Object class, `clone()`, `equals()`, `hashCode()`, `notify()`, `notifyAll()`, and `wait()`, are generally not used in conjunction with ActionEvent objects.

EXAMPLE

Example 6.1 demonstrates how ActionEvent objects are generated by various GUI components and illustrates how ActionListener objects can receive and process those events.

The ActionEventDemo class is a Frame that contains three GUI components that can generate ActionEvents. There is a TextField component that generates an ActionEvent when it has focus and the Return or Enter key is pressed. There is also a Button component that generates an ActionEvent when pressed. The Frame contains a MenuBar with one Menu that contains one MenuItem. The MenuItem will generate an ActionEvent when it is selected.

The button is intended to terminate the program when pressed. The ActionListener that does this is implemented as an anonymous class and is used as an argument when the button calls the `addActionListener()` method.

The ActionEventDemo class implements the ActionListener interface, which means that it will be sent ActionEvent objects from sources to which it is registered. The `actionPerformed()` method is implemented by the ActionEventDemo class. The `enterTF` textfield and the MenuItem register the ActionListener provided by the ActionEventDemo class.

A second, read-only textfield is used to display the contents of the `enterTF` textfield. When an ActionEvent is generated by either the `enterTF` textfield or the MenuItem, it is sent to the `actionPerformed()` method defined in the ActionEventDemo class. If the action command associated with the ActionEvent is `clear`, the event was generated by the MenuItem and the contents of the read-only textfield are cleared. Otherwise, the event was generated by the `enterTF` textfield and its contents are copied to the read-only textfield.

EXAMPLE 6.1 ACTIONEVENT CLASS

```
import java.awt.*;
import java.awt.event.*;

//   The ActionEventDemo class, which is a Frame, also serves
//   as an ActionListener.

public class ActionEventDemo extends Frame implements ActionListener
{
   Button button;
   MenuBar mb;
   Menu editMenu;
   MenuItem clearMI;
   TextField enterTF, displayTF;

   public ActionEventDemo() {

   //  A button is created that is intended to terminate the
   //  application when it is pressed.  The button registers
   //  an ActionListener that is implemented as an anonymous inner class.
   //  When the button is pressed, the actionPerformed() method defined
   //  in the anonymous inner class is called and the program termi-
   nates.

       button = new Button("Quit");
       button.addActionListener(new ActionListener() {
```

```java
            public void actionPerformed(ActionEvent ae) {
                System.exit(0);
            }
        });

    // Two TextFields are created.  The first one, enterTF, is for
    // the user to type in some text.  When the Return key is pressed,
    // the contents of enterTF will be displayed in the second textfield.
    // The TextFields register the ActionListener implemented
    // by the ActionEventDemo class.  The addActionListener() method is
    // passed the "this" reference meaning the ActionEventDemo object.

        enterTF = new TextField(20);
        enterTF.addActionListener(this);

        displayTF = new TextField(20);
        displayTF.setEditable(false);

    // A MenuBar is created that contains one Menu that contains one
    // MenuItem.  Then the MenuItem is selected, the contents of the
    // TextField at the bottom of the Frame are cleared.

        clearMI = new MenuItem("clear");
        clearMI.addActionListener(this);

        editMenu = new Menu("Edit");
        editMenu.add(clearMI);

        mb = new MenuBar();
        mb.add(editMenu);
        setMenuBar(mb);

        Panel cp = new Panel();
        cp.add(enterTF);
        cp.add(button);
        Panel sp = new Panel();
        sp.add(displayTF);
        add(cp, BorderLayout.CENTER);
        add(sp, BorderLayout.SOUTH);

        setBounds(100, 100, 300, 200);
        setVisible(true);
    }

    // The ActionEventDemo class serves as an ActionListener and must
    // implement the actionPerformed() method.  If the action command
    // associated with the ActionEvent is "clear" that means the button
    // has been pressed and the contents of the displayTF TextField are
    // cleared.  Otherwise, the ActionEvent was generated by the TextField
    // and the content of the displayTF TextField is set to be the text
    // contained by the enterTF TextField.
```

```
   public void actionPerformed(ActionEvent ae)
   {
      if ( ae.getActionCommand().equals("clear") ) {
         displayTF.setText("");
      }else {
         displayTF.setText(enterTF.getText());
      }
   }

   public static void main(String args[])
   {
      ActionEventDemo aed = new ActionEventDemo();
   }
}
```

When you run this example, type some text into the upper textfield and hit the carriage return. The input text will appear in the lower textfield. Now, select the `clear` menu item. The text in the lower textfield will disappear. Finally, press the "Quit" button and the application will terminate. All of these occurrences took place because ActionEvent objects were generated and processed.

ActiveEvent Interface

The ActiveEvent interface is implemented by events that know how to dispatch themselves. ActiveEvents can be used to execute a block of code from the event dispatch thread. An ActiveEvent can be placed upon the event queue using the `invokeAndWait()` and `invokeLater()` methods defined in the EventQueue and SwingUtilities classes. The ActiveEvent interface declares one method, `dispatch()`. When the ActiveEvent reaches the front of the system event queue, its `dispatch()` method is called. This method can be implemented to call the `run()` method of a Runnable object.

ActiveEvents can be used to prevent deadlocks. If a thread is inside a synchronized method or block and tries to call another synchronized block of code, a deadlock can occur. An ActiveEvent can be used to run the second block of code at another time, thus avoiding the deadlock. If there is a monitor conflict, the second thread will simply block (wait) until any other competing threads have finished.

The InvocationEvent class is an example of an event class that implements the ActiveEvent interface.

Syntax:	public interface ActiveEvent
Package:	java.awt
Interface hierarchy:	ActiveEvent
	The ActiveEvent interface does not inherit from any other interfaces.
Introduced:	JDK 1.2

ActiveEvent Class Methods

public void `dispatch()`

`dispatch()` sends the invoking ActiveEvent to its target destination or performs other operations defined by the event class that implements the ActiveEvent interface.

EXAMPLE

In Example 6.2, a poorly written banking application experiences a deadlock condition. An ActiveEvent object is used to avoid the deadlock. The application transfers money between two Account objects. The Account class defines an account name and an account balance. The Account class defines methods for adding and subtracting a value from the balance and for returning the account name and current balance.

The Account class also defines a synchronized method named `transfer()` that is used to transfer money from one Account object to another. The `transfer()` method first subtracts a specified amount from the invoking Account object and then adds the same amount to another Account object passed to the `transfer()` method as an argument. Both the `subtractBalance()` and `addBalance()` methods are synchronized. Calling a synchronized method from within a synchronized method can lead to deadlock. The `transfer()` method also has a one second delay that (intentionally) makes deadlock more likely.

EXAMPLE 6.2 ACTIVEEVENT INTERFACE: ACCOUNT CLASS

```
public class Account
{
   int balance;
   String name;

   public Account(int amt, String nm)
   {
```

```
      balance = amt;
      name = nm;
   }

/* The transfer() method is used to transfer money from the invoking    */
/* Account object to the one passed as an argument to the method.       */
/* The transfer() method is synchronized.  It first subtracts the       */
/* specified amount from the invoking Account object and then adds      */
/* the same amount to the other Account object.  The subtractBalance()  */
/* and addBalance() methods are synchronized.  Calling a synchronized   */
/* method from within a synchronized method can lead to deadlock.       */

   public synchronized void transfer(Account acctB, int amount)
   {
      subtractBalance(amount);

      try
      {
         Thread.sleep(1000);
      }
      catch (Exception e) {}

      System.out.println(Thread.currentThread().getName()+
                        " trying to call addBalance()");

      acctB.addBalance(amount);
   }

   public synchronized void addBalance(int amt)
   {
      balance += amt;
   }

   public synchronized void subtractBalance(int amt)
   {
      balance -= amt;
   }

   public int getBalance()
   {
      return balance;
   }

   public String getName()
   {
      return name;
         }
      }
```

The Deadlock class (Example 6.3) is the driver class for this application. It creates two Account objects and then starts two transactions as separate threads. The first thread transfers 50 (dollars? yen? rubles?) from Account acct1 to Account acct2. The second thread transfers 75 from acct2 to acct1. Both of the threads invoke the `run()` method from the TransferAtoB class. Inside the `run()` method, one of the Account objects invokes the `transfer()` method, passing the other Account object as an argument.

The Deadlock class does nothing to prevent a deadlock from occurring. When it is run, because of the way the Account class was written, a deadlock will take place.

EXAMPLE 6.3 ACTIVEEVENT INTERFACE: DEADLOCK CLASS

```
import java.awt.event.*;
import java.awt.*;

public class Deadlock
{
   Account acct1, acct2;

   public Deadlock(int amt1, int amt2)
   {
/*   Two Account objects are created    */

      acct1 = new Account(amt1, "account one");
      acct2 = new Account(amt2, "account two");

/*   Two transactions are executed as separate threads.  The first   */
/*   transfers money from Account acct1 to Account acct2.  The       */
/*   second transaction transfers money from acct2 to acct1.         */

      Thread thread1 = new Thread(new TransferAtoB(acct1, acct2,
50));
      thread1.setName("Thread 1");
      thread1.start();
      System.out.println(thread1.getName()+" started");

      Thread thread2 = new Thread(new TransferAtoB(acct2, acct1,
75));
      thread2.setName("Thread 2");
      thread2.start();
      System.out.println(thread2.getName()+" started");

   }

   public static void main(String args[])
```

```
   {
      Deadlock demo = new Deadlock(100, 200);
   }
}
```

Example 6.4 is the code listing for the TransferAtoB class.

EXAMPLE 6.4 ACTIVEEVENT INTERFACE: TRANSFERATOB CLASS

```
class TransferAtoB implements Runnable
{
   Account acctA, acctB;
   int amount;

   public TransferAtoB(Account a, Account b, int amt)
   {
      acctA = a;
      acctB = b;
      amount = amt;
   }

/* The run() method has one of the Account objects invoke the   */
/* transfer() method passing the other Account object and the   */
/* amount of the transaction as arguements.                     */
   public void run()
   {
      acctA.transfer(acctB,amount);
      printBalances();
   }

   public void printBalances()
   {
      System.out.println(Thread.currentThread().getName()+
                        " transaction complete.");
      System.out.println(
              "   balance of "+acctA.getName()+" = 
"+acctA.getBalance()+
              "   balance of "+acctB.getName()+" = 
"+acctB.getBalance());
   }
}
```

Start this application. The progress of each thread is printed on the screen. You will see that both threads start, enter the `transfer()` method, and then stop. No further progress occurs and the transaction does not run to completion.

What has happened is that because of the one-second delay in the `transfer()` method, both threads are in the `transfer()` method at the same time. The first thread has the monitor on Account acct1 and needs the monitor for Account acct2 before it can continue. The second thread has the monitor on Account acct2 and needs the monitor for Account acct1 before it can continue. The program is deadlocked.

This is where the use of an ActiveEvent comes in handy. An ActiveEvent can be used to send the second transaction to the event queue where its `run()` method will be executed by the event-dispatcher thread. When the monitor conflict appears, the second transaction waits until the first transaction is finished. The ActiveEvent can be placed on the event queue, using the `invokeAndWait()` and `invokeLater()` methods. Example 6.5 is the code listing for the DeadlockFree class, which uses the ActiveEvent.

EXAMPLE 6.5 ACTIVEEVENT INTERFACE: DEADLOCKFREE CLASS

```
import java.awt.event.*;
import java.awt.*;

public class DeadlockFree
{
   Account acct1, acct2;

   public DeadlockFree(int amt1, int amt2)
     {
        acct1 = new Account(amt1, "account one");
        acct2 = new Account(amt2, "account two");

/* The first transaction is done as before.    */

        Thread thread1 = new Thread(new TransferAtoB(acct1, acct2,
50));
        thread1.setName("Thread 1");
        thread1.start();
        System.out.println(thread1.getName()+" starting");

/* The second transaction is now placed on the event queue using  */
/* the invokeAndWait() method.                                    */

        EventQueue eq = Toolkit.getDefaultToolkit().
getSystemEventQueue();
        try
        {
          System.out.println("ActiveEvent dispatched");
          eq.invokeAndWait(new TransferAtoB(acct2, acct1, 75));
        }
        catch (Exception e) {}
```

```
   }

   public static void main(String args[])
   {
      DeadlockFree demo = new DeadlockFree(100, 200);
   }
}
```

At first glance, this code listing looks odd because there is no reference to an ActiveEvent. The `invokeAndWait()` method is passed a reference to the TransferAtoB object, just as the second thread was in the Deadlock class. What happens is that the TransferAtoB object is bundled into an InvocationEvent by the system and placed on the event queue, using the `postEvent()` method. Thus, in a sense, you can create and dispatch an ActiveEvent object without doing any of the dirty work yourself—which is nice.

Run the DeadlockFree code and see what happens. The first thread starts and enters the `transfer()` method. The second transaction is placed on the event queue, where it detects a monitor conflict and waits until the first transaction is finished. It then executes the `run()` method assigned to it. Both transactions complete and the deadlock problem has disappeared.

A couple of other notes about this example and ActiveEvents in general: You will notice that although the transactions completed successfully, the program did not terminate. This is because the `invokeAndWait()` and `invokeLater()` methods activate the AWT thread when they are called. Once the AWT thread is active, the JVM will stay active until the AWT thread is killed. The CTRL-C sequence will do the trick.

A final comment about dispatching ActiveEvents is that the `invokeAndWait()` and `invokeLater()` methods cannot be called from the event-dispatcher thread. This becomes an issue when working with GUIs because the event-dispatcher thread will be the active thread inside event listener methods. One way around this is to create a separate thread inside the event listener method and dispatch the ActiveEvent from this new thread.

AdjustmentEvent Class

An AdjustmentEvent is a semantic (high-level) event generated by an object that implements the Adjustable interface. These objects have a component, such as a slider, that can be moved left-to-right or up-and-down. For instance, a

ScrollBar or JScrollBar object will generate an AdjustmentEvent object if the position of the slider is changed.

The thing to look for is the Adjustable interface. An object that implements the Adjustable interface will likely generate AdjustmentEvent objects. An AdjustmentEvent object will contain information about the source that generated the event, the ID constant of the event, and the current value of the Adjustable object that generated the event. This information allows a registered listener to determine what was adjusted and what the current value of that component is.

When an AdjustmentEvent object is generated, it is sent to every registered AdjustmentListener object. The AdjustmentListener object provides an implementation of the `adjustmentValueChanged()` method. This method is overridden to contain the code that processes the event.

Syntax: public class AdjustmentEvent extends AWTEvent

Package: java.awt.event

Class hierarchy: Object—EventObject—AWTEvent—AdjustmentEvent

The AdjustmentEvent class is part of the AWTEvent hierarchy. An AdjustmentEvent object has access to the methods defined in the AWTEvent, EventObject, and Object classes.

Introduced: JDK 1.1

Constructors

```
public AdjustmentEvent(Adjustable source, int id,
int type, int value)
```

Most of the time, AdjustmentEvents are generated by the system. The AdjustmentEvent class provides a public constructor to create AdjustmentEvent objects. The `source` is the GUI component that generated the event. For AdjustmentEvents, this source will be a component that implements the Adjustable interface. The `id` parameter identifies the AdjustmentEvent type. With a system-generated AdjustmentEvent, this will be the `ADJUSMENT_VALUE_CHANGED` field described next, under "Constants." The `type` indicates how the AdjustmentEvent was generated. It will be one of the AdjustmentEvent class constants. The `value` parameter contains the current value of the slider.

Constants

public static final int ADJUSTMENT_FIRST
public static final int ADJUSTMENT_LAST
public static final int ADJUSMENT_VALUE_CHANGED
public static final int BLOCK_DECREMENT
public static final int BLOCK_INCREMENT
public static final int UNIT_DECREMENT
public static final int UNIT_INCREMENT
public static final int TRACK

The ADJUSTMENT_FIRST and ADJUSTMENT_LAST constants represent the range of system-provided IDs for AdjustmentEvent objects. There is only one ID, so both of these constants have the same value as ADJUSTMENT_VALUE_CHANGED.

The ADJUSTMENT_VALUE_CHANGED parameter will be the ID for all system-generated AdjustmentEvent objects. It has a numerical value of 601.

The remaining field constants are used to specify the type of AdjustmentEvent. The BLOCK_DECREMENT and BLOCK_INCREMENT constants indicate that the scrollbar value was changed by clicking inside the scrollbar area.

The UNIT_DECREMENT and UNIT_INCREMENT parameters are for when the scrollbar value is changed by clicking the up- or down-arrow.

The TRACK constant indicates that the value was changed by dragging the slider.

Fields

Beyond those constants described in the preceding section, the AdjustmentEvent class does not define any additional fields. An AdjustmentEvent object has access to the fields defined in the AWTEvent and EventObject classes.

AdjustmentEvent Class Methods

public Adjustable getAdjustable()
public int getAdjustmentType()

public int `getValue()`
public String `paramString()`

`getAdjustable()` is a more AdjustmentEvent-specific version of the `getSource()` method defined in the EventObject class. It returns a reference to the Adjustable object that generated the event. Remember that an Adjustable object is one that implements the Adjustable interface.

`getAdjustmentType()` returns the type of AdjustmentEvent. For system-generated AdjustmentEvents, the return value will be one of the AdjustmentEvent class field constants described previously.

`getValue()` returns the value of the AdjustmentEvent. For system-generated events, this will be the current value of the Scrollbar or JScrollBar object that generated the event.

`paramString()` overrides the method defined in the AWTEvent class and returns a parameter String that identifies the AdjustmentEvent. This is generally used for event-logging and debugging purposes. When an AdjustmentEvent object calls the `toString()` method, the return value of the `paramString()` method is incorporated in the return value of the `toString()` method.

Methods Inherited from the java.awt.AWTEvent Class

protected void `consume()`
protected void `finalize()` throws Throwable
public int `getID()`
protected boolean `isConsumed()`
public String `toString()`

An AdjustmentEvent object has access to thethese methods defined in the AWTEvent class. For a description of these methods, see the section "AWTEvent Class" in this chapter.

Methods Inherited from the java.util.EventObject Class

public Object `getSource()`

`getSource()` returns a reference to the object that generated the invoking event. This method can be used to determine which component generated the invoking AdjustmentEvent object. The AdjustmentEvent class provides a similar method, `getAdjustable()`, for returning a reference to the event source.

Methods Inherited from the java.lang.Object Class

public final Class getClass()

`getClass()` returns a Class object representing the runtime class of the invoking object. In this case, it would return an object representing the java.awt.event.AdjustmentEvent class.

The other methods inherited from the Object class, `clone()`, `equals()`, `hashCode()`, `notify()`, `notifyAll()`, and `wait()` are generally not used in conjunction with AdjustmentEvent objects.

EXAMPLE

In this example, AdjustmentEvent objects generated by a JScrollBar object are used to set the background darkness level of a JPanel. The event also serves to update the text shown inside a JTextField to the current level of the JScrollBar. The JScrollBar object registers an AdjustmentListener that is implemented as an inner class. The `adjustmentValueChanged()` method of the AdjustmentListener contains code to update the text inside the JTextField and to change the background color of the JPanel. The code listing is shown in Example 6.6.

EXAMPLE 6.6 ADJUSTMENTEVENT CLASS

```
import javax.swing.*;
import java.awt.*;
import java.awt.event.*;

public class AdjEventDemo extends JFrame
{
   private JScrollBar jsb;
   private JTextField jtf;
   private JLabel label;
   private JPanel panel;

   public AdjEventDemo()
   {
```

```java
    /* The JScrollBar registers an AdjustmentListener   */

        jsb = new JScrollBar(JScrollBar.VERTICAL, 255, 5, 0, 260);
        jsb.addAdjustmentListener(new JScrollBarListener());

        jtf = new JTextField(3);
        jtf.setEditable(false);
        jtf.setText(""+jsb.getValue());

        label = new JLabel("Darkness Level");
        label.setForeground(Color.black);

        panel = new JPanel();
        panel.setBackground(Color.white);
        panel.add(label);
        panel.add(jtf);
        panel.add(jsb);

        getContentPane().add(panel);

        setDefaultCloseOperation(JFrame.EXIT_ON_CLOSE);
        setBounds(100, 100, 300, 200);
        setVisible(true);
    }

    /* The AdjustmentListener is implemented as an inner class.        */
    /* In the adjustmentValueChanged() method, the AdjustmentEvent     */
    /* is used to obtain the value of the Adjustable object that created */
    /* the event, in this case the JScrollBar.  The darkness level of */
    /* the JPanel background is set to current JScrollBar level.       */

    class JScrollBarListener implements AdjustmentListener
    {
        public void adjustmentValueChanged(AdjustmentEvent event)
        {
           int level = event.getValue();
           jtf.setText(""+level);
            panel.setBackground(new Color(level, level, level));
        }
    }

    public static void main(String args[])
    {
       AdjEventDemo adj = new AdjEventDemo();
    }
}
```

When you run this example, the panel background color is initially white. Adjust the slider value either by clicking on the arrow, clicking in the JScrollBar area, or dragging the slider up or down. Every time the slider value is changed, an AdjustmentEvent is generated and sent to the `adjustmentValueChanged()` method. The AdjustmentEvent obtains the current value of the JScrollBar, and the JTextField and background color are updated to reflect this level.

By default, the vertical scrollbar component in Java will have its range of values go from top to bottom, with the minimum value on top. This may or may not be what you want. It is fairly simple to build in logic so it appears as though the minimum scrollbar value is at the bottom. This wasn't done in this example for the purpose of simplifying the code listing.

AncestorEvent Class

An AncestorEvent is a low-level event generated when a change occurs to a component hierarchy. A component hierarchy consists of the component itself and any ancestors to the component. Recall that an ancestor is the component's container, its container's container, and so on. An AncestorEvent occurs if a component or any of its ancestors is added or removed from the component hierarchy, is moved, or has its visible state changed.

An AncestorEvent object contains information about the source of the AncestorEvent, the ancestor component that caused the event, the parent of that ancestor component, and the type of AncestorEvent. This information allows an AncestorListener to determine the cause and nature of the event.

AncestorEvent objects are generated only by Swing GUI components, those that are subclasses of the JComponent class. The GUI components from the java.awt package will not generate these events.

When an AncestorEvent is generated, it is sent to any registered AncestorListener. The AncestorListener provides implementation of the methods used to process AncestorEvents.

Syntax: public class AncestorEvent extends AWTEvent
Package: javax.swing.event
Class hierarchy: Object—EventObject—AWTEvent—AncestorEvent

While the AncestorEvent class is contained in the javax.swing.event package, it is really part of the AWTEvent hierarchy, as it is a direct subclass of AWTEvent. An AncestorEvent object has access to the methods defined in the AWTEvent, EventObject, and Object classes.

Introduced: JDK 1.3

Constructors

```
public AncestorEvent(JComponent source, int id, Container ancestor, Container parent)
```

The AncestorEvent class provides one public constructor for creating AncestorEvent objects. The `source` is the component that generated the event. The `id` identifies the type of AncestorEvent. For system-generated AncestorEvents, it will be one of the ID constants described next. The `ancestor` parameter is the container whose position or visibility changed. The `parent` is a reference to the ancestor's parent container.

Constants

```
public static final int ANCESTOR_ADDED
public static final int ANCESTOR_MOVED
public static final int ANCESTOR_REMOVED
```

These constants are used to identify the type of AncestorEvent. The `ANCESTOR_ADDED` and `ANCESTOR_REMOVED` constants refer to the hierarchy of visible objects currently being displayed. The `ANCESTOR_ADDED` constant indicates that an ancestor was added to the hierarchy of visible objects. The `ANCESTOR_REMOVED` constant signifies that an ancestor was hidden from the hierarchy of visible objects. The `ANCESTOR_MOVED` constant indicates that an ancestor component has changed its position on the screen.

Fields

Beyond those constants described in the preceding section, the AncestorEvent class does not define any additional fields. An AncestorEvent object does have access to the fields defined in the AWTEvent and EventObject classes.

AncestorEvent Class Methods:

public Container `getAncestor()`
public Container `getAncestorParent()`
public JComponent `getComponent()`

`getAncestor()` returns a reference to the ancestor container whose change initiated the event.

`getAncestorParent()` returns a reference to the parent container of the ancestor whose change initiated the event. This method is especially useful for `ANCESTOR_REMOVED` events, where the ancestor may no longer be part of the container hierarchy.

`getComponent()` returns a reference to the object that generated the AncestorEvent. Note that this is not the component that had its status changed. AncestorEvents are generated by a component when some aspect of one of its ancestors changes.

Methods Inherited from the java.awt.AWTEvent Class:

protected void `consume()`
protected void `finalize()` throws Throwable
public int `getID()`
protected boolean `isConsumed()`
public String `paramString()`
public String `toString()`

An AncestorEvent object has access to the methods defined in the AWTEvent class. For a description of these methods, see the section "AWTEvent Class" in this chapter.

Methods Inherited from the java.util.EventObject Class

public Object `getSource()`

`getSource()` returns a reference to the object that generated the AncestorEvent. An AncestorEvent object could also use the `getComponent()` method for this purpose.

Methods Inherited from the java.lang.Object classClass

public final Class `getClass()`

`getClass()` returns a Class object representing the runtime class of the invoking object. In this case, it would return an object representing the javax.swing.event.AncestorEvent class.

The other methods inherited from the Object class, `clone()`, `equals()`, `hashCode()`, `notify()`, `notifyAll()`, and `wait()`, are generally not used in conjunction with AncestorEvent objects.

EXAMPLE

In Example 6.7, AncestorEvent objects are used to keep track of the position of a JFrame. The AncestorEvents are generated by a JButton that is placed on the JFrame. The JButton registers an AncestorListener. The JFrame is part of the JButton object's ancestor hierarchy. Whenever the JFrame is moved, the JButton generates an AncestorEvent that is sent to the `ancestorMoved()` method. A JTextField at the bottom of the JFrame is updated with the new position of the frame.

EXAMPLE 6.7 ANCESTOREVENT CLASS

```
import javax.swing.*;
import javax.swing.event.*;
import java.awt.*;

public class AncEventDemo extends JFrame implements AncestorListener
{
   JButton button;
   JTextField jtf;

   public AncEventDemo()
   {
/*   A JButton is created and placed on a JFrame.  The JButton       */
/*   registers an AncestorListener.  Because the AncEventDemo class */
```

```
      /*    serves as the AncestorListener, the addAncestorListener()    */
      /*    method is passed the "this" reference.                       */

         button = new JButton("help");
         button.setBorder(BorderFactory.createRaisedBevelBorder());
         button.addAncestorListener(this);

         jtf = new JTextField(15);
         jtf.setEditable(false);

         JPanel panel = new JPanel();
         panel.add(button);

         getContentPane().add(panel, BorderLayout.CENTER);
         getContentPane().add(jtf, BorderLayout.SOUTH);

         setName("frame");
         setDefaultCloseOperation(JFrame.EXIT_ON_CLOSE);
         setBounds(100, 100, 300, 200);
         setVisible(true);
      }

   /*  The AncEventDemo class serves as the AncestorListener so the      */
   /*  implementations of the methods declared in the AncestorListener   */
   /*  interface are provided inside the AncEventDemo class. If the      */
   /*  JFrame is moved, the JButton generates an AncestorEvent which     */
   /*  is sent to the ancestorMoved() method.                            */

      public void ancestorMoved(AncestorEvent event)
      {
         Container ancestor = event.getAncestor();
         if ( ancestor.getName().equals("frame") )
         {
            jtf.setText("frame was moved to ("+ancestor.getX()+","+
                     ancestor.getY()+")");
         }
      }

      public void ancestorAdded(AncestorEvent event) {}
      public void ancestorRemoved(AncestorEvent event){}

      public static void main(String args[])
      {
         AncEventDemo demo = new AncEventDemo();
      }
   }
```

When the application is started, the JFrame appears on the screen. Move the frame to a new location. The textfield will indicate where the JFrame now is. Remember that the events used to update the frame location in the JTextField are generated by the JButton, not the JFrame.

AWTEvent Class

AWTEvent is the parent class of all the event classes in the java.awt.event package and some of the events in the javax.swing.event package. It defines a series of field constants for identifying and selecting different event types. It also provides the `getID()` method, which returns an int identifying the event type, the `paramString()` method, which returns a String representing the state of the event, and an overridden version of the `toString()` method from the EventObject class.

Syntax:	public abstract class AWTEvent extends EventObject
Package:	java.awt
Class hierarchy:	Object—EventObject—AWTEvent
	The AWTEvent class is part of the AWT Event hierarchy. Any subclasses of AWTEvent will have access to the methods defined in the AWTEvent, EventObject, and Object classes.
Introduced:	JDK 1.1

Constructors

```
public AWTEvent(Event event)
public AWTEvent(Object source, int id)
```

AWTEvent is an abstract class, so you can't ever instantiate an AWTEvent object. The AWTEvent class does provide two constructors for use with subclasses of AWTEvent. A user-defined event that was a subclass of AWTEvent, for instance, could simply call the AWTEvent constructor in its constructor. The first version is for events using the Java 1.0.2 event model. The second version is for events under the Java 1.1 event model.

Constants

public static final long ACTION_EVENT_MASK
public static final long ADJUSTMENT_EVENT_MASK
public static final long COMPONENT_EVENT_MASK
public static final long CONTAINER_EVENT_MASK
public static final long FOCUS_EVENT_MASK
public static final long HIERARCHY_BOUNDS_EVENT_MASK
public static final long HIERARCHY_EVENT_MASK
public static final long INPUT_METHOD_EVENT_MASK
public static final long INVOCATION_EVENT_MASK
public static final long ITEM_EVENT_MASK
public static final long KEY_EVENT_MASK
public static final long MOUSE_EVENT_MASK
public static final long MOUSE_MOTION_EVENT_MASK
public static final long PAINT_EVENT_MASK
public static final long RESERVED_ID_MAX
public static final long TEXT_EVENT_MASK
public static final long WINDOW_EVENT_MASK

The EVENT_MASK constants are used in conjunction with the enableEvent() and disableEvent() methods defined in the Component class. A component that is enabled to receive a certain type of event will receive that event whether it has a listener registered for that event type or not.

The RESERVED_ID_MAX constant has the highest event ID value of any constants used by the system: the numerical value of 1999. Any events defined outside of the java.awt.event package (user-defined events, for instance) should set their ID values to be greater than this number.

Fields

protected boolean consumed
protected int id

The `consumed` field contains the consumed state of the event.

The `id` field is the identification constant for the event.

In addition to the `consumed` and `id` fields, a subclass of AWTEvent would have access to the `source` field defined in the EventObject class.

AWTEvent Class Methods

protected void `consume()`
protected void `finalize()`
public int `getID()`
protected boolean `isConsumed()`
public String `paramString()`
public String `toString()`

`consume()` marks the invoking event as being consumed. A consumed event will be ignored by the source component's peer. Only mouse and keyboard events can be consumed using this method. It can be used, for instance, to limit the types of characters that can be typed into a textfield. The `consume()` method is only relevant for events generated by AWT GUI components. Swing GUI components are pure Java, have no component peer, and are unaffected by `consume()`.

`finalize()` is called by the garbage collector when it determines there are no more references to an object. It is used to return the resources allocated to the object back to the system. This method can be overridden for some other user-defined cleanup operation.

`getID()` returns the ID for a given event. Oftentimes, there is more than one way to generate a given event. For example, a ComponentEvent can be caused by a component being hidden, moved, resized, or made visible. The ID for an event can be used to determine how the event was generated.

`isConsumed()` returns true if the invoking event has been marked as having been consumed.

`paramString()` returns a parameter String that identifies the event. This is generally used for event-logging and debugging purposes. When an event object calls the `toString()` method, the return value of the `paramString()` method is incorporated in the return value of the `toString()` method.

`toString()` overrides the `toString()` method defined in the EventObject class to return a String representation of the invoking event object.

Methods Inherited from the java.util.EventObject Class

public Object `getSource()`

`getSource()` returns a reference to the object that generated the event. subclass objects can use this method to determine the event source.

Methods Inherited from the java.lang.Object Class

public final Class `getClass()`

`getClass()` returns a Class object representing the runtime class of the invoking object.

The other methods inherited from the Object class, `clone()`, `equals()`, `hashCode()`, `notify()`, `notifyAll()`, and `wait()`, are generally not used in conjunction with event objects.

CaretEvent Class

A CaretEvent is a semantic (high-level) event generated by Swing text components (JEditorPane, JPasswordField, JTextArea, JTextField) when their caret position is changed. The caret is the cursor that appears inside the text area of the component, indicating the insertion point for new text. The CaretEvent class is an abstract class. The system will generate CaretEvents when required, but the user cannot instantiate a CaretEvent object.

CaretEvent objects are useful for keeping track of where the caret is in a Swing text component. You don't need to access the component's caret directly. A CaretEvent can provide information about the current status of the caret. The information a CaretEvent contains includes the event source, the location of the caret, and the location of the end of any selected text.

CaretEvent objects are only generated by Swing GUI text components, those that are subclasses of the JTextComponent class. The GUI text components from the java.awt package will not generate these events.

CaretEvent Class

When a CaretEvent is generated, it is sent to any registered CaretListener. The CaretListener provides implementation of the `caretUdpate()` method, which is overridden to contain the code used to process the event.

Syntax: public abstract class CaretEvent extends EventObject

Package: javax.swing.event

Class hierarchy: Object—EventObject—CaretEvent

The CaretEvent class is not part of the AWTEvent hierarchy as it is a direct subclass of EventObject. A CaretEvent object has access to the methods defined in the EventObject and Object classes.

Introduced: JDK 1.2

Constructors

```
public CaretEvent(Object source)
```

While the CaretEvent class is abstract, the class does provide one public constructor for CaretEvent subclasses. The `source` is the component that generated the event.

Constants

The CaretEvent class does not contain any identification constants.

Fields

The CaretEvent class does not define any fields. A CaretEvent object has access to the `source` field from the EventObject class.

CaretEvent Class Methods

```
public abstract int getDot()
```
```
public abstract int getMark()
```

The CaretEvent class uses two properties, `dot` and the `mark`. The `dot` is the current position of the caret. The `mark` indicates the index at the other end of the range of any selected text relative to the caret. For example, if the range of selected text goes from index 2 to index 6 and the caret is at index 2, the `mark` will be at index 6. If there is no selected text, the `mark` will be the same value as the `dot`.

`getDot()` returns the current location of the caret.

`getMark()` returns the location of the other end of the selected text relative to the caret. For instance, if the selected range is from index 2 to index 6 and the caret is at index 6, `getMark()` will return 2. If there is no selected text, the method returns the current location of the caret.

Methods Inherited from the java.util.EventObject Class

public Object `getSource()`
public String `toString()`

`getSource()` returns a reference to the object that generated the CaretEvent.

`toString()` returns a String representation of the CaretEvent object.

Methods Inherited from the java.lang.Object Class

public final Class `getClass()`

`getClass()` returns a Class object representing the runtime class of the invoking object. In this case, it would return an object representing the javax.swing.event.CaretEvent class.

The other methods inherited from the Object class, `clone()`, `equals()`, `hashCode()`, `notify()`, `notifyAll()`, and `wait()`, are generally not used in conjunction with CaretEvent objects.

EXAMPLE

In Example 6.8, CaretEvents are used to keep track of the caret position and range of selected text of a JTextField component. The JTextField is placed on a JFrame and registers a CaretListener. Every time the caret position of the JTextField is changed, or if text is selected in the JTextField, a CaretEvent is generated and sent to the `caretUpdate()` method.

Example 6.8 CaretEvent Class

```java
import javax.swing.*;
import javax.swing.event.*;
import java.awt.*;

public class CaretEventDemo extends JFrame implements CaretListener
{
   JTextField jtf, jtf1, jtf2;

   public CaretEventDemo()
   {
/* A JTextField is created and placed on a JFrame.  The JTextField */
/* registers a CaretListener.  The CaretEventDemo class serves as  */
/* the CaretListener, so the addCaretListener() method is passed   */
/* the "this" argument.                                            */

      jtf = new JTextField(20);
      jtf.setBorder(BorderFactory.createLineBorder(Color.black));
      jtf.addCaretListener(this);

      jtf1 = new JTextField(15);
      jtf1.setEditable(false);

      jtf2 = new JTextField(15);
      jtf2.setEditable(false);

      JPanel centerPanel = new JPanel();
      centerPanel.add(jtf);

      JPanel southPanel = new JPanel();
      southPanel.add(jtf1);
      southPanel.add(jtf2);

      getContentPane().add(centerPanel, BorderLayout.CENTER);
      getContentPane().add(southPanel, BorderLayout.SOUTH);

      setDefaultCloseOperation(JFrame.EXIT_ON_CLOSE);
      setBounds(100, 100, 400, 200);
      setVisible(true);
   }

/* Since the CaretEventDemo class is the CaretListener, it provides */
/* an implementation of the caretUpdate() method.  Whenever the caret */
/* of the upper JTextField is changed, a CaretEvent is generated and */
/* sent to this method.  The current caret position and range of any */
/* selected text are written to textfields at the bottom of the frame.*/

   public void caretUpdate(CaretEvent event)
```

```
    {
       jtf1.setText("caret at "+event.getDot());
       jtf2.setText("selected range ("+event.getMark()+
                                    ","+event.getDot()+")");
    }
    public static void main(String args[])
    {
       CaretEventDemo demo = new CaretEventDemo();
    }
}
```

When this example is run, a JTextField appears at the top of the frame. Type some text into it. Notice how the caret position is updated in a textfield at the bottom of the frame. Now select some text. The range of selected text is listed in another textfield at the bottom of the frame.

ChangeEvent Class

A ChangeEvent is a semantic (high-level) event generated by some Swing components when a component property changes. For example, if the action command of a JButton component is changed, a ChangeEvent object is generated. ChangeEvents are generated by the following components:

- JButton
- JCheckBox
- JCheckBoxMenuItem
- JProgressBar
- JRadioButton
- JRadioButtonMenuItem
- JSlider
- JTabbedPane
- JTable
- JToggleButton
- JViewPort

A ChangeEvent can be thought of as a poor-person's PropertyChangeEvent. A PropertyChangeEvent has information about the property name and the old and new values of the property. A ChangeEvent only contains information about the source that generated the event. A ChangeEvent has no information about the nature of the property change that caused the event.

ChangeEvent objects are generated only by Swing GUI components. The GUI components from the java.awt package will not generate these events. When a ChangeEvent is generated, it is sent to any registered ChangeListener. The ChangeListener provides implementation of the `stateChanged()` method, which is overridden to contain the code used to process the event.

Syntax: public class ChangeEvent extends EventObject

Package: javax.swing.event

Class hierarchy: Object—EventObject—ChangeEvent

The ChangeEvent class is not part of the AWTEvent hierarchy, as it is a direct subclass of EventObject. A ChangeEvent object has access to the methods defined in the EventObject and Object classes.

Introduced: JDK 1.2

Constructors

`public ChangeEvent(Object source)`

The ChangeEvent class provides one public constructor for creating ChangeEvent objects. The `source` is the component that generated the event.

Constants

The ChangeEvent class does not contain any identification constants.

Fields

The ChangeEvent class defines no fields. A ChangeEvent object has access to the `source` field from the EventObject class.

ChangeEvent Class Methods

The ChangeEvent class does not define any methods.

Methods Inherited from the java.util.EventObject Class

public Object getSource()
public String toString()

getSource() returns a reference to the object that generated the ChangeEvent.

toString() returns a String representation of the ChangeEvent object.

Methods Inherited from the java.lang.Object Class

public final Class getClass()

getClass() returns a Class object representing the runtime class of the invoking object. In this case, it would return an object representing the javax.swing.event.ChangeEvent class.

The other methods inherited from the Object class, clone(), equals(), hashCode(), notify(), notifyAll(), and wait(), are generally not used in conjunction with ChangeEvent objects.

EXAMPLE

In Example 6.9, a ChangeEvent is used to monitor the value of a JSlider. The JSlider is placed on a JFrame and registers a ChangeListener. Whenever the slider is moved, thereby changing the value property of the JSlider, a ChangeEvent is generated and sent to the stateChanged() method. This method updates a JTextField at the bottom of the frame with the current value of the JSlider.

EXAMPLE 6.9 CHANGEEVENT CLASS

```
import javax.swing.*;
import java.awt.*;
import javax.swing.event.*;

public class ChangeEventDemo extends JFrame
{
   JSlider slider;
   JTextField jtf;

   public ChangeEventDemo() {
```

```
/* A JSlider is created and placed on a JFrame.  The JSlider   */
/* registers a ChangeListener.                                 */

    slider = new JSlider(JSlider.VERTICAL, 0, 10, 0);
    slider.setMajorTickSpacing(5);
    slider.setMinorTickSpacing(1);
    slider.setPaintTicks(true);
    slider.setPaintLabels(true);
    slider.setForeground(Color.black);
    slider.setBorder(BorderFactory.createLineBorder(Color.black));
    slider.addChangeListener(new ChangeHandler());

    jtf = new JTextField(15);
    jtf.setText("Value is "+slider.getValue());
    jtf.setEditable(false);

    JPanel p = new JPanel();
    p.add(slider);

    getContentPane().add(p, BorderLayout.CENTER);
    getContentPane().add(jtf, BorderLayout.SOUTH);

    setDefaultCloseOperation(JFrame.EXIT_ON_CLOSE);
    setBounds(100, 100, 300, 300);
    setVisible(true);
 }

/* The ChangeListener is implemented as an inner class.  Whenever */
/* the slider value is changed, a ChangeEvent is generated and    */
/* sent to the stateChanged() method.  A JTextField at the bottom */
/* of the JFrame is updated to indicate the current value of the  */
/* JSlider.                                                       */

   class ChangeHandler implements ChangeListener
   {
      public void stateChanged(ChangeEvent event)
      {
         JSlider js = (JSlider)event.getSource();
         jtf.setText("Value is "+js.getValue());
      }
   }

   public static void main(String args[]) {
      ChangeEventDemo demo = new ChangeEventDemo();
   }
}
```

When the program is run, a vertical JSlider appears on the frame. Move the slider up and down and notice how the textfield indicates the current value of the JSlider.

ComponentEvent Class

A ComponentEvent is a low-level event generated whenever a component is shown, hidden, moved, or re-sized. This is also the parent class for the ContainerEvent, FocusEvent, InputEvent, and WindowEvent classes. This event type is used for notification purposes only. The AWT will handle component movements, re-sizings, or visibility changes automatically whether the ComponentEvents are listened to or not. Any Component subclass object can generate a ComponentEvent.

A ComponentEvent contains information about the component that generated the event and the type of ComponentEvent. ComponentEvents can be used to constrain the movements, re-sizing, or visibility changes of a component. For instance, a ComponentEvent can be used to detect if a container has been resized too small to fit its child components.

When a ComponentEvent object is generated, it is sent to every registered ComponentListener object. The ComponentListener object provides .imethods used to process the ComponentEvent.

Syntax:	public class ComponentEvent extends AWTEvent
Package:	java.awt.event
Class hierarchy:	Object—EventObject—AWTEvent—ComponentEvent
	The ComponentEvent class is part of the AWT Event hierarchy. A ComponentEvent object has access to the methods defined in the AWTEvent, EventObject, and Object classes.
Introduced:	JDK 1.1

Constructors

```
public ComponentEvent(Component source, int id)
```

The system will generate a ComponentEvent whenever a Component subclass object is shown, hidden, moved, or resized. The ComponentEvent class defines one public constructor to create ComponentEvent objects. The `source` is the GUI component that generated the event. The `id` parameter identifies the type of ComponentEvent. Its value will be one of the following ComponentEvent class constants.

Constants

public static final int `COMPONENT_HIDDEN`
public static final int `COMPONENT_MOVED`
public static final int `COMPONENT_RESIZED`
public static final int `COMPONENT_SHOWN`
public static final int `COMPONENT_FIRST`
public static final int `COMPONENT_LAST`

The first four field constants represent the types of ComponentEvents. Their names are pretty much self-explanatory.

The `COMPONENT_MOVED` constant has a numerical value of 100.

The `COMPONENT_RESIZED` constant has a numerical value of 101.

The `COMPONENT_SHOWN` parameter has a numerical value of 102.

The `COMPONENT_HIDDEN` constant has a numerical value of 103.

The `COMPONENT_FIRST` and `COMPONENT_LAST` constants represent the range of system-provided IDs for ComponentEvent objects. They have numerical values of 100 and 103 respectively.

Fields

Beyond the identification constants described previously, the ComponentEvent class does not define any additional fields. A ComponentEvent object has access to the fields defined in the AWTEvent and EventObject classes. Noteable among these are the `id` and `source` fields.

ComponentEvent Class Methods

public Component `getComponent()`
public String `paramString()`

`getComponent()` is similar to the `getSource()` method defined in the EventObject class. It returns a reference to the component that generated the event.

`paramString()` overrides the method defined in the AWTEvent class and returns a parameter String that identifies the ComponentEvent. This is generally used for event-logging and debugging purposes. When a ComponentEvent object calls the `toString()` method, the return value of the `paramString()` method is incorporated in the return value of the `toString()` method.

Methods Inherited from the java.awt.AWTEvent Class

protected void `consume()`
protected void `finalize()` throws Throwable
public int `getID()`
protected boolean `isConsumed()`
public String `toString()`

A ComponentEvent object has access to the methods defined in the AWTEvent class. For a description of these methods, see the section "AWTEvent Class" in this chapter.

Methods Inherited from the java.util.EventObject Class

public Object `getSource()`

`getSource()` returns a reference to the object that generated the invoking event. This method can be used to determine which component generated the invoking ComponentEvent object. The ComponentEvent class provides a similar method, `getComponent()`, for returning a reference to the event source.

Methods Inherited from the java.lang.Object Class

public final Class `getClass()`

`getClass()` returns a Class object representing the runtime class of the invoking object. In this case, it would return an object representing the java.awt.event.ComponentEvent class.

The other methods inherited from the Object class, `clone()`, `equals()`, `hashCode()`, `notify()`, `notifyAll()`, and `wait()`, are generally not used in conjunction with ComponentEvent objects.

EXAMPLE

In Example 6.10, a ComponentEvent object is used to ensure that a resize operation performed on a JFrame does not truncate a long label contained inside the JFrame. The program uses a ComponentListener that is implemented as an inner class that extends the ComponentAdapter class.

EXAMPLE 6.10 COMPONENTEVENT CLASS

```java
import javax.swing.*;
import java.awt.*;
import java.awt.event.*;

public class ComponentEventDemo extends JFrame
{
   private JLabel label;

   public ComponentEventDemo()
   {
/* A very long label is created and placed on a JFrame   */

      label = new JLabel("This is a very, very long label");
      label.setFont(new Font("Serif", Font.BOLD, 14));
      label.setForeground(Color.black);

      JPanel panel = new JPanel();
      panel.add(label);
      getContentPane().add(panel);

/* The JFrame registers a ComponentListener   */

      addComponentListener(new CompListener());
      setDefaultCloseOperation(JFrame.EXIT_ON_CLOSE);
      setBounds(100, 100, 300, 200);
      setVisible(true);
   }

/* We're only really interested in the componentResized() method   */
/* so the ComponentListener is implemented as an inner class       */
```

```
/* that extends the ComponentAdapter class.  When the JFrame is   */
/* resized, a ComponentEvent is generated and sent to the         */
/* componentResized() method.  This method tests to see if the    */
/* JFrame width is smaller than the JLabel width.  If it is, the  */
/* JFrame is resized so it is wider than the JLabel.              */

   class CompListener extends ComponentAdapter
   {
     public void componentResized(ComponentEvent event)
     {
       Component comp = event.getComponent();
       if ( comp.getWidth() < label.getWidth() )
       {
          comp.setSize( label.getWidth()+100, comp.getHeight() );
       }
     }
   }

   public static void main(String args[])
   {
      ComponentEventDemo adj = new ComponentEventDemo();
   }
}
```

When this code is initially started, the JLabel is contained within the bounds of the JFrame. If the JFrame is re-sized, it generates a ComponentEvent, which is sent to the `componentResized()` method of the ComponentListener. This method determines if the current width of the JFrame is less than the width of the JLabel. If it is, the JFrame is resized so it is larger than the JLabel.

ContainerEvent Class

A ContainerEvent is a low-level event generated by Container subclass objects (frames, windows, dialogs, etc.). A ContainerEvent is generated whenever the contents of a container have changed because a component was added or removed. As with ComponentEvents, this event type is used for notification purposes only. The AWT handles changes to a container's contents automatically, whether the resulting ContainerEvent objects are listened to or not.

A ContainerEvent contains information about the container that generated the event, the type of ContainerEvent, and the child component that was added or removed from the container. ContainerEvents can be used to keep track of the number of child components a container has.

When a ContainerEvent object is generated, it is sent to every registered ContainerListener object. The ContainerListener object provides an implementation of the `componentAdded()` and `componentRemoved()` methods.

Syntax: public class ContainerEvent extends ComponentEvent

Package: java.awt.event

Class hierarchy: Object—EventObject—AWTEvent—ComponentEvent—ContainerEvent

The ContainerEvent class is part of the AWTEvent hierarchy. A ContainerEvent object has access to the methods defined in the ComponentEvent, AWTEvent, EventObject, and Object classes.

Introduced: JDK 1.1

Constructors

```
public ContainerEvent(Component source, int id, Component child)
```

ContainerEvent objects are generated by the system whenever a component is added or removed from a container. The ContainerEvent class defines one public constructor for creating ContainerEvent objects. The `source` is the container object that generated the event. The `id` parameter identifies the type of ContainerEvent. This will be either the COMPONENT_ADDED or COMPONENT_REMOVED constants described next. The `child` is the component that was added or removed from the container.

Constants

public static final int COMPONENT_ADDED
public static final int COMPONENT_REMOVED
public static final int CONTAINER_FIRST
public static final int CONTAINER_LAST

The COMPONENT_ADDED parameter will be the ID for all system-generated ContainerEvent objects caused when a component is added to a container. It has a numerical value of 300.

The COMPONENT_REMOVED parameter indicates that the event was caused by having a component removed from a container. It has a numerical value of 301.

The `CONTAINER_FIRST` and `CONTAINER_LAST` constants represent the range of system-provided IDs for ContainerEvent objects. These have numerical values of 300 and 301 respectively.

Fields

Beyond the identification constants described previously, the ContainerEvent class does not define any additional fields. A ContainerEvent object has access to the fields defined in the ComponentEvent, AWTEvent, and EventObject classes including the `id` and `source` fields.

ContainerEvent Class Methods

public Component `getChild()`
public Container `getContainer()`
public String `paramString()`

`getChild()` returns a reference to the component that was added or removed from the container.

`getContainer()` is similar to the `getSource()` method defined in the EventObject class. It returns a reference to the container that generated the event.

`paramString()` overrides the method defined in the ComponentEvent class and returns a parameter String that identifies the ContainerEvent. This is generally used for event-logging and debugging purposes. When a ContainerEvent object calls the `toString()` method, the return value of the `paramString()` method is incorporated in the return value of the `toString()` method.

Methods Inherited from the java.awt.event.ComponentEvent Class

public Component `getComponent()`

`getComponent()` is used to obtain a reference to the component that generated the event. While a ContainerEvent object has access to this method, it could also use the `getContainer()` method for this purpose.

Methods Inherited from the java.awt.AWTEvent Class

protected void `consume()`
protected void `finalize()` throws Throwable
public int `getID()`
protected boolean `isConsumed()`
public String `toString()`

A ContainerEvent object has access to the methods defined in the AWTEvent class. For a description of these methods, see the section "AWTEvent Class" in this chapter.

Methods Inherited from the java.util.EventObject Class

public Object `getSource()`

`getSource()` returns a reference to the object that generated the ContainerEvent. A ContainerEvent object could also use either the `getComponent()` or `getContainer()` methods for this purpose.

Methods Inherited from the java.lang.Object Class

public final Class `getClass()`

`getClass()` returns a Class object representing the runtime class of the invoking object. In this case, it would return an object representing the java.awt.event.ContainerEvent class.

The other methods inherited from the Object class, `clone()`, `equals()`, `hashCode()`, `notify()`, `notifyAll()`, and `wait()`, are generally not used in conjunction with ContainerEvent objects.

EXAMPLE

In Example 6.11, a ContainerEvent object is used to obtain information about buttons that are placed on a frame. An "add" button and a JTextField are placed in the Ssouth quadrant of a JFrame. When the "add" button is pressed, a new JButton is created and placed on a JPanel in the center quadrant of the JFrame.

When a button is added to the center panel, a ContainerEvent is generated. Because the center panel has a registered ContainerListener, the ContainerEvent is sent to the componentAdded() method. The ContainerEvent is used to return a reference to the button that was added, and the JTextField is updated to show which button this was.

EXAMPLE 6.11 CONTAINEREVENT CLASS

```java
import javax.swing.*;
import java.awt.*;
import java.awt.event.*;

public class ContainerEventDemo extends JFrame
                  implements ContainerListener, ActionListener
{
   private JButton addButton;
   private JTextField jtf;
   private JPanel southPanel, centerPanel;
   private int count;

   public ContainerEventDemo()
   {
      count = 0;

/* A JButton and a JTextField are added to a JPanel.          */
/* The JPanel is placed in the South quadrant of the frame.   */

      addButton = new JButton("add");
      addButton.addActionListener(this);

      jtf = new JTextField(20);
      jtf.setEditable(false);

      southPanel = new JPanel();
      southPanel.add(addButton);
      southPanel.add(jtf);

/* The centerPanel registers a ContainerListener.             */
/* The ContainerEventDemo class itself serves as the          */
/* ContainerListener so the addContainerListener() method     */
/* is passed the "this" reference.                            */

      centerPanel = new JPanel();
      centerPanel.addContainerListener(this);

      getContentPane().add(southPanel, BorderLayout.SOUTH);
      getContentPane().add(centerPanel, BorderLayout.CENTER);

      setDefaultCloseOperation(JFrame.EXIT_ON_CLOSE);
```

```
      setBounds(100, 100, 500, 200);
      setVisible(true);
   }

/* When the "add" button is pressed, a new JButton is placed    */
/* on the centerPanel.  This action generates a ContainerEvent  */
/* which is sent to the componentAdded() method. When a button  */
/* is added to the frame, the display won't automatically be    */
/* updated.  The revalidate() method causes the display to be   */
/* updated.                                                     */

   public void actionPerformed(ActionEvent event)
   {
      centerPanel.add(new JButton("Button "+count));
      centerPanel.revalidate();
      ++count;
   }

/* The componentAdded() method obtains a reference to the JButton */
/* that was added to the centerPanel and updates the JTextField   */
/* to indicate which button was added.                            */

   public void componentAdded(ContainerEvent event)
   {
      JButton button = (JButton)event.getChild();
      jtf.setText(button.getText()+" was added");
   }

/* The componentRemoved() method is not used in this example but */
/* an implementation must be provided anyway.  It is implemented */
/* as a stub method.  This could have been avoided if the        */
/* ContainerAdapter class had been used.                         */

   public void componentRemoved(ContainerEvent event) {}

   public static void main(String args[])
   {
      ContainerEventDemo adj = new ContainerEventDemo();
   }
}
```

Initially when this example is run, the center panel and textfield are blank. Start pressing the "add" button to add buttons to the center panel. The resulting ContainerEvent objects are used to update the text inside the textfield.

DocumentEvent Interface

A DocumentEvent object is a semantic (high-level) event used to provide detailed information to a Document observer about how a Document has changed. This is one of two event types that indicate a change has been made to a Document; the other is the UndoableEditEvent class. Unlike the other Swing events, a DocumentEvent is implemented in the API as an interface instead of a class. The DocumentEvent interface defines two inner elements, the DocumentEvent.ElementChange interface and the DocumentEvent.EventType class.

The Swing Document model is fairly complex and a complete description of it and how to apply it are beyond the scope of this book. Please consult a good Swing reference for more details on this model. This section will provide a fairly simple example of how to use a DocumentListener to receive DocumentEvents.

A DocumentEvent object contains information about the source of the DocumentEvent, the type of DocumentEvent, any changes made to a parent element of the Document, the length of the change, and the offset from the start of the Document where the change was made. DocumentEvents are used to monitor and respond to changes made to Swing text components that employ a document model.

When a DocumentEvent is generated, it is sent to any registered DocumentListener. The DocumentListener provides implementation of the `changedUpdate()`, `insertUpdate()`, and `removeUpdate()` methods that are used to process the different types of DocumentEvents.

Syntax:	public interface DocumentEvent
Package:	javax.swing.event
Interface hierarchy:	DocumentEvent
	The DocumentEvent interface is contained in the javax.swing.event package but is not part of any hierarchy. It stands alone.
Introduced:	JDK 1.2

Methods Declared in the DocumentEvent Interface

public `DocumentEvent.ElementChange getChange(Element e)`
public `Document getDocument()`
public int `getLength()`
public int `getOffset()`
public `DocumentEvent.EventType getType()`

`getChange()` returns a DocumentEvent.ElementChange object containing information about any elements that were added to or removed from a parent element of the Document. If there were no such changes, this method returns null.

`getDocument()` returns a reference to the Document that generated the DocumentEvent.

`getLength()` returns the number of characters that were involved in the change.

`getOffset()` gives the position of the beginning of the change relative to the start of the Document.

`getType()` returns a DocumentEvent.EventType object that identifies the type of DocumentEvent.

EXAMPLE

Example 6.12 uses DocumentEvent objects to monitior changes made to the text contained inside a JTextArea object. The JTextArea is added to a JFrame. The Document object associated with the JTextArea registers a Document-Listener. Whenever text is inserted or removed from the JTextArea, DocumentEvent objects are generated and sent to either the `insertUpdate()` or `changeUpdate()` methods of the DocumentListener. The length and position of the change are printed inside a textfield at the bottom of the frame.

EXAMPLE 6.12 DOCUMENTEVENT INTERFACE

```
import javax.swing.*;
import java.awt.*;
import javax.swing.event.*;
```

```java
public class DocumentEventDemo extends JFrame
{
   private JTextArea jta;
   private JTextField jtf;

   public DocumentEventDemo()
   {

/* A JTextArea is created and placed on a JFrame.  The Document   */
/* associated with the JTextArea is obtained and registers        */
/* a DocumentListener.                                            */

      jta = new JTextArea(5,15);
      jta.setLineWrap(true);
      jta.setWrapStyleWord(true);
      jta.getDocument().addDocumentListener(new DocumentHandler());

      jtf = new JTextField(15);
      jtf.setEditable(false);

      JPanel p = new JPanel();
      p.add(new JScrollPane(jta));

      getContentPane().add(p, BorderLayout.CENTER);
      getContentPane().add(jtf, BorderLayout.SOUTH);

      setDefaultCloseOperation(JFrame.EXIT_ON_CLOSE);
      setBounds(100, 100, 300, 250);
      setVisible(true);
   }

/* The DocumentListener is implemented as an inner class.  When    */
/* text is added to or removed from the JTextArea, a DocumentEvent */
/* is generated and sent to either the insertUpdate() or           */
/* removeUpdate() methods.  The length and position of the change  */
/* is written to a JTextField at the bottom of the frame.  The     */
/* changedUpdate() method is not used so it is implemented as a stub.*/

   class DocumentHandler implements DocumentListener
   {
      public void insertUpdate(DocumentEvent event)
      {
         int length = event.getLength();
         if ( length == 1 )
         {
         jtf.setText("1 character inserted at position "+
                                             event.getOffset());
         }
         else
         {
            jtf.setText(""+event.getLength()+
```

```
                    " characters inserted at position "+event.getOffset());
            }
        }

        public void removeUpdate(DocumentEvent event)
        {
            jtf.setText(""+event.getLength()+
                    " characters deleted at position "+event.getOffset());
        }

        public void changedUpdate(DocumentEvent event) {}
    }

    public static void main(String args[])
    {
        DocumentEventDemo demo = new DocumentEventDemo();
    }
}
```

When you run this application, a blank text area appears on the frame. Type some text into the text area. Insert some text in the middle of the text you previously wrote. The textfield at the bottom of the frame updates how many characters were inserted and where they were inserted. Now delete some of the text. The textfield now indicates how many characters were removed and from what position. Select a series of characters and press the delete key. Notice what the message is in the textfield.

DOCUMENTEVENT.ELEMENTCHANGE INTERFACE

The DocumentEvent.ElementChange interface is an inner interface of the DocumentEvent interface. It declares four methods for retrieving information when elements are added or removed from a specific parent element of the Document. The `getChange()` method from the DocumentEvent interface returns a DocumentEvent.ElementChange object.

Syntax:	public static interface DocumentEvent.ElementChange
Package:	javax.swing.event
Interface hierarchy:	DocumentEvent.ElementChange
	The DocumentEvent.ElementChange interface does not inherit from any other interface.
Introduced:	JDK 1.2

Methods Declared in the DocumentEvent.ElementChange Interface

public Element[] getChildrenAdded()
public Element[] getChildrenRemoved()
public Element getElement()
public int getIndex()

getChildrenAdded() returns an array of Element objects that were added to a parent Element. The parent Element is part of a Document.

getChildrenRemoved() returns an array of Element objects that were removed from a parent Element. The parent Element is part of a Document.

getElement() returns a reference to the parent Element.

getIndex() returns the position inside the parent Element that the child Elements were added or removed.

DocumentEvent.EventType Class

The DocumentEvent.EventType class is an inner class contained in the DocumentEvent interface. It defines three fields that are used to identify the type of DocumentEvent. It declares no public constructors. The getType() method from the DocumentEvent interface returns a DocumentEvent.EventType object containing the type of DocumentEvent.

Syntax: public static final class DocumentEvent.EventType extends Object

Package: javax.swing.event

Class hierarchy: Object—DocumentEvent.EventType

Introduced: JDK 1.2

Constructors

The DocumentEvent.EventType class defines no constructors.

Constants

```
public static final DocumentEvent.EventType INSERT
```
```
public static final DocumentEvent.EventType REMOVE
```
```
public static final DocumentEvent.EventType CHANGE
```

These constants are used to identify the type of DocumentEvent. The `INSERT` parameter indicates that content has been inserted into the Document. The `REMOVE` parameter indicates that content has been removed from the Document. The `CHANGE` parameter indicates that a Document attribute has changed.

DocumentEvent.EventType Class Methods

```
public String toString()
```

`toString()` returns a String representation of a DocumentEvent.EventType object.

Methods Inherited from the java.lang.Object Class

```
public final Class getClass()
```

`getClass()` returns a Class object representing the runtime class of the invoking object. In this case, it would return an object representing the javax.swing.event.DocumentEvent.EventType class.

The other methods inherited from the Object class, `clone()`, `equals()`, `hashCode()`, `notify()`, `notifyAll()`, and `wait()`, are generally not used in conjunction with DocumentEvent.EventType objects.

EventObject Class

The EventObject class is the parent class of all Java event classes. It defines methods that can be used by any event object. It implements the Serializable interface, which means that event objects can be saved and restored using Java I/O streams.

Syntax:	public class EventObject extends Object implements Serializable
Package:	java.util
Class hierarchy:	Object—EventObject
	The EventObject class is at the top of the event class hierarchy. It is a direct subclass of the Object class.
Introduced:	JDK 1.1

Constructors

```
public EventObject(Object source)
```

You generally would not create an EventObject object, but the EventObject class does provide one public constructor that could be accessed by EventObject subclasses. The `source` parameter is the object that generated the event.

Fields

```
protected transient Object source
```

`source` represents the source that generated the event. The EventObject class provides the `getSource()` method to return a reference to this object.

EventObject Class Methods

```
public Object getSource()
```
```
public String toString()
```

`getSource()` returns a reference to the object that generated the event. This can be useful for many things. For instance, sometimes you will need to determine which component among several possibilities generated the event.

`toString()` returns a String representation of the event object. This method overrides the version of this method defined in the Object class.

Methods Inherited from the java.lang.Object Class

```
public final Class getClass()
```

`getClass()` returns a Class object representing the runtime class of the invoking object.

The other methods inherited from the Object class, `clone()`, `equals()`, `hashCode()`, `notify()`, `notifyAll()`, and `wait()`, are generally not used in conjunction with event objects.

FocusEvent Class

A FocusEvent is a low-level event generated whenever a component gains or loses keyboard focus. The component has focus when it is the current active component and is ready to receive input. The change in focus can be permanent or temporary. A temporary change in focus can occur as a result of some other operation, for instance, when a JOptionPane appears on the screen. The focus is restored to the object that had it when the temporary operation is complete. A permanent change of focus occurs when the focus is directly moved from one component to another.

FocusEvent objects contain information about the component that generated the event, whether the event source gained or lost focus, and whether the focus change was permanent or temporary. As the name implies, FocusEvents can be used to manage, control, or respond to focus changes in GUI components.

Whether the focus change is temporary or permanent, a FocusEvent is sent to every registered FocusListener object when it is generated. The FocusListener provides an implementation of the `focusGained()` and `focusLost()` methods. These methods are overridden to contain the code used to process the FocusEvent.

Syntax: public class FocusEvent extends ComponentEvent

Package: java.awt.event

Class hierarchy: Object—EventObject—AWTEvent—ComponentEvent—FocusEvent

The FocusEvent class is part of the AWTEvent hierarchy. A FocusEvent object has access to the methods defined in the ComponentEvent, AWTEvent, EventObject, and Object classes.

Introduced: JDK 1.1

Constructors

```
public FocusEvent(Component source, int id)
```

```
public FocusEvent(Component source, int id, boolean temporary)
```

FocusEvent objects are generated by the system whenever a component gains or loses focus. The FocusEvent class defines two public constructors for creating FocusEvent objects. The `source` is a reference to the object that gained or lost focus. The `id` parameter identifies the type of FocusEvent. This will be either the FOCUS_GAINED or FOCUS_LOST constants described next. The `temporary` parameter is true if the focus change is temporary. The default is for the event to represent a permanent change in focus.

Constants

```
public static final int FOCUS_GAINED
```

```
public static final int FOCUS_LOST
```

```
public static final int FOCUS_FIRST
```

```
public static final int FOCUS_LAST
```

The FOCUS_GAINED parameter will be the ID for all system-generated FocusEvent objects caused when a component gains focus. It has a numerical value of 1004.

The FOCUS_LOST parameter indicates that the event was caused by a component losing focus. It has a numerical value of 1005.

The FOCUS_FIRST and FOCUS_LAST constants represent the range of system-provided IDs for FocusEvent objects. These have numerical values of 1004 and 1005 respectively.

Fields

Beyond those constants described in the preceding section, the FocusEvent class does not define any additional fields. A FocusEvent object has access to the fields defined in the AWTEvent and EventObject classes, including the `id` and `source` fields.

FocusEvent Class Methods

public boolean `isTemporary()`
public String `paramString()`

`isTemporary()` returns true if the invoking FocusEvent object represents a temporary change in focus.

`paramString()` overrides the method defined in the ComponentEvent class and returns a parameter String that identifies the FocusEvent. This is generally used for event-logging and debugging purposes. When a FocusEvent object calls the `toString()` method, the return value of the `paramString()` method is incorporated in the return value of the `toString()` method.

Methods Inherited from the java.awt.event.ComponentEvent Class

public Component `getComponent()`

`getComponent()` is used to obtain a reference to the component that generated the event.

Methods Inherited from the java.awt.AWTEvent Class

protected void `consume()`
protected void `finalize()` throws Throwable
public int `getID()`
protected Bboolean `isConsumed()`
public String `toString()`

A FocusEvent object has access to thesethe methods defined in the AWTEvent class. For a description of these methods, see the section "AWTEvent Class" in this chapter.

Methods Inherited from the java.util.EventObject Class

public Object `getSource()`

`getSource()` returns a reference to the object that generated the FocusEvent. A FocusEvent object could also use the `getComponent()` method for this purpose.

Methods Inherited from the java.lang.Object Class

> **public final Class** `getClass()`

`getClass()` returns a Class object representing the runtime class of the invoking object. In this case, it would return an object representing the java.awt.event.FocusEvent class.

The other methods inherited from the Object class, `clone()`, `equals()`, `hashCode()`, `notify()`, `notifyAll()`, and `wait()`, are generally not used in conjunction with FocusEvent objects.

EXAMPLE

Example 6.13 uses FocusEvent objects to highlight the component that has keyboard focus. Two JTextField objects are placed on a JFrame. The JTextFields register a FocusListener that is implemented as an inner class.

Whenever one of the JTextField objects gains focus, a FocusEvent is generated and sent to the `focusGained()` method. The FocusEvent is used to get a reference to the JTextField that generated the event, and the background color of the JTextField is set to pink. Similarly, when one of the JTextField objects loses keyboard focus, the resulting FocusEvent is sent to the `focusLost()` method and the background color of the JTextField is set to light gray.

EXAMPLE 6.13 FOCUSEVENT CLASS

```
import javax.swing.*;
import java.awt.*;
import java.awt.event.*;

public class FocusEventDemo extends JFrame
{
   private JTextField jtf1, jtf2;
   private JLabel label1, label2;

   public FocusEventDemo()
   {
```

```
    /*   Two JLabels and two JTextFields are created    */

        jtf1 = new JTextField(20);
        jtf1.setBorder(BorderFactory.createLineBorder(Color.black));
        jtf1.setBackground(Color.lightGray);
        jtf1.addFocusListener(new FocusHandler());

        jtf2 = new JTextField(20);
        jtf2.setBorder(BorderFactory.createLineBorder(Color.black));
        jtf2.setBackground(Color.lightGray);
        jtf2.addFocusListener(new FocusHandler());

        label1 = new JLabel("Line 1");
        label1.setForeground(Color.black);

        label2 = new JLabel("Line 2");
        label2.setForeground(Color.black);

    /*   The components are placed on the JFrame using a BoxLayout    */

        JPanel p1 = new JPanel();
        p1.add(label1);
        p1.add(jtf1);

        JPanel p2 = new JPanel();
        p2.add(label2);
        p2.add(jtf2);

        JPanel panel = new JPanel();
        panel.setLayout(new BoxLayout(panel, BoxLayout.Y_AXIS));
        panel.add(p1);
        panel.add(p2);

        getContentPane().add(panel);

        setDefaultCloseOperation(JFrame.EXIT_ON_CLOSE);
        setBounds(100, 100, 400, 200);
        setVisible(true);
    }

    /*   The FocusListener is implemented as an inner class.  Whenever   */
    /*   one of the JTextField objects gains keyboard focus, a FocusEvent*/
    /*   is generated and sent to the focusGained() method.              */
    /*   The background color of the JTextField that generated the event */
    /*   is set to pink.  Similarly, if a JTextField loses keyboard      */
    /*   focus the focusLost() method is called and the background color */
    /*   is set to light gray.                                           */

       class FocusHandler implements FocusListener
```

```
    {
       public void focusGained(FocusEvent event)
       {
          JTextField tf = (JTextField)event.getComponent();
          tf.setBackground(Color.pink);
       }

       public void focusLost(FocusEvent event)
       {
          JTextField tf = (JTextField)event.getComponent();
          tf.setBackground(Color.lightGray);
       }
    }

    public static void main(String args[])
    {
       FocusEventDemo demo = new FocusEventDemo();
    }
}
```

When the code is first run, neither JTextField has keyboard focus. Click in the text area of one of the JTextFields. This component now has focus and can accept keyboard input. The FocusEvent object that resulted from this component gaining focus is used to turn the background color pink. Switch back and forth between the JTextField objects. The background color changes to reflect which component currently has keyboard focus.

HierarchyEvent Class

A HierarchyEvent is a low-level event generated by a component when some aspect of its component hierarchy changes. The hierarchy consists of the component itself, a component's container, its container's container, and so on. For example, say there is a frame that contains a panel, and the panel contains a textfield. If the frame is re-sized, both the panel and the textfield will generate a HierarchyEvent. HierarchyEvents are intended for notification purposes only. The AWT automatically takes care of changes to the component hierarchy whether these events are processed or not.

A HierarchyEvent object contains information about the component that generated the event, the component that is at the top of the event source's component hierarchy, the parent component of the component at the top of the event source's component hierarchy, and the type of HierarchyEvent. While the HierarchyEvent class is intended for notification purposes only, a

HierarchyEvent can be used to have a component respond to some change in its component hierarchy.

There are two general types of HierarchyEvents. *Ancestor reshape events* occur when an ancestor in the component hierarchy changes its size or is moved. These events are sent to any registered HierarchyBoundsListener objects. HierarchyEvents caused by the addition or removal of an ancestor or by a change in the hierarchy visibility are known as *hierarchy change events*. This type of HierarchyEvent is sent to any registered HierarchyListener objects.

Syntax: public class HierarchyEvent extends AWTEvent

Package: java.awt.event

Class hierarchy: Object—EventObject—AWTEvent—HierarchyEvent

The HierarchyEvent class is part of the AWTEvent family. A HierarchyEvent object has access to the methods defined in the AWTEvent, EventObject, and Object classes.

Introduced: JDK 1.3

Constructors

```
public HierarchyEvent(Component source, int id, Component changed, Container parent)
public HierarchyEvent(Component source, int id, Component changed, Container parent, long changeFlags)
```

HierarchyEvent objects are generated by the system when some aspect of a component's hierarchy changes. The HierarchyEvent class defines two public constructors for creating HierarchyEvent objects. The `source` is a reference to the object that generated the event. The `id` parameter identifies the type of HierarchyEvent being generated. This will be one of the HierarchyEvent class constants described next. The `changed` parameter is the component at the top of the hierarchy. The `parent` is the parent container of the changed component. The `changeFlags` parameter is a bit mask that indicates the type of HierarchyEvent being generated. This will most likely be one of the change flags described under "Constants."

Constants

public static final int HIERARCHY_CHANGED
public static final int ANCESTOR_MOVED
public static final int ANCESTOR_RESIZED
public static final int DISPLAYABILITY_CHANGED
public static final int PARENT_CHANGED
public static final int SHOWING_CHANGED
public static final int HIERARCHY_FIRST
public static final int HIERARCHY_LAST

The first three of these constants are used to identify the HierarchyEvent object. The HIERARCHY_CHANGED constant indicates that this is a hierarchy change event. It has a numerical value of 1400. The ANCESTOR_MOVED parameter indicates that this is an ancestor reshape event in which an ancestor has been moved. It has a numerical value of 1401. The ANCESTOR_RESIZED parameter indicates that this is an ancestor reshape event in which an ancestor has been re-sized. It has a numerical value of 1402.

The next three constants are change flags that define the nature of a hierarchy change event. The PARENT_CHANGED constant indicates that a parent-child relationship in the hierarchy has changed. The DISPLAYABILITY_CHANGED constant specifies that the displayable property of the hierarchy has changed. The SHOWING_CHANGED parameter indicates a change in either the displayability or visibility of the hierarchy.

The HIERARCHY_FIRST and HIERARCHY_LAST constants represent the range of system-provided IDs for HierarchyEvent objects. These have numerical values of 1400 and 1402 respectively.

Fields

Beyond those constants described in the preceding section, the HierarchyEvent class does not define any additional fields. A HierarchyEvent object has access to the fields defined in the AWTEvent and EventObject classes, including the id and source fields.

HierarchyEvent Class Methods

public Component `getChanged()`
public Container `getChangedParent()`
public long `getChangeFlags()`
public Component `getComponent()`
public String `paramString()`

`getChanged()` returns a reference to the component at the top of the hierarchy that was changed.

`getChangedParent()` goes one level above the `getChanged()` method and returns the parent of the component at the top of the hierarchy that was changed.

`getChangeFlags()` returns a bit mask that indicates the type of HierarchyEvent.

`getComponent()` returns the object that generated the event. This is similar to the `getSource()` method defined in the EventObject class.

`paramString()` overrides the method defined in the AWTEvent class and returns a parameter String that identifies the HierarchyEvent. This is generally used for event-logging and debugging purposes. When a HierarchyEvent object calls the `toString()` method, the return value of the `paramString()` method is incorporated in the return value of the `toString()` method.

Methods Inherited from the java.awt.AWTEvent Class

protected void `consume()`
protected void `finalize()` throws Throwable
public int `getID()`
protected boolean `isConsumed()`
public String `toString()`

A HierarchyEvent object has access to these the methods defined in the AWTEvent class. For a description of these methods, see the section "AWTEvent Class" in this chapter.

Methods Inherited from the java.util.EventObject Class

public Object `getSource()`

`getSource()` returns a reference to the object that generated the HierarchyEvent. A HierarchyEvent object could also use the `getComponent()` method for this purpose.

Methods Inherited from the java.lang.Object Class

public final Class `getClass()`

`getClass()` returns a Class object representing the runtime class of the invoking object. In this case, it would return an object representing the java.awt.event.HierarchyEvent class.

The other methods inherited from the Object class, `clone()`, `equals()`, `hashCode()`, `notify()`, `notifyAll()`, and `wait()`, are generally not used in conjunction with HierarchyEvent objects.

EXAMPLE

In Example 6.14, a HierarchyEvent is used to maintain the proportional size of a JButton relative to its parent container, a JFrame. The button is placed on the frame with some initial width and height. It also registers a HierarchyBoundsListener that will be notified if some part of the button's component hierarchy is moved or resized.

The HierarchyBoundsListener is implemented as an inner class that extends the HierarchyBoundsAdapter class and only overrides the `ancestorResized()` method. When the JFrame is resized, a HierarchyEvent generated by the JButton is sent to this method. The HierarchyEvent is used to obtain a reference to the event source, the button, and to the top of the event source's hierarchy, which is the frame. The JButton is then resized the same relative amount as was the frame.

The general component hierarchy of the JButton component is JButton–JPanel—JFrame. This is a slight simplification. A JFrame object, like all higher-level Swing containers, contains a JRootPane object, which itself contains a number of subcontainers, including the layered pane and content pane. When the JFrame is resized, these additional containers are also resized (thereby generating HierarchyEvents) and, strictly speaking, the JRootPane and its subcontainers should be considered part of the component hierarchy.

Example 6.14 HierarchyEvent Class

```java
import java.awt.*;
import java.awt.event.*;
import javax.swing.*;

public class HierEventDemo extends JFrame
{
   private JButton button;
   private int frameInitWidth, frameInitHeight;
   private int buttonInitWidth, buttonInitHeight;

   public HierEventDemo()
   {
      buttonInitWidth = 70;
      buttonInitHeight = 70;
      frameInitWidth = 300;
      frameInitHeight = 200;

/* A JButtons is placed on a JFrame.  The button registers   */
/* a HierarchyBoundsListener.                                */

      button = new JButton("Button");
      button.setPreferredSize(
            new Dimension(buttonInitWidth, buttonInitHeight));
      button.setBorder(BorderFactory.createRaisedBevelBorder());
      button.addHierarchyBoundsListener(new HierBndsListener());

      JPanel panel = new JPanel();
      panel.add(button);

      getContentPane().add(panel);

      setDefaultCloseOperation(JFrame.EXIT_ON_CLOSE);
      setBounds(100, 100, frameInitWidth, frameInitHeight);
      setVisible(true);
   }

/* A HierarchyBoundsListener is implemented as an inner class that */
/* extends the HierarchyBoundsAdapter class.  If the frame is      */
/* re-sized, HierarchyEvents generated by the button are sent to the */
/* ancestorResized() method.  This method resizes the button so its */
/* size relative to the frame remains the same.                    */

   class HierBndsListener extends HierarchyBoundsAdapter
   {
      public void ancestorResized(HierarchyEvent event)
      {
         Component top = event.getChanged();
         JButton source = (JButton)event.getComponent();
```

```
        int width = top.getWidth();
        int height = top.getHeight();

        source.setPreferredSize(
            new Dimension(buttonInitWidth*width/frameInitWidth,
buttonInitHeight*height/frameInitHeight));
        }
    }

    public static void main(String args[])
    {
       HierEventDemo demo = new HierEventDemo();
    }
}
```

When the example is run, a JButton with an initial size is placed on a JFrame. If the JFrame is resized larger, a HierarchyEvent is generated, which causes the button to be resized larger as well. If the JFrame is resized smaller, the button becomes smaller too.

HTMLFrameHyperlinkEvent Class

An HTMLFrameHyperlinkEvent object is a semantic (high-level) event generated by JEditorPane components when something has happened with respect to a hyperlink inside an HTML frame displayed by the JEditorPane. Usually, this means that the user has clicked on a hyperlink inside the frame. The HTMLFrameHyperlinkEvent class has access to an inner class, HyperlinkEvent.EventType, which contains information about the nature of the HTMLFrameHyperlinkEvent.

HTMLFrameHyperlinkEvent objects contain information about the JEditorPane object that is responsible for the event: the type of HTMLFrameHyperlinkEvent, the URL to which the link refers, a description of the hyperlink as a String, the element of the HTML frame element that generated the event, and the target frame on which to display the updated HTML page. HTMLFrameHyperlinkEvents are used to facilitate the hyperlink capability of a JEditorPane that is displaying an HTML frame document.

When an HTMLFrameHyperlinkEvent is generated, it is sent to any registered HyperlinkListener. The HyperlinkListener provides implementation of the `hyperlinkUdpate()` method, which is overridden to contain the code used to process the event. The code used to process HTMLFrameHyperlinkEvents is more involved than with HyperlinkEvents because a change in the display of an HTML frame involves changing the HTMLDocument associated with the frame. The Example 6.15 at the bottom of this section demonstrates how this can be done.

Syntax: public class HTMLFrameHyperlinkEvent extends HyperlinkEvent

Package: javax.swing.text.html

Class hierarchy: Object—EventObject—HyperlinkEvent—HTMLFrameHyperlinkEvent

The HTMLFrameHyperlinkEvent class is a subclass of HyperlinkEvent. An HTMLFrameHyperlinkEvent object has access to the methods defined in the HyperlinkEvent, EventObject, and Object classes.

Introduced: JDK 1.2

Constructors

```
public HTMLFrameHyperlinkEvent(Object source,
HyperlinkEvent.EventType type, URL targetUrl, String targetFrame)
public HTMLFrameHyperlinkEvent(Object source,
HyperlinkEvent.EventType type, URL targetUrl, String desc, String
targetFrame)
public HTMLFrameHyperlinkEvent(Object source,
HyperlinkEvent.EventType type, URL targetUrl, Element
sourceElement, String targetFrame)
public HTMLFrameHyperlinkEvent(Object source,
HyperlinkEvent.EventType type, URL targetUrl, String desc,
Element sourceElement, String targetFrame)
```

The HTMLFrameHyperlinkEvent class provides four constructors for creating HTMLFrameHyperlinkEvent objects. The source is the component that is responsible the event—the JEditorPane, in most cases. The type identifies the type of HyperlinkEvent. The url is the URL corresponding to the target destination of the hyperlink. The description is a String describing the link. The `sourceElement` is the element in the HTML frame that generated the event. The `targetFrame` is the HTML frame in which the HTML page corresponding to the hyperlink will be displayed.

Constants

The HTMLFrameHyperlinkEvent class does not contain any identification constants. These are provided by the HyperlinkEvent.EventType class.

Fields

The HTMLFrameHyperlinkEvent class defines no new fields. An HTMLFrameHyperlinkEvent object has access to the `source` field from the EventObject class.

HTMLFrameHyperlinkEvent Class Methods

public Element `getSourceElement()`
public String `getTarget()`

`getSourceElement()` returns an Element object corresponding to the source of the event. The Element object will be a leaf element containing the tag HTML.Tag.Frame.

`getTarget()` returns a String description of the target destination. The return value will either be `_self`, `_parent`, `_top`, or the name of another target frame.

Methods Inherited from the javax.swing.event.HyperlinkEvent Class

public String `getDescription()`
public HyperlinkEvent.EventType `getEventType()`
public URL `getURL()`

`getDescription()` returns a String that describes the link. This is typically the URL text string. This is useful if the URL object associated with the HTMLFrameHyperlinkEvent is null or improperly formed.

`getEventType()` provides a HyperlinkEvent.EventType object containing information about the type of HTMLFrameHyperlinkEvent.

`getURL()` returns a URL object containing the URL associated with the hyperlink.

Methods Inherited from the java.util.EventObject Class

public Object `getSource()`
public String `toString()`

`getSource()` returns a reference to the object that generated the HTMLFrameHyperlinkEvent.

`toString()` returns a String representation of the HTMLFrameHyperlink-Event object.

Methods Inherited from the java.lang.Object Class

public final Class `getClass()`

`getClass()` returns a Class object representing the runtime class of the invoking object. In this case, it would return an object representing the javax.swing.text.html.HTMLFrameHyperlinkEvent class.

The other methods inherited from the Object class, `clone()`, `equals()`, `hashCode()`, `notify()`, `notifyAll()`, and `wait()`, are generally not used in conjunction with HTMLFrameHyperlinkEvent objects.

EXAMPLE

In Example 6.15, a JEditorPane is used to display HTML pages inside an HTML frame. The HTML frame is loaded into the JEditorPane. The JEditorPane registers a HyperlinkListener to detect HyperlinkEvent or HTMLFrameHyperlinkEvent objects.

The `hyperlinkUpdate()` method of the HyperlinkListener has been written such that it can process both HyperlinkEvent and HTMLFrameHyperlinkEvent objects. When a hyperlink in either of the frames is selected, an event is generated and sent to the `hyperlinkUpdate()` method. This method first determines if the event is a HyperlinkEvent.-

EventType.ACTIVATED type event. If it is, the method then checks to see if the event is an HTMLFrameHyperlinkEvent (which it will be in this example). If the event is an HTMLFrameHyperlinkEvent, the HTMLDocument associated with the JEditorPane is accessed. The HTMLDocument object calls the `processHTMLFrameHyperlinkEvent()` method, which processes the event and displays the HTML page corresponding to the hyperlink in the frame in which the link was selected.

Note that the JEditorPane is initialized with a path to the HTML frame that is to be displayed. You will have to change this path to whatever is appropriate for your system.

EXAMPLE 6.15 HTMLFRAMEHYPERLINKEVENT CLASS

```
import javax.swing.*;
import javax.swing.event.*;
import javax.swing.text.html.*;
import java.io.*;

public class HTMLFrameDemo extends JFrame implements
HyperlinkListener
{
   private JEditorPane jep = null;

   public HTMLFrameDemo()
   {
/*   A JEditorPane object is initialized with an HTML frame.    */
/*   The JEditorPane registers a HyperlinkListener              */
/*   and is added to the content pane of a JFrame.              */

      try
      {
         jep = new JEditorPane(
"file:/usr/people/palmer/Java_Event/Part2/javax.swing.event/Frame.html");
         jep.setContentType("text/html");
         jep.setEditable(false);
      }
      catch (IOException ioe)
      {
         ioe.printStackTrace(System.err);
         System.exit(1);
      }

      jep.addHyperlinkListener(this);
```

HTMLFrameHyperlinkEvent Class

```
            getContentPane().add(new JScrollPane(jep));

            setDefaultCloseOperation(JFrame.EXIT_ON_CLOSE);
            setBounds(100, 100, 400, 400);
            setVisible(true);
        }

     /* When the user clicks on a hyperlink in one of the HTML pages,   */
     /* a HyperlinkEvent is generated and sent to the hyperlinkUpdate() */
     /* method.  The event is tested to see if it is a plain old        */
     /* HyperlinkEvent or an HTMLFrameHyperlinkEvent. If it is the      */
     /* latter, the HTMLDocument associated with the JEditorPane is     */
     /* used to process the event and update the display.  Otherwise,   */
     /* the display is updated by calling the setPage() methods.        */

        public void hyperlinkUpdate(HyperlinkEvent event)
        {
            if ( event.getEventType() == HyperlinkEvent.EventType.ACTIVATED )
            {
                JEditorPane pane = (JEditorPane)event.getSource();
                if ( event instanceof HTMLFrameHyperlinkEvent )
                {
                    HTMLFrameHyperlinkEvent evt = (HTMLFrameHyperlinkEvent)event;
                    HTMLDocument document = (HTMLDocument)pane.getDocument();
                    document.processHTMLFrameHyperlinkEvent(evt);
                }
                else
                {
                    try
                    {
                        jep.setPage(event.getURL());
                    }
                    catch (IOException ioe)
                    {
                        ioe.printStackTrace(System.err);
                    }
                }
            }
        }

        public static void main(String args[])
        {
            HTMLFrameDemo demo = new HTMLFrameDemo();
        }
    }
```

When you run this program, the Frame.html page is initially displayed on the JEditorPane. The Frame.html page in turn displays two copies of the TheBoys.html page. Now click on a hyperlink in either frame and see what happens. The display inside the frame changes to the hyperlink destination. The HTMLDocument associated with the JEditorPane has used the HTMLFrameHyperlinkEvent to display the HTML page associated with the hyperlink.

The HTML pages used in this example are listed in Example 6.16. When you run this example, you will have to change the paths to the HTML files to whatever the correct path is for your system.

EXAMPLE 6.16 HTML PAGES USED FOR HTMLFRAMEHYPERLINKEVENT CLASS EXAMPLE

Frame.html

```
<HTML>
<HEAD><TITLE>Frameset</TITLE></HEAD>
<FRAMESET cols="50%,50%">
<FRAME name="JRP" src="TheBoys.html">
<FRAME name="ZGP" src="TheBoys.html">
</FRAMESET>
</HTML>
```

TheBoys.html

```
<HTML>
<!- TheBoys.html -->
<HEAD><TITLE>The Boys</TITLE></HEAD>
<BODY>
<H2> Jackson and Zachary </H2>
<P>
<A HREF="file:/usr/people/palmer/Java_Event/Part2/Jackson.html">
Jackson </A> and
<A HREF="file:/usr/people/palmer/Java_Event/Part2/Zachary.html">
Zachary </A> are two high
spirited boys that live with their mother and
father in Chandler, Arizona. </P>
</BODY>
</HTML>
```

Jackson.html

```
<HTML>
<!- Jackson.html -->
<HEAD><TITLE>Jackson</TITLE></HEAD>
```

```
<BODY>
<H2> Jackson </H2>
<P>
Jackson joined a soccer team and played in a
game every Saturday.  Jackson liked to play
goalie, but so did everyone else.  In the
last game of the season, Jackson almost scored
a goal</P><BR><BR>
<A HREF="file:/usr/people/palmer/Java_Event/Part2/TheBoys.html">
Return </A> to main page.
</BODY>
</HTML>
```

Zachary.html

```
<HTML>
<!-  Zachary.html  ->
<HEAD><TITLE>Zachary</TITLE></HEAD>
<BODY>
<H2> Zachary </H2>
<P>
Zachary loves cars, both model cars and
real ones.  Every day when we walk Jackson
to school, we have to stand in the parking
lot for several minutes watching the cars
go by. </P><BR><BR>
<A HREF="file:/usr/people/palmer/Java_Event/Part2/TheBoys.html">
Return </A> to main page.
</BODY>
</HTML>
```

HyperlinkEvent Class

A HyperlinkEvent object is a semantic (high-level) event generated by JEditorPane components when something has happened with respect to a hyperlink. Usually, this means that the user has clicked on a hyperlink inside the JEditorPane. Under JDK 1.3, a HyperlinkEvent is also generated if the mouse enters or exits the bounding area of the hyperlink. The HyperlinkEvent class contains an inner class, the HyperlinkEvent.EventType, which contains information about the nature of the HyperlinkEvent.

HyperlinkEvent objects contain information about the JEditorPane object that generated the event, a description of the link as a String, the type of HyperlinkEvent, and the URL to which the link refers. HyperlinkEvents are used to facilitate the hyperlink capability of a JEditorPane.

When a HyperlinkEvent is generated, it is sent to any registered HyperlinkListener. The HyperlinkListener provides implementation of the `hyperlinkUdpate()` method, which is overridden to contain the code used to process the event.

Syntax: public class HyperlinkEvent extends EventObject

Package: javax.swing.event

Class hierarchy: Object—EventObject—HyperlinkEvent

The HyperlinkEvent class is not part of the AWTEvent hierarchy as it is a direct subclass of EventObject. A HyperlinkEvent object has access to the methods defined in the EventObject and Object classes.

Introduced: JDK 1.2

Constructors

```
public HyperlinkEvent(Object source,
HyperlinkEvent.EventType type, URL url)
public HyperlinkEvent(Object source,
HyperlinkEvent.EventType type, URL url, String description)
```

The HyperlinkEvent class provides two constructors for creating HyperlinkEvent objects. The `source` is the component that generated the event. The `type` identifies the `type` (ACTIVATED, ENTERED, EXITED) of HyperlinkEvent. The `url` is the URL corresponding to the hyperlink. The `description` is a String describing the link.

Constants

The HyperlinkEvent class does not contain any identification constants. These are provided by the HyperlinkEvent.EventType class.

Fields

The HyperlinkEvent class defines no new fields. A HyperlinkEvent object has access to the `source` field from the EventObject class.

HyperlinkEvent Class Methods

public String `getDescription()`
public `HyperlinkEvent.EventType getEventType()`
public URL `getURL()`

`getDescription()` returns a String that describes the link. This is typically the URL text string. This is useful if the URL object associated with the HyperlinkEvent is null or improperly formed.

`getEventType()` provides a HyperlinkEvent.EventType object containing information about the type of HyperlinkEvent.

`getURL()` returns a URL object containing the URL associated with the hyperlink.

Methods Inherited from the java.util.EventObject Class

public Object `getSource()`
public String `toString()`

`getSource()` returns a reference to the object that generated the HyperlinkEvent.

`toString()` returns a String representation of the HyperlinkEvent object.

Methods Inherited from the java.lang.Object Class

public final Class `getClass()`

`getClass()` returns a Class object representing the runtime class of the invoking object. In this case, it would return an object representing the javax.swing.event. HyperlinkEvent class.

The other methods inherited from the Object class, `clone()`, `equals()`, `hashCode()`, `notify()`, `notifyAll()`, and `wait()`, are generally not used in conjunction with HyperlinkEvent objects.

EXAMPLE

In Example 6.17, a JEditorPane is used to display HTML pages inside a JFrame. The initial HTML page displayed by the JEditorPane contains hyperlinks to two other pages. In order for the hyperlinks to work, the JEditorPane must register a HyperlinkListener. Every time the user clicks on one of the hyperlinks, a HyperlinkEvent is generated and sent to the `hyperlinkUpdate()` method. The event is used to obtain the URL associated with the hyperlink, and the `setPage()` method is called to update the HTML page displayed by the JEditorPane.

A HyperlinkEvent is generated if the link is selected or if the mouse enters or exits the bounding area of the hyperlink. We don't want to react to the entering or exiting type HyperlinkEvents in this example, so we use the `getEventType()` method to filter out these events. The entering and exiting type HyperlinkEvents might be used, for instance, to update a status bar.

Note that the JEditorPane is initialized with a path to the HTML file that is to be displayed. You will have to change this path to whatever is appropriate for your system.

EXAMPLE 6.17 HYPERLINKEVENT CLASS

```
import javax.swing.*;
import javax.swing.event.*;
import java.io.*;

public class HyperlinkDemo extends JFrame implements
HyperlinkListener
{
   private JEditorPane jep = null;

   public HyperlinkDemo()
   {
/* A JEditorPane object is initialized with an HTML file.      */
/* The JEditorPane registers a HyperlinkListener and is added  */
/* to the content pane of a JFrame.                            */

      try
      {
         jep = new JEditorPane(
 "file:/usr/people/palmer/Java_Event/Part2/javax.swing.event/
TheBoys.html");
         jep.setContentType("text/html");
         jep.setEditable(false);
      }
```

```
      catch (IOException ioe)
      {
         ioe.printStackTrace(System.err);
         System.exit(1);
      }

      jep.addHyperlinkListener(this);

      getContentPane().add(new JScrollPane(jep));

      setDefaultCloseOperation(JFrame.EXIT_ON_CLOSE);
      setBounds(100, 100, 400, 400);
      setVisible(true);
   }

/* When the user clicks on a hyperlink in one of the HTML pages,  */
/* a HyperlinkEvent is generated and sent to the hyperlinkUpdate() */
/* method.  The event is used to obtain the URL associated with   */
/* the hyperlink and the HTML page displayed by the JEditorPane   */
/* is changed to be the one represented by the hyperlink.         */

   public void hyperlinkUpdate(HyperlinkEvent event)
   {
      try
      {
         if ( event.getEventType() ==
HyperlinkEvent.EventType.ACTIVATED )
         {
            jep.setPage(event.getURL());
         }
      }
      catch (IOException ioe)
      {
         ioe.printStackTrace(System.err);
      }
   }

   public static void main(String args[])
   {
      HyperlinkDemo demo = new HyperlinkDemo();
   }
}
```

When you run this program, the TheBoys.html page is initially displayed on the JEditorPane. Now click on one of the two hyperlinks and see what happens. A HyperlinkEvent has been used to change the HTML page that is displayed.

The HTML pages used in Example 6.17 are listed in Example 6.18. When you run this example, you will have to change the paths to the HTML files to whatever the correct path is for your system.

EXAMPLE 6.18 HTML PAGES USED FOR HYPERLINKEVENT CLASS EXAMPLE

TheBoys.html

```
<HTML>
<!-  TheBoys.html  ->
<HEAD><TITLE>The Boys</TITLE></HEAD>
<BODY>
<H2> Jackson and Zachary </H2>
<P>
<A HREF="file:/usr/people/palmer/Java_Event/Part2/Jackson.html">
Jackson </A> and
<A HREF="file:/usr/people/palmer/Java_Event/Part2/Zachary.html">
Zachary </A> are two high
spirited boys that live with their mother and
father in Chandler, Arizona. </P>
</BODY>
</HTML>
```

Jackson.html

```
<HTML>
<!-  Jackson.html  ->
<HEAD><TITLE>Jackson</TITLE></HEAD>
<BODY>
<H2> Jackson </H2>
<P>
Jackson joined a soccer team and played in a
game every Saturday.  Jackson liked to play
goalie, but so did everyone else.  In the
last game of the season, Jackson almost scored
a goal</P><BR><BR>
<A HREF="file:/usr/people/palmer/Java_Event/Part2/TheBoys.html">
Return </A> to main page.
</BODY>
</HTML>
```

Zachary.html

```
<HTML>
<!-  Zachary.html  ->
<HEAD><TITLE>Zachary</TITLE></HEAD>
<BODY>
<H2> Zachary </H2>
```

```
<P>
Zachary loves cars, both model cars and
real ones.  Every day when we walk Jackson
to school, we have to stand in the parking
lot for several minutes watching the cars
go by. </P><BR><BR>
<A HREF="file:/usr/people/palmer/Java_Event/Part2/TheBoys.html">
Return </A> to main page.
</BODY>
</HTML>
```

HyperlinkEvent.EventType Class

The HyperlinkEvent.EventType class is an inner class of the HyperlinkEvent class. It defines three fields that are used to identify the type of HyperlinkEvent and provides an overridden version of the toString() method to return a String representation of the type.

The HyperlinkEvent.EventType class contains no constructors. A HyperlinkEvent.EventType object can be obtained from the getEventType() method defined in the HyperlinkEvent class.

Syntax:	public static final class HyperlinkEvent.EventType extends Object
Package:	javax.swing.event
Class hierarchy:	Object—HyperlinkEvent.EventType
Introduced:	JDK 1.2

Constructors

The HyperlinkEvent.EventType class defines no constructors.

Constants

public static final HyperlinkEvent.EventType ACTIVATED

public static final HyperlinkEvent.EventType ENTERED

public static final HyperlinkEvent.EventType EXITED

These constants are used to identify the type of HyperlinkEvent. The `ACTIVATED` constant indicates that the user has clicked on a hyperlink. The `ENTERED` and `EXITED` constants were unused before JDK 1.3. As of JDK 1.3, a HyperlinkEvent is generated if the mouse enters or exits the bounding area of a hyperlink.

HyperlinkEvent.EventType Class Methods

public String `toString()`

`toString()` returns a String representation of a HyperlinkEvent.EventType object.

Methods Inherited from the java.lang.Object Class

public final Class `getClass()`

`getClass()` returns a Class object representing the runtime class of the invoking object. In this case, it would return an object representing the javax.swing.event.HyperlinkEvent.EventType class.

The other methods inherited from the Object class, `clone()`, `equals()`, `hashCode()`, `notify()`, `notifyAll()`, and `wait()`, are generally not used in conjunction with HyperlinkEvent.EventType objects.

EXAMPLE

See Example 6.17, where the identification constants defined in the HyperlinkEvent.EventType class are used to identify a HyperlinkEvent.

InputEvent Class

This is the parent class of the KeyEvent and MousEvent classes. It provides methods used by both KeyEvent and MouseEvent objects. InputEvent is an abstract class, so an InputEvent object is never created.

Input events are treated differently than other types of events in that they are delivered to listeners before going through the normal Java event life cycle. This allows the events to be consumed. An event that is marked consumed is ignored by the component peer.

InputEvent Class

Syntax:	public abstract class InputEvent extends ComponentEvent
Package:	java.awt.event
Class hierarchy:	Object—EventObject—AWTEvent—ComponentEvent—InputEvent
	The InputEvent class is part of the AWT event family. An InputEvent object has access to the methods defined in the Component, AWTEvent, EventObject, and Object classes.
Introduced:	JDK 1.1

Constructors

The InputEvent class provides no constructors.

Constants

public static final int ALT_GRAPH_MASK
public static final int ALT_MASK
public static final int BUTTON1_MASK
public static final int BUTTON2_MASK
public static final int BUTTON3_MASK
public static final int CTRL_MASK
public static final int META_MASK
public static final int SHIFT_MASK

These constants are used to identify which modifier keys were pressed when an InputEvent object is generated.

InputEvent Class Methods

public void consume()
public int getModifiers()
public long getWhen()
public boolean isAltDown()
public boolean isAltGraphDown()
public boolean isConsumed()

public boolean `isControlDown()`
public boolean `isMetaDown()`
public boolean `isShiftDown()`

`consume()` is used to mark an event as being consumed. A consumed event will not be processed in the default manner by the invoking component.

`getModifiers()` will return a bitwise flag containing the modifiers for this InputEvent. The modifiers will include which modifier keys were pressed and, for mouse events, which mouse button was pressed.

`getWhen()` returns the time in milliseconds from January 1, 1970 when the event occurred.

`isAltDown()` returns true if the ALT key was pressed when the event was generated.

`isAltGraphDown()` returns true if the ALT-Graph key was pressed when the event was generated.

`isConsumed()` returns true if the invoking event has been consumed.

`isControlDown()` returns true if the CTRL key was pressed when the event was generated.

`isMetaDown()` returns true if the Meta key was pressed when the event was generated.

`isShiftDown()` returns true if the Shift key was pressed when the event was generated.

Methods Inherited from the java.awt.event.ComponentEvent Class

public Component `getComponent()`
public String `paramString()`

`getComponent()` is used to obtain a reference to the component that generated the event.

`paramString()` returns a parameter String that identifies the InputEvent. This is generally used for event-logging and debugging purposes. When an InputEvent subclass object calls the `toString()` method, the return value of the `paramString()` method is incorporated in the return value of the `toString()` method.

Methods Inherited from the java.awt.AWTEvent Class

protected void `finalize()` throws Throwable
public int getID()
public String `toString()`

An InputEvent subclass object has access to the methods defined in the AWTEvent class. For a description of these methods, see the section "AWTEvent Class" in this chapter.

Methods Inherited from the java.util.EventObject Class

public `Object getSource()`

`getSource()` returns a reference to the object that generated the InputEvent.

Methods Inherited from the java.lang.Object Class

public final Class `getClass()`

`getClass()` returns a Class object representing the runtime class of the invoking object.

The other methods inherited from the Object class, `clone()`, `equals()`, `hashCode()`, `notify()`, `notifyAll()`, and `wait()`, are generally not used in conjunction with InputEvent objects.

InputMethodEvent Class

An InputMethodEvent is a high-level event generated by an input method when the text that is being composed by the input method changes. Input methods are components that allow for alternate forms of composition. For instance, an input method might provide support when Chinese character documents are created on PCs with a western-style keyboard. The input method would translate various combinations of letters into the desired glyph. A detailed look at input methods is beyond the scope of this book. See an appropriate Java reference for more details on this subject.

An InputMethodEvent object contains information about the component that generated the event, the type of InputMethodEvent, the number of committed characters in the text, and whether or not the event has been consumed. The InputMethodEvent object will contain both committed text and composed text. Committed text represents a final change to the text. Composed text can reflect some ongoing editing operations.

InputMethodEvents are sent to any registered InputMethodListener objects when they are generated. The InputMethodListener will provide an implementation of the `caretPositionChanged()` and `inputMethodTextChanged()` methods to process the event.

Syntax: public abstract class InputMethodEvent extends AWTEvent
Package: java.awt.event
Class hierarchy: Object—EventObject—AWTEvent—InputMethodEvent

The InputMethodEvent class is part of the AWT event AWTEvent family. An InputMethodEvent object has access to the methods defined in the AWTEvent, EventObject, and Object classes.

Introduced: JDK 1.2

Constructors

```
public InputMethodEvent(Component source, int id,
AttributedCharacterIterator text, int
committedCharacterCount, TextHitInfo caret, TextHitInfo
visiblePosition)
```

```
public InputMethodEvent(Component source, int id, int
committedCharacterCount, TextHitInfo visiblePosition)
```

The InputMethodEvent class provides two public constructors for creating InputMethodEvent objects. The `source` is the object that generated the event. The `id` identifies the type of InputMethodEvent. It will be one of the InputMethodEvent class constants described next. The `text` parameter contains the committed and composed text. The `committedCharacterCount` (as you may expect) is the number of committed characters in the text. The `caret` represents the position of the cursor within the text component. The `visiblePosition` is a recommendation of which text is to be made visible within the currently composed text.

Constants

public static final int `CARET_POSITION_CHANGED`
public static final int `INPUT_METHOD_TEXT_CHANGED`
public static final int `INPUT_METHOD_FIRST`
public static final int `INPUT_METHOD_LAST`

The `CARET_POSITION_CHANGED` constant is used to identify an InputMethodEvent caused by a change to the caret position. The caret is the cursor that appears within the text component, indicating the insertion point for added text. This constant has a numerical value of 1101.

The `INPUT_METHOD_TEXT_CHANGED` parameter indicates that an InputMethodEvent object was generated as a result of the text inside an input method changing. It has a numerical value of 1100.

The `INPUT_METHOD_FIRST` and `INPUT_METHOD_LAST` constants represent the range of system-provided IDs for InputMethodEvent objects. These have numerical values of 1100 and 1101 respectively.

Fields

Beyond those constants described in the preceding section, the InputMethodEvent class does not define any additional fields. An InputMethodEvent object has access to the fields defined in the AWTEvent and EventObject classes, including the `id` and `source` fields.

InputMethodEvent Class Methods

public void `consume()`
public TextHitInfo `getCaret()`
public int `getCommittedCharacterCount()`
public `AttributedCharacterIterator getText()`
public TextHitInfo `getVisiblePosition()`
public boolean `isConsumed()`
public String `paramString()`

`consume()` is used to mark an event as being consumed. A consumed event will not be processed in the default manner by the invoking component.

`getCaret()` will return a TextHitInfo object containing information about the caret. The TextHitInfo class is contained in the java.awt.font package.

`getCommittedCharacterCount()` returns the number of committed characters in the text.

`getText()` returns an AttributedCharacterInfo object containing the committed and composed text. The AttributedCharacterInfo class is contained in the java.text package.

`getVisiblePosition()` returns a TextHitInfo object containing the location of the text that has been designated as the most important to be visible.

`isConsumed()` returns true if the invoking event has been consumed.

`paramString()` returns a parameter String that identifies the InputMethodEvent. This is generally used for event-logging and debugging purposes. When an InputMethodEvent object calls the `toString()` method, the return value of the `paramString()` method is incorporated in the return value of the `toString()` method.

Methods Inherited from the java.awt.AWTEvent Class

protected void `finalize()` throws Throwable
public int `getID()`
public String `toString()`

An InputMethodEvent object has access to the methods defined in the AWTEvent class. For a description of these methods, see the section "AWTEvent Class" in this chapter.

Methods Inherited from the java.util.EventObject Class

public Object `getSource()`

`getSource()` returns a reference to the object that generated the InputMethodEvent.

Methods Inherited from the java.lang.Object Class

public final Class getClass()

getClass() returns a Class object representing the runtime class of the invoking object. In this case, it would return an object representing the java.awt.event.InputMethodEvent class.

The other methods inherited from the Object class, clone(), equals(), hashCode(), notify(), notifyAll(), and wait(), are generally not used in conjunction with InputMethodEvent objects.

EXAMPLE

Creating an input method example is difficult, because their implementation is platform-specific and not all platforms support the use of input methods. Consult an appropriate specialized Java reference book for an example of using an input method.

INTERNALFRAMEEVENT CLASS

An InternalFrameEvent is a semantic (high-level) event indicating that the state of a JInternalFrame object has changed. A JInternalFrame is a frame that is contained inside another Java container. The JInternalFrame object is managed by its parent container like a child component would be.

An InternalFrameEvent contains information about the source of the event and the type of InternalFrameEvent. An InternalFrameEvent has very similar functionality as a WindowEvent. The JInternalFrame class is not a subclass of Window, so JInternalFrame objects do not generate WindowEvents. The InternalFrameEvent class gives JInternalFrames the same event capability as a Window.

When an InternalFrameEvent is generated it is sent to any registered InternalFrameListener. The InternalFrameListener provides implementation of the methods used to process InternalFrameEvents.

Syntax: public class InternalFrameEvent extends AWTEvent
Package: javax.swing.event

Class hierarchy: Object—EventObject—AWTEvent—InternalFrameEvent

While the InternalFrameEvent class is contained in the javax.swing.event package it is really part of the AWTEvent hierarchy as it is a direct subclass of AWTEvent. An InternalFrameEvent object has access to the methods defined in the AWTEvent, EventObject, and Object classes.

Introduced: JDK 1.2

Constructors

```
public InternalFrameEvent(Component source, int id)
```

The InternalFrameEvent class provides one public constructor for creating InternalFrameEvent objects. The `source` is the component that generated the event. The `id` identifies the type of InternalFrameEvent. For system-generated InternalFrameEvents, it will be one of the ID constants described next.

Constants

```
public static final int INTERNAL_FRAME_ACTIVATED
public static final int INTERNAL_FRAME_CLOSED
public static final int INTERNAL_FRAME_CLOSING
public static final int INTERNAL_FRAME_DEACTIVATED
public static final int INTERNAL_FRAME_DEICONIFIED
public static final int INTERNAL_FRAME_ICONIFIED
public static final int INTERNAL_FRAME_OPENED
public static final int INTERNAL_FRAME_FIRST
public static final int INTERNAL_FRAME_LAST
```

The first seven constants are used to identify an InternalFrameEvent. Most of the names are self-explanatory. The `INTERNAL_FRAME_CLOSING` constant is for an InternalFrameEvent that results from a user attempting to close a JInternalFrame. The `INTERNAL_FRAME_CLOSED` constant is for a InternalFrameEvent generated after the frame has been successfully closed. The numerical values for these constants range from 25549 for `INTERNAL_FRAME_OPENED` to 25555 for `INTERNAL_FRAME_DEACTIVATED`.

The `INTERNAL_FRAME_FIRST` and `INTERNAL_FRAME_LAST` constants represent the range of system-provided ID's for InternalFrameEvent objects. They have numerical values of 25549 and 25555 respectively.

Fields

Beyond the identification constants previously described, the InternalFrameEvent class does not define any additional fields. An InternalFrameEvent object has access to the fields defined in the AWTEvent and EventObject classes including the `source` and `id` fields.

InternalFrameEvent Class Methods

public JInternalFrame `getInternalFrame()`
public String `paramString()`

`getInternalFrame()` returns a reference to the JInternalFrame that generated the event. It is similar in nature to the `getSource()` method from the EventObject class.

`paramString()` returns a parameter String that identifies the InternalFrameEvent. This is generally used for event-logging and debugging purposes. When an InternalFrameEvent subclass object calls the `toString()` method, the return value of the `paramString()` method is incorporated in the return value of the `toString()` method.

Methods Inherited from the java.awt.AWTEvent Class

protected void `consume()`
protected void `finalize()` throws Throwable
public int `getID()`
protected void `isConsumed()`
public String `toString()`

An InternalFrameEvent object has access to these the methods defined in the AWTEvent class. For a description of these methods, see the section "AWTEvent Class" in this chapter.

Methods Inherited from the java.util.EventObject Class

public Object `getSource()`

`getSource()` returns a reference to the object that generated the InternalFrameEvent.

Methods Inherited from the java.lang.Object Class

public final Class `getClass()`

`getClass()` returns a Class object representing the runtime class of the invoking object.

The other methods inherited from the Object class, `clone()`, `equals()`, `hashCode()`, `notify()`, `notifyAll()`, and `wait()`, are generally not used in conjunction with InternalFrameEvent objects.

EXAMPLE

In Example 6.19, InternalFrameEvents are used to keep track of the iconified state of a JInternalFrame. A JInternalFrame is placed on a JFrame and registers an InternalFrameListener. Whenever the JInternalFrame is iconified or de-iconified, an InternalFrameEvent is generated and sent to either the `internalFrameIconified()` or `internalFrameDeiconified()` methods. The current iconified state of the JInternalFrame is listed inside a JTextField placed at the bottom of the frame.

JInternalFrames are normally used in conjunction with, and managed by, JDesktopPane objects. It is presented here as a more standalone object to demonstrate and emphasize how to handle InternalFrameEvents.

Note that this example uses an image file that is placed inside the internal frame. You can substitute any image file on your system to run this example.

EXAMPLE 6.19 INTERNALFRAMEEVENT CLASS

```
import javax.swing.*;
import javax.swing.event.*;
import java.awt.*;
import java.awt.event.*;

public class IntFrameEventDemo extends JFrame implements ActionListener
{
```

```
      private JInternalFrame jif;
      private JTextField jtf;
      private JButton button;

      public IntFrameEventDemo()
      {
/*  A JInternalFrame object is created and placed on a JFrame.      */
/*  The JInternalFrame registers an InternalFrameListener.          */

         jif = new JInternalFrame("Bailey", true, true, true, true);
         jif.getContentPane().add(new JLabel(new
ImageIcon("Bailey.jpg")));
         jif.setSize(200, 100);
         jif.setDefaultCloseOperation(WindowConstants.HIDE_ON_CLOSE);
         jif.addInternalFrameListener(new InternalFrameHandler());

         button = new JButton("show");
         button.setBorder(BorderFactory.createRaisedBevelBorder());
         button.addActionListener(this);

         jtf = new JTextField(20);
         jtf.setEditable(false);

         JPanel centerPanel = new JPanel();
         centerPanel.add(jif);

         JPanel southPanel = new JPanel();
         southPanel.add(jtf);
         southPanel.add(button);

         getContentPane().add(centerPanel, BorderLayout.CENTER);
         getContentPane().add(southPanel, BorderLayout.SOUTH);

         setDefaultCloseOperation(JFrame.EXIT_ON_CLOSE);
         setBounds(100, 100, 300, 300);
         setVisible(true);
      }

/*  The InternalFrameListener is implemented as an inner class.     */
/*  If the JInternalFrame is iconified or de-inconified, an         */
/*  InternalFrameEvent is generated and sent to the appropriate     */
/*  method where the iconified state of the JInternalFrame is      */
/*  displayed in a JTextField.  The other five methods declared    */
/*  in the InternalFrameListener interface aren't used in this     */
/*  application but must be given some implementation.  They are   */
/*  implemented as stub methods.                                    */

      class InternalFrameHandler implements InternalFrameListener
      {
         public void internalFrameDeiconified(InternalFrameEvent event)
         {
            jtf.setText("internal frame deiconified");
            invalidate();
```

```
         validate();
      }

      public void internalFrameIconified(InternalFrameEvent event)
      {
         jtf.setText("internal frame iconified");
         invalidate();
         validate();
      }

      public void internalFrameActivated(InternalFrameEvent event) {}
      public void internalFrameClosed(InternalFrameEvent event) {}
      public void internalFrameClosing(InternalFrameEvent event) {}
      public void internalFrameDeactivated(InternalFrameEvent event) {}
      public void internalFrameOpened(InternalFrameEvent event) {}
   }

/* When the "show" button is pressed, the JInternalFrame is made  */
/* visible.                                                       */

      public void actionPerformed(ActionEvent event)
      {
         jif.show();
      }

      public static void main(String args[])
      {
         IntFrameEventDemo demo = new IntFrameEventDemo();
      }
}
```

When you first run this code, the JInternalFrame is not visible. Press the "show" button and the JInternalFrame appears. Press the "iconify" symbol at the top of the internal frame. The frame is iconified and the textfield displays this fact at the bottom of the JFrame. Clicking on the icon deiconifies the JInternalFrame and an InternalFrameEvent object is used to update the textfield.

INVOCATIONEVENT CLASS

An InvocationEvent is a unique type of event that is used to execute the `run()` method of an object that implements the Runnable interface. The InvocationEvent class implements the ActiveEvent interface. This interface is for events that can dispatch themselves. It defines one method, `dispatch()`, which calls the `run()` method of a Runnable object.

InvocationEvents can be used to execute the `run()` method of a Runnable object directly, but they can also be used to execute the `run()` method of a Runnable object from the event dispatch thread. The InvocationEvent is placed on the system event queue using the `invokeLater()` and `invokeAndWait()` methods. These methods are defined in the EventQueue and SwingUtilities classes. When the InvocationEvent method reaches the front of the event queue, its `dispatch()` method is called.

InvocationEvents are always user-generated. An InvocationEvent has information about the event source, the Runnable object that is to be executed, and any objects whose `notifyAll()` will be called when the Runnable object's `run()` method returns.

No event listeners are used with InvocationEvent objects. They know what it is they have to do and do it when dispatched.

Syntax: public abstract class InvocationEvent extends AWTEvent implements ActiveEvent

Package: java.awt.event

Class hierarchy: Object—EventObject—AWTEvent—InvocationEvent

The InvocationEvent class is part of the AWT event AWTEvent family. An InvocationEvent object has access to the methods defined in the AWTEvent, EventObject, and Object classes.

Introduced: JDK 1.2

Constructors

```
protected InvocationEvent(Object source, int id, Runnable runnable, Object notifier, boolean catchExceptions)
public InvocationEvent(Object source, Runnable runnable)
public InvocationEvent(Object source, Runnable runnable, Object notifier, boolean catchExceptions)
```

The InvocationEvent class provides one protected and two public constructors for creating InvocationEvent objects. The `source` is the object that generated the event. The `id` identifies the type of InvocationEvent. It will be one of the InvocationEvent class constants described next. The `runnable` is the Runnable object whose `run()` method will be executed when the event is dispatched. The `notifier` is an object whose `notifyAll()` method will be called after the `run()` method has returned. The `notifyAll()` method wakes up all existing threads that are waiting for execution. If `catchExceptions` is true, the `dispatch()` method will catch any exceptions that occur during the execution of the Runnable object's `run()` method.

Constants

public static final int `INVOCATION_DEFAULT`
public static final int `INVOCATION_FIRST`
public static final int `INVOCATION_LAST`

The `INVOCATION_DEFAULT` constant is the default ID for Invocation-Events. It has a numerical value of 1200.

The `INVOCATION_FIRST` and `INVOCATION_LAST` constants represent the range of system-provided ID's for InvocationEvent objects. There is only one ID, so these also have the numerical value of 1200.

Fields

protected boolean `catchExceptions`
protected Object `notifier`
protected Runnable `runnable`

The InvocationEvent class defines the following fields. They are all protected and there are no class methods to access them. In addition to these fields, an InvocationEvent object has access to the fields defined in the AWTEvent and EventObject classes.

`catchExceptions` is true if the `dispatch()` method will catch any exceptions thrown by the Runnable's `run()` method.

`notifier` is a reference to the Object (if any) whose `notifyAll()` method will be called when the Runnable's `run()` method returns. The `notifyAll()` method will tell any threads that are waiting for the `run()` method to finish that it has finished.

`runnable` is a reference to the Runnable object associated with the InvocationEvent.

InvocationEvent Class Methods:

public void `dispatch()`
public `Exception getException()`
public String `paramString()`

`dispatch()` executes the Runnable object's `run()` method and will notify the notifier object, if any, when the `run()` method returns.

`getException()` returns any exceptions caught by the `dispatch()` method. This method will return null if there were no exceptions caught or if `catchExceptions` was set to false.

`paramString()` returns a parameter String that identifies the InvocationEvent. This is generally used for event-logging and debugging purposes. When an InvocationEvent subclass object calls the `toString()` method, the return value of the `paramString()` method is incorporated in the return value of the `toString()` method.

Methods Inherited from the java.awt.AWTEvent Class

protected void `consume()`
protected void `finalize()` throws Throwable
public int `getID()`
protected boolean `isConsumed()`
public String `toString()`

An InvocationEvent object has access to these the methods defined in the AWTEvent class. For a description of these methods, see the section "AWTEvent Class" in this chapter.

Methods Inherited from the java.util.EventObject Class

public Object `getSource()`

`getSource()` returns a reference to the object that generated the InvocationEvent.

Methods Inherited from the java.lang.Object Class

public final Class `getClass()`

`getClass()` returns a Class object representing the runtime class of the invoking object. In this case it would return an object representing the java.awt.event.InvocationEvent class.

The other methods inherited from the Object class, `clone()`, `equals()`, `hashCode()`, `notify()`, `notifyAll()`, and `wait()`, are generally not used in conjunction with InvocationEvent objects.

EXAMPLE

In Example 6.20, an InvocationEvent object is used to execute the `run()` method of the GetTime class. This occurs when the "Time" button is pressed. The `run()` method creates an instance of the Date class, which is used to display the time.

To see an example of how an InvocationEvent can be used to prevent a deadlock condition in a multithreaded application, look at Example 6.2 in the "ActiveEvent Interface" section.

EXAMPLE 6.20 INVOCATIONEVENT CLASS

```
import java.awt.*;
import java.awt.event.*;
import javax.swing.*;
import java.util.*;

public class InvocEventDemo extends JFrame implements ActionListener
{
   private JLabel label;
   private JButton button;
   private JPanel southPanel, centerPanel;

   public InvocEventDemo()
   {
      button = new JButton("Time");
      button.setBorder(BorderFactory.createRaisedBevelBorder());
      button.addActionListener(this);

      label = new JLabel("");
      label.setFont(new Font("Serif", Font.PLAIN, 12));
      label.setForeground(Color.black);

      southPanel = new JPanel();
```

```
         southPanel.add(button);

         centerPanel = new JPanel();
         centerPanel.add(label);

         getContentPane().add(southPanel, BorderLayout.SOUTH);
         getContentPane().add(centerPanel, BorderLayout.CENTER);

         setDefaultCloseOperation(JFrame.EXIT_ON_CLOSE);
         setBounds(100, 100, 300, 200);
         setVisible(true);
      }

/*   When the JButton is pressed, an ActionEvent is generated and    */
/*   sent to the actionPerformed() method.  This method creates an   */
/*   InvocationEvent object which is then dispatched.  The event     */
/*   calls the run() method of the GetTime class which displays      */
/*   the current time.                                               */
      public void actionPerformed(ActionEvent event)
      {
         InvocationEvent ie =
                 new InvocationEvent(this, new GetTime());
         ie.dispatch();
      }

      class GetTime implements Runnable
      {
         public void run()
         {
             Date d = new Date();
             label.setText(d.toString());
             centerPanel.invalidate();
             centerPanel.validate();
         }
      }

      public static void main(String args[])
      {
         InvocEventDemo demo = new InvocEventDemo();
      }
}
```

When the code is started, the center panel is initially blank. When the "Time" button is pressed, an InvocationEvent is instantiated. This event is then dispatched and executes the run() program.

ItemEvent Class

An ItemEvent is a semantic (high-level) event generated by components that represent an item that can be selected or de-selected. The event is generated when the selected state of the item changes. ItemEvent objects are generated by:

1. Checkbox or JCheckBox objects when the box is checked or unchecked.
2. JToggleButton objects when the button is toggled up or down.
3. CheckboxMenuItem or JCheckBoxMenuItem objects when the box is checked or unchecked.
4. Choice objects when the selected item changes.
5. List objects when a selection is single-clicked.
6. JComboBox objects when the selection is changed for any reason.
7. JRadioButton or JRadioButtonMenuItem objects when the button is toggled on or off.

The thing to look for is the ItemSelectable interface. An object that implements the ItemSelectable interface will likely generate ItemEvents.

An ItemEvent contains information about the component that generated the event, the element that was selected or deselected, and whether the event was caused by an item being selected or by an item being deselected. ItemEvents are commonly used events used to indicate or update one or more user selections.

ItemEvents are sent to any registered ItemListener objects when they are generated. The ItemListener will provide an implementation of the `itemStateChanged()` methods to process the event.

Syntax:	public class ItemEvent extends AWTEvent
Package:	java.awt.event
Class hierarchy:	Object—EventObject—AWTEvent—ItemEvent
	The ItemEvent class is part of the AWT event family. An ItemEvent object has access to the methods defined in the AWTEvent, EventObject, and Object classes.
Introduced:	JDK 1.1

Constructors

```
public ItemEvent(ItemSelectable source, int id, Object
item, int stateChange)
```

The ItemEvent class provides one public constructor for creating ItemEvent objects. The `source` is the ItemSelectable object that generated the event. The `id` identifies the type of ItemEvent. For system-generated ItemEvents, it will be the `ITEM_STATE_CHANGED` constant described next. The `item` is the object representing the selection or de-selection. This will vary from component to component. The `stateChange` parameter indicates if the item was selected or deselected. It will be either the `SELECTED` or `DESELECTED` constants described here.

Constants

```
public static final int ITEM_STATE_CHANGED
public static final int SELECTED
public static final int DESELECTED
public static final int ITEM_FIRST
public static final int ITEM_LAST
```

The `ITEM_STATE_CHANGED` constant is the default ID for ItemEvent objects. It has a numerical value of 701.

The `SELECTED` and `DESELECTED` constants represent the state of the ItemSelectable item that generated the event.

The `ITEM_FIRST` and `ITEM_LAST` constants represent the range of system-provided IDs for ItemEvent objects. There is only one ID, so both of these constants have the numerical value of 701.

Fields

Besides the constants described in the previous section, the ItemEvent class defines no additional fields. An ItemEvent object does have access to the fields defined in the AWTEvent and EventObject classes.

ItemEvent Class Methods

public Object `getItem()`
public ItemSelectable `getItemSelectable()`
public int `getStateChange()`
public String `paramString()`

`getItem()` returns an object that represents some aspect of the event. The return type is component-specific. For example, when a Checkbox generates an ItemEvent, the `getItem()` method returns a String containing the name of the Checkbox. When a List object generates an ItemEvent, the `getItem()` method returns an Integer object representing the index of the selected item, and so on.

`getItemSelectable()` returns a reference to the ItemSelectable object that generated the event. This method is similar to the `getSource()` method defined in the EventObject class.

`getStateChange()` returns the selected state of the object that generated the event. The return value will either be `ItemEvent.SELECTED` or `ItemEvent.DESELECTED`.

`paramString()` returns a parameter String that identifies the ItemEvent. This is generally used for event-logging and debugging purposes. When an ItemEvent object calls the `toString()` method, the return value of the `paramString()` method is incorporated in the return value of the `toString()` method.

Methods Inherited from the java.awt.AWTEvent Class

protected void `consume()`
protected void `finalize()` throws Throwable
public int `getID()`
protected boolean `isConsumed()`
public String `toString()`

An ItemEvent object has access to the methods defined in the AWTEvent class. For a description of these methods, see the section "AWTEvent Class" in this chapter.

Methods Inherited from the java.util.EventObject Class

public Object `getSource()`

`getSource()` returns a reference to the object that generated the ItemEvent. An ItemEvent object could also use the `getItemSelectable()` method for this purpose.

Methods Inherited from the java.lang.Object Class

public final Class `getClass()`

`getClass()` returns a Class object representing the runtime class of the invoking object. In this case, it would return an object representing the java.awt.event.ItemEvent class.

The other methods inherited from the Object class, `clone()`, `equals()`, `hashCode()`, `notify()`, `notifyAll()`, and `wait()`, are generally not used in conjunction with ItemEvent objects.

EXAMPLE

Example 6.21 is a simple example that shows how an ItemEvent can be used to indicate a selection change in a JComboBox. A JComboBox containing three choices of foods is placed on a JFrame. The JComboBox registers an ItemListener. When the user makes a selection, an ItemEvent is generated and sent to the `itemStateChanged()` method. This method updates a JTextField to indicate the current selection.

EXAMPLE 6.21 ITEMEVENT CLASS

```
import java.awt.*;
import java.awt.event.*;
import javax.swing.*;

public class ItemEventDemo extends JFrame
{
   private JComboBox jcb;
   private JTextField jtf;

   public ItemEventDemo()
   {
      jtf = new JTextField(20);
      jtf.setText("Selection is ");
      jtf.setEditable(false);
```

```
/* A JComboBox is created and placed on a JFrame.  The JComboBox  */
/* registers an ItemListener.                                     */

    String[] food = {"hamburger", "pizza", "lentil soup"};
    jcb = new JComboBox(food);
    jcb.setBorder(BorderFactory.createLineBorder(Color.black));
    jcb.addItemListener(new ItemEventHandler());

    JPanel southPanel = new JPanel();
    southPanel.add(jtf);

    JPanel centerPanel = new JPanel();
    centerPanel.add(jcb);

    getContentPane().add(southPanel, BorderLayout.SOUTH);
    getContentPane().add(centerPanel, BorderLayout.CENTER);

    setDefaultCloseOperation(JFrame.EXIT_ON_CLOSE);
    setBounds(100, 100, 300, 200);
    setVisible(true);
}

/* The ItemListener is implemented as an inner class.  When the user */
/* makes a selection, an ItemEvent is generated and sent to the      */
/* itemStateChanged() method.  This method updtates the JTextField   */
/* to indicate the new selection.                                    */

    class ItemEventHandler implements ItemListener
    {
        public void itemStateChanged(ItemEvent event)
        {
            jtf.setText("Selection is "+event.getItem());
        }
    }

    public static void main(String args[])
    {
        ItemEventDemo demo = new ItemEventDemo();
    }
}
```

Run the code and change the selected element of the JComboBox. Note how the JTextField updates any change in selection.

In some situations, two ItemEvents will be generated when the user changes a selection. For example, a series of JRadioButtons grouped together with a ButtonGroup will generate one ItemEvent for the radio button that was selected and one for the radio button that was de-selected. In this situation, the `getStateChange()` method could be used to identify which ItemEvent was which. See the "Stagnation Point Heating Code" example in Chapter 13, "Putting It All Together," to see how this can be used.

KeyEvent Class

A KeyEvent is a low-level event generated by the component that has focus when the user types on the keyboard. There are three general types of KeyEvents. These occur when a key is pressed, released, or typed. The first two, pressed and released, represent a single keystroke. A typed KeyEvent can represent a combination of keystrokes. For example, G is a combination of the Shift and *g* keystrokes. Key typed events are not generated for keys, such as the modifier keys, that don't generate characters.

The KeyEvent class also defines some quantities that are used to characterize the event. The virtual key code represents which individual key was pressed. It will not represent a combination of keystrokes used to generate a character (Shift and -*g*). The mapping of virtual key codes to specific keys on the keyboard is platform and locality dependent. The KeyEvent class also defines a method to return the Unicode character that was typed.

A key pressed or key released KeyEvent has information about the virtual key code and character associated with the event, the object that was the source of the event, and any modifier keys that were pressed during the event. A key typed KeyEvent does not have virtual key code or modifier key information. KeyEvent objects are very versatile and can be used to implement all kinds of interesting things.

KeyEvents are sent to any registered KeyListener objects when they are generated. The KeyListener will provide an implementation of methods used to process the different types of KeyEvents.

Syntax:	public class KeyEvent extends InputEvent
Package:	java.awt.event
Class hierarchy:	Object—EventObject—AWTEvent—ComponentEvent—InputEvent—KeyEvent

The KeyEvent class is part of the AWTEvent family. An KeyEvent object has access to the methods defined in the InputEvent, ComponentEvent, AWTEvent, EventObject, and Object classes.

Introduced: JDK 1.1

Constructors

```
public KeyEvent(Component source, int id, long when, int modifiers, int virtualKeyCode)
public KeyEvent(Component source, int id, long when, int modifiers, int virtualKeyCode, char keyChar)
```

The KeyEvent class provides two public constructors for creating KeyEvent objects. The `source` is the component that generated the event. The `id` identifies the type of KeyEvent. For system-generated KeyEvents, it will be one of the ID constants described in Table 6.1. The `when` parameter is the time in milliseconds from January 1, 1970 that the event occurred. The `modifiers` constant provides a bit mask of the modifier keys pressed when the event was generated. The mask constants are described in the InputEvent class section. The `virtualKeyCode` parameter is the virtual key code corresponding to the keystroke that caused the event. The `keyChar` parameter is the Unicode character generated by the keystroke.

Identification Constants

```
public static final int KEY_PRESSED
public static final int KEY_RELEASED
public static final int KEY_TYPED
public static final int KEY_FIRST
public static final int KEY_LAST
```

The first three constants are used to identify a KeyEvent.

The `KEY_PRESSED` and `KEY_RELEASED` constants represent a single key being pressed or released. They have numerical values of 401 and 402 respectively.

The `KEY_TYPED` constant may represent a combination of keystrokes. It has a numerical value of 400.

The `KEY_FIRST` and `KEY_LAST` constants represent the range of system-provided ID's for KeyEvent objects. They have numerical values of 400 and 402 respectively.

Virtual Key Code Constants

The KeyEvent class defines a large number of virtual key code constants representing all the different types of keys that can generate a KeyEvent. They all have the general form public static final int VK_XXXX, as listed in Table 6.1.

TABLE 6.1 VIRTUAL KEY CODE CONSTANTS

Numbers	VK_0 – VK_9	
Letters	VK_A – VK_Z	
Meta keys	VK_ALT	VK_SHIFT
	VK_CONTROL	
Punctuation	VK_ASTERISK	VK_INVERTED_EXCLAMATION_MARK
	VK_BACK_QUOTE	VK_PERIOD
	VK_COLON	VK_QUOTE
	VK_COMMA	VK_QUOTEDBL
	VK_EXCLAMATION_MARK	VK_SEMICOLON
Special characters	VK_AT	VK_EURO
	VK_AMPERSAND	VK_LEFT_PARENTHESIS
	VK_BACK_SLASH	VK_NUMBER_SIGN
	VK_BACK_SPACE	VK_OPEN_BRACKET
	VK_BRACELEFT	VK_RIGHT_PARENTHESIS
	VK_BRACERIGHT	VK_SLASH
	VK_CLOSE_BRACKET	VK_SPACE
	VK_DELETE	VK_TAB
	VK_DOLLAR	VK_UNDERSCORE
	VK_ENTER	
Math	VK_DECIMAL	VK_MINUS
	VK_DIVIDE	VK_MULTIPLY
	VK_EQUALS	VK_PLUS
	VK_GREATER	VK_SUBTRACT
	VK_LESS	

TABLE 6.1 VIRTUAL KEY CODE CONSTANTS (CONTINUED)

Keypad functions	VK_KP_DOWN VK_KP_LEFT VK_KP_RIGHT VK_KP_UP VK_NUMPAD0 – VK_NUMPAD9 VK_HELP	VK_HOME VK_PAGE_DOWN VK_PAGE_UP VK_PAUSE VK_PRINTSCREEN VK_SCROLL_LOCK
Editing	VK_COPY VK_CUT	VK_PASTE
Function keys	VK_F1 – VK_F24 VK_ACCEPT VK_ALL_CANDIDATES VK_ALPHANUMERIC VK_ALT_GRAPH VK_CODE_INPUT VK_COMPOSE VK_CONVERT VK_FULL_WIDTH	VK_HALF_WIDTH VK_JAPANESE_HIRAGANA VK_JAPANESE_KATAKANA VK_JAPANESE_ROMAN VK_KANA_LOCK VK_KATAKANA VK_NONCONVERT VK_PREVIOUS_CANDIDATE VK_ROMAN_CHARACTERS
Undefined key	VK_UNDEFINED	

Fields

public static final char CHAR_UNDEFINED

CHAR_UNDEFINED is the keyChar value for KEY_PRESSED and KEY_RELEASED events that do not map to a valid Unicode character.

A KeyEvent object also has access to the fields defined in the InputEvent, ComponentEvent, AWTEvent, and EventObject classes.

KeyEvent Class Methods

public char getKeyChar()

public int getKeyCode()

public static String getKeyModifiersText(int modifiers)

public static String getKeyText(int virtualKeyCode)

public boolean isActionKey()

public String paramString()

```
public void setKeyChar(char keyChar)
public void setKeyCode(int virtualKeyCode)
public void setModifiers(int modifiers)
public void setSource(Object newSource)
```

`getKeyChar()` returns the character represented by the event. For instance, if a key-typed event is created by pressing the Shift and G keys, this method would return G.

`getKeyCode()` returns the virtual key code for this event. The return value will be one of the virtual key code constants described in Table 6.1.

`getKeyModifiersText()` is a static method that returns a String representation of the bitwise modifier key mask. For instance, the following syntax would return the String "`Ctrl`":

```
KeyEvent.getKeyModifiersText(InputEvent.CTRL_MASK);
```

`getKeyText()` is a static method that returns a String describing a virtual key code. For instance, the following syntax returns the String "`NumPad-0`":

```
KeyEvent.getKeyText(InputEvent.VK_NUMPAD0);
```

`isActionKey()` returns true if the KeyEvent was generated by typing an action key (arrow, keypad, or function).

`paramString()` returns a parameter String that identifies the KeyEvent. This is generally used for event-logging and debugging purposes. When a KeyEvent object calls the `toString()` method, the return value of the `paramString()` method is incorporated in the return value of the `toString()` method.

`setKeyChar()` is used to change the UNICODE character associated with the invoking the KeyEvent.

`setKeyCode()` is used to specify the virtual key code associated with invoking the KeyEvent.

`setModifiers()` changes the modifier keys associated with invoking the KeyEvent.

Methods Inherited from the java.awt.event.InputEvent Class

public void `consume()`
public int `getModifiers()`
public long `getWhen()`
public boolean `isAltDown()`
public boolean `is AltGraphDown()`
public boolean `isConsumed()`
public boolean `isControlDown()`
public boolean `isMetaDown()`
public boolean `isShiftDown()`

A KeyEvent object has access to the events defined in the InputEvent class. For a description of these methods, see the section "InputEvent Class" in this chapter.

Methods Inherited from the java.awt.event.ComponentEvent Class

public Component `getComponent()`

`getComponent()` returns a reference to the component that generated the KeyEvent.

Methods Inherited from the java.awt.AWTEvent Class

protected void `finalize()` throws Throwable
public int `getID()`
public String `toString()`

A KeyEvent object has access to the methods defined in the AWTEvent class. For a description of these methods, see the section "AWTEvent Class" in this chapter.

Methods Inherited from the java.util.EventObject Class

public Object `getSource()`

`getSource()` returns a reference to the object that generated the KeyEvent. A KeyEvent object could also use the `getComponent()` method for this purpose.

Methods Inherited from the java.lang.Object Class

public final Class `getClass()`

`getClass()` returns a Class object representing the runtime class of the invoking object. In this case, it would return an object representing the java.awt.event.KeyEvent class.

The other methods inherited from the Object class, `clone()`, `equals()`, `hashCode()`, `notify()`, `notifyAll()`, and `wait()`, are generally not used in conjunction with KeyEvent objects.

EXAMPLE

In Example 6.22, KeyEvents are used to manipulate a JFrame. The JFrame registers a KeyListener. Every time a key is typed when the JFrame has keyboard focus, a KeyEvent is generated and sent to the `keyTyped()` method of the KeyListener. The KeyEvent is used to determine which key was typed to generate the event. If a *b* is typed, the JFrame is resized larger. If an *s* is typed, the JFrame is resized smaller. If a *q* is typed, the application quits.

EXAMPLE 6.22 KEYEVENT CLASS

```
import java.awt.*;
import java.awt.event.*;
import javax.swing.*;

public class KeyEventDemo extends JFrame
{
   public KeyEventDemo()
   {
/*  An empty JFrame is created and registers a KeyListener    */

      addKeyListener(new KeyEventHandler());
      setDefaultCloseOperation(JFrame.EXIT_ON_CLOSE);
      setBounds(100, 100, 300, 200);
      setVisible(true);
   }

/*  The KeyListener is implemented as an inner class that extends  */
/*  the KeyAdapter class.  When the JFrame has keyboard focus and  */
/*  a key is typed, a KeyEvent is generated and sent to the        */
```

```
/* keyTyped() method.  If a 'b' is typed, the JFrame is resized    */
/* bigger.  If a 's' is typed, the JFrame is resized smaller.      */
/* If a 'q' is typed, the application quits.                       */

   class KeyEventHandler extends KeyAdapter
   {
      public void keyTyped(KeyEvent event)
      {
         if ( event.getKeyChar() == 'b' )
         {
            setSize( (int)(getWidth()*1.1), (int)(getHeight()*1.1) );
         }
         if ( event.getKeyChar() == 's' )
         {
            setSize( (int)(getWidth()*0.9), (int)(getHeight()*0.9) );
         }
         if ( event.getKeyChar() == 'q' )
         {
            System.exit(0);
         }
      }
   }

   public static void main(String args[])
   {
      KeyEventDemo demo = new KeyEventDemo();
   }
}
```

When the program is run, a blank JFrame appears on the screen. Place the mouse cursor inside the JFrame (thus giving it keyboard focus) and type some letters. A *b* makes the frame larger. An *s* makes the frame smaller. A *q* quits the application. Any other key has no effect.

LISTDATAEVENT CLASS

A ListDataEvent is a semantic (high-level) event generated when a change is made to the contents of a list. The change can be the insertion of a list element, the removal of a list element, or the alteration of a list element. This is one of two event classes used with Swing list components; the other is the ListSelectionEvent class.

A ListDataEvent contains information about the event source, the range of indices that were changed, and whether list elements were changed, added, or removed.

ListDataEvent Class

ListDataEvents will be generated by any class that implements the ListModel interface or by any object that uses the DefaultComboBoxModel class. The most likely objects to do this are JList and JComboBox objects. One thing to note is that ListDataEvents are generated by the list model, not by the components themselves. It is the list model that must register the listener.

When a ListDataEvent is generated, it is sent to any registered ListDataListener. The ListDataListener provides implementation of methods used to process ListDataEvents.

Syntax: public class ListDataEvent extends EventObject

Package: javax.swing.event

Class hierarchy: Object—EventObject—ListDataEvent

The ListDataEvent class is not part of the AWTEvent hierarchy as it is a direct subclass of EventObject. A ListDataEvent object has access to the methods defined in the EventObject and Object classes.

Introduced: JDK 1.2

Constructors

```
public ListDataEvent(Object source, int type, int indexStart, int indexEnd)
```

The ListDataEvent class provides one public constructor for creating ListDataEvent objects. The `source` is the component that generated the event. The `type` identifies the type of ListDataEvent. It will be one of the ListDataEvent constants described next. The `indexStart` is the lower index in the range of the elements that have changed. The `indexEnd` is the upper index in the range of elements that have changed.

Constants

```
public static final int CONTENTS_CHANGED
public static final int INTERVAL_ADDED
public static final int INTERVAL_REMOVED
```

These constants are used as identifiers for ListDataEvents.

The CONTENTS_CHANGED constant indicates that one or more list elements have been altered.

The INTERVAL_ADDED parameter indicates the ListDataEvent was caused by the addition of one or more elements to the list.

The INTERVAL_REMOVED constants indicates that one or more elements was removed from the list.

Fields

Beyond the identification constants described previously, the ListDataEvent class defines no new constants. A ListDataEvent object has access to the source field defined in the EventObject class.

ListDataEvent Class Methods

public int getIndex0()
public int getIndex1()
public int getType()

getIndex0() returns the lower index of the range of elements that were changed.

getIndex1() returns the upper index of the range of elements that were changed.

getType() is used to identify the type of ListDataEvent. The return value will be one of the ListDataEvent class constants described previously.

Methods Inherited from the java.util.EventObject Class

public Object getSource()
public String toString()

getSource() returns a reference to the object that generated the ListDataEvent.

toString() returns a String representation of the ListDataEvent object.

Methods Inherited from the java.lang.Object Class

public final Class getClass()

`getClass()` returns a Class object representing the runtime class of the invoking object. In this case, it would return an object representing the javax.swing.event.ListDataEvent class.

The other methods inherited from the Object class, `clone()`, `equals()`, `hashCode()`, `notify()`, `notifyAll()`, and `wait()`, are generally not used in conjunction with ListDataEvent objects.

EXAMPLE

Example 6.23 uses ListDataEvent objects to manage the elements of a JList. A list model is created using a DefaultListModel object. The DefaultListModel is initialized with a list of names. The JList is placed on a JFrame. At the bottom of the frame are a JTextField and JButton. When the button is pressed, whatever text is in the textfield will be added as an element to the JList.

The DefaultListModel registers a ListDataListener. When an element is added to the list, a ListDataEvent is generated and sent to the `intervalAdded()` method. This method checks to see if the element already exists in the list. If it does, the element is removed from the list. This action generates another ListDataEvent object, which is sent to the `intervalRemoved()` method. This method displays a message dialog informing the user that the element is already part of the list.

EXAMPLE 6.23 LISTDATAEVENT CLASS

```
import javax.swing.*;
import javax.swing.event.*;
import java.awt.*;
import java.awt.event.*;

public class ListDataEventDemo extends JFrame implements ActionListener
{
    private JButton button;
    private JTextField jtf;
    private JList list;
```

```java
        private DefaultListModel model;

        public ListDataEventDemo()
        {
/*   A JList object is created by first initializing a DefaultListModel*/
/*   with a list of names.  The DefaultListModel registers a           */
/*   ListDataListener.                                                 */

            model = new DefaultListModel();
            model.addElement("Mark");
            model.addElement("Maria");
            model.addElement("Scott");
            model.addElement("Diana");
            model.addElement("Stephanie");
            model.addListDataListener(new ListDataHandler());

            list = new JList(model);
            list.setVisibleRowCount(7);

            button = new JButton("Add");
            button.setBorder(BorderFactory.createRaisedBevelBorder());
            button.addActionListener(this);

            jtf = new JTextField(15);
            jtf.setBorder(BorderFactory.createLineBorder(Color.black));

            JPanel centerPanel = new JPanel();
            centerPanel.add(new JScrollPane(list,
                    ScrollPaneConstants.VERTICAL_SCROLLBAR_ALWAYS,
                    ScrollPaneConstants.HORIZONTAL_SCROLLBAR_AS_NEEDED));

            JPanel southPanel = new JPanel();
            southPanel.add(jtf);
            southPanel.add(button);

            getContentPane().add(centerPanel, BorderLayout.CENTER);
            getContentPane().add(southPanel, BorderLayout.SOUTH);

            setDefaultCloseOperation(JFrame.EXIT_ON_CLOSE);
            setBounds(100, 100, 300, 300);
            setVisible(true);
        }

/*   When the "Add" button is pressed, the text in the JTextField is */
/*   added as an element to the JList.                               */

        public void actionPerformed(ActionEvent event)
        {
            if ( jtf.getText().length() != 0 )
```

```java
      {
         model.addElement(jtf.getText());
      }
   }

   /* The ListDataListener is implemented as an inner class. Whenever */
   /* an element is added to the list, a ListDataEvent is generated and */
   /* sent to the intervalAdded() method.  This method checks to see if */
   /* the element is already in the list.  If it is, the element is    */
   /* removed.  This action generates another ListDataEvent that is    */
   /* sent to the intervalRemoved() method.  This method displays a    */
   /* message dialog informing the user that the name is already part  */
   /* of the list.                                                     */

   class ListDataHandler implements ListDataListener
   {
      public void intervalAdded(ListDataEvent event)
      {
         for(int i=0; i<event.getIndex0(); ++i)
         {
            String element = (String)model.elementAt(i);
            String newElement =
(String)model.elementAt(event.getIndex0());
            if ( newElement.equals(element) )
            {
               model.removeElementAt(event.getIndex0());
               break;
            }
         }
         jtf.setText("");
      }

      public void intervalRemoved(ListDataEvent event)
      {
         JOptionPane.showMessageDialog(list, "Name already in list");
      }

      public void contentsChanged(ListDataEvent event) {}
   }

   public static void main(String args[])
   {
      ListDataEventDemo demo = new ListDataEventDemo();
   }
}
```

When you run this program, an initial list of five names appears on the screen. Type in another name in the textfield and press the Add button. The new name will appear as an element of the list. Now type in one of the names that is already in the list. The name is not added to the list a second time, and a message dialog appears telling you that the name is already part of the list. The functionality of disallowing duplicate list entries is facilitated by using ListDataEvents.

ListSelectionEvent Class

A ListSelectionEvent is a semantic (high-level) event indicating a change in the current selection of a list. It does not identify what the change was, only that a change has occurred. ListSelectionEvent objects are generated by JList and JTable components as well as by any other component of a class that implements either the ListSelectionModel or DefaultListSelectionModel interface.

A ListSelectionEvent object contains information about the event source, the range of indices of the selection change, and whether the event is part of a series of associated events. An example of this would be dragging the mouse down a list or table.

When a ListSelectionEvent is generated, it is sent to any registered ListSelectionListener. The ListSelectionListener provides an implementation of the `valueChanged()` method that is used to process the event. The ListSelectionListener can be registered either to the component itself or to the list selection model.

Syntax:	public class ListSelectionEvent extends EventObject
Package:	javax.swing.event
Class hierarchy:	Object—EventObject—ListSelectionEvent
	The ListSelectionEvent class is not part of the AWTEvent hierarchy as it is a direct subclass of EventObject. A ListSelectionEvent object has access to the methods defined in the EventObject and Object classes.
Introduced:	JDK 1.2

ListSelectionEvent Class

Constructors

```
public ListSelectionEvent(Object source, int indexStart,
int indexEnd, boolean isAdjusting)
```

The ListSelectionEvent class provides one public constructor for creating ListSelectionEvent objects. The `source` is the component that generated the event. The `indexStart` is the lower index in the range of the elements that have had their selection status changed. The `indexEnd` is the upper index in the range of elements that have had their selection status changed. If `isAdjusting` is true, the ListSelectionEvent represents one of a series of events, such as when a user drags the mouse down a list of elements. These events are often ignored because they indicate that the user hasn't finished making the selection.

Constants

The ListSelectionEvent class defines no constants.

Fields

The ListSelectionEvent class defines no additional fields. A ListSelectionEvent object has access to the `source` field defined in the EventObject class.

ListSelectionEvent Class Methods

```
public int getFirstIndex()
```
```
public int getLastIndex()
```
```
public boolean getValueIsAdjusting()
```
```
public String toString()
```

`getFirstIndex()` returns the lower index of the range of elements whose selection state changed.

`getLastIndex()` returns the upper index of the range of elements whose selection state changed.

`getValueIsAdjusting()` returns true if the invoking ListSelectionEvent represents one of a rapid series of associated events. This might occur, for instance, if the user was dragging the mouse down a list or table.

toString() provides a String containing the index and valueIsAdjusting properties of the ListSelectionEvent.

Methods Inherited from the java.util.EventObject Class

> public Object getSource()

getSource() returns a reference to the object that generated the ListSelectionEvent.

Methods Inherited from the java.lang.Object Class

> public final Class getClass()

getClass() returns a Class object representing the runtime class of the invoking object. In this case, it would return an object representing the javax.swing.event.ListSelectionEvent class.

The other methods inherited from the Object class, clone(), equals(), hashCode(), notify(), notifyAll(), and wait(), are generally not used in conjunction with ListSelectionEvent objects.

EXAMPLE

In this Example 6.24, ListSelectionEvents are used to monitor the changes in the selected item of a JList. A JList is created and placed on a JFrame. The JList registers a ListSelectionListener. Whenever the selected item of the JList changes, a ListSelectionEvent is generated and sent to the valueChanged() method. This method updates a JTextField at the bottom of the frame with the currently selected item.

EXAMPLE 6.24 LISTSELECTIONEVENT CLASS

```
import javax.swing.*;
import javax.swing.event.*;
import java.awt.*;
import java.awt.event.*;

public class ListSelectionDemo extends JFrame
                    implements ListSelectionListener
```

```
{
   private JTextField jtf;
   private JList list;
   private DefaultListModel model;

   public ListSelectionDemo()
   {
/*  A JList object is created by first initializing a
DefaultListModel   */
/*  with a list of names.  The JList object registers a         */
/*  ListDataListener.  The ListSelectionDemo class serves as the */
/*  ListDataListener, so the addListSelectionListener() method is */
/*  passed the "this" reference as an argument.                   */

      model = new DefaultListModel();
      model.addElement("Lisa");
      model.addElement("Angela");
      model.addElement("Diana");

      list = new JList(model);
      list.setVisibleRowCount(5);
      list.setSelectionMode(ListSelectionModel.SINGLE_SELECTION);
      list.addListSelectionListener(this);

      jtf = new JTextField(15);
      jtf.setEditable(false);

      JPanel centerPanel = new JPanel();
      centerPanel.add(new JScrollPane(list));

      JPanel southPanel = new JPanel();
      southPanel.add(jtf);

      getContentPane().add(centerPanel, BorderLayout.CENTER);
      getContentPane().add(southPanel, BorderLayout.SOUTH);

      setDefaultCloseOperation(JFrame.EXIT_ON_CLOSE);
      setBounds(100, 100, 300, 250);
      setVisible(true);
   }

/*  The ListSelectionDemo class serves as the ListSelectionListener */
/*  so it implements the valueChanged() method.  When the user      */
/*  changes the list selection, a ListSelectionEvent is generated   */
/*  and sent to this method.  The method displays the currently     */
/*  selected item in a textfield at the bottom of the frame.        */

   public void valueChanged(ListSelectionEvent event)
   {
      jtf.setText("Selection is "+
```

```
                (String)model.elementAt(list.getSelectedIndex()));
    }
    public static void main(String args[])
    {
        ListSelectionDemo demo = new ListSelectionDemo();
    }
}
```

When you run this program, a list of items appears on the screen. Make a selection. Change your selection. The textfield indicates what the currently selected item is.

MenuDragMouseEvent Class

Swing menu items generate a MenuDragMouseEvent when the mouse is dragged into, out of, or within a menu component's display area. It is also generated if the mouse is dragged into a menu component's display area and then released.

A MenuDragMouseEvent contains information about the event source, the type of MenuDragMouseEvent, any modifier keys that were held down at the time of the event, the x- and y-location of the event origin, and whether the event is the trigger for a popup menu.

When a MenuDragMouseEvent is generated, it is sent to any registered MenuDragMouseListener objects. The MenuDragMouseListener provides four methods, one of which is called to process the MenuDragMouseEvent.

Syntax:	public class MenuDragMouseEvent extends MouseEvent
Package:	javax.swing.event
Class hierarchy:	Object—EventObject—AWTEvent—ComponentEvent—InputEvent—MouseEvent—MenuDragMouseEvent
	The MenuDragMouseEvent class is part of the AWTEvent family and has quite an involved hierarchy. A MenuDragMouseEvent object has access to the methods defined in the MouseEvent, InputEvent, ComponentEvent, AWTEvent, EventObject, and Object classes.
Introduced:	JDK 1.2

Constructors

```
public MenuDragMouseEvent(Component source, int id, long
when, int modifiers, int x, int y, int clickCount,
boolean popupTrigger, MenuElement[] path,
MenuSelectionManager manager)
```

The MenuDragMouseEvent class provides one public constructor for creating MenuDragMouseEvent objects. It requires a whole slew of parameters. The `source` is the component that generated the event. The `id` identifies the type of MenuDragMouseEvent. For system-generated MenuDragMouseEvents, it will be one of the MouseEvent class ID constants described in the MouseEvent class section. The `when` parameter is the time in milliseconds from January 1, 1970 that the event occurred. The `modifiers` constant provides a bit mask of the modifier keys pressed when the event was generated. The `x` and `y` parameters are the x- and y-location of the mouse when the event occurred. The `clickCount` parameter contains the number of clicks associated with the MouseEvent. The `popupTrigger` parameter is true if the event is a trigger for a popup menu. The `path` is an array of MenuElements representing the path to the menu item that generated the event. The MenuSelectionManager is provided as a means to handle selections.

Constants

The MenuDragMouseEvent class does not define any new identification constants. A MenuDragMouseEvent object uses those constants defined in the MouseEvent class for identification purposes.

Fields

The MenuDragMouseEvent class does not define any new fields. A MenuDragMouseEvent object has access to the fields defined in the MouseEvent, InputEvent, ComponentEvent, AWTEvent, and EventObject classes.

MenuDragMouseEvent Class Methods

```
public MenuElement[] getPath()
```
```
public MenuSelectionManager getMenuSelectionManager()
```

These methods are used to retrieve information about or properties of a MenuDragMouseEvent.

`getPath()` provides an array of MenuElements representing the path to the menu item that generated the event.

`getMenuSelectionManager()` returns the current menu selection manager.

Methods Inherited from the java.awt.event.MouseEvent Class

public int `getClickCount()`
public Point `getPoint()`
public int `getX()`
public int `getY()`
public boolean `isPopupTrigger()`
public String `paramString()`
public void `translatePoint(int x, int y)`

A MenuDragMouseEvent object has access to the methods defined in the MouseEvent class. For a description of these methods, see the section "MouseEvent Class" in this chapter.

Methods Inherited from the java.awt.event.InputEvent Class

public void `consume()`
public int `getModifiers()`
public long `getWhen()`
public boolean `isAltDown()`
public boolean `isAltGraphDown()`
public boolean `isConsumed()`
public boolean `isControlDown()`
public boolean `isMetaDown()`
public boolean `isShiftDown()`

A MenuDragMouseEvent object has access to the events defined in the InputEvent class. For a description of these methods, see the section "InputEvent Class" in this chapter.

Methods Inherited from the java.awt.event.ComponentEvent Class

public Component getComponent()

getComponent() returns a reference to the component that generated the MenuDragMouseEvent.

Methods Inherited from the java.awt.AWTEvent Class

protected void finalize() throws Throwable
public int getID()
public String toString()

A MenuDragMouseEvent object has access to the methods defined in the AWTEvent class. For a description of these methods, see the section "AWTEvent Class" in this chapter.

Methods Inherited from the java.util.EventObject Class

public Object getSource()

getSource() returns a reference to the object that generated the MenuDragMouseEvent. A MenuDragMouseEvent object could also use the getComponent() method for this purpose.

Methods Inherited from the java.lang.Object Class

public final Class getClass()

getClass() returns a Class object representing the runtime class of the invoking object. In this case, it would return an object representing the javax.swing.event.MenuDragMouseEvent class.

The other methods inherited from the Object class, clone(), equals(), hashCode(), notify(), notifyAll(), and wait(), are generally not used in conjunction with MenuDragMouseEvent objects.

EXAMPLE

In Example 6.25, MenuDragMouseEvent objects are used to dynamically update the font size of a JLabel that is placed on a JFrame. A Font Size menu is created with three JMenuItems corresponding to different font sizes. The menu items register a MenuDragMouseListener.

When the user drags the mouse through the Font Size menu, MenuDragMouseEvents are generated and sent to the `menuDragMouseDragged()` method. This method sets the font of the label to be the size corresponding to the menu item that generated the event.

EXAMPLE 6.25 MENUDRAGMOUSEEVENT CLASS

```
import javax.swing.*;
import javax.swing.event.*;
import java.awt.*;
import java.awt.event.*;

public class MenuDragDemo extends JFrame
{
   private JMenuBar menuBar;
   private JMenu menu;
   private JMenuItem font10, font12, font14;
   private JLabel label;

   public MenuDragDemo()
   {
/*  A "Font Size" menu is created with three menu items.  The menu  */
/*  is intended to set the font size of a label. The three JMenuItem */
/*  objects register a MenuDragMouseListener.                        */

      font10 = new JMenuItem("10");
      font10.addMenuDragMouseListener(new MenuDragHandler());

      font12 = new JMenuItem("12");
      font12.addMenuDragMouseListener(new MenuDragHandler());

      font14 = new JMenuItem("14");
      font14.addMenuDragMouseListener(new MenuDragHandler());

      menu = new JMenu("Font Size");
      menu.add(font10);
      menu.add(font12);
      menu.add(font14);

      menuBar = new JMenuBar();
```

MenuDragMouseEvent Class

```java
        menuBar.add(menu);

        label = new JLabel("The Rain in Spain");
        label.setFont(new Font("Serif", Font.PLAIN, 12));
        label.setForeground(Color.black);
        label.setVerticalAlignment(SwingConstants.CENTER);
        label.setHorizontalAlignment(SwingConstants.CENTER);

        JPanel panel = new JPanel();
        panel.add(label);

        getContentPane().add(menuBar, BorderLayout.NORTH);
        getContentPane().add(panel, BorderLayout.CENTER);

        setDefaultCloseOperation(JFrame.EXIT_ON_CLOSE);
        setBounds(100, 100, 300, 200);
        setVisible(true);
    }

    /* The MenuDragMouseListener is implemented as an inner class.   */
    /* When the user drags the mouse through the items in the        */
    /* "Font Size" menu, MenuDragMouseEvents are generated and       */
    /* sent to the menuDragMouseEntered() method.  The font size     */
    /* of the label is updated to correspond with the menu item      */
    /* that generated the event.  The other three methods declared   */
    /* in the MenuDragMouseListener interface aren't used in this    */
    /* program, so they are implemented as stub methods.             */

    class MenuDragHandler implements MenuDragMouseListener
    {
        public void menuDragMouseEntered(MenuDragMouseEvent event)
        {
            JMenuItem item = (JMenuItem)event.getComponent();
            label.setFont(new Font("Serif", Font.PLAIN,
                      Integer.parseInt(item.getActionCommand())));
            invalidate();
            validate();
        }

        public void menuDragMouseDragged(MenuDragMouseEvent event) {}
        public void menuDragMouseExited(MenuDragMouseEvent event) {}
        public void menuDragMouseReleased(MenuDragMouseEvent event) {}
    }

    public static void main(String args[])
    {
        MenuDragDemo demo = new MenuDragDemo();
    }
}
```

When you run the code, you will notice the initial font size of the label. Now, drag the mouse through the Font Size menu. Note how the font size of the label changes. If you release the mouse, the font size will remain whatever the last selected value was.

MenuEvent Class

A MenuEvent is a semantic (high-level) event generated when a JMenu object is been selected, deselected, or removed from the screen. This is a very simple event type. The MenuEvent class defines no identification constants or methods. A MenuEvent only contains information about the event source.

When a MenuEvent is generated it is sent to any registered MenuListener. The MenuListener provides an implementation of three methods, one of which is called to process the MenuEvent

Syntax: public class MenuEvent extends EventObject

Package: javax.swing.event

Class hierarchy: Object—EventObject—MenuEvent

The MenuEvent class is not part of the AWTEvent hierarchy as it is a direct subclass of EventObject. A MenuEvent object has access to the methods defined in the EventObject and Object classes.

Introduced: JDK 1.2

Constructors

```
public MenuEvent(Object source)
```

The MenuEvent class provides one public constructor for creating MenuEvent objects. The `source` is the component that generated the event.

Constants

The MenuEvent class defines no constants.

Fields

The MenuEvent class defines no fields. A MenuEvent object has access to the `source` field defined in the EventObject class.

MenuEvent Class Methods

The MenuEvent class defines no methods.

Methods Inherited from the java.util.EventObject Class

public Object `getSource()`
public String `toString()`

`getSource()` returns a reference to the object that generated the MenuEvent.

`toString()` provides a String representation of the MenuEvent object.

Methods Inherited from the java.lang.Object Class

public final Class `getClass()`

`getClass()` returns a Class object representing the runtime class of the invoking object. In this case, it would return an object representing the javax.swing.event. MenuEvent class.

The other methods inherited from the Object class, `clone()`, `equals()`, `hashCode()`, `notify()`, `notifyAll()`, and `wait()`, are generally not used in conjunction with MenuEvent objects.

EXAMPLE

In Example 6.26, MenuEvent objects are used to keep track of the selected state of two JMenu objects. The JMenus are placed on a JMenuBar that is placed on a JFrame. The JMenus register a MenuEventListener. Whenever a menu is selected or deselected, a MenuEvent is generated and sent to either the `menuSelected()` or `menuDeselected()` methods. These methods determine the event source and print a message concerning the nature of the event in a JTextField at the bottom of the frame.

EXAMPLE 6.26 MENUEVENT CLASS

```
import javax.swing.*;
import javax.swing.event.*;
import java.awt.*;
```

```java
import java.awt.event.*;

public class MenuEventDemo extends JFrame
{
   private JMenuBar menuBar;
   private JMenu fontMenu, fileMenu;
   private JTextField jtf;

   public MenuEventDemo()
   {
/*  Two JMenu objects are created and placed on a Frame. The menus  */
/*  register a MenuEventListener.                                   */

      fileMenu = new JMenu("File");
      fileMenu.setFont(new Font("Serif", Font.BOLD, 12));
      fileMenu.add(new JMenuItem("Open"));
      fileMenu.add(new JMenuItem("Quit"));
      fileMenu.addMenuListener(new MenuHandler());

      fontMenu = new JMenu("Font Size");
      fontMenu.setFont(new Font("Serif", Font.BOLD, 12));
      fontMenu.add(new JMenuItem("10"));
      fontMenu.add(new JMenuItem("12"));
      fontMenu.add(new JMenuItem("14"));
      fontMenu.addMenuListener(new MenuHandler());

      menuBar = new JMenuBar();
      menuBar.add(fileMenu);
      menuBar.add(fontMenu);

      jtf = new JTextField(15);
      jtf.setEditable(false);

      getContentPane().add(menuBar, BorderLayout.NORTH);
      getContentPane().add(jtf, BorderLayout.SOUTH);

      setDefaultCloseOperation(JFrame.EXIT_ON_CLOSE);
      setBounds(100, 100, 300, 200);
      setVisible(true);
   }

/*  The MenuListener is implemented as an inner class.  If one of   */
/*  the menus is selected or deselected, a MenuEvent is generated   */
/*  and sent to either the menuDeselected() or menuSelected()       */
/*  methods.  These methods determine the event source and print    */
/*  a message about the nature of the event in a JTextField.        */
/*  The menuCanceled() method is not used in this example, so it    */
/*  is implemented as a stub method.                                */

   class MenuHandler implements MenuListener
   {
```

```
            public void menuDeselected(MenuEvent event)
            {
               JMenu menu = (JMenu)event.getSource();
               jtf.setText(menu.getActionCommand()+" menu deselected");
            }

            public void menuSelected(MenuEvent event)
            {
               JMenu menu = (JMenu)event.getSource();
               jtf.setText(menu.getActionCommand()+" menu selected");
            }

            public void menuCanceled(MenuEvent event) {}
      }

      public static void main(String args[])
      {
         MenuEventDemo demo = new MenuEventDemo();
      }
}
```

When you run this program, two menus appear at the top of the frame. Try selecting and deselecting the menus. MenuEvents are used to keep track of which menu has been selected or deselected.

MenuKeyEvent Class

A MenuKeyEvent is a semantic (high-level) event generated whenever a Swing menu item receives a KeyEvent. This occurs if a keystroke is pressed when the menu popup display is made visible on the screen.

A MenuKeyEvent object contains information about the event source, the type of MenuKeyEvent, which keys were pressed when the event was generated, and any modifier keys that were pressed when the event was generated. MenuKeyEvents can be used to provide a wide range of keystroke-induced functionality to menu items.

MenuKeyEvents are sent to any registered MenuKeyListener objects when they are generated. The MenuKeyListener will provide an implementation of three methods to process the different types of MenuKeyEvents.

Syntax: public class MenuKeyEvent extends KeyEvent
Package: javax.swing.event

Class hierarchy: Object—EventObject—AWTEvent—ComponentEvent—InputEvent—KeyEvent—MenuKeyEvent

The MenuKeyEvent class is part of the AWT event family and, like the MenuDragMouseEvent class, has quite an extensive hierarchy. A MenuKeyEvent object has access to the methods defined in the KeyEvent, InputEvent, ComponentEvent, AWTEvent, EventObject, and Object classes.

Introduced: JDK 1.2

Constructors

```
public MenuKeyEvent(Component source, int id, long when,
int modifiers, int virtualKeyCode, char keyChar,
MenuElement[] path, MenuSelectionManager manager)
```

The MenuKeyEvent class provides two public constructors for creating MenuKeyEvent objects. The `source` is the component that generated the event. The `id` identifies the type of MenuKeyEvent. For system-generated MenuKeyEvents, it will be one of the KeyEvent ID constants described in the "KeyEvent Class" section. The `when` parameter is the time in milliseconds from January 1, 1970 that the event occurred. The `modifiers` constant provides a bit mask of the modifier keys pressed when the event was generated. The mask constants are described in the "InputEvent Class" section. The `virtualKeyCode` parameter is the virtual key code corresponding to the keystroke that caused the event. The `keyChar` parameter is the Unicode character generated by the keystroke. The `path` is an array of MenuElements representing the path to the menu item that generated the event. The MenuSelectionManager is provided as a means to handle selections.

Constants

The MenuKeyEvent class defines no new identification constants. A MenuKeyEvent object uses the ID constants defined in the KeyEvent class.

Fields

The MenuKeyEvent class defines no new fields. A MenuKeyEvent object has access to the wide range of fields defined in the KeyEvent, InputEvent, ComponentEvent, AWTEvent, and EventObject classes.

MenuKeyEvent Class Methods

public MenuElement[] getPath()
public MenuSelectionManager getMenuSelectionManager()

These methods are used to retrieve information about or properties of a MenuKeyEvent.

getPath() provides an array of MenuElements representing the path to the menu item that generated the event.

getMenuSelectionManager() returns the current menu selection manager.

Methods Inherited from the java.awt.event.KeyEvent Class

public char getKeyChar()
public int getKeyCode()
public static String getKeyModifiersText(int modifiers)
public static String getKeyText(int virtualKeyCode)
public boolean isActionKey()
public String paramString()
public void setKeyChar(char keyChar)
public void setKeyCode(int virtualKeyCode)
public void setModifiers(int modifiers)
public void setSource(Object newSource)

A MenuKeyEvent object has access to the methods defined in the KeyEvent class. For a description of these methods, see the section "KeyEvent Class" in this chapter.

Methods Inherited from the java.awt.event.InputEvent Class

public void consume()
public int getModifiers()
public long getWhen()
public boolean isAltDown()

public boolean `isAltGraphDown()`
public boolean `isConsumed()`
public boolean `isControlDown()`
public boolean `isMetaDown()`
public boolean `isShiftDown()`

A MenuKeyEvent object has access to the events defined in the InputEvent class. For a description of these methods, see the section "InputEvent Class" in this chapter.

Methods Inherited from the java.awt.event.ComponentEvent Class

public Component `getComponent()`

`getComponent()` returns a reference to the component that generated the MenuKeyEvent.

Methods Inherited from the java.awt.AWTEvent Class

protected void `finalize()` throws Throwable
public int `getID()`
public String `toString()`

A MenuKeyEvent object has access to the methods defined in the AWTEvent class. For a description of these methods, see the section "AWTEvent Class" in this chapter.

Methods Inherited from the java.util.EventObject Class

public Object `getSource()`

`getSource()` returns a reference to the object that generated the MenuKeyEvent. A MenuKeyEvent object could also use the `getComponent()` method for this purpose.

Methods Inherited from the java.lang.Object Class

> **public final Class** `getClass()`

`getClass()` returns a Class object representing the runtime class of the invoking object. In this case, it would return an object representing the javax.swing.event.MenuKeyEvent class.

The other methods inherited from the Object class, `clone()`, `equals()`, `hashCode()`, `notify()`, `notifyAll()`, and `wait()`, are generally not used in conjunction with MenuKeyEvent objects.

EXAMPLE

In Example 6.27, a MenuKeyEvent is used to set the style of a label font. Three JMenuItem objects are placed inside a JMenu. The JMenuItems are used to set the size of the font used to display a JLabel. The JMenu object registers a MenuKeyListener.

When the JMenu is selected and a keystroke is pressed, a MenuKeyListener object is generated and sent to the `menuKeyPressed()` method. If the keystroke was *b*, the font style is set to `Font.BOLD`. If the keystroke was *p*, the font style is set to `Font.PLAIN`.

EXAMPLE 6.27 MENUKEYEVENT CLASS

```
import javax.swing.*;
import javax.swing.event.*;
import java.awt.*;
import java.awt.event.*;

public class MenuKeyEventDemo extends JFrame implements
ActionListener
{
   private JMenuBar menuBar;
   private JMenu menu;
   private JMenuItem font10, font12, font14;
   private JLabel label;
   private int fontStyle, fontSize;

   public MenuKeyEventDemo()
   {
      fontStyle = Font.PLAIN;
```

```
        fontSize = 12;

/* A "Font Size" menu is created with three menu items.  The menu  */
/* is intended to set the font size of a label. The three JMenuItem */
/* objects register an ActionListener.                              */

        font10 = new JMenuItem("10");
        font10.addActionListener(this);

        font12 = new JMenuItem("12");
        font12.addActionListener(this);

        font14 = new JMenuItem("14");
        font14.addActionListener(this);

/* The three JMenuItem objects are placed inside a JMenu.  The JMenu */
/* registers a MenuKeyListener.                                      */

        menu = new JMenu("Font Size");
        menu.add(font10);
        menu.add(font12);
        menu.add(font14);
        menu.addMenuKeyListener(new MenuKeyHandler());

        menuBar = new JMenuBar();
        menuBar.add(menu);

        label = new JLabel("Java, Java, Java");
        label.setFont(new Font("Serif", fontStyle, fontSize));
        label.setForeground(Color.black);

        JPanel panel = new JPanel();
        panel.add(label);

        getContentPane().add(menuBar, BorderLayout.NORTH);
        getContentPane().add(panel, BorderLayout.CENTER);

        setDefaultCloseOperation(JFrame.EXIT_ON_CLOSE);
        setBounds(100, 100, 300, 200);
        setVisible(true);
    }

/* The MenuKeyListener is implemented as an inner class. Whenever   */
/* the menu display is visible and the user presses a key, the      */
/* JMenu will generate a MenuKeyEvent and send it to the            */
/* menuKeyPressed() method.  If the keystroke was 'b', the font     */
/* type is set to Font.BOLD.  If the keystroke was 'p', the font    */
/* type is set to Font.PLAIN.  The menuKeyReleased() and            */
/* menuKeyTyped() methods are not used in this example, so they     */
/* implemented as stub methods.                                     */
```

```java
class MenuKeyHandler implements MenuKeyListener
{
   public void menuKeyPressed(MenuKeyEvent event)
   {
      if ( event.getKeyCode() == KeyEvent.VK_B )
      {
         fontStyle = Font.BOLD;
      }
      if ( event.getKeyCode() == KeyEvent.VK_P )
      {
         fontStyle = Font.PLAIN;
      }
   }

   public void menuKeyReleased(MenuKeyEvent event) {}
   public void menuKeyTyped(MenuKeyEvent event) {}
}

/* When a menu item is selected, it generates an ActionEvent that is */
/* sent to the actionPerformed() method.  This method re-sets the   */
/* font size of the label.                                          */

public void actionPerformed(ActionEvent event)
{
   fontSize = Integer.parseInt(event.getActionCommand());
   label.setFont(new Font("Serif", fontStyle, fontSize));
   invalidate();
   validate();
}

public static void main(String args[])
{
   MenuKeyEventDemo demo = new MenuKeyEventDemo();
}
}
```

When you run this program, the font style for the label "Java, Java, Java" that appears on the screen is plain font. Select the Font Size menu and choose another font size. The font size of the label changes. Now select the Font Size menu and press the *b* key. When you release the mouse, the font style of the label will have changed to bold.

MouseEvent Class

A MouseEvent is a low-level event generated by a component when the mouse performs an action over the components' bounding area. There are two general types of MouseEvents. The first type is a non-motion-oriented MouseEvent and occurs when the mouse is pressed, released, clicked (pressed and released), or enters or exits the bounding area of a component. The second type, referred to as a mouse motion event, occurs when the mouse is moved or dragged through the bounding area of a component.

A MouseEvent has information about the source that generated the event, the type of MouseEvent, the x- and y-location relative to the source component where the event occurred, the number of mouse clicks associated with the event, and whether the event was the trigger for a popup menu to appear. MouseEvents are very versatile events that can be used to implement a wide range of functionality into a program.

Non-motion-oriented MouseEvents are sent to any registered MouseListener objects when they are generated. Motion-oriented MouseEvents are sent to any registered MouseMotionListener objects. The javax.swing.event package also defines a MouseInputListener that provides a one-stop listener for all types of MouseEvents.

Syntax: public class MouseEvent extends InputEvent

Package: java.awt.event

Class hierarchy: Object—EventObject—AWTEvent—ComponentEvent—InputEvent—MouseEvent

The MouseEvent class is part of the AWTEvent family. A MouseEvent object has access to the methods defined in the InputEvent, ComponentEvent, AWTEvent, EventObject, and Object classes.

Introduced: JDK 1.1

Constructors

```
public MouseEvent(Component source, int id, long when,
int modifiers, int x, int y, int clickCount, boolean
popupTrigger)
```

The MouseEvent class provides one public constructor for creating MouseEvent objects. The `source` is the component that generated the event. The `id` identifies the type of MouseEvent. For system-generated MouseEvents, it will be one of the ID constants described next. The `when` parameter is the time in milliseconds from January 1, 1970 that the event occurred. The `modifiers` constant provides a bit mask of the modifier keys pressed when the event was generated. The `x` and `y` parameters are the x- and y-location of the mouse when the event occurred. The `clickCount` parameter contains the number of clicks associated with the MouseEvent. This parameter is only relevant for the `MOUSE_CLICKED`, `MOUSE_PRESSED`, and `MOUSE_RELEASED` types of MouseEvents. The `popupTrigger` parameter is true if the event is a trigger for a popup menu.

Constants

public static final int MOUSE_CLICKED
public static final int MOUSE_DRAGGED
public static final int MOUSE_EXITED
public static final int MOUSE_MOVED
public static final int MOUSE_PRESSED
public static final int MOUSE_RELEASED
public static final int MOUSE_FIRST
public static final int MOUSE_LAST

The first six constants are used to identify a MouseEvent. The names are pretty much self-explanatory. The numerical values for these constants range from 500 for `MOUSE_CLICKED` to 506 for `MOUSE_DRAGGED`.

The `MOUSE_FIRST` and `MOUSE_LAST` constants represent the range of system-provided IDs for MouseEvent objects. They have numerical values of 500 and 506 respectively.

Fields

Beyond the constants defined previously, the MouseEvent class defines no additional fields. A MouseEvent object has access to the fields defined in the InputEvent, ComponentEvent, AWTEvent, and EventObject classes. The fields include the modifier and mouse button masks, the `source` field, and the `id` field.

MouseEvent Class Methods

public int `getClickCount()`
public Point `getPoint()`
public int `getX()`
public int `getY()`
public boolean `isPopupTrigger()`
public String `paramString()`
public void `translatePoint(int x, int y)`

`getClickCount()` returns the number of mouse clicks associated with the invoking MouseEvent. This parameter is only relevant for the `MOUSE_CLICKED`, `MOUSE_PRESSED`, and `MOUSE_RELEASED` types of MouseEvents. Motion-oriented MouseEvents have a click count of 0.

`getPoint()` returns a Point object containing the x- and y-location of the mouse relative to the source component when the event was generated.

`getX()` returns the x-location of the mouse relative to the source component when the event was generated.

`getY()` returns the y-location of the mouse relative to the source component when the event was generated.

`isPopupTrigger()` returns true if this MouseEvent serves as a trigger for a popup-menu.

`paramString()` returns a parameter String that identifies the MouseEvent. This is generally used for event-logging and debugging purposes. When a MouseEvent object calls the `toString()` method, the return value of the `paramString()` method is incorporated in the return value of the `toString()` method.

`translatePoint()` modifies the x- and y-coordinates of the invoking event by the specified x- and y-offsets.

Methods Inherited from the java.awt.event.InputEvent Class

public void `consume()`
public int `getModifiers()`
public long `getWhen()`

```
public boolean isAltDown()
public boolean isAltGraphDown()
public boolean isConsumed()
public boolean isControlDown()
public boolean isMetaDown()
public boolean isShiftDown()
```

A MouseEvent object has access to the events defined in the InputEvent class. For a description of these methods, see the section "InputEvent Class" in this chapter.

Methods Inherited from the java.awt.event.ComponentEvent Class

```
public Component getComponent()
```

`getComponent()` returns a reference to the component that generated the MouseEvent.

Methods Inherited from the java.awt.AWTEvent Class

```
protected void finalize() throws Throwable
public int getID()
public String toString()
```

A MouseEvent object has access to the methods defined in the AWTEvent class. For a description of these methods, see the section "AWTEvent Class" in this chapter.

Methods Inherited from the java.util.EventObject Class

```
public Object getSource()
```

`getSource()` returns a reference to the object that generated the MouseEvent. A MouseEvent object could also use the `getComponent()` method for this purpose.

Methods Inherited from the java.lang.Object Class

public final Class `getClass()`

`getClass()` returns a Class object representing the runtime class of the invoking object. In this case, it would return an object representing the java.awt.event.MouseEvent class.

The other methods inherited from the Object class, `clone()`, `equals()`, `hashCode()`, `notify()`, `notifyAll()`, and `wait()`, are generally not used in conjunction with MouseEvent objects.

EXAMPLE

In Example 6.28, MouseEvents are used to implement a doodle pad. A Canvas object is placed on a Frame. When the mouse is dragged inside the frame, a line is drawn along the course the mouse takes. The canvas registers both a MouseListener and a MouseMotionListener. When the mouse is pressed, a MouseEvent is generated and sent to the `mousePressed()` method. The event is used to obtain the current position of the mouse. This position is used as the starting position of the line.

When the mouse is then dragged inside the frame, MouseEvents are generated and sent to the `mouseDragged()` method. These events are used to draw a continuous line that tracks the trajectory of the mouse. If the mouse is released, the line drawing stops.

EXAMPLE 6.28 MOUSEEVENT CLASS

```
import java.awt.*;
import java.awt.event.*;

public class MouseEventDemo extends Frame
{
   private Canvas canvas;
   private int startX, startY, endX, endY;

   public MouseEventDemo()
   {
/*   A Canvas object is placed on a Frame and registers a    */
/*   MouseListener and a MouseMotionListener.                */

      canvas = new Canvas();
```

```
      canvas.addMouseListener(new MouseHandler());
      canvas.addMouseMotionListener(new MouseMotionHandler());

      add(canvas);

      addWindowListener(new WinAdapter());
      setBounds(100, 100, 300, 200);
      setVisible(true);
   }

/* Both the MouseListener and the MouseMotionListener are written   */
/* as extensions of the corresponding adapter class.  The purpose of */
/* the listeners is to draw a line on the Canvas when the mouse is   */
/* dragged.  When the mouse is pressed, this indicates the starting  */
/* point of the line.  A MouseEvent is generated and sent to the     */
/* mousePressed() method.  The event is used to get the current      */
/* position of the mouse and set the starting point of the line.     */

   class MouseHandler extends MouseAdapter
   {
      public void mousePressed(MouseEvent event)
      {
         startX = event.getX();
         startY = event.getY();
         endX = startX;
         endY = startY;
      }
   }

/* When the mouse is dragged across the Canvas, MouseEvents are      */
/* generated and set to the mouseDragged() method.  A line is drawn  */
/* on the Canvas that tracks the motion of the mouse.                */

   class MouseMotionHandler extends MouseMotionAdapter
   {
      public void mouseDragged(MouseEvent event)
      {
         startX = endX;
         startY = endY;
         endX = event.getX();
         endY = event.getY();
         canvas.getGraphics().drawLine(startX, startY, endX, endY);
      }
   }

   public static void main(String args[])
   {
      MouseEventDemo demo = new MouseEventDemo();
   }
```

```
}

/* This makes sure the application terminates if the window is
closed   */

class WinAdapter extends WindowAdapter
{
   public void windowClosing(WindowEvent event)
   {
      System.exit(0);
   }
}
```

Initially, the canvas is blank. Try drawing a line by pressing and dragging the mouse around the frame. If the mouse is released, the line stops. If the mouse is moved to a new position and then pressed and dragged, a new line begins. Have a little fun with this one. Write your name. Have your 5-year-old draw a picture.

PaintEvent Class

A PaintEvent is a special type of event that does not use the normal event listener model. It is used to ensure the serialization of paint/update method calls with other events delivered from the event queue. The user will probably never have to access or manipulate PaintEvents.

Syntax:	public class PaintEvent extends ComponentEvent
Package:	java.awt.event
Class hierarchy:	Object—EventObject—AWTEvent—ComponentEvent—PaintEvent
	The PaintEvent class is part of the AWTEvent family. A PaintEvent object has access to the methods defined in the InputEvent, ComponentEvent, AWTEvent, EventObject, and Object classes.
Introduced:	JDK 1.1

PopupMenuEvent Class

A PopupMenuEvent is a semantic (high-level) event generated by a JPopupMenu object before the popup menu becomes visible, before it becomes invisible, or when it is canceled. This is a very simple event type. The PopupMenuEvent class defines no identification constants or methods. A PopupMenuEvent object contains information only about the event source.

When a PopupMenuEvent is generated, it is sent to any registered PopupMenuListener. The PopupMenuListener provides an implementation of three methods, one of which is called to process the PopupMenuEvent.

Syntax: public class PopupMenuEvent extends EventObject

Package: javax.swing.event

Class hierarchy: Object—EventObject—PopupMenuEvent

The PopupMenuEvent class is not part of the AWTEvent hierarchy as it is a direct subclass of EventObject. A PopupMenuEvent object has access to the methods defined in the EventObject and Object classes.

Introduced: JDK 1.2

Constructors

```
public PopupMenuEvent(Object source)
```

The PopupMenuEvent class provides one public constructor for creating PopupMenuEvent objects. The `source` is the component that generated the event.

Constants

The PopupMenuEvent class defines no constants.

Fields

The PopupMenuEvent class defines no fields. A PopupMenu object has access to the `source` field defined in the EventObject class.

PopupMenuEvent Class Methods

The PopupMenuEvent class defines no methods.

Methods Inherited from the java.util.EventObject Class

> public Object `getSource()`
>
> public String `toString()`

`getSource()` returns a reference to the object that generated the PopupMenuEvent.

`toString()` provides a String representation of the PopupMenuEvent object.

Methods Inherited from the java.lang.Object Class

> public final Class `getClass()`

`getClass()` returns a Class object representing the runtime class of the invoking object. In this case, it would return an object representing the javax.swing.event.PopupMenuEvent class.

The other methods inherited from the Object class, `clone()`, `equals()`, `hashCode()`, `notify()`, `notifyAll()`, and `wait()`, are generally not used in conjunction with PopupMenuEvent objects.

EXAMPLE

In Example 6.29, a JPopupMenu is associated with a JLabel. The JPopupMenu has a registered PopupMenuListener. When a PopupMenuEvent is generated by the menu, the event is sent to one of the three PopupMenuListener methods. A JTextField at the bottom of the frame is updated with the type of PopupMenuEvent.

EXAMPLE 6.29 POPUPMENUEVENT CLASS

```
import javax.swing.*;
import javax.swing.event.*;
import java.awt.*;
import java.awt.event.*;

public class PopupMenuDemo extends JFrame
{
   private JLabel label;
   private JPopupMenu menu;
   private JTextField jtf;
```

```java
      public PopupMenuDemo()
      {
/* A JPopupMenu is created with two menu items.  The JPopupMenu   */
/* registers a PopupMenuListener.                                 */

         menu = new JPopupMenu("menu");
         menu.add(new JMenuItem("open"));
         menu.add(new JMenuItem("quit"));
         menu.addPopupMenuListener(new PopupMenuHandler());

         label = new JLabel("Menu");
         label.setFont(new Font("Serif", Font.BOLD, 12));
         label.setForeground(Color.black);
         label.setBorder(BorderFactory.createEmptyBorder(20,20,20,20));
         label.addMouseListener(new MouseHandler());

         jtf = new JTextField(15);
         jtf.setEditable(true);

         JPanel centerPanel = new JPanel();
         centerPanel.add(label);

         getContentPane().add(centerPanel, BorderLayout.CENTER);
         getContentPane().add(jtf, BorderLayout.SOUTH);

         setDefaultCloseOperation(JFrame.EXIT_ON_CLOSE);
         setBounds(100, 100, 300, 200);
         setVisible(true);
      }

/* The PopupMenuListener is implemented as an inner class.     */
/* When a PopupMenuEvent is generated, it is sent to one       */
/* of the three listener methods.  The type of event is        */
/* printed inside a textfield at the bottom of the frame.      */

      class PopupMenuHandler implements PopupMenuListener
      {
         public void popupMenuCanceled(PopupMenuEvent event)
         {
            jtf.setText("menu canceled");
         }

         public void popupMenuWillBecomeInvisible(PopupMenuEvent event)
         {
            jtf.setText("menu becoming invisible");
         }

         public void popupMenuWillBecomeVisible(PopupMenuEvent event)
         {
            jtf.setText("menu becoming visible");
         }
      }
```

```
/*  The MouseListener is used to detect the popup menu trigger  */
/*  When that happens, the popup menu is made visible.  All     */
/*  three types of non-motion oriented MouseEvents are tested   */
/*  because the popup menu trigger may be platform dependent.   */

   class MouseHandler extends MouseAdapter
   {
      public void mousePressed(MouseEvent event)
      {
         testEvent(event);
      }

      public void mouseReleased(MouseEvent event)
      {
         testEvent(event);
      }

      public void mouseClicked(MouseEvent event)
      {
         testEvent(event);
      }

      private void testEvent(MouseEvent event)
      {
         if ( event.isPopupTrigger() )
         {
            menu.show(label, event.getX(), event.getY());
         }
      }
   }

   public static void main(String args[])
   {
      PopupMenuDemo demo = new PopupMenuDemo();
   }
}
```

When you run this example, you will initially see the label *Menu* on the screen. This label has a popup menu associated with it. Place the mouse over the label and press the mouse buttons until you activate the popup trigger (the trigger is system-dependent). Before the menu becomes visible, a PopupMenuEvent is generated and sent to the `popupMenuWillBecomeVisible()` method. The textfield will indicate that the menu is becoming visible. When you leave the popup menu, the textfield will indicate that the menu is becoming invisible.

PropertyChangeEvent Class

A PropertyChangeEvent object is a powerful event type that indicates a change to a component property. Initially, PropertyChangeEvents were only used to implement the bound and constrained property functionality of a Java Bean. With more recent releases of the J2SE, a wide variety of AWT and Swing components in the Java API can also fire PropertyChangeEvents.

As a brief review, a bound property is one that is shared among multiple components. If the value of the bound property is changed, the change is implemented for all components that share the property. A constrained property is one that has limits to the changes that can occur. If a change is attempted outside of the acceptable range, the change will be vetoed.

PropertyChangeEvent objects resulting from a change to a bound property are sent to any registered PropertyChangeListener. PropertyChangeEvents resulting from a change to a constrained property are sent to any registered VetoableChangeListener. These listeners provide implementation of either the `propertyChange()` or `vetoableChange()` methods.

A PropertyChangeEvent object contains information about the object that generated the event, the name of the property that was changed, and the old and new values of the property.

Syntax:	public class PropertyChangeEvent extends EventObject
Package:	java.beans
Class hierarchy:	Object—EventObject—PropertyChangeEvent
	The PropertyChangeEvent is defined in the java.beans package and is not part of any other event hierarchy. A PropertyChangeEvent object has access to the methods defined in the EventObject and Object classes.
Introduced:	JDK 1.2

Constructors

```
public PropertyChangeEvent(Object source, String
propertyName, Object oldValue, Object newValue)
```

The PropertyChangeEvent class provides one public constructor to create PropertyChangeEvent objects. The `source` is the component that generated the event. The `propertyName` is the name of the property that is being changed. The `oldValue` and `newValue` are the old and new values of the property.

Constants

The PropertyChangeEvent class defines no identification constants.

Fields

The PropertyChangeEvent class defines no new fields but does inherit the `source` field from the EventObject class.

PropertyChangeEvent Class Methods

public Object `getNewValue()`
public Object `getOldValue()`
public Object `getPropagationId()`
public String `getPropertyName()`
public void `setPropagationId(Object idObject)`

`getNewValue()` returns the new value of the property. The return value is of type Object, which can be cast to another class type if desired.

`getOldValue` returns the previous value of the property. The return value is of type Object, which can be cast to another class type if desired.

`getPropagationId()` would return the `propagationId` field if such a thing existed. Currently, the `propagationId` field and this method are reserved for future use.

`getPropertyName()` returns the name of the property.

`setPropagationId()` is reserved for future use.

Methods Inherited from the java.util.EventObject Class

public Object `getSource()`
public String `toString()`

`getSource()` returns a reference to the object that generated the invoking event. This method can be used to determine which component generated the invoking PropertyChangeEvent object.

`toString()` returns a String representation of the PropertyChangeEvent object.

Methods Inherited from the java.lang.Object Class

> public final Class `getClass()`

`getClass()` returns a Class object representing the runtime class of the invoking object. In this case it would return an object representing the java.beans.PropertyChangeEvent class.

The other methods inherited from the Object class, `clone()`, `equals()`, `hashCode()`, `notify()`, `notifyAll()`, and `wait()`, are generally not used in conjunction with PropertyChangeEvent objects.

EXAMPLE

Example 6.30 uses PropertyChangeEvent objects to implement a font color as a bound property of a JLabel. When the color is changed, every JLabel that uses that color for its font color also changes. This example comes in three parts, so let's look at each part separately.

The first class to look at it is the FontColor class. This class is a Java Bean that contains a Color object as a data member. It also contains a PropertyChangeSupport object that is used to implement the Color as a bound property. When the value of the Color is changed, every JLabel object that uses a FontColor object to set its font color will also change. This is done by having the PropertyChangeSupport object fire a PropertyChangeEvent in the `setColor()` method of the FontColor class.

In order for instances of the FontColor class to add or remove a PropertyChangeListener from its listener list, the FontColor class must define the `addPropertyChangeListener()` and `removePropertyChange-Listener()` methods. The PropertyChangeSupport object is used to maintain the list of registered listeners.

EXAMPLE 6.30 PROPERTYCHANGEEVENT CLASS: FONTCOLOR CLASS

```
import javax.swing.*;
import java.awt.*;
```

```java
import java.beans.*;

public class FontColor
{
   private Color color;
   private PropertyChangeSupport pcs;

   public FontColor(Color c)
   {
      color = c;
      pcs = new PropertyChangeSupport(this);
   }

   public Color getColor()
   {
      return color;
   }

/* The Color object is implemented as a bound property. When the   */
/* setColor() method is called, the PropertyChangeSupport object   */
/* is used to fire a PropertyChangeEvent.                          */

   public void setColor(Color c)
   {
      Color oldColor = color;
      color = c;
      pcs.firePropertyChange("color", oldColor, color);
   }

/* For the FontColor class to be able to register and/or disconnect */
/* PropertyChangeListeners, it has to provide methods to add        */
/* and remove PropertyChangeListeners.  The PropertyChangeSupport   */
/* is used to manage the listener list.                             */

   public void addPropertyChangeListener(PropertyChangeListener listener)
   {
      pcs.addPropertyChangeListener(listener);
   }

   public void removePropertyChangeListener(PropertyChangeListener listener)
   {
      pcs.removePropertyChangeListener(listener);
   }
}
```

The second class used in this example is the NewLabel class. A NewLabel is a JLabel that also maintains an instance of the FontColor class. The FontColor object is used to set the text color of the label. The FontColor object associated with a NewLabel registers a PropertyChangeListener in the NewLabel class constructor. Whenever the color of the FontColor object is changed, the FontColor object fires a PropertyChangeEvent to this listener.

The NewLabel class also serves as a PropertyChangeListener and as such implements the `propertyChange()` method. If the incoming PropertyChangeEvent was due to a change in the `color` property of a FontColor object, the text color of the NewLabel is changed. The source code for the NewLabel class is given in Example 6.31.

EXAMPLE 6.31 PROPERTYCHANGEEVENT CLASS: NEWLABEL CLASS

```
import javax.swing.*;
import java.awt.*;
import java.beans.*;

public class NewLabel extends JLabel implements
PropertyChangeListener
{
   private FontColor fontColor;

   public NewLabel(String str, FontColor fc)
   {
      super(str);
      fontColor = fc;
      setForeground(fontColor.getColor());

/*  When a NewLabel object is created, its FontColor object    */
/*  registers a PropertyChangeListener.  When the Color object */
/*  associated with the FontColor object is changed, the       */
/*  FontColor object will fire a PropertyChangeEvent that will */
/*  be sent to this listener.                                  */

      fontColor.addPropertyChangeListener(this);
   }

   public FontColor getFontColor()
   {
      return fontColor;
   }

   public void setFontColor(FontColor fc)
   {
      fontColor = fc;
   }

/*  The NewLabel class serves as a PropertyChangeListener and thus */
/*  provides an implementation of the propertyChange() method.  If */
```

```
/* the PropertyChangeEvent was due to a change in the "color"  */
/* property, the text color of the NewLabel is changed.        */

   public void propertyChange(PropertyChangeEvent event)
   {
      if ( event.getPropertyName().equals("color") )
      {
         setForeground( (Color)event.getNewValue() );
      }
   }
}
```

The PropChangeEventDemo class is the driver class for this example. This class creates a FontColor object, which is used to initialize three NewLabel objects. The NewLabel objects are placed on a JFrame along with a JComboBox. The JComboBox is used to select a new font color and has a registered ItemListener.

When the user makes a color selection in the JComboBox, an ItemEvent is generated and sent to the `itemStateChanged()` method. In this method, the FontColor object that was used to initialize the NewLabel objects calls its `setColor()` method, passing the method the color that was selected. The `setColor()` method changes the color of the FontColor object and fires a PropertyChangeEvent.

The source code for the PropChangeEventDemo class is given in Example 6.32.

EXAMPLE 6.32 PROPERTYCHANGEEVENT CLASS: PROPCHANGEEVENTDEMO CLASS

```
import javax.swing.*;
import java.awt.*;
import java.awt.event.*;

public class PropChangeEventDemo extends JFrame implements
ItemListener
{
   NewLabel label1, label2, label3;
   FontColor fontColor;
   JComboBox jcb;

   public PropChangeEventDemo()
   {
/* A FontColor object is created. This object maintains a Color  */
/* object as a bound property.                                   */
```

```
            fontColor = new FontColor(Color.black);

   /* Three NewLabel objects are created and placed on a JFrame. The */
   /* NewLabel class is a JLabel that uses a FontColor object to set */
   /* the color of the label text.                                   */

            label1 = new NewLabel("hello", fontColor);
            label1.setFont(new Font("Serif", Font.BOLD, 14));

            label2 = new NewLabel("there", fontColor);
            label2.setFont(new Font("Serif", Font.BOLD, 14));

            label3 = new NewLabel("boys", fontColor);
            label3.setFont(new Font("Serif", Font.BOLD, 14));

   /* A JComboBox is used to change the color of the NewLabel object text */
   /* The JComboBox registers an ItemListener.                            */

            String[] colorList = {"black", "red", "blue", "green"};
            jcb = new JComboBox(colorList);
            jcb.setSelectedIndex(0);
            jcb.addItemListener(this);

            JPanel centerPanel = new JPanel();
            centerPanel.add(label1);
            centerPanel.add(label2);
            centerPanel.add(label3);

            JPanel southPanel = new JPanel();
            southPanel.add(jcb);

            getContentPane().add(centerPanel, BorderLayout.CENTER);
            getContentPane().add(southPanel, BorderLayout.WEST);

            setDefaultCloseOperation(JFrame.EXIT_ON_CLOSE);
            setBounds(100, 100, 300, 200);
            setVisible(true);
       }

   /* Since the PropChangeEventDemo class serves as the ItemListener,*/
   /* it provides an implementation of the itemStateChanged() method.*/
   /* The FontColor object calls its setColor() method passing it the */
   /* selected color.                                                 */

       public void itemStateChanged(ItemEvent event)
       {
            JComboBox comboBox = (JComboBox)event.getItemSelectable();
            String color = (String)comboBox.getSelectedItem();
            if ( color.equals("black") )
                 fontColor.setColor(Color.black);
```

```
        if ( color.equals("red") )
            fontColor.setColor(Color.red);
        if ( color.equals("blue") )
            fontColor.setColor(Color.blue);
        if ( color.equals("green") )
            fontColor.setColor(Color.green);
    }
    public static void main(String args[])
    {
       PropChangeEventDemo demo = new PropChangeEventDemo();
    }
}
```

When you run this example, a frame appears with a JComboBox and the text "Hello there boys." The text is actually comprised of three different labels. Select a different color in the JComboBox. The color of the three labels is automatically updated. This is because the three labels share a bound property.

TableColumnModelEvent Class

A TableColumnModelEvent is a semantic (high-level) event indicating that some aspect of a table column model has changed. This change might be the result of a column being added, moved, or removed.

A TableColumnModelEvent object has information about the event source and the column or columns that were moved, added, or removed.

When a TableColumnModelEvent is generated, it is sent to any registered TableColumnModelListener objects. The TableColumnModelListener provides five methods, one for each type of TableColumnModelEvent.

Syntax: public class TableColumnModelEvent extends EventObject

Package: javax.swing.event

Class hierarchy: Object—EventObject—TableColumnModelEvent

The TableColumnModelEvent class is not part of the AWTEvent family, as it is a direct subclass of the EventObject class. A TableColumnModelEvent object has access to the methods defined in the EventObject and Object classes.

Introduced: JDK 1.2

TableColumnModelEvent Class

Constructors

```
public TableColumnModelEvent(TableColumnModel source, int from, int to)
```

The TableColumnModelEvent class provides one public constructor for creating TableColumnModelEvent objects. The source is a reference to the TableColumnModel that generated the event. The from parameter is an int specifying the first row in a range of affected rows. The to parameter is an int specifying the last row in a range of affected rows.

Constants

The TableColumnModelEvent class provides no identification constants.

Fields

```
protected int fromIndex
protected int toIndex
```

fromIndex is the index of the first in the range of columns associated with the event.

toIndex is the index of the last of the range of columns associated with the event.

TableColumnModelEvent Class Methods

```
public int getFromIndex()
public int getToIndex()
```

These methods are used for TableColumnModelEvents that are generated due to a column being moved, removed, or added.

getFromIndex() returns the original index of the column. This method is valid for move or remove events.

`getToIndex()` returns the destination index of the column. This method is valid for move or add events.

Methods Inherited from the java.util.EventObject Class

public Object `getSource()`
public String `toString()`

`getSource()` returns a reference to the object that generated the TableColumnModelEvent.

`toString()` provides a String representation of the TableColumnModelEvent object.

Methods Inherited from the java.lang.Object Class

public final Class `getClass()`

`getClass()` returns a Class object representing the runtime class of the invoking object. In this case, it would return an object representing the javax.swing.event.TableColumnModelEvent class.

The other methods inherited from the Object class, `clone()`, `equals()`, `hashCode()`, `notify()`, `notifyAll()`, and `wait()`, are generally not used in conjunction with TableColumnModelEvent objects.

EXAMPLE

In Example 6.33, TableColumnModelEvent objects are used to monitor movements of the columns in a JTable. The table column model of the JTable is obtained and registers a TableColumnModelListener. Whenever the user moves a column or causes a column to be moved (by having two columns switch places, for instance), a TableColumnModelEvent is generated and sent to the `columnMoved()` method. A JTextField is updated to indicate which column was moved.

EXAMPLE 6.33 TABLECOLUMNMODELEVENT CLASS

```java
import javax.swing.*;
import javax.swing.event.*;
import java.awt.*;
import java.awt.event.*;
import javax.swing.table.*;

public class TableColumnDemo extends JFrame
{
   private JTable table;
   private DefaultTableModel model;
   private JTextField jtf;

   public TableColumnDemo()
   {
      Object[][] data = {
         {"Jackson", new Integer(12345), "555-123-4567"},
         {"Zachary", new Integer(65432), "555-567-1234"} };
      String[] headers = { "Name", "ID number", "Phone" };

/* A simple table is created and placed on a JFrame.      */
/* The TableColumnModel of the table registers a          */
/* TableColumnModelListener.                              */

      model = new DefaultTableModel(data, headers);

      table = new JTable(model);
      TableColumnModel columnModel = table.getColumnModel();
      columnModel.addColumnModelListener(new ColumnModelHandler());

      jtf = new JTextField(20);
      jtf.setEditable(false);

      JPanel centerPanel = new JPanel();
      centerPanel.add(new JScrollPane(table));

      JPanel southPanel = new JPanel();
      southPanel.add(jtf);

      getContentPane().add(centerPanel, BorderLayout.CENTER);
      getContentPane().add(southPanel, BorderLayout.SOUTH);

      setDefaultCloseOperation(JFrame.EXIT_ON_CLOSE);
      setBounds(100, 100, 600, 300);
      setVisible(true);
   }

/* The TableColumnModelListener is implemented as an inner class */
/* In this case, the listener only monitors column movements, so */
/* the other methods are implemented as stub methods. Whenever   */
/* the user moves a column or causes a column to be moved, a     */
```

```
/* TableColumnModelEvent is generated and sent to the      */
/* columnMoved() method.                                    */

   class ColumnModelHandler implements TableColumnModelListener
   {
      public void columnMoved(TableColumnModelEvent event)
      {
         jtf.setText("column "+event.getFromIndex()+" moved");
      }

      public void columnAdded(TableColumnModelEvent event) {}
      public void columnMarginChanged(ChangeEvent event) {}
      public void columnRemoved(TableColumnModelEvent event) {}
      public void columnSelectionChanged(ListSelectionEvent event) {}
   }

   public static void main(String args[])
   {
      TableColumnDemo demo = new TableColumnDemo();
   }
}
```

When you run this example, a table with two rows and three columns appears on the screen. Try moving one of the columns by dragging it to the left or right. The identity of the column that was moved appears in the textfield.

TableModelEvent Class

A TableModelEvent is a semantic (high-level) event indicating that some aspect of a table model has changed. This could happen if a row or some part of a row is changed, added, removed, moved, or reordered. The difference between TableModelEvents and TableColumnModelEvents is that TableModelEvents generally deal with changes to rows whereas TableColumnModelEvents deal with changes to columns.

A TableModelEvent object contains information about the event source, the type of TableModelEvent, and the rows and columns that were changed.

When a TableModelEvent is generated, it is sent to any registered TableModelListener objects. The TableModelListener provides an implementation of the `tableChanged()` method, which is used to process the event.

Syntax: public class TableModelEvent extends EventObject

Package: javax.swing.event

Class hierarchy: Object—EventObject—TableModelEvent

The TableModelEvent class is not part of the AWTEvent family as it is a direct subclass of the EventObject class. A TableModelEvent object has access to the methods defined in the EventObject and Object classes.

Introduced: JDK 1.2

Constructors

public TableModelEvent(TableModel source)
public TableModelEvent(TableModel source, int row)
public TableModelEvent(TableModel source, int firstRow, int lastRow)
public TableModelEvent(TableModel source, int firstRow, int lastRow, int column)
public TableModelEvent(TableModel source, int firstRow, int lastRow, int column, int type)

The TableModelEvent class provides five public constructors for creating TableModelEvent objects. The `source` is a reference to the TableModel that generated the event. If only the `row` parameter is provided, it indicates that that row of data has been changed. If `firstRow` and `lastRow` are specified, it means that the data between `firstRow` and `lastRow` for every column has been changed. If `firstRow`, `lastRow`, and `column` are given, it indicates that the data between `firstRow` and `lastRow` for the specified column has been changed. The `type` will be one of the `DELETE`, `INSERT`, or `UPDATE` identification constants described next.

Constants

public static final int ALL_COLUMNS
public static final int DELETE
public static final int HEADER_ROW
public static final int INSERT
public static final int UPDATE

The `DELETE`, `INSERT`, and `UPDATE` constants are used to identify the type of TableModelEvent. The `ALL_COLUMNS` constant indicates that the change occurs over all of the columns in the table model. The `HEADER_ROW` refers to the metadata (names, types, and order of columns) for the table.

Fields

protected int `column`
protected int `firstRow`
protected int `lastRow`
protected int `type`

The `column`, `firstRow`, and `lastRow` fields store information about the region of the table that was changed, causing the TableModelEvent. The `type` field contains the type of TableModelEvent and will be one of the identification constants described previously.

TableModelEvent Class Methods

public int `getFirstRow()`
public int `getLastRow()`
public int `getColumn()`
public int `getType()`

These methods are used to obtain information about the action that generated the TableModelEvent.

`getFirstRow()` returns the index of the first row that was changed. This method might also return the `HEADER_ROW` constant.

`getLastRow()` returns the index of the last row that was changed.

`getColumn()` returns the column that is associated with the event or `ALL_COLUMNS` if every column is associated with the event.

`getType()` returns the type of TableModelEvent. The return value will be one either the `DELETE`, `INSERT`, or `UPDATE` constants.

Methods Inherited from the java.util.EventObject Class

public Object `getSource()`
public String `toString()`

`getSource()` returns a reference to the object that generated the TableModelEvent.

`toString()` provides a String representation of the TableModelEvent object.

Methods Inherited from the java.lang.Object Class

public final Class `getClass()`

`getClass()` returns a Class object representing the runtime class of the invoking object. In this case, it would return an object representing the javax.swing.event.TableModelEvent class.

The other methods inherited from the Object class, `clone()`, `equals()`, `hashCode()`, `notify()`, `notifyAll()`, and `wait()`, are generally not used in conjunction with TableModelEvent objects.

EXAMPLE

Example 6.34 uses TableModelEvent objects to monitor changes in the data contained in a JTable. The table model of the JTable registers a TableModelListener. When the user changes the data in one of the table cells, a TableModelEvent is generated and sent to the `tableChanged()` method. The location of the change and the new data of that cell are printed inside a JTextField at the bottom of the frame.

EXAMPLE 6.34 TABLEMODELEVENT CLASS

```
import javax.swing.*;
import javax.swing.event.*;
import java.awt.*;
import java.awt.event.*;
import javax.swing.table.*;

public class TableModelDemo extends JFrame implements
TableModelListener
{
    private JTable table;
```

```
      private DefaultTableModel model;
      private JTextField jtf;

      public TableModelDemo()
      {
         Object[][] data = {
            {"Jackson", new Integer(12345), "555-123-4567"},
            {"Zachary", new Integer(65432), "555-567-1234"} };
         String[] headers = { "Name", "ID number", "Phone" };

/* A simple table is created and placed on a JFrame. The TableModel */
/* of the table registers a TableColumnModelListener.               */

         model = new DefaultTableModel(data, headers);
         model.addTableModelListener(this);

         table = new JTable(model);

         jtf = new JTextField(25);
         jtf.setEditable(false);

         JPanel centerPanel = new JPanel();
         centerPanel.add(new JScrollPane(table));

         JPanel southPanel = new JPanel();
         southPanel.add(jtf);

         getContentPane().add(centerPanel, BorderLayout.CENTER);
         getContentPane().add(southPanel, BorderLayout.SOUTH);

         setDefaultCloseOperation(JFrame.EXIT_ON_CLOSE);
         setBounds(100, 100, 600, 300);
         setVisible(true);
      }

/* The TableModelDemo class serves as the TableModelListener so it  */
/* provides an implementation of the tableChanged() method. When    */
/* the user changes the data in one of the table cells, a           */
/* TableModelEvent is generated and sent to the tableChanged()      */
/* method. The location of the change and the change itself is      */
/* displayed inside a JTextField.                                   */

      public void tableChanged(TableModelEvent event)
      {
         if ( event.getType() == TableModelEvent.UPDATE )
         {
            int row = event.getFirstRow();
            int column = event.getColumn();
            jtf.setText("data at ("+row+","+column+") is now "+
                        model.getValueAt(row,column));
```

```
      }
   }

   public static void main(String args[])
   {
      TableModelDemo demo = new TableModelDemo();
   }
}
```

When you run this example, a small table appears on the screen. Edit the data in one of the cells and press the Enter key. The location of the change and the new cell data appears in the textfield at the bottom of the frame.

TextEvent Class

A TextEvent is a semantic (high-level) event generated by AWT text components when the text they contain changes. TextEvent objects can be generated by TextComponent subclasses such as TextField and TextArea objects. TextEvents are fired only by AWT text components.

A TextEvent object contains information about the source that generated the event and the event ID. For TextEvents, there is only one ID, TEXT_VALUE_CHANGED.

TextEvents are delivered to any registered TextListener objects when the event is generated. The TextListener will provide an implementation of the `textValueChanged()` method to process the event.

Syntax: public class TextEvent extends AWTEvent

Package: java.awt.event

Class hierarchy: Object—EventObject—AWTEvent—TextEvent

The TextEvent class is part of the AWTEvent family. A TextEvent object has access to the methods defined in the AWTEvent, EventObject, and Object classes.

Introduced: JDK 1.1

Constructors

```
public TextEvent(Component source, int id)
```

    The TextEvent class provides one public constructor for creating TextEvent objects. The `source` is the component that generated the event. The `id` identifies the type of TextEvent. For system-generated TextEvents, it will be the `TEXT_VALUE_CHANGED` constant.

Constants

public static final int `TEXT_VALUE_CHANGED`
public static final int `TEXT_FIRST`
public static final int `TEXT_LAST`

The `TEXT_VALUE_CHANGED` constant is the default system ID for TextEvents. It has a numerical value of 900.

The `TEXT_FIRST` and `TEXT_LAST` constants represent the range of system-provided IDs for TextEvent objects. There is only one ID, so `TEXT_FIRST` and `TEXT_LAST` have the same numerical value of 900.

Fields

Beyond those constants described in the preceding section, the TextEvent class does not define any additional fields. A TextEvent object does have access to the fields defined in the AWTEvent and EventObject classes, including the `source` and `id` fields.

TextEvent Class Methods

```
public String paramString()
```

`paramString()` returns a parameter String that identifies the TextEvent. This is generally used for event-logging and debugging purposes. When a TextEvent object calls the `toString()` method, the return value of the `paramString()` method is incorporated in the return value of the `toString()` method.

Methods Inherited from the java.awt.AWTEvent Class

protected void `consume()`
protected void `finalize()` throws Throwable
public int `getID()`
protected void `isConsumed()`
public String `toString()`

A TextEvent object has access to the methods defined in the AWTEvent class. For a description of these methods, see the section "AWTEvent Class" in this chapter.

Methods Inherited from the java.util.EventObject Class

public Object `getSource()`

`getSource()` returns a reference to the object that generated the TextEvent.

Methods Inherited from the java.lang.Object Class

public final Class `getClass()`

`getClass()` returns a Class object representing the runtime class of the invoking object. In this case, it would return an object representing the java.awt.event.TextEvent class.

The other methods inherited from the Object class, `clone()`, `equals()`, `hashCode()`, `notify()`, `notifyAll()`, and `wait()`, are generally not used in conjunction with TextEvent objects.

EXAMPLE

TextEvents are not as functional as they could be because the TextEvent class defines no methods for accessing the text that was changed. To find the current text, the TextEvent object must get a reference to the event source. In Example 6.35, a TextField is placed on top of a Frame. The textfield then registers a TextListener. When text is added to, removed from, or substituted in the textfield, a TextEvent is generated and sent to the `textValueChanged()` method. A second textfield placed at the bottom of the Frame is updated to reflect the current contents of the first textfield.

EXAMPLE 6.35 TEXTEVENT CLASS

```java
import java.awt.*;
import java.awt.event.*;

public class TextEventDemo extends Frame
{
   private TextField tf1, tf2;

   public TextEventDemo()
   {
/* A TextField is created and placed on a Frame.  It registers   */
/* a TextListener.  A second TextField is used to reflect        */
/* changes in the text contained by the first TextField.         */

      tf1 = new TextField(25);
      tf1.addTextListener(new TextEventHandler());

      tf2 = new TextField(25);
      tf2.setEditable(false);

      Panel panel = new Panel();
      panel.add(tf1);

      add(panel, BorderLayout.NORTH);
      add(tf2, BorderLayout.SOUTH);

      addWindowListener(new WinAdapter());
      setBounds(100, 100, 300, 200);
      setVisible(true);
   }

/* The TextListener is implemented as an inner class.  Whenever  */
/* the text inside the top TextField is changed, a TextEvent is  */
/* generated and sent to the textValueChanged() method.          */

   class TextEventHandler implements TextListener
   {
      public void textValueChanged(TextEvent event)
      {
         TextField tf = (TextField)event.getSource();
         tf2.setText("Text is: "+tf.getText());
      }
   }

   public static void main(String args[])
   {
      TextEventDemo demo = new TextEventDemo();
   }
}
```

```
/* This makes sure the application terminates if the window is
closed    */

class WinAdapter extends WindowAdapter
{
   public void windowClosing(WindowEvent event)
   {
      System.exit(0);
   }
}
```

When this program starts, the top textfield is initially blank. Type some text into it. TextEvents are used to update the bottom textfield every time the text in the first textfield is changed. This happens if text is added, removed, or substituted.

TreeExpansionEvent Class

A TreeExpansionEvent is a semantic (high-level) event generated by a JTree object whenever a path in the tree has been expanded or collapsed.

A TreeExpansionEvent object contains information about the event source and the path to the node that has expanded or collapsed. The system will handle the basic aspects of expanding or collapsing tree nodes. TreeExpansionEvents can be used to react to or add some additional functionality to these occurrences.

There are two kinds of listeners used with TreeExpansionEvents. A TreeExpansionListener is notified after a node has been expanded or collapsed. A TreeWillExpandListener is called before a node has been expanded or collapsed. The TreeWillExpandListener can be used to get user confirmation, check permission, and if necessary veto the expansion before the expansion change takes place.

When a TreeExpansionEvent is generated, it is sent to any registered TreeExpansionListener or TreeWillExpandListener objects. The listeners provide implementation of methods used to process the event.

Syntax:	public class TreeExpansionEvent extends EventObject
Package:	javax.swing.event
Class hierarchy:	Object—EventObject—TreeExpansionEvent
	The TreeExpansionEvent class is not part of the AWTEvent family, as it is a direct subclass of the EventObject class. A

TreeExpansionEvent object has access to the methods defined in the EventObject and Object classes.

Introduced: JDK 1.2

Constructors

```
public TreeExpansionEvent(Object source, TreePath path)
```

The TreeExpansionEvent class provides one public constructor for creating TreeExpansionEvent objects. The `source` is a reference to the object that generated the event. This will generally be a JTree object. The `path` parameter is a TreePath object representing the path to the node that was expanded or collapsed.

Constants

The TreeExpansionEvent class defines no identification constants.

Fields

```
protected TreePath path
```

The `path` field represents the path to the node that was expanded or collapsed.

TreeExpansionEvent Class Methods

```
public TreePath getPath()
```

`getPath()` returns a TreePath object containing the path to the node that was expanded or collapsed.

Methods Inherited from the java.util.EventObject Class

```
public Object getSource()
```
```
public String toString()
```

`getSource()` returns a reference to the object that generated the TreeExpansionEvent.

`toString()` provides a String representation of the TreeExpansionEvent object.

Methods Inherited from the java.lang.Object Class

public final Class `getClass()`

`getClass()` returns a Class object representing the runtime class of the invoking object. In this case, it would return an object representing the javax.swing.event.TreeExpansionEvent class.

The other methods inherited from the Object class, `clone()`, `equals()`, `hashCode()`, `notify()`, `notifyAll()`, and `wait()`, are generally not used in conjunction with TreeExpansionEvent objects.

EXAMPLE

In Example 6.36, TreeExpansionEvents are used to determine if a user has permission to expand a node of a JTree. A JTree representing a soccer league is created and placed on a JFrame. The JTree registers a TreeWillExpandListener. A JCheckBox is used to specify permission to expand a tree node.

When the user attempts to expand a node, a TreeExpansionEvent is generated and sent to the `treeWillExpand()` method. The method checks to see if the "permission" checkbox is checked. If it is, the expansion is allowed to proceed. If the checkbox is not checked, an ExpandVetoException is thrown, which cancels the expansion.

EXAMPLE 6.36 TREEEXPANSIONEVENT CLASS

```
import javax.swing.*;
import javax.swing.tree.*;
import javax.swing.event.*;
import java.awt.*;
import java.awt.event.*;

public class TreeExpansionDemo extends JFrame
                               implements TreeWillExpandListener
{
   private JTree tree;
   private JCheckBox jcb;
   private JTextField jtf;

   public TreeExpansionDemo()
   {
/* A Collection of DefaultMutableTreeNode objects are created that */
/* will form the components of a tree.                             */

      DefaultMutableTreeNode league =
             new DefaultMutableTreeNode("Soccer League");
```

```
        DefaultMutableTreeNode north =
                new DefaultMutableTreeNode("North Division");
        DefaultMutableTreeNode south =
                new DefaultMutableTreeNode("South Division");

        DefaultMutableTreeNode jets =
                    new DefaultMutableTreeNode("Jets");
        DefaultMutableTreeNode raiders =
                    new DefaultMutableTreeNode("Raiders");
        DefaultMutableTreeNode fins =
                    new DefaultMutableTreeNode("Fins");
        DefaultMutableTreeNode shooters =
                    new DefaultMutableTreeNode("Shooters");
        DefaultMutableTreeNode lions =
                    new DefaultMutableTreeNode("Lions");
        DefaultMutableTreeNode tigers =
                    new DefaultMutableTreeNode("Tigers");

/* The node hierarchy is loaded into a DefaultTreeModel object.  */

        DefaultTreeModel dtm = new DefaultTreeModel(league);
        dtm.insertNodeInto(north, league, 0);
        dtm.insertNodeInto(south, league, 1);
        dtm.insertNodeInto(jets, north, 0);
        dtm.insertNodeInto(raiders, north, 1);
        dtm.insertNodeInto(fins, north, 2);
        dtm.insertNodeInto(shooters, south, 0);
        dtm.insertNodeInto(lions, south, 1);
        dtm.insertNodeInto(tigers, south, 2);

/* A JTree object is created using the previously created tree model. */
/* The JTree registers a TreeWillExpandListener.  The                 */
/* TreeExpansionDemo class serves as the TreeWillExpandListener, so   */
/* the "this" reference is passed to the addTreeWillExpandListener()  */
/* method.                                                            */

        tree = new JTree(dtm);
        tree.setShowsRootHandles(true);
        tree.addTreeWillExpandListener(this);

        jcb = new JCheckBox("permission");
        jcb.setBorder(BorderFactory.createLineBorder(Color.black));
        jcb.setBorderPainted(true);
        jcb.setPreferredSize(new Dimension(100, 30));

        jtf = new JTextField(20);
        jtf.setEditable(false);

        JPanel panel = new JPanel();
            panel.add(jcb);
```

```
         panel.add(jtf);

         getContentPane().add( new JScrollPane(tree),
BorderLayout.CENTER );
         getContentPane().add( panel, BorderLayout.SOUTH );

         setDefaultCloseOperation(JFrame.EXIT_ON_CLOSE);
         setBounds(100, 100, 400, 300);
         setVisible(true);
      }

/*   The TreeExpansionDemo class provides implementation of the    */
/*   treeWillExpand() method.  The method checks to see if the     */
/*   "permission" checkbox is checked.  If it is, the expansion    */
/*   is allowed to proceed.  If the checkbox is not checked, an    */
/*   ExpandVetoException is thrown and the expansion is canceled.  */
/*   The treeWillCollapse() method is not used in this example so  */
/*   it is implemented as a stub method.                           */

      public void treeWillExpand(TreeExpansionEvent event)
                                  throws ExpandVetoException
      {
         if ( jcb.isSelected() )
         {
            TreePath path = event.getPath();
            jtf.setText(""+path.getLastPathComponent()+" node ex-
panded");
         }
         else
         {
            jtf.setText("permission denied");
            throw new ExpandVetoException(event);
         }

      }

      public void treeWillCollapse(TreeExpansionEvent event)
                                  throws ExpandVetoException {}

      public static void main(String args[])
      {
         TreeExpansionDemo demo = new TreeExpansionDemo();
      }
}
```

When you initially start this example, the JCheckBox is not checked. Try expanding a node. A "permission denied" message will appear in the JTextField. Now check the "permission" checkbox and try to expand a node. You now have "permission" and the expansion is allowed to take place.

TreeModelEvent Class

A TreeModelEvent is a semantic (high-level) event indicating that a change has been made to the tree model of a tree. Possible changes include inserting, removing, or altering a node in a tree, or a change in the structure of the tree structure below a given node.

A TreeModelEvent object contains information about the event source, the path to the parent component of the changed nodes, and the child nodes of the changed node. TreeModelEvents are used to monitor and react to any changes in the tree structure.

When a TreeModelEvent is generated, it is sent to any registered TreeModelListener objects. The TreeModelListener provides an implementation of four methods, one for each type of TreeModelEvent.

Syntax: public class TreeModelEvent extends EventObject

Package: javax.swing.event

Class hierarchy: Object—EventObject—TreeModelEvent

The TreeModelEvent class is not part of the AWTEvent family, as it is a direct subclass of the EventObject class. A TreeModelEvent object has access to the methods defined in the EventObject and Object classes.

Introduced: JDK 1.2

Constructors

```
public TreeModelEvent(Object source, Object[] path)
public TreeModelEvent(Object source, Object[] path, int[] changedIndices, Object[] nodes)
public TreeModelEvent(Object source, TreePath path)
public TreeModelEvent(Object source, TreePath path, int[] changedIndices, Object[] nodes)
```

The TreeModelEvent class provides four public constructors for creating TreeModelEvent objects. The `source` is a reference to the object that generated the event. If the event represents a change to the node structure, only the path parameter is provided. This can be done either through an array of Objects or by using a TreePath object. If the TreeModelEvent is due to one or more nodes being inserted, removed, or changed, an array containing the indices of the modified nodes and an array containing the modified node objects themselves are provided.

Constants

The TreeModelEvent class defines no identification constants.

Fields

protected int[] childIndices
protected Object[] children
protected TreePath path

The childIndices field is an int array containing the indices of the child nodes of the node that caused the event. The children field is an Object array containing the child nodes of the node that caused the event. The path field is the path to the parent node of the nodes that were changed.

TreeModelEvent Class Methods

public int getChildIndices()
public Object[] getChildren()
public Object[] getPath()
public TreePath getTreePath()
public String toString()

These methods are used to obtain information about the changes to the tree model that precipitated the TreeModelEvent.

getChildIndices() returns an int array containing the indices of the child nodes of the node that caused the event. If the event was due to a node being removed, this method will return the index of the removed node.

getChildren() returns the child nodes of the node returned by the getPath() or getTreePath() methods. If the event was caused by a node being removed, this method will return the removed node.

`getPath()` returns an Object array representing the path to the parent of the changed nodes. For events resulting from a change to the tree structure, this method returns the path to the ancestor of the structure that has changed.

`getTreePath()` does the same thing as `getPath()` but returns the path as a TreePath object.

`toString()` provides a String representation of the TreeModelEvent object.

Methods Inherited from the java.util.EventObject Class

> public Object `getSource()`

`getSource()` returns a reference to the object that generated the TreeModelEvent.

Methods Inherited from the java.lang.Object Class

> public final Class `getClass()`

`getClass()` returns a Class object representing the runtime class of the invoking object. In this case, it would return an object representing the javax.swing.event.TreeModelEvent class.

The other methods inherited from the Object class, `clone()`, `equals()`, `hashCode()`, `notify()`, `notifyAll()`, and `wait()`, are generally not used in conjunction with TreeModelEvent objects.

EXAMPLE

Example 6.37 uses TreeModelEvent objects to give the user a chance to confirm a node removal operation. A JTree is created and placed on a JFrame. The tree model associated with the JTree registers a TreeModelListener. A JButton is also placed on the frame. When the user presses the button, the selected node of the JTree is removed from the tree. This generates a TreeModelEvent that is sent to the `treeNodesRemoved()` method. This method uses the event to get a reference to the node that was removed, its parent node, and its index. A confirm dialog appears on the screen. If the user rejects the removal, the node is placed back inside the tree.

EXAMPLE 6.37 TREEMODELEVENT CLASS

```
import javax.swing.*;
import javax.swing.tree.*;
import javax.swing.event.*;
import java.awt.*;
import java.awt.event.*;

public class TreeModelEventDemo extends JFrame implements
ActionListener
{
   private JTree tree;
   private JButton button;
   private DefaultTreeModel model;

   public TreeModelEventDemo()
      {
/*   A Collection of DefaultMutableTreeNode objects are created that  */
/*   will form the components of a tree.                              */

      DefaultMutableTreeNode league =
            new DefaultMutableTreeNode("Soccer League");

      DefaultMutableTreeNode north =
             new DefaultMutableTreeNode("North Division");
      DefaultMutableTreeNode south =
             new DefaultMutableTreeNode("South Division");

      DefaultMutableTreeNode jets =
                 new DefaultMutableTreeNode("Jets");
      DefaultMutableTreeNode raiders =
                 new DefaultMutableTreeNode("Raiders");
      DefaultMutableTreeNode fins =
                 new DefaultMutableTreeNode("Fins");
      DefaultMutableTreeNode shooters =
                 new DefaultMutableTreeNode("Shooters");
      DefaultMutableTreeNode lions =
                 new DefaultMutableTreeNode("Lions");
      DefaultMutableTreeNode tigers =
                 new DefaultMutableTreeNode("Tigers");

/*   The node hierarchy is loaded into a DefaultTreeModel object.    */
/*   The tree model registers a TreeModelListener.                   */

      model = new DefaultTreeModel(league);
      model.insertNodeInto(north, league, 0);
      model.insertNodeInto(south, league, 1);
      model.insertNodeInto(jets, north, 0);
      model.insertNodeInto(raiders, north, 1);
      model.insertNodeInto(fins, north, 2);
```

```
        model.insertNodeInto(shooters, south, 0);
        model.insertNodeInto(lions, south, 1);
        model.insertNodeInto(tigers, south, 2);
        model.addTreeModelListener(new TreeModelHandler());

/* A JTree object is created using the previously created tree model. */

        tree = new JTree(model);
        tree.setShowsRootHandles(true);
        tree.expandRow(1);

        button = new JButton("remove");
        button.setBorder(BorderFactory.createRaisedBevelBorder());
        button.addActionListener(this);

        JPanel panel = new JPanel();
        panel.add(button);

        getContentPane().add( new JScrollPane(tree),
BorderLayout.CENTER );
        getContentPane().add( panel, BorderLayout.SOUTH );

        setDefaultCloseOperation(JFrame.EXIT_ON_CLOSE);
        setBounds(100, 100, 400, 300);
        setVisible(true);
    }

/* The TreeModelListener is implemented as an inner class.         */
/* When the user removes a tree node, a TreeModelEvent is generated */
/* and sent to the treeNodesRemoved() method. This method uses the  */
/* event to obtain a reference to the node that was removed, its    */
/* parent node, and its index.  It then displays a confirm dialog,  */
/* so the user can confirm the removal.  If the user does not       */
/* confirm the  removal, the node is placed back inside the         */
/* tree. The other methods declared in the TreeModelListener        */
/* interface are not used, so they are implemented as stub methods. */

    class TreeModelHandler implements TreeModelListener
    {
      public void treeNodesRemoved(TreeModelEvent event)
      {
         Object[] path = event.getPath();
         Object[] child = event.getChildren();
         int[] indices = event.getChildIndices();

         int confirm =
             JOptionPane.showConfirmDialog(tree, "Confirm node
deletion?");

         if ( confirm != JOptionPane.YES_OPTION )
         {
            model.insertNodeInto( (MutableTreeNode)child[0],
```

```
                (MutableTreeNode)path[path.length-1], indices[0]);

         }
      }

      public void treeNodesChanged(TreeModelEvent event) {}
      public void treeNodesInserted(TreeModelEvent event) {}
      public void treeStructureChanged(TreeModelEvent event) {}
   }

/* When the "remove" button is pressed, the selected node is removed */
/* from the tree.  This generates a TreeModelEvent that is sent to    */
/* the TreeModelListener.                                             */

   public void actionPerformed(ActionEvent event)
   {
      DefaultMutableTreeNode node =
         (DefaultMutableTreeNode)tree.getLastSelectedPathComponent();

      if ( !node.isRoot() )
      {
         model.removeNodeFromParent(node);
      }
   }

   public static void main(String args[])
   {
      TreeModelEventDemo demo = new TreeModelEventDemo();
   }
}
```

When you run this program, a JTree appears on your screen. The "North Division" has been expanded. Select one of the team nodes and press the "remove" button. A confirm dialog appears. Press No or Cancel, and the node is returned to the tree. If you press Yes, the node is removed from the tree.

TREESELECTIONEVENT CLASS

A TreeSelectionEvent is a semantic (high-level) event generated whenever the currently selected node of a tree changes. TreeSelectionEvent objects will be created if an unselected node is selected or if a currently selected node is deselected.

A TreeSelectionEvent object contains information about the event source, the current and previous lead selection path, the path to the currently selected node, and whether the event was due to a selection or a deselection.

TreeSelectionEvents are used to monitor and respond to changes in the selected nodes of a tree.

When a TreeSelectionEvent is generated, it is sent to any registered TreeSelectionListener objects. The TreeSelectionListener provides an implementation of the `valueChanged()` method, which is used to process the event.

Syntax:	public class TreeSelectionEvent extends EventObject
Package:	javax.swing.event
Class hierarchy:	Object—EventObject—TreeSelectionEvent
	The TreeSelectionEvent class is not part of the AWTEvent family as it is a direct subclass of the EventObject class. A TreeSelectionEvent object has access to the methods defined in the EventObject and Object classes.
Introduced:	JDK 1.2

Constructors

```
public TreeSelectionEvent(Object source, TreePath path,
boolean isNew, TreePath oldLeadSelectionPath, TreePath
newLeadSelectionPath)

public TreeSelectionEvent(Object source, TreePath[]
paths, boolean[] areNew, TreePath oldLeadSelectionPath,
TreePath newLeadSelectionPath)
```

The TreeSelectionEvent class provides two public constructors for creating TreeSelectionEvent objects. The `source` is a reference to the object that generated the event. The `path` parameter is the path to the change in selection. If more than one change in selection is involved, an array of paths can be specified. The `isNew` parameter is true if the event represents a selection and false if it represents a deselection. The `oldLeadSelectionPath` is the path to the lead selected item before the change that generated the event occurred. The `newLeadSelectionPath` is the path to the lead selected item after the change that generated the event occurred. Either of these can be null if the old or new paths don't exist.

Constants

The TreeSelectionEvent class defines no identification constants.

Fields

protected `boolean[] areNew`
protected `TreePath newLeadSelectionPath`
protected `TreePath oldLeadSelectionPath`
protected `TreePath[] paths`

The `areNew` field is a boolean array for every path associated with the event. If a path represents a new selection, its element in the boolean array is true. The `newLeadSelectionPath` and `oldLeadSelectionPath` fields are the current and former lead selection paths. The `paths` field contains all of the paths associated with the event.

TreeSelectionEvent Class Methods

public `Object cloneWithSource(Object newSource)`
public `TreePath getNewLeadSelectionPath()`
public `TreePath getOldLeadSelectionPath()`
public `TreePath getPath()`
public `TreePath[] getPaths()`
public `boolean isAddedPath()`
public `boolean isAddedPath(int index)`
public `boolean isAddedPath(TreePath path)`

These methods are used to obtain information about the changes to the selected state of a tree that generated the TreeSelectionEvent.

`cloneWithSource()` is used to generate a clone of the invoking TreeSelectionEvent object with a modified event source. This is useful for an object that uses a tree to display itself on the screen. The underlying component can be designated as the source of the event.

`getNewLeadSelectionPath()` returns the current lead selection path.

`getOldLeadSelectionPath()` returns the previous lead selection path. The return value of this method will be null if there is no old lead selection path.

`getPath()` returns the path to the currently selected node.

`getPaths()` returns an array of TreePath objects representing the paths to all selected nodes. This method is used if there is more than one node selected.

`isAddedPath()` returns true if the TreeSelectionEvent represents an addition to the current selection and false if it represents a deselection. If no argument is provided, the method will only check the first path element. If a path index or TreePath object is specified, the method will check that path.

Methods Inherited from the java.util.EventObject Class

public Object `getSource()`
public String `toString()`

`getSource()` returns a reference to the object that generated the TreeSelectionEvent.

`toString()` provides a String representation of the TreeSelectionEvent.

Methods Inherited from the java.lang.Object Class

public final Class `getClass()`

`getClass()` returns a Class object representing the runtime class of the invoking object. In this case, it would return an object representing the javax.swing.event.TreeSelectionEvent class.

The other methods inherited from the Object class, `clone()`, `equals()`, `hashCode()`, `notify()`, `notifyAll()`, and `wait()`, are generally not used in conjunction with TreeSelectionEvent objects.

EXAMPLE

In Example 6.38, TreeSelectionEvents are used to monitor the currently selected node of a JTree. The JTree registers a TreeSelectionListener. When the user selects a node of the tree, a TreeSelectionEvent is generated and sent to the `valueChanged()` method. This method prints the name of the currently selected node in a textfield at the bottom of the frame.

EXAMPLE 6.38 TREESELECTIONEVENT CLASS

```
import javax.swing.*;
import javax.swing.tree.*;
import javax.swing.event.*;
import java.awt.*;
import java.awt.event.*;

public class TreeSelectionDemo extends JFrame
                               implements TreeSelectionListener
{
   private JTree tree;
   private JTextField jtf;

   public TreeSelectionDemo()
   {
/* A Collection of DefaultMutableTreeNode objects are created that */
/* will form the components of a tree.                             */

      DefaultMutableTreeNode league =
              new DefaultMutableTreeNode("Soccer League");

      DefaultMutableTreeNode north =
              new DefaultMutableTreeNode("North Division");
      DefaultMutableTreeNode south =
              new DefaultMutableTreeNode("South Division");

      DefaultMutableTreeNode jets =
                  new DefaultMutableTreeNode("Jets");
      DefaultMutableTreeNode raiders =
                  new DefaultMutableTreeNode("Raiders");
      DefaultMutableTreeNode fins =
                  new DefaultMutableTreeNode("Fins");
      DefaultMutableTreeNode shooters =
                  new DefaultMutableTreeNode("Shooters");
      DefaultMutableTreeNode lions =
                  new DefaultMutableTreeNode("Lions");
      DefaultMutableTreeNode tigers =
                  new DefaultMutableTreeNode("Tigers");

   /* The node hierarchy is loaded into a DefaultTreeModel object.  */

      DefaultTreeModel dtm = new DefaultTreeModel(league);
      dtm.insertNodeInto(north, league, 0);
      dtm.insertNodeInto(south, league, 1);
      dtm.insertNodeInto(jets, north, 0);
      dtm.insertNodeInto(raiders, north, 1);
      dtm.insertNodeInto(fins, north, 2);
      dtm.insertNodeInto(shooters, south, 0);
      dtm.insertNodeInto(lions, south, 1);
      dtm.insertNodeInto(tigers, south, 2);

   /* A JTree object is created using the previously created tree model.*/
```

```
         /* The JTree registers a TreeSelectionListener.            */

            tree = new JTree(dtm);
            tree.setShowsRootHandles(true);
            tree.expandRow(1);
            tree.getSelectionModel().setSelectionMode(
                      TreeSelectionModel.SINGLE_TREE_SELECTION);
            tree.addTreeSelectionListener(this);

            jtf = new JTextField(20);
            jtf.setEditable(false);

            getContentPane().add( new JScrollPane(tree),
    BorderLayout.CENTER );
            getContentPane().add( jtf, BorderLayout.SOUTH );

            setDefaultCloseOperation(JFrame.EXIT_ON_CLOSE);
            setBounds(100, 100, 300, 300);
            setVisible(true);
         }

   /* The TreeSelectionDemo class serves as the TreeSelectionListener, */
   /* so it provides an implementation of the valueChanged() method.   */
   /* When the user selects a node, a TreeSelectionEvent is generated  */
   /* and sent to the valueChanged() method.  The identity of the      */
   /* currently selected node is printed inside a JTextField.          */

         public void valueChanged(TreeSelectionEvent event)
         {
            TreePath path = event.getPath();
            jtf.setText("Current selection is
    "+path.getLastPathComponent());
         }

         public static void main(String args[])
         {
            TreeSelectionDemo demo = new TreeSelectionDemo();
         }
    }
```

When you run this program, a JTree appears on the screen. Select one of the nodes. The identity of this node appears inside the textfield.

UndoableEditEvent Class

An UndoableEditEvent is generated by components that support the undo functionality when an action that can be undone has occurred. The undo capability is particularly useful in text editors because it allows users to recover from mistakes.

An UndoableEditEvent object contains information about the event source and the undoable edit that generated the event. UndoableEditEvents are used to implement the undo capability and can respond or provide additional functionality when undoable edits occur.

When an UndoableEditEvent is generated, it is sent to any registered UndoableEditListener objects. The UndoableEditListener provides an implementation of the `undoableEditHappened()` method, which is used to process the event.

Syntax:	public class UndoableEditEvent extends EventObject
Package:	javax.swing.event
Class hierarchy:	Object—EventObject—UndoableEditEvent
	The UndoableEditEvent class is not part of the AWTEvent family, as it is a direct subclass of the EventObject class. A UndoableEditEvent object has access to the methods defined in the EventObject and Object classes.
Introduced:	JDK 1.2

Constructors

```
public UndoableEditEvent(Object source, UndoableEdit edit)
```

The UndoableEditEvent class provides one public constructor for creating UndoableEditEvent objects. The `source` is a reference to the object that generated the event. The `edit` parameter contains the edit that caused the event.

Constants

The UndoableEditEvent class defines no identification constants.

Fields

The UndoableEditEvent class defines no fields. An UndoableEditEvent object has access to the `source` field defined in the EventObject class.

UndoableEvent Class Methods

```
public UndoableEdit getEdit()
```

`getEdit()` returns an UndoableEdit object encapsulating the edit that caused the event.

Methods Inherited from the java.util.EventObject Class

public Object `getSource()`
public String `toString()`

`getSource()` returns a reference to the object that generated the UndoableEditEvent.

`toString()` provides a String representation of the UndoableEditEvent.

Methods Inherited from the java.lang.Object Class

public final Class `getClass()`

`getClass()` returns a Class object representing the runtime class of the invoking object. In this case, it would return an object representing the javax.swing.event.UndoableEditEvent class.

The other methods inherited from the Object class `clone()`, `equals()`, `hashCode()`, `notify()`, `notifyAll()`, and `wait()`, are generally not used in conjunction with UndoableEditEvent objects.

EXAMPLE

Example 6.39 uses UndoableEditEvent objects to implement the undo capability to a JTextArea. The JTextArea is placed on a JFrame and registers an UndoableEditListener. An UndoManager is also provided to manage the list of undoable edits. An Edit menu is created with undo and redo menu items. These menu items initiate the undo and redo operations. The redo operation undoes the undo.

When the user executes an undoable edit inside the text area, an UndoableEditEvent is generated and sent to the `undoableEdit Happened()` method. An undoable edit might involve typing some text into the textfield, deleting some existing text, or pasting some text into the text area. The `undoableEditHappened()` method adds the undoable edit to the list managed by the UndoManager. The undo and redo menu items are enabled or disabled depending on whether this edit can be undone or redone.

The user can then select one of the menu items, if it is enabled, to undo or redo the edit. The UndoManager takes care of these operations. The enabled state of the menu items is updated every time an undo or redo takes place.

EXAMPLE 6.39 UNDOABLEEDITEVENT CLASS

```
import javax.swing.*;
import java.awt.*;
import java.awt.event.*;
import javax.swing.event.*;
import javax.swing.undo.*;

public class UndoableEditDemo extends JFrame
                    implements UndoableEditListener,
ActionListener
{
   private JTextArea jta;
   protected UndoManager undoManager;
   private JTextField jtf;
   private JMenuBar menuBar;
   private JMenu menu;
   private JMenuItem undoItem, redoItem;

   public UndoableEditDemo()
     {
/*  An UndoManager is created to manage undo and redo operations.  */

      undoManager = new UndoManager();

/*  A JTextArea is created and placed on a JFrame.  The Document    */
/*  associated with the JTextArea is obtained.  The Document        */
/*  registers an UndoableEventListener.                             */

      jta = new JTextArea(5,15);
      jta.setLineWrap(true);
      jta.setWrapStyleWord(true);
      jta.getDocument().addUndoableEditListener(this);

      jtf = new JTextField(15);
      jtf.setEditable(false);

/*  An "Edit" menu is created with "undo" and "redo" menu items.    */
/*  These menu items will initiate undo and redo actions to the     */
/*  text in the text area. The menu items are initially disabled    */
/*  since there is initially no text in the JTextArea.              */

      undoItem = new JMenuItem("undo");
      undoItem.setEnabled(false);
      undoItem.addActionListener(this);

      redoItem = new JMenuItem("redo");
```

```java
            redoItem.setEnabled(false);
            redoItem.addActionListener(this);

            menu = new JMenu("Edit");
            menu.add(undoItem);
            menu.add(redoItem);

            menuBar = new JMenuBar();
            menuBar.add(menu);

            getContentPane().add(new JScrollPane(jta), BorderLayout.CENTER);
            getContentPane().add(menuBar, BorderLayout.NORTH);
            getContentPane().add(jtf, BorderLayout.SOUTH);

            setDefaultCloseOperation(JFrame.EXIT_ON_CLOSE);
            setBounds(100, 100, 300, 250);
            setVisible(true);
        }

/*    The UndoableEditDemo class serves as the UndoableEditListener,     */
/*    so it provides an implementation of the undoableEditHappened()     */
/*    method.  When the user executes an undoable edit in the text       */
/*    area, an UndoableEditEvent is generated and sent to this method.   */
/*    The method adds the edit to the list managed by the UndoManager.   */
/*    The "undo" and "redo" menu items are enabled or disabled depending */
/*    on whether subsequent undo and redo operations are possible.       */

        public void undoableEditHappened(UndoableEditEvent event)
        {
            undoManager.addEdit(event.getEdit());
            redoItem.setEnabled(undoManager.canRedo());
            undoItem.setEnabled(undoManager.canUndo());
        }

/*    The actionPerformed() method responds to the selection of the      */
/*    "undo" and "redo" menu items.  If the "undo" menu item was         */
/*    selected, the UndoManager attempts to undo the last undoable       */
/*    edit in its list.  If the "redo" menu item was chosen, the         */
/*    UndoManager tries to redo (undo the undo).  After the actions      */
/*    are taken, the menu items are enabled or disabled depending        */
/*    on whether subsequent undo and redo operations are possible.       */

        public void actionPerformed(ActionEvent event)
        {
            if ( event.getActionCommand().equals("undo") )
            {
                try
                {
                    undoManager.undo();
                    redoItem.setEnabled(undoManager.canRedo());
                        undoItem.setEnabled(undoManager.canUndo());
                }
                    catch (CannotUndoException cue)
```

```
               {
                  jtf.setText("Can't perform undo");
               }
            }
            if ( event.getActionCommand().equals("redo") )
            {
               try
               {
                  undoManager.redo();
                  redoItem.setEnabled(undoManager.canRedo());
                  undoItem.setEnabled(undoManager.canUndo());
               }
               catch (CannotRedoException cre)
               {
                  jtf.setText("Can't perform redo");
               }
            }
         }

         public static void main(String args[])
         {
            UndoableEditDemo demo = new UndoableEditDemo();
         }
      }
```

When you run this example, an empty text area appears on your screen. Type some text into the text area. Every time you type a character, an UndoableEditEvent is generated. Now select the undo menu option. The last character typed is removed. If you select the redo menu item, this character is restored. Select a portion of the text and delete it. Now try the undo and redo menu items.

WindowEvent Class

A WindowEvent is a low-level event indicating that a window has been activated, deactivated, iconified, deiconified, opened, or closed. WindowEvent objects can be generated by Dialog, Frame, JDialog, JFrame, JWindow, and Window objects.

A WindowEvent object contains information about the event source and the type of window event. WindowEvents can be used to monitor and manage all types of Window operations. One of the most common usages involves determining what is to happen when a window is going to be closed.

WindowEvents are sent to any registered WindowListener objects when the event is generated. The WindowListener will implement methods to process the WindowEvent.

Syntax: public class WindowEvent extends ComponentEvent

Package: java.awt.event

Class hierarchy: Object—EventObject—AWTEvent—ComponentEvent—WindowEvent

The WindowEvent class is part of the AWTEvent family. A WindowEvent object has access to the methods defined in the Component, AWTEvent, EventObject, and Object classes.

Introduced: JDK 1.1

Constructors

```
public WindowEvent(Component source, int id)
```

The WindowEvent class provides one public constructor for creating WindowEvent objects. The `source` is the component that generated the event. The `id` identifies the type of WindowEvent. For system-generated WindowEvents, it will be one of the ID constants described next.

Constants

public static final int WINDOW_ACTIVATED
public static final int WINDOW_CLOSED
public static final int WINDOW_CLOSING
public static final int WINDOW_DEACTIVATED
public static final int WINDOW_DEICONIFIED
public static final int WINDOW_ICONIFIED
public static final int WINDOW_OPENED
public static final int WINDOW_FIRST
public static final int WINDOW_LAST

The first seven constants are used to identify a WindowEvent. Most of the names are self-explanatory. The `WINDOW_CLOSING` constant identifies a

WindowEvent that results from a user attempting to close a window from the window's system menu. The `WINDOW_CLOSED` constant identifies a WindowEvent that was generated after the window has been successfully closed. The numerical values for these constants range from 200 for `WINDOW_OPENED` to 206 for `WINDOW_DEACTIVATED`.

The `WINDOW_FIRST` and `WINDOW_LAST` constants represent the range of system-provided IDs for WindowEvent objects. They have numerical values of 200 and 206 respectively.

Fields

Beyond those constants described in the preceding section, the WindowEvent class does not define any additional fields. A WindowEvent object does have access to the fields defined in the AWTEvent and EventObject classes including the `source` and `id` fields.

WindowEvent Class Methods

public Window `getWindow()`
public String `paramString()`

`getWindow()` returns a reference to the Window that generated the event. It is similar in nature to the `getComponent()` and `getSource()` methods from the ComponentEvent and EventObject classes.

`paramString()` returns a parameter String that identifies the WindowEvent. This is generally used for event-logging and debugging purposes. When a WindowEvent subclass object calls the `toString()` method, the return value of the `paramString()` method is incorporated in the return value of the `toString()` method.

Methods Inherited from the java.awt.event.ComponentEvent Class

public Component `getComponent()`

`getComponent()` is used to obtain a reference to the component that generated the event. A WindowEvent object could also use the `getWindow()` method for this purpose.

Methods Inherited from the java.awt.AWTEvent Class

protected void `consume()`

protected void `finalize()` throws Throwable
public int `getID()`
protected void `isConsumed()`
public String `toString()`

A WindowEvent object has access to the methods defined in the AWTEvent class. For a description of these methods, see the section "AWTEvent Class" in this chapter.

Methods Inherited from the java.util.EventObject Class

public Object `getSource()`

`getSource()` returns a reference to the object that generated the WindowEvent.

Methods Inherited from the java.lang.Object Class

public final Class `getClass()`

The `getClass()` method returns a Class object representing the runtime class of the invoking object.

The other methods inherited from the Object class, `clone()`, `equals()`, `hashCode()`, `notify()`, `notifyAll()`, and `wait()`, are generally not used in conjunction with WindowEvent objects.

EXAMPLE

Example 6.40 shows a common use of WindowEvents, namely insuring that a program will terminate if a window is closed. In this case, a Frame component registers a WindowListener. When an attempt is made to close the frame window, a WindowEvent is generated and sent to the `windowClosing()` method. This method terminates the program.

If the frame did not have the previously described WindowListener registered to it and the frame window was closed, the application would continue to run. What is worse, there would no longer be any graceful way of terminating the program.

Certain Swing containers (JFrame, JInternalFrame, JDialog) can use the `setDefaultCloseOperation()` method as an alternative to using this type of WindowListener.

Example 6.40 WindowEvent Class

```
import java.awt.*;
import java.awt.event.*;

public class WindowEventDemo extends Frame
{
   public WindowEventDemo()
   {
/*  The Frame registers a WindowListener.   */

      addWindowListener(new WinAdapter());
      setBounds(100, 100, 300, 200);
      setVisible(true);
   }

   public static void main(String args[])
   {
      WindowEventDemo demo = new WindowEventDemo();
   }
}

/*  This WindowListener does not need access to the private data   */
/*  members of the WindowEventDemo class (if there were any), so   */
/*  it can be implemented as a separate class that extends the     */
/*  WindowAdapter class.  The windowClosing() method is overridden */
/*  to terminate the program if the window is closed.              */

class WinAdapter extends WindowAdapter
{
   public void windowClosing(WindowEvent event)
   {
      System.exit(0);
   }
}
```

When this program is run, a blank frame appears. Close the frame window. The application will terminate. Try commenting out the `addWindowListener()` syntax and recompile and run the program. When the frame window is closed now, the application does not terminate. It continues to run and requires a CTRL-C or similar sequence to terminate it.

Other Event Classes in the J2SE

The following is a brief description of other event classes contained in the J2SE that are not described in detail by this book. These events are generated by a BeanContext, by a drag-and-drop operation, by a change to a namespace or naming/directory service, or as part of the Java sound API.

java.beans.beancontext.BeanContextEvent—parent class of all events that are related to or generated by a BeanContext.

java.beans.beancontext.BeanContextMembershipEvent—occurs when a child object or a list of child objects is added to or removed from a BeanContext.

java.beans.beancontext.BeanContextServiceRevokedEvent—generated when a service is made no longer available to a BeanContext.

java.beans.beancontext.BeanContextServiceAvailableEvent—generated when a service is registered with a BeanContext.

java.awt.dnd.DragGestureEvent—generated when a DragGestureRecognizer detects that a drag initiating gesture has occurred.

java.awt.dnd.DragSourceEvent—parent class of the DragSourceDragEvent and DragSourceDropEvent classes.

java.awt.dnd.DragSourceDragEvent—generated during a drag-over operation.

java.awt.dnd.DragSourceDropEvent—generated when a drag-and-drop process is completed.

java.awt.dnd.DropTargetEvent—parent class of the DropTargetDragEvent and DropTargetDropEvent classes. It contains the current state of the DropTargetContext.

java.awt.dnd. DropTargetDragEvent—generated when a drag-over operation enters or passes through the drop target.

java.awt.dnd. DropTargetDropEvent—generated when a drag-and-drop process is completed.

javax.sound.sampled.LineEvent—generated when a line representing an audio feed opens, closes, starts, or stops.

javax.naming.event.NamingEvent—generated when a change is made to a namespace or to a naming/directory service.

javax.naming.event.NamingExceptionEvent—generated when the code used to collect information for notifying listeners of NamingEvents throws a NamingException.

javax.naming.ldap.UnsolicitedNotificationEvent—generated in response to an unsolicited notification sent by the Lightweight Directory Access Protocol (LDAP) server.

7

EVENT SUPPORT CLASSES

Implementing bound or constrained properties from scratch is a fairly complex and tedious process. The Java Bean or other component that supports these properties must maintain a list of VetoableChangeListeners and/or PropertyChangeListeners, including logic to determine if a listener already exists in the list. The object must also implement methods to fire PropetyChange events. These methods must instantiate the appropriate PropertyChangeEvent object and send it to every PropertyChangeListener or VetoableChangeListener in the list.

Fortunately, the Java language provides three utility classes that do much of the dirty work of implementing bound and constrained properties. They provide methods to fire property change and vetoable change events. They also have the ability to manage a listener list for the object and provide methods to add or remove listeners from the list.

To use one of the property change event support classes, simply include an instance of it in the class definition of the object that will generate PropertyChangeEvents. The object can use this instance to access the methods provided by the event support classes.

The javax.swing.undo package also contains the UndoableEditSupport class. This class defines methods that can be used to create components that support the undoable edit feature. This class is not used by Swing text components that have a built-in undo-redo capability, but are usually used to extend an undo-redo capability to a component that wouldn't normally support it. An example in the section "UndoableEditSupport Class" in this chapter shows how this might be done.

PropertyChangeSupport Class

The PropertyChangeSupport class is a utility class that makes it easier for Java Beans or other components to fire property change events associated with changes to bound properties and allows these components to easily manage a list of registered PropertyChangeListeners. To use the PropertyChangeSupport class, a PropertyChangeSupport object should be included as a data member of the object that will generate the PropertyChangeEvent.

Syntax:	public class PropertyChangeSupport extends Object implements Serializable
Package:	java.beans
Class hierarchy:	Object—PropertyChangeSupport
	PropertyChangeSupport is a direct subclass of Object. A PropertyChangeSupport object has access to Object class methods.
Introduced:	JDK 1.1

Constructors

```
public PropertyChangeSupport(Object source)
```

The PropertyChangeSupport class provides one public constructor for creating PropertyChangeSupport objects. The `source` parameter identifies the object that is designated as the source of any PropertyChangeEvents generated by the PropertyChangeSupport object.

Fields

The PropertyChangeSupport class defines no fields.

PropertyChangeSupport Class Methods

public void addPropertyChangeListener(PropertyChangeListener listener)
public void addPropertyChangeListener(String propertyName, PropertyChangeListener listener)
public void firePropertyChange(PropertyChangeEvent event)
public void firePropertyChange(String propertyName, boolean oldValue, boolean newValue)
public void firePropertyChange(String propertyName, int oldValue, int newValue)
public void firePropertyChange(String propertyName, Object oldValue, Object newValue)
public boolean hasListeners(String propertyName)
public void removePropertyChangeListener(PropertyChangeListener listener)
public void removePropertyChangeListener(String propertyName, PropertyChangeListener listener)

addPropertyChangeListener() adds the specified PropertyChangeListener to the listener list managed by the PropertyChangeSupport object. If a property name is given, the listener will only be called when the firePropertyChange() method is used with that property name. If no property name is provided, the listener is registered for all properties.

firePropertyChange() sends a PropertyChangeEvent to any registered listeners. It can do this either by using an existing PropertyChangeEvent or by sending the property name along with the old and new values.

hasListeners() returns true if there are any listeners registered to the specified property.

removePropertyChangeListener() removes a PropertyChangeListener from the listener list managed by the PropertyChangeSupport object. If a property name is provided, the method will only remove the listener for that property. Otherwise, it will remove the listener from all properties.

Methods Inherited from the java.lang.Object Class

> public final Class getClass()

getClass() returns a Class object representing the runtime class of the invoking object. In this case, it would return an object representing the java.beans.PropertyChangeSupport class.

The other methods inherited from the Object class, clone(), equals(), hashCode(), notify(), notifyAll(), and wait(), are generally not used in conjunction with PropertyChangeSupport objects.

EXAMPLE

See Chapter 6, "Event Classes and Interfaces," Example 6.30, where a PropertyChangeSupport object is used to make a Color object a bound property.

SwingPropertyChangeSupport Class

The SwingPropertyChangeSupport class is a utility class that makes it easier for Swing components to fire property change events and allows them to easily manage a list of registered PropertyChangeListeners. This is a subclass of the PropertyChangeSupport class found in the java.beans package and mimics the behavior of that class. The SwingPropertyChangeSupport class does not insure thread safety. Sacrificing thread safety reduces memory consumption and increases performance.

Syntax:	public final class SwingPropertyChangeSupport extends PropertyChangeSupport
Package:	javax.swing.event
Class hierarchy:	Object—PropertyChangeSupport—SwingPropertyChangeSupport
Introduced:	JDK 1.2

Constructors

> public SwingPropertyChangeSupport(Object source)

The SwingPropertyChangeSupport class provides one public constructor for creating SwingPropertyChangeSupport objects. The `source` parameter identifies the object that is designated as the source of all PropertyChangeEvents generated by the SwingPropertyChangeSupport object.

SwingPropertyChangeSupport Class Methods

public void addPropertyChangeListener(PropertyChange-Listener listener)
public void addPropertyChangeListener(String propertyName, PropertyChangeListener listener)
public void firePropertyChange(PropertyChangeEvent event)
public void firePropertyChange(String propertyName, Object oldValue, Object newValue)
public boolean hasListeners(String propertyName)
public void removePropertyChangeListener(PropertyChange-Listener listener)
public void removePropertyChangeListener(String propertyName, PropertyChangeListener listener)

`addPropertyChangeListener()` adds the specified PropertyChangeListener to the listener list. If a property name is given, the listener will only be called when the `firePropertyChange()` method is used with that property name. If no property name is provided, the listener is registered for all properties.

`firePropertyChange()` sends a PropertyChangeEvent to any registered listeners. It can do this either by using an existing PropertyChangeEvent or by sending the property name along with the old and new values.

`hasListeners()` returns true if there are any listeners registered to the specified property.

`removePropertyChangeListener()` removes a PropertyChangeListener from the listener list. If a property name is provided, the method will only remove the listener for that property. Otherwise, it will remove the listener from all properties.

Methods Inherited from the PropertyChangeSupport Class

public void firePropertyChange(String propertyName, boolean oldValue, boolean newValue)

public void firePropertyChange(String propertyName, int oldValue, int newValue)

firePropertyChange() sends a PropertyChangeEvent to any registered listeners. These methods require the property name and the old and new values of the property.

Methods Inherited from the java.lang.Object Class

public final Class getClass()

getClass() returns a Class object representing the runtime class of the invoking object. In this case. it would return an object representing the javax.swing.event.SwingPropertyChangeSupport class.

The other methods inherited from the Object class, clone(), equals(), hashCode(), notify(), notifyAll(), and wait(), are generally not used in conjunction with SwingPropertyChangeSupport objects.

EXAMPLE

Let us modify Example 6.30 (found in Chapter 6) to use a SwingPropertyChangeSupport object instead of a PropertyChangeSupport object. The required changes are very minor. In the FontColor class, you must simply import the javax.swing.event package (or just the SwingPropertyChangeSupport class from that package) and instantiate a SwingPropertyChangeSupport object. The modified FontColor class code listing is shown in Example 7.1.

EXAMPLE 7.1 FONTCOLOR CLASS

```
import javax.swing.*;
import javax.swing.event.*;
```

```java
import java.awt.*;
import java.beans.*;

public class FontColor
{
   private Color color;
   private SwingPropertyChangeSupport pcs;

   public FontColor(Color c)
   {
      color = c;
      pcs = new SwingPropertyChangeSupport(this);
   }

   public Color getColor()
   {
      return color;
   }

/* The Color object is implemented as a bound property. When the  */
/* setColor() method is called, the PropertyChangeSupport object  */
/* is used to fire a PropertyChangeEvent.                         */

   public void setColor(Color c)
   {
      Color oldColor = color;
      color = c;
      pcs.firePropertyChange("color", oldColor, color);
   }

/* For the FontColor class to be able to register and/or disconnect */
/* PropertyChangeListeners, it has to provide methods to add        */
/* and remove PropertyChangeListeners.  The PropertyChangeSupport   */
/* is used to manage the listener list.                             */

   public void addPropertyChangeListener(PropertyChangeListener listener)
   {
      pcs.addPropertyChangeListener(listener);
   }

   public void removePropertyChangeListener(PropertyChangeListener listener)
   {
      pcs.removePropertyChangeListener(listener);
   }
}
```

The NewLabel and PropChangeEventDemo class code listings are the same as in Examples 6.31 and 6.32 in Chapter 6.

When you first run this program, a frame appears with a JComboBox and the text "Hello there boys." The text is actually comprised of three different labels. Select a different color in the JComboBox. The color of the three labels is automatically updated. This is because the three labels share a bound property. You may not be able to tell, but this code should respond faster to changes than does Example 6.30, which used the more resource-intensive PropertyChangeSupport class.

UndoableEditSupport Class

The UndoableEditSupport class is a utility class that provides methods for managing UndoableEditListeners, firing UndoableEditEvents, and combining multiple undoable edits into a single CompoundEdit. The Swing text components (JTextField, JTextArea, JPasswordField, JEditorPane) don't use the UndoableEditSupport class because they inherit the undoable edit capability from the TextComponent class. The UndoableEditSupport class is generally used to add an undoable edit functionality to a component that wouldn't normally have it.

Syntax:	public class UndoableEditSupport extends Object
Package:	javax.swing.undo
Class hierarchy:	Object—UndoableEditSupport
	UndoableEditSupport is a direct subclass of Object. An UndoableEditSupport object has access to Object class methods.
Introduced:	JDK 1.2

Constructors

```
public UndoableEditSupport()
public UndoableEditSupport(Object eventSource)
```

The UndoableEditSupport class provides two public constructors for creating UndoableEditSupport objects. If the `eventSource` parameter is provided, this will be the source for any UndoableEditEvents fired by the UndoableEditSupport object. Otherwise, the UndoableEditSupport object itself will be the event source.

Fields

protected int `updateLevel`
protected CompoundEdit `compoundEdit`
protected Vector `listeners`
protected Object `realSource`

`updateLevel` indicates the current nesting level of `beginUpdate()`—`endUpdate()` method calls. If the `beginUpdate()` method is called, the `updateLevel` field is incremented by one. If the `endUpdate()` method is called, the `updateLevel` field is decremented by one.

`compoundEdit` is a CompoundEdit object containing a series of smaller undoable edits.

`listeners` contains the listener list of the UndoableEditSupport object.

`realSource` represents the event source for any UndoableEditEvents fired by the UndoableEditSupport object. This will either be the UndoableEditSupport object itself or some other object that was specified in the UndoableEditSupport constructor.

UndoableEditSupport Class Methods

protected void `_postEdit(UndoableEdit edit)`
public void `addUndoableEditListener(UndoableEditListener listener)`
public void `beginUpdate()`
protected CompoundEdit `createCompoundEdit()`
public void `endUpdate()`
public int `getUpdateLevel()`
public void `postEdit(UndoableEdit edit)`
public void `removeUndoableEditListener(UndoableEditListener listener)`
public String `toString()`

`_postEdit()` is called by the `postEdit()` and `endUpdate()` methods. This method creates an UndoableEditEvent object and sends it to all registered UndoableEditListeners.

`addUndoableEditListener()` adds an UndoableEditListener to the listener list managed by the UndoableEditSupport object.

`beginUpdate()` increments the `updateLevel` field by one. If the `updateLevel` field was zero, the `createCompoundEdit()` method is called to create a CompoundEdit object.

`createCompoundEdit()` is called only by the `beginUpdate()` method. It returns a CompoundEdit object that will contain subsequent edits.

`endUpdate()` decrements the `updateLevel` field by one. If the `updateLevel` field was one, the `_postEdit()` method is called to fire an UndoableEditEvent.

`getUpdateLevel()` returns the current value of the `updateLevel` field.

`postEdit()` checks the current value of the `updateLevel` field. If the `updateLevel` field is zero, the `postEdit()` method calls the `_postEdit()` method to fire an UndoableEditEvent. If the `updateLevel` field is not zero, it adds the UndoableEdit that was passed to the method to a CompoundEdit object to be fired later.

`removeUndoableEditListener()` removes the specified UndoableEditListener from the listener list managed by the UndoableEditSupport object.

`toString()` overrides the `toString()` method from the Object class to return a String representation of the UndoableEditSupport object.

Methods Inherited from the java.lang.Object Class

public final Class `getClass()`

`getClass()` returns a Class object representing the runtime class of the invoking object. In this case, it would return an object representing the javax.swing.undo.UndoableEditSupport class.

The other methods inherited from the Object class, `clone()`, `equals()`, `hashCode()`, `notify()`, `notifyAll()`, and `wait()`, are generally not used in conjunction with UndoableEditSupport Support objects.

EXAMPLE

In Example 7.2, an UndoableEditSupport object is used to give an "undoable" capability to a JCheckBox. The intent is that when a change is made to the selected state of a JCheckBox, the change is stored as an undoable edit. The UndoableJCheckBox class extends JCheckBox and adds an UndoableEditSupport object. This object allows the UndoableJCheckBox to register UndoableEditListeners and to fire UndoableEditEvents.

EXAMPLE 7.2 UNDOABLEJCHECKBOX CLASS

```
import javax.swing.*;
import java.awt.event.*;
import javax.swing.event.*;
import javax.swing.undo.*;

public class UndoableJCheckBox extends JCheckBox
{
/*  The UndoableJCheckBox class uses an UndoableEditSupport object */
/*  to provide an undoable capability to a JCheckBox.               */

   private UndoableEditSupport undoSupport;

/*  The constructor calls the JCheckBox constructor and then       */
/*  initializes the UndoableEditSupport object. The event source    */
/*  is set to be the UndoableJCheckBox object.                      */

   public UndoableJCheckBox(String title)
   {
      super(title);
      undoSupport = new UndoableEditSupport(this);
   }

/*  The UndoableEditSupport object is used to implement the methods */
/*  to add or remove an UndoableEditListener from the UndoableJCheckBox.*/

   public void addUndoableEditListener(UndoableEditListener listener)
   {
      undoSupport.addUndoableEditListener(listener);
   }

   public void removeUndoableEditListener(UndoableEditListener listener)
   {
      undoSupport.removeUndoableEditListener(listener);
   }

/*  The fireActionPerformed() method is overridden so that when the mouse  */
```

```
/* is pressed over the UndoableJCheckBox, an UndoableJCheckBoxEdit object */
/* is created and sent to any registered UndoableEditListeners.           */

   protected void fireActionPerformed(ActionEvent event)
   {
     super.fireActionPerformed(event);
     undoSupport.postEdit(new UndoableJCheckBoxEdit(this));
   }
}
```

An UndoableJCheckBox object needs to fire an UndoableEdit that contains some information about the selected state of the UndoableJCheckBox. This is accomplished by creating a user-defined undoable edit class that has this capability. The UndoableJCheckBoxEdit class extends the AbstractUndoableEdit class and adds variables to track and update the selected state of the UndoableJCheckBox object that generated the event. The UndoableJCheckBoxEdit is passed as an argument to the `postEdit()` method. The UndoableJCheckBoxEdit class listing is shown in Example 7.3.

EXAMPLE 7.3 UNDOABLEJCHECKBOXEDIT CLASS

```
import javax.swing.*;
import javax.swing.undo.*;

public class UndoableJCheckBoxEdit extends AbstractUndoableEdit
{
/* The UndoableJCheckBoxEdit class defines two variables, an    */
/* UndoableJCheckBox which serves as a reference to the object  */
/* that generated the event and a boolean which represents the  */
/* selected state of the event source.                          */

   private boolean selected;
   private UndoableJCheckBox jcb;

/* The UndoableJCheckBoxEdit constructor is passed a reference   */
/* to the object that generated the event.  The selected variable */
/* is set based on the selected state of the event source.       */

   public UndoableJCheckBoxEdit(UndoableJCheckBox checkbox)
   {
     jcb = checkbox;
     selected = jcb.isSelected();
   }

/* The redo() method is overridden to include a change to the   */
/* selected state of the event source.                          */
```

UndoableEditSupport Class

```
   public void redo() throws CannotRedoException
   {
      super.redo();
      jcb.setSelected(selected);
   }
/* The undo() method is overridden to include a change to the   */
/* selected state of the event source.                          */
   public void undo() throws CannotRedoException
   {
      super.undo();
      jcb.setSelected(!selected);
   }
}
```

The UndoableSuppDemo class shown in Example 7.4 demonstrates the use of our user-defined UndoableJCheckBox object. An UndoableJCheckBox object is placed on a JFrame and registers an UndoableEditListener. An UndoManager object is used to manage the list of undoable edits generated by the UndoableJCheckBox. A JMenu containing menu items to undo or redo the most recent edit is placed on top of the frame.

This class is very similar to the one used in Example 6.39 in the section "UndoableEditEvent Class" in Chapter 6. That example used a JTextArea, which inherits its undoable edit capability from the JTextComponent class.

EXAMPLE 7.4 UndoableSuppDemo Class

```
import javax.swing.*;
import java.awt.*;
import java.awt.event.*;
import javax.swing.event.*;
import javax.swing.undo.*;

public class UndoableSuppDemo extends JFrame
           implements UndoableEditListener, ActionListener
{
   private UndoableJCheckBox jcb;
   protected UndoManager undoManager;
   private JTextField jtf;
   private JMenuBar menuBar;
   private JMenu menu;
   private JMenuItem undoItem, redoItem;
```

```java
    public UndoableSuppDemo()
    {
/*  An UndoManager is created to manage undo and redo operations.    */

        undoManager = new UndoManager();

/*  An UndoableJCheckBox is created and placed on a JFrame.           */
/*  Because the UndoableJCheckBox class uses an UndoableEditSupport   */
/*  object, an UndoableJCheckBox object can register an               */
/*  UndoableEventListener.                                            */

        jcb = new UndoableJCheckBox("Jackson");
        jcb.addUndoableEditListener(this);

        jtf = new JTextField(15);
        jtf.setEditable(false);

/*  An "Edit" menu is created with "undo" and "redo" menu items.      */
/*  These menu items will initiate undo and redo actions to the       */
/*  text in the text area. The menu items are initially disabled      */
/*  until the user interacts with the UndoableJCheckBox object.       */

        undoItem = new JMenuItem("undo");
        undoItem.setEnabled(false);
        undoItem.addActionListener(this);

        redoItem = new JMenuItem("redo");
        redoItem.setEnabled(false);
        redoItem.addActionListener(this);

        menu = new JMenu("Edit");
        menu.add(undoItem);
        menu.add(redoItem);

        menuBar = new JMenuBar();
        menuBar.add(menu);

        JPanel panel = new JPanel();
        panel.add(jcb);

        getContentPane().add(panel, BorderLayout.CENTER);
        getContentPane().add(menuBar, BorderLayout.NORTH);
        getContentPane().add(jtf, BorderLayout.SOUTH);

        setDefaultCloseOperation(JFrame.EXIT_ON_CLOSE);
        setBounds(100, 100, 300, 250);
        setVisible(true);
    }
```

```
/* The UndoableEditDemo class serves as the UndoableEditListener,   */
/* so it provides an implementation of the undoableEditHappened()   */
/* method.  When the user checks or unchecks the UndoableJCheckBox, */
/* an UndoableEditEvent is generated and sent to this method.       */
/* The method adds the edit to the list managed by the UndoManager. */
/* The "undo" and "redo" menu items are enabled or disabled depending */
/* on whether subsequent undo and redo operations are possible.     */

   public void undoableEditHappened(UndoableEditEvent event)
   {
      undoManager.addEdit(event.getEdit());
      redoItem.setEnabled(undoManager.canRedo());
      undoItem.setEnabled(undoManager.canUndo());
   }

/* The actionPerformed() method responds to the selection of the    */
/* "undo" and "redo" menu items.  If the "undo" menu item was       */
/* selected, the UndoManager attempts to undo the last undoable     */
/* edit in its list.  If the "redo" menu item was chosen, the       */
/* UndoManager tries to redo (undo the undo).  After the actions    */
/* are taken, the menu items are enabled or disabled depending      */
/* on whether subsequent undo and redo operations are possible.     */

   public void actionPerformed(ActionEvent event)
   {
      if ( event.getActionCommand().equals("undo") )
      {
         try
         {
            undoManager.undo();
            redoItem.setEnabled(undoManager.canRedo());
            undoItem.setEnabled(undoManager.canUndo());
         }
         catch (CannotUndoException cue)
         {
            jtf.setText("can't undo");
         }
      }
      if ( event.getActionCommand().equals("redo") )
      {
         try
         {
            undoManager.redo();
            redoItem.setEnabled(undoManager.canRedo());
            undoItem.setEnabled(undoManager.canUndo());
         }
```

```
         catch (CannotRedoException cre)
         {
            jtf.setText("can't redo");
         }
      }
   }

   public static void main(String args[])
   {
      UndoableSuppDemo demo = new UndoableSuppDemo();
   }
}
```

When you run this example, a frame with a checkbox appears on your screen. Select the Edit menu. Initially, neither of the menu options are enabled. Select the checkbox with the mouse. Now look at the Edit menu. The undo option has become available. Select the undo option. The checkbox becomes unchecked, the undo option becomes disabled, and the redo option now becomes available. The UndoManager object can store any number of checkbox selections and deselections. Try checking and unchecking the checkbox several times. Now, when you select the undo option, both the undo and redo options become available, meaning that you can go both forward and backwards in the undoable edit chain.

This is a relatively simple example using a simple component, but there is no reason why any component can't be given an undoable capability using the UndoableEditSupport class.

VetoableChangeSupport Class

The VetoableChangeSupport class is a utility class that makes it easier for Java Beans or other components to fire property change events associated with attempts to change constrained properties and allows these components to easily manage a list of registered VetoableChangeListeners. To use the VetoableChangeSupport class, a VetoableChangeSupport object should be included as a data member of the object that will generate the vetoable PropertyChangeEvent.

Syntax: public class VetoableChangeSupport extends Object implements Serializable

Package:	java.beans
Class hierarchy:	Object—VetoableChangeSupport
	VetoableChangeSupport is a direct subclass of Object. A VetoableChangeSupport object has access to Object class methods.
Introduced:	JDK 1.1

Constructors

```
public VetoableChangeSupport(Object source)
```

The VetoableChangeSupport class provides one public constructor for creating VetoableChangeSupport objects. The `source` parameter identifies the object that is designated to be the source of any PropertyChangeEvents generated by the VetoableChangeSupport object.

VetoableChangeSupport Class Methods

public void addVetoableChangeListener(VetoableChangeListener listener)
public void addVetoableChangeListener(String propertyName, VetoableChangeListener listener)
public void fireVetoableChange(PropertyChangeEvent event)
public void fireVetoableChange(String propertyName, boolean oldValue, boolean newValue)
public void fireVetoableChange(String propertyName, int oldValue, int newValue)
public void fireVetoableChange(String propertyName, Object oldValue, Object newValue)
public boolean hasListeners(String propertyName)
public void removeVetoableChangeListener(VetoableChangeListener listener)
public void removeVetoableChangeListener(String propertyName, VetoableChangeListener listener)

`addVetoableChangeListener()` adds the specified VetoableChange‑Listener to the listener list managed by the VetoableChangeSupport object. If a property name is given, the listener will only be called when the `firePropertyChange()` method is used with that property name. If no property name is provided, the listener is registered for all properties.

`fireVetoableChange()` sends a PropertyChangeEvent to any registered listeners. It can do this either by using an existing PropertyChangeEvent or by sending the property name along with the old and new values.

`hasListeners()` returns true if there are any listeners registered to the specified property.

`removeVetoableChangeListener()` removes a VetoableChangeListener from the listener list managed by the VetoableChangeSupport object. If a property name is provided, the method will only remove the listener for that property. Otherwise, it will remove the listener from all properties.

Methods Inherited from the java.lang.Object Class

> public final Class `getClass()`

`getClass()` returns a Class object representing the runtime class of the invoking object. In this case, it would return an object representing the java.beans.VetoableChangeSupport class.

The other methods inherited from the Object class, `clone()`, `equals()`, `hashCode()`, `notify()`, `notifyAll()`, and `wait()`, are generally not used in conjunction with VetoableChangeSupport objects.

EXAMPLE

Example 7.5 is a revision of Example 6.30 in the "PropertyChangeEvent Class" of Chapter 6. The color property in the FontColor object is now implemented as a constrained property. Any changes to the color are first checked to see if they are acceptable before they are implemented.

The constrained property functionality is provided by a VetoableChangeSupport object. This object is an instance variable of the FontColor2 class. The VetoableChangeSupport object can fire vetoable PropertyChangeEvents and manages a list of VetoableChangeListener objects.

As with Example 6.30, this program consists of three classes. The first class, FontColor2, is a Java Bean that contains Color, PropertyChangeSupport, and VetoableChangeSupport objects as instance variables. The Color object is intended to serve as the text color for a JLabel and is meant to be a constrained property.

When a FontColor2 object calls its `setColor()` method, the VetoableChangeSupport object is used to determine if the change is acceptable. In this example, any change that is not to the color green is acceptable. The VetoableChangeSupport object fires a PropertyChangeEvent containing the proposed change to any registered VetoableChangeListener objects. If the change is unacceptable, an exception is thrown. If the change is acceptable, the color associated with the FontColor2 object is updated and the PropertyChangeSupport object fires a PropertyChangeEvent to any registered PropertyChangeListeners.

The VetoableChangeSupport and PropertyChangeSupport objects are also used to maintain a list of any registered VetoableChangeListener and PropertyChangeListener objects. The code listing for the FontColor2 class is given in Example 7.5.

EXAMPLE 7.5 FONTCOLOR2 CLASS

```
import javax.swing.*;
import java.awt.*;
import java.beans.*;

public class FontColor2
{
   private Color color;
   private PropertyChangeSupport pcs;
   private VetoableChangeSupport vcs;
   private Component parent;

   public FontColor2(Color c, Component p)
   {
/* The FontColor2 constructor initializes the Color variable as well  */
/* as PropertyChangeSupport and VetoableChangeSupport objects.        */
/* A parent component is passed to the constructor so a JOptionPane   */
/* can be displayed if a an attempt is made to change the color to    */
/* a forbidden value.  In this example, the color green is forbidden  */

      color = c;
      pcs = new PropertyChangeSupport(this);
      vcs = new VetoableChangeSupport(this);
```

```
      parent = p;
   }

   public Color getColor()
   {
      return color;
   }

/* The Color object is implemented as a constrained property. When  */
/* the setColor() method is called, the VetoableChangeSupport       */
/* object fires a PropertyChangeEvent object to any registered      */
/* VetoableChangeListeners.  These listeners determine if the       */
/* proposed change is acceptable.  If it is not, a                  */
/* PropertyVetoException is thrown.  If the change is acceptable,   */
/* the color instance variable is updated with the change and a     */
/* PropertyChangeEvent is sent to any registered                    */
/* PropertyChangeListeners.                                         */

   public void setColor(Color c)
   {
      Color oldColor = color;
      try
      {
         vcs.fireVetoableChange("color", oldColor, c);
         color = c;
      }
      catch (PropertyVetoException pve)
      {
         JOptionPane.showMessageDialog(parent, pve.getMessage());
      }

      pcs.firePropertyChange("color", oldColor, color);
   }

/* For the FontColor2 class to be able to register and/or disconnect */
/* a PropertyChangeListener or VetoableChangeListener, it has to     */
/* provide methods to add and remove those listeners.  The           */
/* PropertyChangeSupport object is used to manage the                */
/* PropertyChangeListener lists and the VetoableChangeSupport object */
/* is used to manage the VetoableChangeListener lists.               */

   public void addPropertyChangeListener(PropertyChangeListener listener)
   {
      pcs.addPropertyChangeListener(listener);
   }
```

```
    public void removePropertyChangeListener(PropertyChangeListener listener)
    {
       pcs.removePropertyChangeListener(listener);
    }

    public void addVetoableChangeListener(VetoableChangeListener listener)
    {
       vcs.addVetoableChangeListener(listener);
    }

    public void removeVetoableChangeListener(VetoableChangeListener listener)
    {
       vcs.removeVetoableChangeListener(listener);
    }
}
```

The NewLabel2 class in Example 7.6 is a JLabel that uses a FontColor2 object to initialize and update the text color of the label. The FontColor2 object registers both a PropertyChangeListener and VetoableChangeListener in the FontColor2 constructor.

The NewLabel2 class serves as its own VetoableChangeListener by implementing the `vetoableChange()` method. When a PropertyChangeEvent is sent to this method, it determines whether the change is acceptable. In this case, it is not acceptable to change the Color object associated with a FontColor2 object to green. If an attempt is made to do this, a PropertyVetoException is thrown.

EXAMPLE 7.6 NEWLABEL2 CLASS

```
import javax.swing.*;
import java.awt.*;
import java.beans.*;

public class NewLabel2 extends JLabel implements PropertyChangeListener,
                                                 VetoableChangeListener
{
   private FontColor2 fontColor;

   public NewLabel2(String str, FontColor2 fc)
   {
      super(str);
      fontColor = fc;
      setForeground(fontColor.getColor());
```

```
   /* When a NewLabel2 object is created, its FontColor object registers  */
   /* both a PropertyChangeListener and a VetoableChangeListener.         */
   /* These two listeners are used to implement the color associated      */
   /* with the FontColor object as a constrained property.                */

      fontColor.addPropertyChangeListener(this);
      fontColor.addVetoableChangeListener(this);
   }

   public FontColor2 getFontColor()
   {
      return fontColor;
   }

   public void setFontColor(FontColor2 fc)
   {
      fontColor = fc;
   }

   /* The NewLabel2 class serves as a PropertyChangeListener and thus */
   /* provides an implementation of the propertyChange() method.  If */
   /* the PropertyChangeEvent was due to a change in the "color"     */
   /* property, the text color of the NewLabel is changed.           */

   public void propertyChange(PropertyChangeEvent event)
   {
      if ( event.getPropertyName().equals("color") )
      {
         setForeground( (Color)event.getNewValue() );
      }
   }


   /* The NewLabel class also serves as a VetoableChangeListener and   */
   /* thus provides an implementation of the vetoableChange() method.  */
   /* This method determines if the proposed change is unacceptable.   */
   /* If it is, a PropertyVetoException is thrown.                     */

   public void vetoableChange(PropertyChangeEvent event)
                   throws PropertyVetoException
   {
      if ( event.getPropertyName().equals("color") )
      {
         Color color = (Color)event.getNewValue();
         if ( color.equals(Color.green) )
         {
            throw new PropertyVetoException("Green is forbidden", event);
         }
      }
   }
}
```

The VetoableChangeDemo class in Example 7.7 is the driver class for this example. This class creates a FontColor2 object, which is used to initialize three NewLabel objects. The NewLabel objects are placed on a JFrame along with a JComboBox. The JComboBox is used to select a new font color and is registered with an ItemListener.

When the user makes a color selection in the JComboBox, and ItemEvent is generated and sent to the `itemStateChanged()` method. In this method, the FontColor object that was used to initialize the NewLabel objects calls its `setColor()` method, passing the method the color that was selected. The `setColor()` method determines if the proposed color change is acceptable and, if so, changes the color of the FontColor object and fires a PropertyChangeEvent.

EXAMPLE 7.7 VETOABLECHANGEDEMO CLASS

```
import javax.swing.*;
import java.awt.*;
import java.awt.event.*;

public class VetoableChangeDemo extends JFrame implements ItemListener
{
   NewLabel2 label1, label2, label3;
   FontColor2 fontColor;
   JComboBox jcb;

   public VetoableChangeDemo()
   {
/* A FontColor2 object is created.  This object maintains a Color   */
/* object as a constrained property.                                */

      fontColor = new FontColor2(Color.black, this);

/* Three NewLabel objects are created and placed on a JFrame.  The  */
/* NewLabel class is a JLabel that uses a FontColor object to set   */
/* the color of the label text.                                     */

      label1 = new NewLabel2("hello", fontColor);
      label1.setFont(new Font("Serif", Font.BOLD, 14));

      label2 = new NewLabel2("there", fontColor);
      label2.setFont(new Font("Serif", Font.BOLD, 14));

      label3 = new NewLabel2("boys", fontColor);
      label3.setFont(new Font("Serif", Font.BOLD, 14));

/* A JComboBox is used to change the color of the NewLabel object text */
/* The JComboBox registers an ItemListener.                            */
```

```java
        String[] colorList = {"black", "red", "blue", "green"};
        jcb = new JComboBox(colorList);
        jcb.setSelectedIndex(0);
        jcb.addItemListener(this);

        JPanel centerPanel = new JPanel();
        centerPanel.add(label1);
        centerPanel.add(label2);
        centerPanel.add(label3);

        JPanel southPanel = new JPanel();
        southPanel.add(jcb);

        getContentPane().add(centerPanel, BorderLayout.CENTER);
        getContentPane().add(southPanel, BorderLayout.WEST);

        setDefaultCloseOperation(JFrame.EXIT_ON_CLOSE);
        setBounds(100, 100, 300, 200);
        setVisible(true);
    }

    /*  Since the VetoableChangeDemo class serves as the ItemListener,   */
    /*  it provides an implementation of the itemStateChanged() method.  */
    /*  The FontColor2 object calls its setColor() method passing it the */
    /*  selected color.                                                  */

    public void itemStateChanged(ItemEvent event)
    {
        JComboBox comboBox = (JComboBox)event.getItemSelectable();
        String color = (String)comboBox.getSelectedItem();
        if ( color.equals("black") )
             fontColor.setColor(Color.black);
        if ( color.equals("red") )
             fontColor.setColor(Color.red);
        if ( color.equals("blue") )
             fontColor.setColor(Color.blue);
        if ( color.equals("green") )
             fontColor.setColor(Color.green);

    /*  If the color change is vetoed, the label text color is reset to  */
    /*  its previous value.  This next block of code insures that the    */
    /*  current selection of the JComboBox will be reset as well.        */

        Color c = fontColor.getColor();
        if ( c.equals(Color.black) )
            comboBox.setSelectedIndex(0);
        if ( c.equals(Color.red) )
            comboBox.setSelectedIndex(1);
        if ( c.equals(Color.blue) )
            comboBox.setSelectedIndex(2);
        if ( c.equals(Color.green) )
            comboBox.setSelectedIndex(3);
    }
```

```
   public static void main(String args[])
   {
      VetoableChangeDemo demo = new VetoableChangeDemo();
   }
}
```

When you run this example, a frame appears with a JComboBox and the text "Hello there boys." The text is actually comprised of three different labels. When you select black, red, or blue in the JComboBox, the color of the labels is updated to that color. Try selecting green in the JComboBox. The color property is constrained to reject the color green, so a JOptionPane dialog appears informing you that green is forbidden. The color of the NewLabels and the selected value in the combo box revert to their former values.

8

EVENT LISTENER INTERFACES

An event listener interface defines the functionality that is implemented by an event listener. The event listener will either implement the listener interface directly or indirectly by extending an event listener adapter class. The listener interfaces declare the methods that must be implemented by an event listener class. The good news is that the methods can be written to do whatever is necessary for a given application. The good news is also that the developer has complete freedom over what the methods do. The bad news is you have to do all of the work yourself. The only default implementation of the methods declared by the listener interfaces are the stub methods provided by the listener adapter classes.

This chapter provides a complete description of the listener interfaces contained in the java.awt.event, javax.swing.event, and java.beans packages. It also provides the specification of the EventListener interface defined in the java.util package, which is the parent interface for all other listener interfaces. The information provided includes the interface syntax, hierarchy, package, and when it was introduced to the Java language. The methods declared by each interface, as well as the methods used to add or remove the listener from the listener list managed by an event source, are presented. An example that demonstrates how to use the listener to create a powerful GUI application is provided for every listener type.

ActionListener Interface

The ActionListener interface declares one method that is used to process ActionEvent objects. The method, `actionPerformed()`, is called whenever an ActionEvent object is generated by an event source that has registered the ActionListener. This method is overridden to contain code to respond to the action that caused the event. Because the ActionListener interface has only one method, it does not have a corresponding adapter class.

Any class object can serve as an ActionListener by implementing the ActionListener interface. The syntax for doing this is

```
public class MyClass implements ActionListener
```

Class MyClass would then provide an implementation of the `actionPerformed()` method.

For an ActionListener to receive an ActionEvent generated by a component, the component must register the ActionListener. The component does this by adding the ActionListener to its listener list using the `addActionListener()` method. To disconnect an ActionListener from a component, the component must remove the ActionListener from its listener list by invoking the `removeActionListener()` method. The ActionListener that was removed will no longer receive ActionEvents generated by the component.

Syntax:	public interface ActionListener extends EventListener
Package:	java.awt.event
Interface hierarchy:	EventListener — ActionListener
	The ActionListener interface is a subinterface of EventListener. The EventListener interface does not declare any methods. It is used as a marker to indicate that its subinterfaces are event listeners.
Introduced:	JDK 1.1

ActionListener Interface Methods

`public void actionPerformed(ActionEvent ae)`

`actionPerformed()` is called when an ActionEvent object is generated by an event source that has registered the ActionListener. The method is passed a reference to the ActionEvent object that was generated.

Listener Registration Methods

```
public void addActionListener(ActionListener al)
public void removeActionListener(ActionListener al)
```

`addActionListener()` adds an ActionListener to the invoking component's listener list. An ActionEvent generated by the component will be sent to the `actionPerformed()` method of the ActionListener.

`removeActionListener()` removes an ActionListener from the invoking component's listener list. The ActionListener will no longer be notified when the component generates an ActionEvent.

The `addActionListener()` and `removeActionListener()` methods are defined in the following classes and interfaces:

- AbstractButton class
- BasicComboBoxEditor class
- Button class
- ButtonModel interface
- ComboBoxEditor interface
- DefaultButtonModel class
- JComboBox class
- JFileChooser class
- JTextField class
- List class
- MenuItem class
- TextField class
- Timer class

EXAMPLE

See Chapter 6, "Event Classes and Interfaces," Example 6.1, in the section "ActionEvent Class," where ActionListeners are used to process ActionEvents generated from several sources.

AdjustmentListener Interface

The AdjustmentListener interface declares one method used to process AdjustmentEvent objects. The method, `adjustmentValueChanged()`, is called whenever an AdjustmentEvent object is generated by an event source that has registered the AdjustmentListener. This method is overridden to contain code that responds to the change in value of the Adjustable object that caused the event. Because the AdjustmentListener interface has only one method, it does not have a corresponding adapter class.

Any class object can serve as an AdjustmentListener by implementing the AdjustmentListener interface. The syntax for doing this is

```
public class MyClass implements AdjustmentListener
```

Class MyClass would then provide an implementation of the `adjustmentValueChanged()` method.

For an AdjustmentListener to receive an AdjustmentEvent generated by a component, the component must register the AdjustmentListener. The component does this by adding the AdjustmentListener to its listener list using the `addAdjustmentListener()` method. To disconnect an AdjustmentListener from a component, the component must remove the AdjustmentListener from its listener list by invoking the `removeAdjustmentListener()` method. The AdjustmentListener that was removed will no longer receive AdjustmentEvents generated by the component.

Syntax:	public interface AdjustmentListener extends EventListener
Package:	java.awt.event
Interface hierarchy:	EventListener—AdjustmentListener
	The AdjustmentListener interface is part of the AWT event listener hierarchy.
Introduced:	JDK 1.1

AdjustmentListener Interface Methods

```
public void adjustmentValueChanged(AdjustmentEvent event)
```

`adjustmentValueChanged()` is called when an AdjustmentEvent object is generated by an event source that has registered the AdjustmentListener. The method is passed a reference to the AdjustmentEvent object that was generated.

Listener Registration Methods

```
public void addAdjustmentListener(AdjustmentListener listener)
public void removeAdjustmentListener(AdjustmentListener listener)
```

`addAdjustmentListener()` adds an AdjustmentListener to the invoking component's listener list. An AdjustmentEvent generated by the component will be sent to the `adjustmentValueChanged()` method of the AdjustmentListener.

`removeAdjustmentListener()` removes an AdjustmentListener from the invoking component's listener list. The AdjustmentListener will no longer be notified when the component generates an AdjustmentEvent.

The `addAdjustmentListener()` and `removeAdjustmentListener()` methods are defined in the following classes and interfaces:

- Adjustable interface
- Scrollbar class
- JScrollBar class

One interesting thing to note is that a JSlider component does not generate AdjustmentEvents when its value is changed. This might seem odd, since a JSlider is an object whose value can be adjusted. The JSlider object will generate a ChangeEvent when this happens.

EXAMPLE

See Chapter 6, Example 6.6, in the section "AdjustmentEvent Class," where an AdjustmentListener is used to react to changes in the value of a JScrollBar.

AncestorListener Interface

The AncestorListener interface declares methods used to process AncestorEvent objects. These occur whenever an ancestor in a Swing component's hierarchy is added, removed, moved, or changes its visible state. An ancestor would be a component's container, its container's container, and so on. The interface defines three methods, one of which will be called whenever an

AncestorEvent is generated from an event source that has registered the AncestorListener. Although the AncestorListener declares three methods, it does not have a corresponding adapter class.

Any class object can serve as an AncestorListener by implementing the AncestorListener interface. The syntax for doing this is

```
public class MyClass implements AncestorListener
```

Class MyClass would then provide an implementation of the methods declared in the AncestorListener interface.

For an AncestorListener to receive an AncestorEvent generated by a component, the component must register the AncestorListener. The component does this by adding the AncestorListener to its listener list using the `addAncestorListener()` method. To disconnect an AncestorListener from a component, the component must remove the AncestorListener from its listener list by invoking the `removeAncestorListener()` method. The AncestorListener that was removed will no longer receive AncestorEvents generated by the component.

Syntax:	public interface AncestorListener extends EventListener
Package:	javax.swing.event
Interface hierarchy:	EventListener—AncestorListener
	The AncestorListener interface is part of the Swing event listener hierarchy.
Introduced:	JDK 1.2

AncestorListener Interface Methods

public void `ancestorAdded(AncestorEvent event)`
public void `ancestorMoved(AncestorEvent event)`
public void `ancestorRemoved(AncestorEvent event)`

These methods are used to process the three types of AncestorEvents. They are implemented by the AncestorListener to contain whatever code is necessary to process the event.

`ancestorAdded()` is called when the event source or an ancestor of the event source becomes visible. This can be accomplished either by the component calling the `setVisible()` method or by it being added to the component hierarchy.

`ancestorMoved()` is invoked when the event source or one of its ancestors is moved.

`ancestorRemoved()` is called when the event source or an ancestor of the event source becomes invisible. This can be accomplished either by the component calling the `setVisible()` method or by it being removed from the component hierarchy.

Listener Registration Methods

> public void addAncestorListener(AncestorListener listener)
>
> public void removeAncestorListener(AncestorListener listener)

`addAncestorListener()` adds an AncestorListener to the invoking component's listener list. An AncestorEvent generated by the component will be sent to one of the three methods defined by the AncestorListener.

`removeAncestorListener()` removes an AncestorListener from the invoking component's listener list. The AncestorListener will no longer be notified when the component generates an AncestorEvent.

The `addAncestorListener()` and `removeAncestorListener()` methods are defined in the JComponent class.

EXAMPLE

See Chapter 6, Example 6.7, in the section "AncestorEvent Class," where an AncestorListener is used to monitor movements of a JButton object's ancestor components.

AWTEventListener Interface

The AWTEventListener interface declares one method, `eventDispatched()`, that is used to receive any event from the AWTEvent hierarchy that is generated from a Component or MenuComponent subclass object. It is used to passively monitor events being dispatched in the AWT.

This is a unique listener class that is used for such things as event recorders for automated testing and facilities such as the Java Accessibility package. Most applications will not use this class.

Syntax: public interface AWTEventListener extends EventListener
Package: java.awt.event
Interface hierarchy: EventListener—AWTEventListener

The AWTEventListener interface is part of the AWT event listener hierarchy.

Introduced: JDK 1.2

AWTEventListener Interface Methods

```
public void eventDispatched(AWTEvent event)
```

The `eventDispatched()` method is called whenever an event is dispatched in the AWT. The method is passed a reference to the AWTEvent object that was generated. This method is overridden by the class that implements the AWTEventListener interface to contain whatever code will be used to process the event.

Listener Registration Methods

```
public void addAWTEventListener(AWTEventListener listener, long eventMask)
```
```
public void removeAWTEventListener(AWTEventListener listener, long eventMask)
```

These methods are defined in the java.awt.Toolkit class and are used to register or disconnect an AWTEventListener to an instance of the Toolkit class. They are passed a reference to the AWTEventListener as an argument, as well as a bit mask of the event types to be received.

EXAMPLE

In Example 8.1, an AWTEventListener is used to passively monitor ActionEvent objects that occur when any of three buttons are pressed. The

AWTEventListener Interface

AWTEventListener is not explicitly registered to one or more components but instead monitors the entire system for ActionEvents. A Toolkit object is used to call the `addAWTEventListener()` method. The Toolkit object is obtained using the static `getDefaultToolkit()` method.

EXAMPLE 8.1 AWTEventListener Interface

```
import java.awt.*;
import java.awt.event.*;

public class AWTEventListenerDemo extends Frame
{
   private Button button1, button2, button3;
   private TextField tf;
   private int count;

   public AWTEventListenerDemo()
   {

/* Three buttons and a TextField are placed on a frame    */

      button1 = new Button("button1");
      button2 = new Button("button1");
      button3 = new Button("button1");

      tf = new TextField(20);
      tf.setEditable(false);

      Panel panel = new Panel();
      panel.add(button1);
      panel.add(button2);
      panel.add(button3);
      add(panel, BorderLayout.CENTER);
      add(tf, BorderLayout.SOUTH);

/* A Toolkit object is obtained and it is used to register an  */
/* AWTEventListener to passively listen for ActionEvents.      */

      Toolkit.getDefaultToolkit().addAWTEventListener(
            new AWTEventHandler(), AWTEvent.ACTION_EVENT_MASK);

      addWindowListener(new WinAdapter());
      setBounds(100, 100, 300, 200);
      setVisible(true);
   }

/* The AWTEventListener is implemented as an inner class.  Whenever  */
/* an ActionEvent is generated by any source, it is sent to the      */
/* eventDispatched() method.  In this case, the method has been      */
```

```
/*   overridden to keep a running count of the number of ActionEvents  */
/*   that have been generated.                                         */

   class AWTEventHandler implements AWTEventListener
   {
      public void eventDispatched(AWTEvent event)
      {
         ++count;
         tf.setText("Buttons pressed "+count+" times");
      }
   }

   public static void main(String args[])
   {
      AWTEventListenerDemo demo = new AWTEventListenerDemo();
   }
}

/*   This makes sure the application terminates if the window is closed   */

class WinAdapter extends WindowAdapter
{
   public void windowClosing(WindowEvent event)
   {
      System.exit(0);
   }
}
```

When the application is run, three buttons and a blank textfield appear on the screen. Whenever a button is pressed, an ActionEvent is generated and sent to the `eventDispatched()` method. This method keeps a running total of the number of ActionEvents that have been generated.

CaretListener Interface

The CaretListener interface declares one method, `caretUpdate()`, that is used to process CaretEvents. These occur when the caret position changes inside a Swing text component. The caret is the cursor that appears inside the text area of a text component. Using a CaretListener is often the easiest way to keep track of the caret position as well as any changes to the selected text within a Swing text component. With a CaretListener, the program does not need to access a Caret component directly.

Any class object can serve as a CaretListener by implementing the CaretListener interface. The syntax for doing this is

```
public class MyClass implements CaretListener
```

Class MyClass would then provide an implementation of the `caretUpdate()` method declared in the CaretListener interface.

For a CaretListener to receive a CaretEvent generated by a Swing text component, the component must register the CaretListener. The component does this by adding the CaretListener to its listener list using the `addCaretListener()` method. To disconnect a CaretListener from a component, the component must remove the CaretListener from its listener list by invoking the `removeCaretListener()` method. The CaretListener that was removed will no longer receive CaretEvents generated by the Swing text component.

Syntax: public interface CaretListener extends EventListener

Package: javax.swing.event

Interface hierarchy: EventListener—CaretListener

The CaretListener interface is part of the Swing event listener hierarchy.

Introduced: JDK 1.2

CaretListener Interface Methods

public void `caretUpdate(CaretEvent event)`

`caretUpdate()` is called whenever the caret position changes in a Swing text component to which the CaretListener has been registered.

Listener Registration Methods

public void `addCaretListener(CaretListener listener)`

public void `removeCaretListener(CaretListener listener)`

`addCaretListener()` adds a CaretListener to the invoking component's listener list. A CaretEvent generated by the component will be sent to the `caretUpdate()` method of the CaretListener.

`removeCaretListener()` removes a CaretListener from the invoking component's listener list. The CaretListener will no longer be notified when the component generates a CaretEvent.

The `addCaretListener()` and `removeCaretListener()` methods are defined in the JTextComponent class.

EXAMPLE

See Chapter 6, Example 6.8, in the section "CaretEvent Class," where a CaretListener is used to monitor changes to the caret position and selected text of a JTextField.

CellEditorListener Interface

The CellEditorListener declares methods that are used to process ChangeEvents that occur when a CellEditor ends or cancels an editing session. A CellEditor is most commonly associated with the JTable and JTree components. The difference between ending and canceling is that when an editing session is canceled, any changes made are not saved. The methods in the CellEditorListener can be overridden to detect the end of an editing session or to provide some additional functionality at the end of a cell editing session.

Any class object can serve as a CellEditorListener by implementing the CellEditorListener interface. The syntax for doing this is

```
public class MyClass implements CellEditorListener
```

Class MyClass would then provide an implementation of the methods declared in the CellEditorListener interface.

For a CellEditorListener to receive a ChangeEvent generated by a CellEditor, the CellEditor must register the CellEditorListener. The CellEditor does this by adding the CellEditorListener to its listener list, using the `addCellEditorListener()` method. To disconnect a CellEditorListener from a CellEditor, the CellEditor must remove the CellEditorListener from its listener list by invoking the `removeCellEditorListener()` method. The CellEditorListener that was removed will no longer receive ChangeEvents generated by the CellEditor.

Syntax:	public interface CellEditorListener extends EventListener
Package:	javax.swing.event
Interface hierarchy:	EventListener—CellEditorListener
	The CellEditorListener interface is part of the Swing event listener hierarchy.
Introduced:	JDK 1.2

CellEditorListener Interface Methods

```
public void editingCanceled(ChangeEvent event)
public void editingStopped(ChangeEvent event)
```

`editingCanceled()` is called whenever the cell editor cancels editing. Any changes that were made are not saved.

`editingStopped()` is called when the cell editor stops editing. When an editor stops editing, any changes made are saved.

Listener Registration Methods

```
public void addCellEditorListener(CellEditorListener listener)
public void removeCellEditorListener(CellEditorListener listener)
```

`addCellEditorListener()` adds a CellEditorListener to the invoking CellEditor's listener list. A ChangeEvent generated by the CellEditor will be sent to either the `editingCanceled()` or `editingStopped()` method of the CellEditorListener.

`removeCellEditorListener()` removes a CellEditorListener from the invoking CellEditor's listener list. The CellEditorListener will no longer be notified when the CellEditor generates a ChangeEvent.

The `addCellEditorListener()` and `removeCellEditorListener()` methods are defined in the following classes and interfaces:

- CellEditor interface
- DefaultTreeCellEditor class
- AbstractCellEditor class

EXAMPLE

Example 8.2 uses a CellEditorListener to determine how a cell editing session has ended. A JTree is placed on a JFrame. A DefaultTreeCellEditor is assigned to the JTree, and the cell editor registers a CellEditorListener.

When a user ends a cell editing session by pressing the Return or Enter key, the editing session is stopped and a ChangeEvent is sent to the `editingStopped()` method. Any changes made to the cell are saved. If the user ends a cell editing session by selecting a different node, the editing session is canceled and a ChangeEvent is sent to the `editingCanceled()` method. Any changes made to the cell are not saved if the editing session is canceled.

EXAMPLE 8.2 CELLEDITORLISTENER INTERFACE

```
import javax.swing.*;
import javax.swing.tree.*;
import javax.swing.event.*;
import java.awt.*;
import java.awt.event.*;

public class CellEditorDemo extends JFrame
{
   private JTree tree;
   private JTextField jtf;
   private DefaultTreeCellEditor editor;

   public CellEditorDemo()
   {
/* A Collection of DefaultMutableTreeNode objects are created that */
/* will form the components of a tree.                             */

      DefaultMutableTreeNode league =
            new DefaultMutableTreeNode("Soccer League");

      DefaultMutableTreeNode north =
             new DefaultMutableTreeNode("North Division");
      DefaultMutableTreeNode south =
             new DefaultMutableTreeNode("South Division");

      DefaultMutableTreeNode jets =
                new DefaultMutableTreeNode("Jets");
      DefaultMutableTreeNode raiders =
                new DefaultMutableTreeNode("Raiders");
      DefaultMutableTreeNode fins =
                new DefaultMutableTreeNode("Fins");
      DefaultMutableTreeNode shooters =
                new DefaultMutableTreeNode("Shooters");
      DefaultMutableTreeNode lions =
                new DefaultMutableTreeNode("Lions");
      DcfaultMutableTreeNode tigers -
                new DefaultMutableTreeNode("Tigers");

/* The node hierarchy is loaded into a DefaultTreeModel object.    */

      DefaultTreeModel model = new DefaultTreeModel(league);
```

CellEditorListener Interface

```
            model.insertNodeInto(north, league, 0);
            model.insertNodeInto(south, league, 1);
            model.insertNodeInto(jets, north, 0);
            model.insertNodeInto(raiders, north, 1);
            model.insertNodeInto(fins, north, 2);
            model.insertNodeInto(shooters, south, 0);
            model.insertNodeInto(lions, south, 1);
            model.insertNodeInto(tigers, south, 2);

   /* A DefaultTreeCellEditor is created and registers a CellEditorListener */

            editor = new DefaultTreeCellEditor(tree,
                             new DefaultTreeCellRenderer());
            editor.addCellEditorListener(new CellEditorHandler());

   /* A JTree object is created using the previously created tree model.  */

            tree = new JTree(model);
            tree.setShowsRootHandles(true);
            tree.expandRow(1);
            tree.setEditable(true);
            tree.setCellEditor(editor);
            tree.setInvokesStopCellEditing(false);

            jtf = new JTextField(20);
            jtf.setEditable(false);

            getContentPane().add( new JScrollPane(tree), BorderLayout.CENTER );
            getContentPane().add( jtf, BorderLayout.SOUTH );

            setDefaultCloseOperation(JFrame.EXIT_ON_CLOSE);
            setBounds(100, 100, 400, 300);
            setVisible(true);
      }

   /* The CellEditorListener is implemented as an inner class.         */
   /* When the user exits the cell editor by pressing the return       */
   /* key or clicking on another node, a ChangeEvent is generated      */
   /* and sent to either the editingCanceled() or editingStopped()     */
   /* methods.  A textfield is updated to indicate which operation     */
   /* has occurred.                                                    */

      class CellEditorHandler implements CellEditorListener
      {
         public void editingCanceled(ChangeEvent event)
         {
            jtf.setText("editing canceled");
         }

         public void editingStopped(ChangeEvent event)
         {
            jtf.setText("editing stopped");
```

```
        }
    }

    public static void main(String args[])
    {
        CellEditorDemo demo = new CellEditorDemo();
    }
}
```

When you run this example, a JTree object appears on your screen. Select a node and enter the cell editor by either clicking on the node three times or performing a click-pause-click operation. Change the name of the node and press the Return or Enter key. The node name is updated and the textfield indicates that the editing has been stopped. Now edit a different node. Change the name of the node and exit the editor by selecting a different node. The name of the edited node goes back to its original value and the textfield indicates that the editing session has been canceled.

ChangeListener Interface

The ChangeListener interface declares one method, `stateChanged()`, that is used to process ChangeEvents. A ChangeEvent is generated by a variety of Swing components when one of their component properties is changed. The `stateChanged()` method is overridden to respond to the property change that caused the event.

Any class object can serve as a ChangeListener by implementing the ChangeListener interface. The syntax for doing this is

```
public class MyClass implements ChangeListener
```

Class MyClass would then provide an implementation of the `stateChanged()` method declared in the ChangeListener interface.

For a ChangeListener to receive a ChangeEvent generated by a Swing component, the component must register the ChangeListener. The component does this by adding the ChangeListener to its listener list using the `addChangeListener()` method. To disconnect a ChangeListener from a Swing component, the component must remove the ChangeListener from its listener list by invoking the `removeChangeListener()` method. The ChangeListener that was removed will no longer receive ChangeEvents generated by the component.

Syntax: public interface ChangeListener extends EventListener
Package: javax.swing.event
Interface hierarchy: EventListener—ChangeListener

The ChangeListener interface is part of the Swing event listener hierarchy.

Introduced: JDK 1.2

ChangeListener Interface Methods

`public void stateChanged(ChangeEvent event)`

`stateChanged()` is called whenever a property has changed from a ChangeEvent source that has registered the ChangeListener.

Listener Registration Methods

`public void addChangeListener(ChangeListener listener)`
`public void removeChangeListener(ChangeListener listener)`

`addChangeListener()` adds a ChangeListener to the invoking component's listener list. A ChangeEvent generated by the component will be sent to the `stateChanged()` method of the ChangeListener.

`removeChangeListener()` removes a ChangeListener from the invoking component's listener list. The ChangeListener will no longer be notified when the component generates a ChangeEvent.

The `addChangeListener()` and `removeChangeListener()` methods are defined in the following classes and interfaces:

- AbstractButton class
- BoundedRangeModel interface
- ButtonModel interface
- Caret interface
- ColorSelectionModel interface
- DefaultBoundedRangeModel class
- DefaultButtonModel class
- DefaultCaret class

- DefaultColorSelectionModel class
- DefaultSingleSelectionModel class
- JProgressBar class
- JSlider class
- JTabbedPane class
- JViewport class
- MenuSelectionManager class
- SingleSelectionModel interface
- Style interface
- StyleContext class
- StyleContext.NamedStyle class

EXAMPLE

See Chapter 6, Example 6.9, in the section "ChangeEvent Class," where a ChangeListener is used to detect changes in the value of a JSlider component.

ComponentListener Interface

The ComponentListener interface declares methods for receiving and processing ComponentEvent objects. A ComponentEvent is generated whenever a component is moved, resized, made visible, or made invisible. The interface declares four methods, one of which is called whenever a ComponentEvent object is generated by an event source that has registered the ComponentListener. The methods in the ComponentListener interface can be overridden to place constraints on the movement, size, or visibility of components. The ComponentListener interface has a corresponding adapter class.

Any class object can serve as a ComponentListener by implementing the ComponentListener interface. The syntax for doing this is

```
public class MyClass implements ComponentListener
```

Class MyClass would then provide an implementation of the methods declared in the ComponentListener interface. A ComponentListener could also be created by extending the ComponentAdapter class.

For a ComponentListener to receive a ComponentEvent generated by a component, the component must register the ComponentListener. The component does this by adding the ComponentListener to its listener list using the `addComponentListener()` method. To disconnect a ComponentListener from a component, the component must remove the ComponentListener from its listener list by invoking the `removeComponentListener()` method. The ComponentListener that was removed will no longer receive ComponentEvents generated by the component.

Syntax: public interface ComponentListener extends EventListener

Package: java.awt.event

Interface hierarchy: EventListener—ComponentListener

The ComponentListener interface is part of the AWT event listener hierarchy.

Introduced: JDK 1.1

ComponentListener Interface Methods

```
public void componentHidden(ComponentEvent event)
public void componentMoved(ComponentEvent event)
public void componentResized(ComponentEvent event)
public void componentShown(ComponentEvent event)
```

These four methods are intended to process the four different types of ComponentEvents. They are implemented by the ComponentListener to contain whatever code is necessary to process the event.

`componentHidden()` is called when a ComponentEvent object is generated as a result of a component becoming invisible.

`componentMoved()` is called when a ComponentEvent object is generated as a result of a component being moved.

`componentResized()` is called when a ComponentEvent object is generated as a result of a component changing its size.

`componentShown()` is called when a ComponentEvent object is generated as a result of a component becoming visible.

Listener Registration Methods

> public void addComponentListener(ComponentListener listener)
>
> public void removeComponentListener(ComponentListener listener)

addComponentListener() adds a ComponentListener to the invoking component's listener list. A ComponentEvent generated by the component will be sent to one of the four methods defined by the ComponentListener.

removeComponentListener() removes a ComponentListener from the invoking component's listener list. The ComponentListener will no longer be notified when the component generates a ComponentEvent.

The addComponentListener() and removeComponentListener() methods are defined in the Component class.

EXAMPLE

Example 8.3 is similar to Example 6.10 from the "ComponentEvent Class" section of Chapter 6, except in this example both the movement and size of a JFrame are restricted. A ComponentListener is implemented as an inner class. The listener overrides the componentMoved() and componentResized() methods.

If the JFrame is resized, a ComponentEvent is generated and sent to the componentResized() method. If the frame has been made smaller such that a label placed on the frame will be truncated, the size of the JFrame is adjusted larger. Similarly, when the JFrame is moved, a ComponentEvent is generated and sent to the componentMoved() method. This method determines if any part of the frame has been moved beyond the limits of the screen. If it has, the method moves the JFrame so all of it is visible again.

EXAMPLE 8.3 COMPONENTLISTENER INTERFACE

```java
import javax.swing.*;
import java.awt.*;
import java.awt.event.*;

public class CompListenerDemo extends JFrame
{
   private JLabel label;

   public CompListenerDemo()
```

```
      {
/* A very long label is created and placed on a JFrame  */

         label = new JLabel("This is a very, very long label");
         label.setFont(new Font("Serif", Font.BOLD, 14));
         label.setForeground(Color.black);

         JPanel panel = new JPanel();
         panel.add(label);
         getContentPane().add(panel);

/* The JFrame registers a ComponentListener    */

         addComponentListener(new CompListener());
         setDefaultCloseOperation(JFrame.EXIT_ON_CLOSE);
         setBounds(100, 100, 300, 200);
         setVisible(true);
      }

/* The ComponentListener is implemented as an inner class.  When      */
/* the JFrame is resized, a ComponentEvent is generated and sent      */
/* to the componentResized() method.  This method tests to see        */
/* if the JFrame width is smaller than the JLabel width.  If it       */
/* is, the JFrame is resized so it is wider than the JLabel.          */
/* If the JFrame is moved, a ComponentEvent is sent to the            */
/* componentMoved() method.  The method determines if the frame       */
/* has been moved off of the screen. If it has, the method moves      */
/* the frame back on to the screen. The componentHidden() and         */
/* componentShown() methods are not used, so they are implemented     */
/* as stub methods.                                                   */

      class CompListener implements ComponentListener
      {
         public void componentResized(ComponentEvent event)
         {
            Component comp = event.getComponent();
            if ( comp.getWidth() < label.getWidth() )
            {
               comp.setSize( label.getWidth()+100, comp.getHeight() );
            }
         }
         public void componentMoved(ComponentEvent event)
         {
            Dimension screenSize =
                  Toolkit.getDefaultToolkit().getScreenSize();

            Component comp = event.getComponent();
            if ( comp.getX() < 0 )
            {
               setLocation(10, comp.getY()+30);
```

```
            }
            if ( comp.getX() > screenSize.width - getWidth() )
            {
                setLocation(screenSize.width-getWidth()-30, comp.getY()+30);
            }
            if ( comp.getY() < 0 )
            {
                setLocation(comp.getX(), 30);
            }
            if ( comp.getY() > screenSize.height - getHeight() )
            {
                setLocation(comp.getX(), screenSize.height-getHeight()-30);
            }
        }
        public void componentHidden(ComponentEvent event){}
        public void componentShown(ComponentEvent event){}
    }

    public static void main(String args[])
    {
        CompListenerDemo demo = new CompListenerDemo();
    }
}
```

When you run this application, a JFrame with a label appears on the screen. Try moving the frame off of the screen, either top, bottom, left, or right. The JFrame will move back so all of it is visible. Try resizing the JFrame so it is smaller than the width of the label. The JFrame will be resized so all of the label is visible.

ContainerListener Interface

The ContainerListener interface declares methods for receiving and processing ContainerEvent objects. These occur when a component is added or removed from a container. The interface declares two methods, one of which is called whenever a ContainerEvent object is generated by an event source that has registered the ContainerListener. These methods can be overridden to contain code that keeps track of the contents of a container. The ContainerListener interface has a corresponding adapter class.

Any class object can serve as a ContainerListener by implementing the ContainerListener interface. The syntax for doing this is

```
public class MyClass implements ContainerListener
```

Class MyClass would then provide an implementation of the methods declared in the ContainerListener interface. A ContainerListener could also be created by extending the ContainerAdapter class.

For a ContainerListener to receive a ContainerEvent generated by a container, the container must register the ContainerListener. The container does this by adding the ContainerListener to its listener list using the `addContainerListener()` method. To disconnect a ContainerListener from a container, the container must remove the ContainerListener from its listener list by invoking the `removeContainerListener()` method. The ContainerListener that was removed will no longer receive ContainerEvents generated by the container.

Syntax: public interface ContainerListener extends EventListener

Package: java.awt.event

Interface hierarchy: EventListener—ContainerListener

The ContainerListener interface is part of the AWT event listener hierarchy.

Introduced: JDK 1.1

ContainerListener Interface Methods

```
public void componentAdded(ContainerEvent event)
public void componentRemoved(ContainerEvent event)
```

These two methods are intended to process the two different types of ContainerEvents. They are implemented by the ContainerListener to contain whatever code is necessary to process the event.

`componentAdded()` is called when a ContainerEvent object is generated as a result of a component being added to a container.

`componentRemoved()` is called when a ContainerEvent object is generated as a result of a component being removed from a container.

Listener Registration Methods

```
public void addContainerListener(ContainerListener listener)
public void removeContainerListener(ContainerListener listener)
```

`addContainerListener()` adds a ContainerListener to the invoking container's listener list. A ContainerEvent generated by the container will be sent to either the `componentAdded()` or `componentRemoved()` method of the ContainerListener.

`removeContainerListener()` removes a ContainerListener from the invoking container's listener list. The ContainerListener will no longer be notified when the container generates a ContainerEvent.

The `addContainerListener()` and `removeContainerListener()` methods are defined in the Container class.

EXAMPLE

See Chapter 6, Example 6.11 in the section "ContainerEvent Class," where a ContainerListener is used to keep track of when child components are added to a JFrame.

DocumentListener Interface

The DocumentListener declares methods that are used to process DocumentEvents. These occur whenever something is added to, removed from, or changed in a Document object. The methods declared in this interface are usually overridden to respond to changes that are made to the contents of a Document or to some of the attributes of the Document.

Any class object can serve as a DocumentListener by implementing the DocumentListener interface. The syntax for doing this is

```
public class MyClass implements DocumentListener
```

Class MyClass would then provide an implementation of the methods declared in the DocumentListener interface.

For a DocumentListener to receive a DocumentEvent generated by a Document, the document must register the DocumentListener. The Document does this by adding the DocumentListener to its listener list, using the `addDocumentListener()` method. To disconnect a DocumentListener from a Document, the Document must remove the DocumentListener from its listener list by invoking the `removeDocumentListener()` method. The DocumentListener that was removed will no longer receive DocumentEvents generated by the Document.

Syntax:	public interface DocumentListener extends EventListener
Package:	javax.swing.event
Interface hierarchy:	EventListener—DocumentListener
	The DocumentListener interface is part of the Swing event listener hierarchy.
Introduced:	JDK 1.2

DocumentListener Interface Methods

```
public void changedUpdate(DocumentEvent event)
public void insertUpdate(DocumentEvent event)
public void removeUpdate(DocumentEvent event)
```

`changedUpdate()` is called if a DocumentEvent was generated because a Document attribute or set of attributes was changed.

`insertUpdate()` is invoked if a text insertion into the Document caused the DocumentEvent.

`removeUpdate()` is called when text has been removed from the Document.

Listener Registration Methods

```
public void addDocumentListener(DocumentListener listener)
public void removeDocumentListener(DocumentListener listener)
```

`addDocumentListener()` adds a DocumentListener to the invoking Document's listener list. A DocumentEvent generated by the Document will be sent to one of the three methods defined by the DocumentListener.

`removeDocumentListener()` removes a DocumentListener from the invoking Document's listener list. The DocumentListener will no longer be notified when the Document generates a DocumentEvent.

The `addDocumentListener()` and `removeDocument-Listener()` methods are defined in the following classes and interfaces:

- AbstractDocument class
- Document interface
- DefaultStyledDocument class

EXAMPLE

See Chapter 6, Example 6.12 in the section "DocumentEvent Class," where a DocumentListener is used to monitor text insertions to and removals from a JTextArea.

EventListener Interface

The EventListener interface is the parent interface of all Java event listeners. It declares no methods but is used as a marker to indicate that a subinterface of EventListener is a listener interface. A user-defined listener interface must extend either EventListener or one of the EventListener subinterfaces.

Syntax:	public interface EventListener
Package:	java.util
Interface hierarchy:	EventListener
	The EventListener interface is at the top of the Java event listener food chain.
Introduced:	JDK 1.1

EventListener Interface Methods

The EventListener interface declares no methods.

FocusListener Interface

The FocusListener interface declares methods for processing FocusEvent objects. These occur when a component gains or loses keyboard focus. The interface declares two methods, one of which is called whenever a FocusEvent object is generated by an event source that has registered the FocusListener. These methods can be overridden to contain code that monitors changes in focus, constrains changes in focus, or changes something else about the GUI due to a change in focus. The FocusListener interface has a corresponding adapter class.

Any class object can serve as a FocusListener by implementing the FocusListener interface. The syntax for doing this is

```
public class MyClass implements FocusListener
```

Class MyClass would then provide an implementation of the methods declared in the FocusListener interface. A FocusListener could also be created by extending the FocusAdapter class.

For a FocusListener to receive a FocusEvent generated by a component, the component must register the FocusListener. The component does this by adding the FocusListener to its listener list using the `addFocusListener()` method. To disconnect a FocusListener from a component, the component must remove the FocusListener from its listener list by invoking the `removeFocusListener()` method. The FocusListener that was removed will no longer receive FocusEvents generated by the component.

Syntax:	public interface FocusListener extends EventListener
Package:	java.awt.event
Interface hierarchy:	EventListener—FocusListener
	The FocusListener interface is part of the AWT event listener hierarchy.
Introduced:	JDK 1.1

FocusListener Interface Methods

```
public void focusGained(FocusEvent event)
public void focusLost(FocusEvent event)
```

These two methods are used to process the two different types of FocusEvents. They are implemented by the FocusListener to contain whatever code is necessary to process the event.

`focusGained()` is called when a FocusEvent object is generated as a result of a component gaining focus.

`focusLost()` is called when a FocusEvent object is generated as a result of a component losing focus.

Listener Registration Methods

> public void addFocusListener(FocusListener listener)
>
> public void removeFocusListener(FocusListener listener)

addFocusListener() adds a FocusListener to the invoking component's listener list. A FocusEvent generated by the component will be sent to either the focusGained() or focusLost() method of the FocusListener. removeFocusListener() removes a FocusListener from the invoking component's listener list. The FocusListener will no longer be notified when the component generates a FocusEvent.

The addFocusListener() and removeFocusListener() methods are defined in the following classes and interfaces:

- AccessibleComponent interface
- Component class
- Component.AccessibleAWTComponent class
- List.AccessibleAWTList.AWTListChild
- JList.AccessibleJList.AccessibleJListChild
- JTable.AccessibleJTable.AccessibleJTableCell
- JTableHeader.AccessibleJTableHeader.AccessibleJTableHeaderEntry
- JTree.AccessibleJTree.AccessibleJTreeNode
- MenuComponent.AccessibleAWTMenuComponent class

EXAMPLE

See Chapter 6, Example 6.13 in the section "FocusEvent Class," where a FocusListener is used to change the background color of the component that has keyboard focus.

HierarchyBoundsListener Interface

The HierarchyBoundsListener interface declares methods for processing HierarchyEvent objects that occur as a result of an ancestor being moved or resized. The interface declares two methods, one of which is called whenever this type of HierarchyEvent object is generated by an event source that has registered the HierarchyBoundsListener. The HierarchyBoundsListener interface has a corresponding adapter class.

Any class object can serve as a HierarchyBoundsListener by implementing the HierarchyBoundsListener interface. The syntax for doing this is

```
public class MyClass implements HierarchyBoundsListener
```

Class MyClass would then provide an implementation of the methods declared in the HierarchyBoundsListener interface. A HierarchyBoundsListener could also be created by extending the HierarchyBoundsAdapter class.

For a HierarchyBoundsListener to receive a bounds-type HierarchyEvent generated by a component, the component must register the HierarchyBoundsListener. The component does this by adding the HierarchyBoundsListener to its listener list using the `addHierarchyBoundsListener()` method. To disconnect a HierarchyBoundsListener from a component, the component must remove the HierarchyBoundsListener from its listener list by invoking the `removeHierarchyBoundsListener()` method. The HierarchyBoundsListener that was removed will no longer receive HierarchyEvents generated by the component.

Syntax:	public interface HierarchyBoundsListener extends EventListener
Package:	java.awt.event
Interface hierarchy:	EventListener—HierarchyBoundsListener
	The HierarchyBoundsListener interface is part of the AWT event listener hierarchy.
Introduced:	JDK 1.3

HierarchyBoundsListener Interface Methods

public void `ancestorMoved(HierarchyEvent event)`
public void `ancestorResized(HierarchyEvent event)`

These two methods are used to process hierarchy bounds events. They are implemented by the HierarchyBoundsListener to contain whatever code is necessary to process the event.

ancestorMoved() is called when a HierarchyEvent object is generated as a result of an ancestor of the source component being moved.

ancestorResized() is called when a HierarchyEvent object is generated as a result of an ancestor of the source component being resized.

Listener Registration Methods

---

public void addHierarchyBoundsListener(HierarchyBoundsListener listener)

public void removeHierarchyBoundsListener(HierarchyBoundsListener listener)

---

addHierarchyBoundsListener() adds a HierarchyBoundsListener to the invoking component's listener list. A bounds-type HierarchyEvent generated by the component will be sent to either the ancestorMoved() or ancestorResized() method of the HierarchyBoundsListener.

removeHierarchyBoundsListener() removes a HierarchyBoundsListener from the invoking component's listener list. The HierarchyBoundsListener will no longer be notified when the component generates a hierarchy bounds event.

The addHierarchyBoundsListener() and removeHierarchyBoundsListener() methods are defined in the Component class.

EXAMPLE

Example 8.4 uses a HierarchyBoundsListener to track movement or size changes to the component hierarchy of a JButton. A JButton is placed on a JPanel that is placed on a JFrame. The JButton registers a HierarchyBoundsListener that is implemented as an inner class.

If the JFrame is moved, the JButton object generates a HierarchyEvent which is sent to the ancestorMoved() method. The new location of the JFrame is written to the text area of a JTextField object placed at the bottom of the JFrame. If the JFrame is resized, the JButton object generates a HierarchyEvent that is sent to the ancestorResized() method. The text of the JTextField is changed to indicate the new dimensions of the JFrame.

Example 8.4 HierarchyBoundsListener Interface

```
import java.awt.*;
import java.awt.event.*;
import javax.swing.*;

public class HBListenerDemo extends JFrame
{
   private JButton button;
   private JTextField jtf;

   public HBListenerDemo()
   {
/*   A JButton is placed on a JFrame.  The button registers   */
/*   a HierarchyBoundsListener.                               */

      button = new JButton("Button");
      button.setBorder(BorderFactory.createRaisedBevelBorder());
      button.addHierarchyBoundsListener(new HierBndsListener());

      jtf = new JTextField(20);
      jtf.setEditable(false);

      JPanel panel = new JPanel();
      panel.add(button);

      getContentPane().add(panel, BorderLayout.CENTER);
      getContentPane().add(jtf, BorderLayout.SOUTH);

      setName("frame");
      setDefaultCloseOperation(JFrame.EXIT_ON_CLOSE);
      setBounds(100, 100, 300, 200);
      setVisible(true);
   }

/*   A HierarchyBoundsListener is implemented as an inner class.   */
/*   If the frame is moved or resized, HierarchyEvents generated   */
/*   by the button are sent to either the ancestorResized() or    */
/*   ancestorMoved() methods.  These methods update the text of a */
/*   JTextField to indicate what has taken place.                 */

   class HierBndsListener implements HierarchyBoundsListener
   {
      public void ancestorResized(HierarchyEvent event)
      {
         Component comp = event.getChanged();
         Dimension d = comp.getSize();
         jtf.setText(comp.getName()+" was resized.  width = "+
                  d.width+" height = "+d.height);
```

```
        }

        public void ancestorMoved(HierarchyEvent event)
        {
            Component comp = event.getChanged();
            jtf.setText(comp.getName()+" was moved to ("+
                        comp.getX()+","+comp.getY()+")");
        }
    }

    public static void main(String args[])
    {
        HBListenerDemo demo = new HBListenerDemo();
    }
}
```

When you run this example, try moving the frame. The location of the frame is continually updated in the textfield. Now try resizing the frame. The new size of the frame is updated in the textfield. The important thing to note here is that while it's the JFrame that is being altered, it's the events generated by the JButton that are being processed.

HierarchyListener Interface

The HierarchyListener interface declares one method, `hierarchyChanged()`, that is used to process HierarchyEvent objects. These occur when the hierarchy of a component changes. This can happen, for instance, if an ancestor is added or removed from the hierarchy or if the hierarchy is made visible or invisible. The addition or removal of a child component will not generate a HierarchyEvent. The HierarchyListener interface declares only one method, so there is no corresponding adapter class.

A HierarchyListener can be used to monitor and detect changes to a component that result from changes to its component hierarchy. For instance, a component that is placed on a panel will become invisible if the panel becomes invisible.

Any class object can serve as a HierarchyListener by implementing the HierarchyListener interface. The syntax for doing this is

```
public class MyClass implements HierarchyListener
```

Class MyClass would then provide an implementation of the `hierarchyChanged()` method that would contain the code to process the HierarchyEvent.

For a HierarchyListener to receive a HierarchyEvent generated by a component, the component must register the HierarchyListener. The component does this by adding the HierarchyListener to its listener list using the `addHierarchyListener()` method. To disconnect a HierarchyListener from a component, the component must remove the HierarchyListener from its listener list by invoking the `removeHierarchyListener()` method. The HierarchyListener that was removed will no longer receive HierarchyEvents generated by the component.

Syntax: public interface HierarchyListener extends EventListener
Package: java.awt.event
Interface hierarchy: EventListener—HierarchyListener

The HierarchyListener interface is part of the AWT event listener hierarchy.

Introduced: JDK 1.3

HierarchyListener Interface Methods

`public void hierarchyChanged(HierarchyEvent event)`

`hierarchyChanged()` is called whenever a HierarchyEvent is generated because the hierarchy of a component is added to, removed from, or had its visibility changed.

Listener Registration Methods

`public void addHierarchyListener(HierarchyListener listener)`
`public void removeHierarchyListener(HierarchyListener listener)`

`addHierarchyListener()` adds a HierarchyListener to the invoking component's listener list. A HierarchyEvent generated by the component will be sent to the `hierarchyChanged()` method of the HierarchyListener.

`removeHierarchyListener()` removes a HierarchyListener from the invoking component's listener list. The HierarchyListener will no longer be notified when the component generates a hierarchy change event.

The `addHierarchyListener()` and `removeHierarchy-Listener()` methods are defined in the Component class.

EXAMPLE

Example 8.5 shows how a HierarchyListener can be used to track visibility changes to a JButton that result from changes in the JButton's component hierarchy. A JButton is placed on a JPanel that is placed in the center region of a JFrame. This JButton registers a HierarchyListener that is implemented as an inner class.

A JTextField and two additional JButtons are placed at the bottom of the frame. The buttons at the bottom of the frame are used to change the visible state of the panel. When the Hide Panel button is pressed, the panel is made invisible. This also makes the JButton contained by the panel become invisible. The JButton fires a HierarchyEvent, which is sent to the `hierarchyChanged()` method of the HierarchyListener. The JTextField is updated to indicate that the JButton has now become invisible.

When the Show Panel button is pressed, the panel is made visible. This also causes the JButton to fire a HierarchyEvent, which is sent to the `hierarchyChanged()` method. The JTextField is updated to indicate that the JButton is now visible.

EXAMPLE 8.5 HIERARCHYLISTENER INTERFACE

```
import java.awt.*;
import java.awt.event.*;
import javax.swing.*;

public class HierListenerDemo extends JFrame implements ActionListener
{
   private JButton button, removePanelButton, removeButton;
   private JPanel centerPanel;
   private JTextField jtf;

   public HierListenerDemo()
   {
/* A JButton is placed on a JFrame.  The button registers   */
/* a HierarchyListener.                                     */

      button = new JButton("Button");
      button.setBorder(BorderFactory.createRaisedBevelBorder());
      button.addHierarchyListener(new HierListener());
```

```java
/* Two more buttons are placed on the JFrame.  These buttons  */
/* are used to change the visibility of the center panel.     */
/* These buttons register an ActionListener.                   */

    removePanelButton = new JButton("Hide Panel");
    removePanelButton.setActionCommand("hide");

removePanelButton.setBorder(BorderFactory.createRaisedBevelBorder());
    removePanelButton.addActionListener(this);

    removeButton = new JButton("Show Panel");
    removeButton.setActionCommand("show");
    removeButton.setBorder(BorderFactory.createRaisedBevelBorder());
    removeButton.addActionListener(this);

    jtf = new JTextField(15);
    jtf.setEditable(false);

    centerPanel = new JPanel();
    centerPanel.setName("center");
    centerPanel.add(button);

    JPanel southPanel = new JPanel();
    southPanel.add(jtf);
    southPanel.add(removePanelButton);
    southPanel.add(removeButton);

    getContentPane().add(centerPanel, BorderLayout.CENTER);
    getContentPane().add(southPanel, BorderLayout.SOUTH);

    setDefaultCloseOperation(JFrame.EXIT_ON_CLOSE);
    setBounds(100, 100, 400, 200);
    setVisible(true);
  }

/* Pressing one of the two buttons on the bottom of the JFrame */
/* changes the visibility of the center panel.  This causes the */
/* JButton contained by the center panel to generate a          */
/* HierarchyEvent.                                              */

  public void actionPerformed(ActionEvent event)
  {
     if ( event.getActionCommand().equals("hide"))
     {
        centerPanel.setVisible(false);
     }
     if ( event.getActionCommand().equals("show"))
     {
        centerPanel.setVisible(true);
     }
```

```
      invalidate();
      validate();
   }

/* The HierarchyListener is implemented as an inner class.  When     */
/* the button on the center panel fires a HierarchyEvent, it is       */
/* sent to the hierarchyChanged() method.  This method determines    */
/* if the event was due to a change in the visibility of some        */
/* part of the component hierarchy.  The JTextField is updated to    */
/* indicate if the JButton has become visible or invisible because   */
/* some part of its component hierarchy (the center panel) has       */
/* become visible or invisible.                                      */

   class HierListener implements HierarchyListener
   {
      public void hierarchyChanged(HierarchyEvent event)
      {
         if ( event.getChangeFlags() == HierarchyEvent.SHOWING_CHANGED )
         {
            if ( event.getChanged().isVisible() )
            {
               jtf.setText("Button is visible");
            }
            else
            {
               jtf.setText("Button is not visible");
            }
         }
      }
   }

   public static void main(String args[])
   {
      HierListenerDemo demo = new HierListenerDemo();
   }
}
```

When this program is run, the upper button is initially visible and the textfield reflects this fact. Now click on the Hide Panel button. The panel and the JButton disappear. The textfield now says "Button is invisible." Now click the Show Panel button. The panel and button are made visible once again. Note that this program processes HierarchyEvents generated by the JButton in response to changes in the visibility of its parent container.

HyperlinkListener Interface

The HyperlinkListener declares one method, `hyperlinkUpdate()`, that is used to process HyperlinkEvents and HTMLFrameHyperlinkEvents. These occur when the user clicks on a hyperlink inside of a JEditorPane object. They can also occur when the mouse enters or exits the bounding area of the hyperlink text. The HyperlinkListener is generally used to execute the hyperlink that was selected. For standalone HTML pages, this is done by having the JEditorPane object call the `setPage()` method, passing this method the URL associated with the HyperlinkEvent. The process of executing the hyperlink is somewhat more complicated for HTML frames.

Any class object can serve as a HyperlinkListener by implementing the HyperlinkListener interface. The syntax for doing this is

```
public class MyClass implements HyperlinkListener
```

Class MyClass would then provide an implementation of the `hyperlinkUpdate()` method declared in the HyperlinkListener interface.

For a HyperlinkListener to receive a HyperlinkEvent or HTMLFrameHyperlinkEvent generated by a JEditorPane, the JEditorPane must register the HyperlinkListener. The JEditorPane does this by adding the HyperlinkListener to its listener list using the `addHyperlinkListener()` method. To disconnect a HyperlinkListener from a JEditorPane, the JEditorPane must remove the HyperlinkListener from its listener list by invoking the `removeHyperlinkListener()` method. The HyperlinkListener that was removed will no longer receive HyperlinkEvents or HTMLFrameHyperlinkEvents generated by the component.

Syntax:	public interface HyperlinkListener extends EventListener
Package:	javax.swing.event
Interface hierarchy:	EventListener—HyperlinkListener
	The HyperlinkListener interface is part of the Swing event listener hierarchy.
Introduced:	JDK 1.2

HyperlinkListener Interface Methods

public void `hyperlinkUpdate(HyperlinkEvent event)`

`hyperlinkUpdate()` is called whenever a HyperlinkEvent event is generated by an event source that has registered the HyperlinkListener.

Listener Registration Methods

> public void addHyperlinkListener(HyperlinkListener listener)
>
> public void removeHyperlinkListener(HyperlinkListener listener)

addHyperlinkListener() adds a HyperlinkListener to the invoking JEditorPane's listener list. A HyperlinkEvent generated by the JEditorPane will be sent to the hyperlinkUpdate() method of the HyperlinkListener.

removeHyperlinkListener() removes a HyperlinkListener from the invoking JEditorPane's listener list. The HyperlinkListener will no longer be notified when the JEditorPane generates a HyperlinkEvent.

The addHyperlinkListener() and removeHyperlinkListener() methods are defined in the JEditorPane class.

EXAMPLE

See Chapter 6, Example 6.17 in the section "HyperlinkEvent Class," where a HyperlinkListener is used to execute hyperlinks contained in an HTML document.

See also Example 6.15 in the section "HTMLFrameHyperlinkEvent Class," where a HyperlinkListener is used to update the display of a JEditorPane displaying an HTML frame.

InputMethodListener Interface

This interface declares methods for processing InputMethodEvents. The InputMethodListener object works in conjunction with the input method and text editing component. The interface defines two methods, one that is called if the caret position within the composed text has changed and the other that is called if the text entered through the input method has changed.

The InputMethodListener interface provides the ability for receiving and processing InputMethodEvent objects. The InputMethodListener object works in conjunction with the input method and text editing component. Although the InputMethodListener interface declares more than one method, it does not have a corresponding adapter class.

Any class object can serve as an InputMethodListener by implementing the InputMethodListener interface. The syntax for doing this is

```
public class MyClass implements InputMethodListener
```

Class MyClass would then provide an implementation of the methods declared in the InputMethodListener interface.

For an InputMethodListener to receive an InputMethodEvent generated by an input method, the input method must register the InputMethodListener. The input method does this by adding the InputMethodListener to its listener list using the `addInputMethodListener()` method. To disconnect an InputMethodListener from an input method, the input method must remove the InputMethodListener from its listener list by invoking the `removeInputMethodListener()` method. The InputMethodListener that was removed will no longer receive InputMethodEvents generated by the input method.

Syntax: public interface InputMethodListener extends EventListener

Package: java.awt.event

Interface hierarchy: EventListener—InputMethodListener

The InputMethodListener interface is part of the AWT event listener hierarchy.

Introduced: JDK 1.2

InputMethodListener Interface Methods

public void `caretPositionChanged(InputMethodEvent event)`

public void `inputMethodTextChanged(InputMethodEvent event)`

These two methods are used to process InputMethodEvents. They are implemented by the InputMethodListener to contain whatever code is necessary to process the event.

`caretPositionChanged()` is called when an InputMethodEvent is generated due to a change in the position of the caret within the composed text. The caret is the cursor that indicates the insertion point within the composed text. `inputMethodTextChanged()` is called whenever an InputMethodEvent is generated because the text entered through an input method has changed.

Listener Registration Methods

```
public void addInputMethodListener(InputMethodListener listener)
public void removeInputMethodListener(InputMethodListener listener)
```

`addInputMethodListener()` adds an InputMethodListener to the invoking input method's listener list. An InputMethodEvent generated by the input method will be sent to either the `caretPositionChanged()` or `inputMethodTextChanged()` method of the InputMethodListener.

`removeInputMethodListener()` removes an InputMethodListener from the invoking input method's listener list. The InputMethodListener will no longer be notified when the component generates a InputMethodEvent.

The `addInputMethodListener()` and `removeInputMethodListener()` methods are defined in the Component and JTextComponent classes.

EXAMPLE

As was stated in Chapter 6 in the section "InputMethodEvent," it is difficult to come up with a generally applicable example of using InputMethodEvents and an InputMethodListener because input methods are platform-specific and some platforms may not even support them. Please consult a specialized Java reference for a complete description of this topic.

INTERNALFRAMELISTENER INTERFACE

The InternalFrameListener interface declares methods for processing InternalFrameEvent objects. These occur whenever a JInternalFrame is opened, closed, closing, activated, deactivated, iconified, or deiconified. The interface defines seven methods, one of which will be called whenever an InternalFrameEvent is generated from an event source that has registered the InternalFrameListener. The InternalFrameListener interface has a corresponding adapter class.

The InternalFrameListener interface is very similar to the WindowListener interface. This is because the JInternalFrame class generates the same types of events as Windows, but since the JInternalFrame class does not inherit from the Window class, it needs its own events (InternalFrameEvent objects) and its own listener (InternalFrameListener).

Any class object can serve as an InternalFrameListener by implementing the InternalFrameListener interface. The syntax for doing this is

```
public class MyClass implements InternalFrameListener
```

Class MyClass would then provide an implementation of the methods declared in the InternalFrameListener interface. An InternalFrameListener could also be created by extending the InternalFrameAdapter class.

For an InternalFrameListener to receive an InternalFrameEvent generated by a JInternalFrame, the JInternalFrame must register the InternalFrameListener. It does this by adding the InternalFrameListener to its listener list using the `addInternalFrameListener()` method. To disconnect an InternalFrameListener from a JInternalFrame, the internal frame must remove the InternalFrameListener from its listener list by invoking the `removeInternalFrameListener()` method. The InternalFrameListener that was removed will no longer receive InternalFrameEvents generated by the JInternalFrame.

Syntax:	public interface InternalFrameListener extends EventListener
Package:	javax.swing.event
Interface hierarchy:	EventListener—InternalFrameListener
	The InternalFrameListener interface is part of the Swing event listener hierarchy.
Introduced:	JDK 1.2

InternalFrameListener Interface Methods

```
public void internalFrameActivated(InternalFrameEvent event)
public void internalFrameClosed(InternalFrameEvent event)
public void internalFrameClosing(InternalFrameEvent event)
public void internalFrameDeactivated(InternalFrameEvent event)
public void internalFrameDeiconified(InternalFrameEvent event)
public void internalFrameIconified(InternalFrameEvent event)
public void internalFrameOpened(InternalFrameEvent event)
```

These methods are used to process the various types of InternalFrameEvents. They are implemented by the InternalFrameListener to contain whatever code is necessary to process the event.

`internalFrameActivated()` is called when an InternalFrameEvent is generated due to an internal frame becoming active. An active internal frame is one that has been brought to the front of the window hierarchy. Child components of the an internal frame can attain keyboard focus.

`internalFrameClosed()` is called when an InternalFrameEvent is generated after an internal frame has been closed.

`internalFrameClosing()` is called when an InternalFrameEvent is generated because a user is attempting to close an internal frame.

`internalFrameDeactivated()` is called when an InternalFrameEvent is generated due to an internal frame becoming deactivated. A deactivated window is one that is no longer at the front of the window hierarchy.

`internalFrameDeiconified()` is called when an InternalFrameEvent is generated due to an internal frame changing from an iconified to normal state.

`internalFrameIconified()` is called when an InternalFrameEvent is generated due to an internal frame becoming iconified. An iconified internal frame will normally appear as a small icon on the screen.

`internalFrameOpened()` is called when an InternalFrameEvent is generated due to an internal frame becoming visible for the first time.

Listener Registration Methods

public void addInternalFrameListener(InternalFrameListener listener)
public void removeInternalFrameListener(InternalFrameListener listener)

`addInternalFrameListener()` adds an InternalFrameListener to the invoking JInternalFrame component's listener list. An InternalFrameEvent generated by the component will be sent to one of the seven methods defined by the InternalFrameListener.

`removeInternalFrameListener()` removes an InternalFrameListener from the invoking JInternalFrame component's listener list. The InternalFrameListener will no longer be notified when the component generates an InternalFrameEvent.

The `addInternalFrameListener()` and `removeInternalFrameListener()` methods are defined in the JInternalFrame class.

EXAMPLE

See Chapter 6, Example 6.19 in the section "InternalFrameEvent Class," where an InternalFrameListener is used to monitor the iconified state of a JInternalFrame object.

ItemListener Interface

The ItemListener interface provides one method, `itemStateChanged()`, that is used to process ItemEvent objects. ItemEvents can be generated in a variety of ways, the manner of which is component-specific, but generally involves the user selecting or deselecting an item. The `itemStateChanged()` method is usually overridden to contain code to react to the user's selection. Because the ItemListener interface has only one method, it does not have a corresponding adapter class.

Any class object can serve as an ItemListener by implementing the ItemListener interface. The syntax for doing this is

```
public class MyClass implements ItemListener
```

Class MyClass would then provide an implementation of the `itemStateChanged()` method.

For an ItemListener to receive an ItemEvent generated by a component, the component must register the ItemListener. The component does this by adding the ItemListener to its listener list using the `addItemListener()` method. To disconnect an ItemListener from a component, the component must remove the ItemListener from its listener list by invoking the `removeItemListener()` method. The ItemListener that was removed will no longer receive ItemEvents generated by the component.

Syntax:	public interface ItemListener extends EventListener
Package:	java.awt.event
Interface hierarchy:	EventListener—ItemListener
	The ItemListener interface is part of the AWT event listener hierarchy.
Introduced:	JDK 1.1

ItemListener Interface Methods

```
public void itemStateChanged(ItemEvent event)
```

The `itemStateChanged()` method is called when an ItemEvent object is generated by an event source that has registered the ItemListener. The method is passed a reference to the ItemEvent object that was generated.

Listener Registration Methods

> public void `addItemListener(ItemListener listener)`
> public void `removeItemListener(ItemListener listener)`

`addItemListener()` adds an ItemListener to the invoking component's listener list. An ItemEvent generated by the component will be sent to the `itemStateChanged()` method of the ItemListener.

`removeItemListener()` removes an ItemListener from the invoking component's listener list. The ItemListener will no longer be notified when the component generates an ItemEvent.

The `addItemListener()` and `removeItemListener()` methods are defined in the following classes and interfaces:

- AbstractButton class
- ButtonModel interface
- Checkbox class
- CheckboxMenuItem class
- Choice class
- DefaultButtonModel class
- ItemSelectable interface
- JComboBox class
- List class

EXAMPLE

See Chapter 6, Example 6.21 in the section "ItemEvent Class," where an ItemListener is used to monitor changes to the selected item of a JComboBox.

KeyListener Interface

The KeyListener interface declares methods for processing KeyEvent objects. These occur when the user presses, releases, or types (presses and releases) a key on the keyboard. The interface declares three methods, one of which is called whenever a KeyEvent object is generated by an event source that has registered the KeyListener. These methods are usually overridden to provide some keyboard-activated functionality to a GUI component. The KeyListener interface has a corresponding adapter class.

Any class object can serve as a KeyListener by implementing the KeyListener interface. The syntax for doing this is

```
public class MyClass implements KeyListener
```

Class MyClass would then provide an implementation of the methods declared in the KeyListener interface. A KeyListener could also be created by extending the KeyAdapter class.

For a KeyListener to receive a KeyEvent generated by a component, the component must register the KeyListener. The component does this by adding the KeyListener to its listener list using the `addKeyListener()` method. To disconnect a KeyListener from a component, the component must remove the KeyListener from its listener list by invoking the `removeKeyListener()` method. The KeyListener that was removed will no longer receive KeyEvents generated by the component.

Syntax:	public interface KeyListener extends EventListener
Package:	java.awt.event
Interface hierarchy:	EventListener—KeyListener
	The KeyListener interface is part of the AWT event listener hierarchy.
Introduced:	JDK 1.1

KeyListener Interface Methods

public void `keyPressed(KeyEvent event)`
public void `keyReleased(KeyEvent event)`
public void `keyTyped(KeyEvent event)`

These three methods are used to process the different types of KeyEvents. They are implemented by the KeyListener to contain whatever code is necessary to process the event.

`keyPressed()` is called when a KeyEvent object is generated as a result of a user pressing a key over the bounding area of a component.

`keyReleased()` is called when a KeyEvent object is generated as a result of a user releasing a key over the bounding area of a component.

`keyTyped()` is called when a KeyEvent object is generated as a result of a user pressing and releasing a key over the bounding area of a component.

Listener Registration Methods

```
public void addKeyListener(KeyListener listener)
```
```
public void removeKeyListener(KeyListener listener)
```

`addKeyListener()` adds a KeyListener to the invoking component's listener list. A KeyEvent generated by the component will be sent to one of the three methods defined by the KeyListener.

`removeKeyListener()` removes a KeyListener from the invoking component's listener list. The KeyListener will no longer be notified when the component generates a KeyEvent.

The `addKeyListener()` and `removeKeyListener()` methods are defined in the Component class.

EXAMPLE

Example 8.6 shows the three types of KeyEvents as they are generated by the user typing input into a JTextField. The JTextField registers a KeyListener that is implemented as an inner class. When the text field has keyboard focus and a key is pressed or released, a KeyEvent is generated and sent to the `keyPressed()` or `keyReleased()` methods. The virtual key code of the keystroke that caused the event is printed on the screen. A key-typed KeyEvent does not have virtual key code information, so the ASCII character that was typed is printed on the screen.

KeyListener Interface

Example 8.6 KeyListener Interface

```
import java.awt.*;
import java.awt.event.*;
import javax.swing.*;

public class KeyListenerDemo extends JFrame
{
   private JTextField jtf, jtf2, jtf3, jtf4;

   public KeyListenerDemo()
   {
/* A JTextField is created and placed on a JFrame.  The JTextField   */
/*    registers a KeyListener.                                        */

      jtf = new JTextField(15);
      jtf.setBorder(BorderFactory.createLineBorder(Color.black));
      jtf.addKeyListener(new KeyHandler());

      jtf2 = new JTextField(12);
      jtf2.setText("key pressed:");
      jtf2.setEditable(false);

      jtf3 = new JTextField(12);
      jtf3.setText("key released:");
      jtf3.setEditable(false);

      jtf4 = new JTextField(12);
      jtf4.setText("key typed:");
      jtf4.setEditable(false);

      JPanel panel = new JPanel();
      panel.add(jtf);

      JPanel panel2 = new JPanel();
      panel2.add(jtf2);
      panel2.add(jtf3);
      panel2.add(jtf4);

      getContentPane().add(panel, BorderLayout.CENTER);
      getContentPane().add(panel2, BorderLayout.SOUTH);

      setDefaultCloseOperation(JFrame.EXIT_ON_CLOSE);
      setBounds(100, 100, 500, 200);
      setVisible(true);
   }

/* The KeyListener is implemented as an inner class.  For key         */
/*    pressed and key released type KeyEvents, the virtual key        */
/*    code of the keystroke that caused the event is written to      */
```

```
/* a textfield.  Key typed events don't have key code or    */
/* modifier information, so the character that was typed is */
/* written to a textfield.  Note that modifier keys are also */
/* processed by the getKeyText() method.                    */

   class KeyHandler implements KeyListener
   {
      public void keyPressed(KeyEvent event)
      {
         jtf2.setText("key pressed: "+
                      event.getKeyText(event.getKeyCode()));
      }

      public void keyReleased(KeyEvent event)
      {
         jtf3.setText("key released: "+
                      event.getKeyText(event.getKeyCode()));
      }

      public void keyTyped(KeyEvent event)
      {
         jtf4.setText("key typed: "+
                      event.getKeyChar());
      }
   }

   public static void main(String args[])
   {
      KeyListenerDemo demo = new KeyListenerDemo();
   }
}
```

When you run this code, type some characters into the upper textfield and note what happens in the `key pressed:`, `key released:`, and `key typed:` textfields. Now try some modifier keys and see what happens.

LISTDATALISTENER INTERFACE

The ListDataListener declares methods to process ListDataEvents. These occur when the contents of a list are added to, removed from, or changed in any other way. One or more of these methods are usually overridden to respond to or manage changes to the contents of a list. The ListDataListener interface does not have a corresponding adapter class.

Any class object can serve as a ListDataListener by implementing the ListDataListener interface. The syntax for doing this is

```
public class MyClass implements ListDataListener
```

Class MyClass would then provide an implementation of the methods declared in the ListDataListener interface.

For a ListDataListener to receive a ListDataEvent generated by an event source, the event source must register the ListDataListener. The event source does this by adding the ListDataListener to its listener list using the `addListDataListener()` method. To disconnect a ListDataListener from an event source, the source must remove the ListDataListener from its listener list by invoking the `removeListDataListener()` method. The ListDataListener that was removed will no longer receive ListDataEvents generated by the event source.

Syntax: public interface ListDataListener extends EventListener

Package: javax.swing.event

Interface hierarchy: EventListener—ListDataListener

The ListDataListener interface is part of the Swing event listener hierarchy.

Introduced: JDK 1.2

ListDataListener Interface Methods

```
public void contentsChanged(ListDataEvent event)
public void intervalAdded(ListDataEvent event)
public void intervalRemoved(ListDataEvent event)
```

`contentsChanged()` is the method of last resort. If a ListDataEvent is generated by a sequence of events that are more complicated than a simple addition or removal of list elements, this method is called.

`intervalAdded()` is called if the ListDataEvent is the result of elements having been added to the list.

`intervalRemoved()` is invoked if list elements have been removed from the list.

Listener Registration Methods

```
public void addListDataListener(ListDataListener listener)
public void removeListDataListener(ListDataListener listener)
```

`addListDataListener()` adds a ListDataListener to the invoking component's listener list. A ListDataEvent generated by the component will be sent to one of the three methods defined by the ListDataListener.

`removeListDataListener()` removes a ListDataListener from the invoking component's listener list. The ListDataListener will no longer be notified when the component generates a ListDataEvent.

The `addListDataListener()` and `removeListDataListener()` methods are defined in the ListModel interface and the AbstractListModel class.

EXAMPLE

See Chapter 6, Example 6.23 in the section "ListDataEvent Class," where a ListDataListener is used to manage changes to the contents of a DefaultListModel.

ListSelectionListener Interface

The ListSelectionListener declares one method, `valueChanged()`, that is used to process ListSelectionEvents. These occur when the selected value of a list changes. The `valueChanged()` method is usually overridden to respond to changes in the selected item or items of a list.

Any class object can serve as a ListSelectionListener by implementing the ListSelectionListener interface. The syntax for doing this is

```
public class MyClass implements ListSelectionListener
```

Class MyClass would then provide an implementation of the method declared in the ListSelectionListener interface.

For a ListSelectionListener to receive a ListSelectionEvent generated by an event source, the event source must register the ListSelectionListener. The event source does this by adding the ListSelectionListener to its listener list using the `addListSelectionListener()` method. To disconnect a ListSelectionListener from an event source, the source must remove the ListSelectionListener from its listener list by invoking the `removeListSelectionListener()` method. The ListSelectionListener that was removed will no longer receive ListSelectionEvents generated by the event source.

Syntax:	public interface ListSelectionListener extends EventListener
Package:	javax.swing.event
Interface hierarchy:	EventListener—ListSelectionListener
	The ListSelectionListener interface is part of the Swing event listener hierarchy.
Introduced:	JDK 1.2

ListSelectionListener Interface Methods

> public void valueChanged(ListSelectionEvent event)

`valueChanged()` is called whenever a ListSelectionEvent is generated from an event source that has registered the ListSelectionListener.

Listener Registration Methods

> public void addListSelectionListener(ListSelectionListener listener)
>
> public void removeListSelectionListener(ListSelectionListener listener)

`addListSelectionListener()` adds a ListSelectionListener to the invoking component's listener list. A ListSelectionEvent generated by the component will be sent to the `valueChanged()` method of the ListSelectionListener.

`removeListSelectionListener()` removes a ListSelectionListener from the invoking component's listener list. The ListSelectionListener will no longer be notified when the component generates a ListSelectionEvent.

The `addListSelectionListener()` and `removeListSelectionListener()` methods are defined in the following classes and interfaces:

- AbstractListModel class
- DefaultListSelectionModel class
- ListModel interface
- OptionListModel (javax.swing.text.html package)

EXAMPLE

See Chapter 6, Example 6.24 in the section "ListSelectionEvent Class," where a ListSelectionListener is used to respond to changes in the selected value of a JList component.

MenuDragMouseListener Interface

The MenuDragMouseListener declares methods used to process MenuDragMouseEvent objects. These occur when the mouse is dragged into or out of the display area of a Swing menu component. One or more of these methods is usually overridden to provide some mouse drag-activated functionality to a menu. Although the MenuDragMouseListener interface declares more than one method, there is no corresponding adapter class.

Any class object can serve as a MenuDragMouseListener by implementing the MenuDragMouseListener interface. The syntax for doing this is

```
public class MyClass implements MenuDragMouseListener
```

Class MyClass would then provide an implementation of the methods declared in the MenuDragMouseListener interface.

For a MenuDragMouseListener to receive a MenuDragMouseEvent generated by a Swing menu component, the menu component must register the MenuDragMouseListener. The Swing menu component does this by adding the MenuDragMouseListener to its listener list using the `addMenuDragMouseListener()` method. To disconnect a MenuDragMouseListener from a Swing menu component, the menu component must remove the MenuDragMouseListener from its listener list by invoking the `removeMenuDragMouseListener()` method. The MenuDragMouse-Listener that was removed will no longer receive MenuDragMouseEvents generated by the menu component.

Syntax: public interface MenuDragMouseListener extends EventListener

Package: javax.swing.event

Interface hierarchy: EventListener—MenuDragMouseListener

The MenuDragMouseListener interface is part of the Swing event listener hierarchy.

Introduced: JDK 1.2

MenuDragMouseListener Interface Methods

```
public void menuDragMouseDragged(MenuDragMouseEvent event)
public void menuDragMouseEntered(MenuDragMouseEvent event)
public void menuDragMouseExited(MenuDragMouseEvent event)
public void menuDragMouseReleased(MenuDragMouseEvent event)
```

`menuDragMouseDragged()` is called when the mouse is dragged inside the display area of a Swing menu component.

`menuDragMouseEntered()` is called when the mouse enters the display area of a Swing menu component.

`menuDragMouseExited()` is called when the mouse leaves the display area of a Swing menu component.

`menuDragMouseReleased()` is called when the a dragged mouse is released inside the display area of a Swing menu component.

Listener Registration Methods

```
public void addMenuDragMouseListener(MenuDragMouseListener listener)
public void removeMenuDragMouseListener(MenuDragMouseListener listener)
```

`addMenuDragMouseListener()` adds a MenuDragMouseListener to the invoking component's listener list. A MenuDragMouseEvent generated by the component will be sent to one of the four method defined by the MenuDragMouseListener.

`removeMenuDragMouseListener()` removes a MenuDragMouseListener from the invoking component's listener list. The MenuDragMouseListener will no longer be notified when the component generates a MenuDragMouseEvent.

The `addMenuDragMouseListener()` and `removeMenuDragMouseListener()` methods are defined in the JMenuItem class.

EXAMPLE

See Chapter 6, Example 6.25 in the section "MenuDragMouseEvent Class," where a MenuDragMouseListener is used to provide a mouse-drag menu item activation to a menu.

MenuKeyListener Interface

The MenuKeyListener declares methods used to process MenuKeyEvent objects. These are generated if a key is pressed, released, or typed while a JMenuItem object or one of its subclasses is selected. One or more of the methods declared in this interface are usually overridden to provide some keystroke-activated functionality to a menu. Although the MenuKeyListener interface declares more than one method, there is no corresponding adapter class.

Any class object can serve as a MenuKeyListener by implementing the MenuKeyListener interface. The syntax for doing this is

```
public class MyClass implements MenuKeyListener
```

Class MyClass would then provide an implementation of the methods declared in the MenuKeyListener interface.

For a MenuKeyListener to receive a MenuKeyEvent generated by a Swing menu component, the menu component must register the MenuKeyListener. The Swing menu component does this by adding the MenuKeyListener to its listener list using the `addMenuKeyListener()` method. To disconnect a MenuKeyListener from a Swing menu component, the menu component must remove the MenuKeyListener from its listener list by invoking the `removeMenuKeyListener()` method. The MenuKeyListener that was removed will no longer receive MenuKeyEvents generated by the menu component.

Syntax: public interface MenuKeyListener extends EventListener
Package: javax.swing.event
Interface hierarchy: EventListener—MenuKeyListener

The MenuKeyListener interface is part of the Swing event listener hierarchy.

Introduced: JDK 1.2

MenuKeyListener Interface Methods

```
public void menuKeyPressed(MenuKeyEvent event)
public void menuKeyReleased(MenuKeyEvent event)
public void menuKeyTyped(MenuKeyEvent event)
```

`menuKeyPressed()` is called if a key is pressed when the Swing menu component is selected.

`menuKeyReleased()` is called if a key is released when the Swing menu component is selected.

`menuKeyPressed()` is called if a key is typed (pressed and released) when the Swing menu component is selected.

Listener Registration Methods

```
public void addMenuKeyListener(MenuKeyListener listener)
public void removeMenuKeyListener(MenuKeyListener listener)
```

`addMenuKeyListener()` adds a MenuKeyListener to the invoking component's listener list. A MenuKeyEvent generated by the component will be sent to one of the three methods defined by the MenuKeyListener.

`removeMenuKeyListener()` removes a MenuKeyListener from the invoking component's listener list. The MenuKeyListener will no longer be notified when the component generates a MenuKeyEvent.

The `addMenuKeyListener()` and `removeMenuKeyListener()` methods are defined in the JMenuItem class.

EXAMPLE

See Chapter 6, Example 6.27 in the section "MenuKeyEvent Class," where a MenuKeyListener is used to provide keystroke-activated changes to the style of a label font.

MenuListener Interface

The MenuListener declares methods used to process MenuEvent objects. These are generated if a JMenu object is selected, deselected, canceled, or removed from the screen. One or more of the methods declared in this interface are usually overridden to respond to changes in the state of a menu. Although the MenuListener interface declares more than one method, there is no corresponding adapter class.

Any class object can serve as a MenuListener by implementing the MenuListener interface. The syntax for doing this is

```
public class MyClass implements MenuListener
```

Class MyClass would then provide an implementation of the methods declared in the MenuListener interface.

For a MenuListener to receive a MenuEvent generated by a JMenu, the JMenu must register the MenuListener. The JMenu does this by adding the MenuListener to its listener list using the `addMenuListener()` method. To disconnect a MenuListener from a JMenu, the JMenu must remove the MenuListener from its listener list by invoking the `removeMenuListener()` method. The MenuListener that was removed will no longer receive MenuEvents generated by the JMenu.

Syntax: public interface MenuListener extends EventListener

Package: javax.swing.event

Interface hierarchy: EventListener—MenuListener

The MenuListener interface is part of the Swing event listener hierarchy.

Introduced: JDK 1.2

MenuListener Interface Methods

public void menuCanceled(MenuEvent event)
public void menuDeselected(MenuEvent event)
public void menuSelected(MenuEvent event)

`menuCanceled()` is called if the MenuEvent represents the JMenu object being canceled or removed from the screen.

`menuDeselected()` is called when the JMenu object is deselected, meaning that the JMenu is no longer the currently active menu.

`menuSelected()` is called when the JMenu object is selected, meaning that the JMenu is the currently active menu.

Listener Registration Methods

> public void addMenuListener(MenuListener listener)
>
> public void removeMenuListener(MenuListener listener)

addMenuListener() adds a MenuListener to the invoking component's listener list. A MenuEvent generated by the component will be sent to one of the three methods defined by the MenuListener.

removeMenuListener() removes a MenuListener from the invoking component's listener list. The MenuListener will no longer be notified when the component generates a MenuEvent.

The addMenuListener() and removeMenuListener() methods are defined in the JMenu class.

EXAMPLE

See Chapter 6, Example 6.26 in the section "MenuEvent Class."

MouseInputListener Interface

The MouseInputListener interface is a convenient interface that declares all of the methods for handling mouse events in one interface. It is literally a combination of the MouseListener and MouseMotionListener interfaces. The MouseInputListener interface has a corresponding adapter class.

Any class object can serve as a MouseInputListener by implementing the MouseInputListener interface. The syntax for doing this is

```
public class MyClass implements MouseInputListener
```

Class MyClass would then provide an implementation of the methods declared in the MouseInputListener interface.

For a MouseInputListener to receive non-motion-oriented MouseEvents from an event source, the source must register the MouseInputListener, using the addMouseListener() method. To receive motion-oriented MouseEvents, the event source would register the MouseInputListener using the addMouseMotionListener() method. This is a quirk in the language in that there is no addMouseInputListener() method. If the event source calls the removeMouseListener() method, the MouseInputListener that was removed will no longer receive non-motion-oriented MouseEvents. If the event source calls the `removeMouseMotionListener()` method, the MouseInputListener that was removed will no longer receive motion-oriented MouseEvents.

Syntax:	public interface MouseInputListener extends MouseListener, MouseMotionListener
Package:	javax.swing.event
Interface hierarchy:	EventListener—MouseListener—MouseInputListener —MouseMotionListener
	The MouseInputListener interface is part of the Swing event listener hierarchy.
Introduced:	JDK 1.2

MouseInputListener Interface Methods

The MouseInputListener interface declares no new methods. It inherits the method declarations from the MouseListener and MouseMotionListener interfaces.

Methods Inherited from the MouseListener Interface

```
public void mouseClicked(MouseEvent event)
public void mouseEntered(MouseEvent event)
public void mouseExited(MouseEvent event)
public void mousePressed(MouseEvent event)
public void mouseReleased(MouseEvent event)
```

These methods are used to process the different types of non-motion-oriented MouseEvents. They are implemented by the MouseListener to contain whatever code is necessary to process the event.

`mouseClicked()` is called when a MouseEvent is generated due to the mouse being clicked (pressed and released) over the bounding area of the event source.

`mouseEntered()` is called when a MouseEvent is generated due to the mouse entering the bounding area of the event source.

`mouseExited()` is called when a MouseEvent is generated due to the mouse leaving the bounding area of the event source.

`mousePressed()` is called when a MouseEvent is generated due to the mouse being pressed over the bounding area of the event source.

`mouseReleased()` is called when a MouseEvent is generated due to the mouse being released over the bounding area of the event source.

Methods Inherited from the MouseMotionListener Interface

public void `mouseDragged(MouseEvent event)`
public void `mouseMoved(MouseEvent event)`

These methods are used to process the two types of motion-oriented MouseEvents. They are implemented by the MouseMotionListener to contain whatever code is necessary to process the event.

`mouseDragged()` is called when a MouseEvent is generated due to the mouse being dragged (moved with one or more mouse buttons pressed) inside the bounding area of the event source.

`mouseMoved()` is called when a MouseEvent is generated due to the mouse moving inside the bounding area of the event source.

Listener Registration Methods

public void `addMouseListener(MouseInputListener listener)`
public void `addMouseMotionListener(MouseInputListener listener)`
public void `removeMouseListener(MouseInputListener listener)`
public void `removeMouseMotionListener(MouseInputListener listener)`

For some reason, the Java API does not define `addMouseInputListener()` and `removeMouseInputListener()` methods. However, a MouseInputListener is also a MouseListener and a MouseMotionListener. To register a MouseInputListener to a GUI component, use either the `addMouseListener()` or `addMouseMotionListener()` methods and pass the method a reference to MouseInputListener.

One note of caution: If you use the `addMouseListener()` method to register the MouseInputListener, the listener will receive only non-motion-oriented mouse events. Similarly, if you use `addMouseMotionListener()`

the MouseInputListener will receive only motion-oriented mouse events. If you want the MouseInputListener to receive all types of events, you have to use both `add()` methods. The syntax for doing that would go something like this:

```
MyMouseInputListener listener = new MyMouseInputListener();
addMouseListener(listener);
addMouseMotionListener(listener);
```

The `removeMouseListener()` and `removeMouseMotionListener()` methods can be used to disconnect the invoking component from the MouseInputListener. The MouseInputListener will no longer be notified when the component generates a MouseEvent.

EXAMPLE

Example 8.7 recreates the doodle pad shown in Chapter 6, Example 6.28 in the section "MouseEvent Class," using a MouseInputListener to receive and process the mouse events. A JPanel is placed on a JFrame and the JPanel registers a MouseInputListener. Whenever the user drags a line across the panel MouseEvents are generated and sent to the `mousePressed()` and `mouseDragged()` methods. These methods draw a line following the path of the mouse.

EXAMPLE 8.7 MOUSEINPUTLISTENER INTERFACE

```
import java.awt.*;
import java.awt.event.*;
import javax.swing.*;
import javax.swing.event.*;

public class MouseInputDemo extends JFrame
{
   private JPanel panel;
   private int startX, startY, endX, endY;

   public MouseInputDemo()
   {
/*   A JPanel object is placed on a Frame and registers a       */
/*   MouseInputListener to receive both motion-oriented and     */
/*   non-motion-oriented MouseEvents.                           */

      panel = new JPanel();
      MouseInputHandler listener = new MouseInputHandler();
      panel.addMouseListener(listener);
      panel.addMouseMotionListener(listener);
```

```java
            getContentPane().add(panel);

            setDefaultCloseOperation(JFrame.EXIT_ON_CLOSE);
            setBounds(100, 100, 300, 200);
            setVisible(true);
        }

        /* The MouseInputListener is implemented as an inner class.  When    */
        /* the user presses the mouse inside the bounding area of the        */
        /* panel, a MouseEvent is generated and sent to the mousePressed()   */
        /* method.  This method sets the starting point for the line.        */
        /* When the mouse is dragged inside the panel, MouseEvents are       */
        /* generated and sent to the mouseDragged() method which draws a     */
        /* line according to the position of the mouse.  Every method       */
        /* declared in the MouseListener and MouseMotionListener interfaces  */
        /* must be given an implementation.  The other five methods are      */
        /* implemented as stub methods.                                      */

        class MouseInputHandler implements MouseInputListener
        {
            public void mousePressed(MouseEvent event)
            {
                startX = event.getX();
                startY = event.getY();
                endX = startX;
                endY = startY;
            }

            public void mouseDragged(MouseEvent event)
            {
                startX = endX;
                startY = endY;
                endX = event.getX();
                endY = event.getY();
                panel.getGraphics().drawLine(startX, startY, endX, endY);
            }

            public void mouseClicked(MouseEvent event) {}
            public void mouseEntered(MouseEvent event) {}
            public void mouseExited(MouseEvent event) {}
            public void mouseReleased(MouseEvent event) {}
            public void mouseMoved(MouseEvent event) {}
        }

        public static void main(String args[])
        {
            MouseInputDemo demo = new MouseInputDemo();
        }
    }
```

When you start this application, a blank frame appears on your screen. Press the mouse and drag it across the frame. A line is drawn. Sign your name. Draw a picture of your dog. When your children are bored, set them up with this doodle pad for hours of entertainment.

MouseListener Interface

The MouseListener interface declares methods for processing non-motion-oriented MouseEvent objects. These occur whenever the mouse is pressed, released, clicked (pressed and released), enters, or leaves the bounding area of a GUI component. The interface defines five methods, one for each of the five non-motion oriented MouseEvent types. The MouseListener interface has a corresponding adapter class.

Any class object can serve as a MouseListener by implementing the MouseListener interface. The syntax for doing this is

```
public class MyClass implements MouseListener
```

Class MyClass would then provide an implementation of the methods declared in the MouseListener interface. A MouseListener could also be created by extending the MouseAdapter class.

For a MouseListener to receive a non-motion-oriented MouseEvent generated by a component, the component must register the MouseListener. The component does this by adding the MouseListener to its listener list using the `addMouseListener()` method. To disconnect a MouseListener from a component, the component must remove the MouseListener from its listener list by invoking the `removeMouseListener()` method. The MouseListener that was removed will no longer receive MouseEvents generated by the component.

Syntax: public interface MouseListener extends EventListener

Package: java.awt.event

Interface hierarchy: EventListener—MouseListener

The MouseListener interface is part of the AWT event listener hierarchy.

Introduced: JDK 1.1

MouseListener Interface Methods

public void mouseClicked(MouseEvent event)
public void mouseEntered(MouseEvent event)
public void mouseExited(MouseEvent event)
public void mousePressed(MouseEvent event)
public void mouseReleased(MouseEvent event)

These methods are used to process the different types of non-motion-oriented MouseEvents. They are implemented by the MouseListener to contain whatever code is necessary to process the event.

`mouseClicked()` is called when a MouseEvent is generated due to the mouse being clicked (pressed and released) over the bounding area of the event source.

`mouseEntered()` is called when a MouseEvent is generated due to the mouse entering the bounding area of the event source.

`mouseExited()` is called when a MouseEvent is generated due to the mouse leaving the bounding area of the event source.

`mousePressed()` is called when a MouseEvent is generated due to the mouse being pressed over the bounding area of the event source.

`mouseReleased()` is called when a MouseEvent is generated due to the mouse being released over the bounding area of the event source.

Listener Registration Methods

public void addMouseListener(MouseListener listener)
public void removeMouseListener(MouseListener listener)

`addMouseListener()` adds a MouseListener to the invoking component's listener list. A non-motion-oriented MouseEvent generated by the component will be sent to one of the five methods defined by the MouseListener.

`removeMouseListener()` removes a MouseListener from the invoking component's listener list. The MouseListener will no longer be notified when the component generates a non-motion-oriented MouseEvent.

The `addMouseListener()` and `removeMouseListener()` methods are defined in the Component class.

EXAMPLE

In Example 8.8, non-motion-oriented MouseEvents are used to change the look of a JButton, depending on what mouse action is occurring. The JButton is placed on a JFrame and registers a MouseListener. Whenever the mouse enters the bounding area of the button, a MouseEvent is generated and sent to the `mouseEntered()` method. This method turns the background color of the button pink. If the mouse is then pressed, the JButton generates a MouseEvent which is sent to the `mousePressed()` method. This method turns the background color of the JButton red.

When the mouse is released, a MouseEvent is sent to the `mouseReleased()` method. This method turns the background color back to pink. When the mouse leaves the bounding area of the JButton, a MouseEvent is sent to the `mouseExited()` method which changes the background color to the default color, light gray. The `mouseClicked()` method is not used with this application, but it must still be implemented in some manner. It is implemented as a stub method.

EXAMPLE 8.8 MOUSELISTENER INTERFACE

```
import java.awt.*;
import java.awt.event.*;
import javax.swing.*;

public class MouseListenerDemo extends JFrame
                         implements MouseListener
{
   private JButton button;

   public MouseListenerDemo()
     {
/*   A JButton is added to a JFrame.  The button registers    */
/*   a MouseListener.  Since the MouseListenerDemo class      */
/*   itself serves as the MouseListener, the addMouseListener() */
/*   method is passed the "this" reference.                   */

      button = new JButton("help");
      button.setBorder(BorderFactory.createRaisedBevelBorder());
      button.setBackground(Color.lightGray);
      button.addMouseListener(this);
```

```
        JPanel panel = new JPanel();
        panel.add(button);

        getContentPane().add(panel);

        setDefaultCloseOperation(JFrame.EXIT_ON_CLOSE);
        setBounds(100, 100, 200, 200);
        setVisible(true);
    }

/*  Since the MouseListenerDemo class serves as the MouseListener    */
/*  all of the implementations of the methods declared in the        */
/*  MouseListener interface are implemented inside the               */
/*  MouseListenerDemo class.  These methods are used to change       */
/*  the background color of the JButton depending on what the        */
/*  mouse is doing.  The mouseClicked() method is not used, so       */
/*  it is implemented as a stub method.                              */

    public void mouseEntered(MouseEvent event)
    {
        button.setBackground(Color.pink);
    }

    public void mouseExited(MouseEvent event)
    {
        button.setBackground(Color.lightGray);
    }

    public void mousePressed(MouseEvent event)
    {
        button.setBackground(Color.red);
    }

    public void mouseReleased(MouseEvent event)
    {
        button.setBackground(Color.pink);
    }

    public void mouseClicked(MouseEvent event) {}

    public static void main(String args[])
    {
        MouseListenerDemo demo = new MouseListenerDemo();
    }
}
```

When this application starts, the button is light gray in color. Now move the mouse arrow over the button. The background color turns pink. Now press the button. The background color is red. If you release the button, the background color turns pink again. When you move the mouse away from the button, the color returns to light gray. All of this is accomplished by non-motion-oriented MouseEvents and simulates the rollover-pressed-selected capability of Swing button components.

MouseMotionListener Interface

The MouseMotionListener interface declares methods used to process motion-oriented MouseEvent objects. These occur whenever the mouse is moved or dragged through the bounding area of a GUI component. The interface defines two methods, one of which will be called whenever a motion-oriented MouseEvent is generated from an event source that has registered the MouseMotionListener. The MouseMotionListener interface has a corresponding adapter class.

Any class object can serve as a MouseMotionListener by implementing the MouseMotionListener interface. The syntax for doing this is

```
public class MyClass implements MouseMotionListener
```

Class MyClass would then provide an implementation of the methods declared in the MouseMotionListener interface. A MouseMotionListener could also be created by extending the MouseMotionAdapter class.

For a MouseMotionListener to receive a motion-oriented MouseEvent generated by a component, the component must register the MouseMotionListener. The component does this by adding the MouseMotionListener to its listener list using the `addMouseMotionListener()` method. To disconnect a MouseMotionListener from a component, the component must remove the MouseMotionListener from its listener list by invoking the `removeMouseMotionListener()` method. The MouseMotionListener that was removed will no longer receive motion-oriented MouseEvents generated by the component.

Syntax:	public interface MouseMotionListener extends EventListener
Package:	java.awt.event
Interface hierarchy:	EventListener—MouseMotionListener
	The MouseMotionListener interface is part of the AWT event listener hierarchy.
Introduced:	JDK 1.1

MouseMotionListener Interface Methods

> public void `mouseDragged(MouseEvent event)`
>
> public void `mouseMoved(MouseEvent event)`

These methods are used to process the two types of motion-oriented MouseEvents. They are implemented by the MouseMotionListener to contain whatever code is necessary to process the event.

`mouseDragged()` is called when a MouseEvent is generated due to the mouse being dragged (moved with one or more mouse buttons pressed) inside the bounding area of the event source.

`mouseMoved()` is called when a MouseEvent is generated due to the mouse moving inside the bounding area of the event source.

Listener Registration Methods

> public void `addMouseMotionListener(MouseMotionListener listener)`
>
> public void `removeMouseMotionListener(MouseMotionListener listener)`

`addMouseMotionListener()` adds a MouseMotionListener to the invoking component's listener list. A motion-oriented MouseEvent generated by the component will be sent to either the `mouseDragged()` or `mouseMoved()` method of the MouseMotionListener.

`removeMouseMotionListener()` removes a MouseMotionListener from the invoking component's listener list. The MouseMotionListener will no longer be notified when the component generates a motion-oriented MouseEvent.

The `addMouseMotionListener()` and `removeMouseMotionListener()` methods are defined in the Component class.

EXAMPLE

In Example 8.9, a MouseMotionListener is used to keep track of the current location of the mouse and to determine whether the mouse is being moved or dragged across the bounding area of a JPanel. The JPanel is placed in the center region of a JFrame. The panel registers a MouseMotionListener. Whenever the mouse is moved or dragged within the bounding area of the JPanel, a MouseEvent is generated and sent to either the `mouseMoved()` or `mouseDragged()` method. The JTextField placed at the bottom of the JFrame is updated with the current mouse position and with type of mouse motion (moved or dragged).

EXAMPLE 8.9 MOUSEMOTIONLISTENER INTERFACE

```
import java.awt.*;
import java.awt.event.*;
import javax.swing.*;

public class MMListenerDemo extends JFrame
{
   private JTextField jtf;

   public MMListenerDemo()
   {
      jtf = new JTextField(20);
      jtf.setEditable(false);

/* A Panel registers a MouseMotionHandler and is added to a JFrame */

      JPanel panel = new JPanel();
      panel.addMouseMotionListener(new MouseMotionHandler());
      panel.setBackground(Color.yellow);

      getContentPane().add(panel, BorderLayout.CENTER);
      getContentPane().add(jtf, BorderLayout.SOUTH);

      setDefaultCloseOperation(JFrame.EXIT_ON_CLOSE);
      setBounds(100, 100, 200, 200);
      setVisible(true);
   }

/* The MouseMotionListener is implemented as an inner class.      */
/* Whenever the mouse is moved or dragged within the bounding     */
/* area of the JPanel, MouseEvents are generated and sent to      */
/* the MouseMotionListener.  The JTextField at the bottom of      */
/* the JFrame is updated with the current position of the mouse.  */

   class MouseMotionHandler implements MouseMotionListener
   {
      public void mouseMoved(MouseEvent event)
      {
         jtf.setText "+mouse moved to event.getX()+","+event.getY());
      }

      public void mouseDragged(MouseEvent event)
      {
```

```
            jtf.setText("mouse dragged to "+event.getX()+","+event.getY());
         }
      }
   }
   public static void main(String args[])
   {
      MMListenerDemo demo = new MMListenerDemo();
   }
}
```

Start this program and move the mouse inside the yellow panel area. Notice how the textfield is updated with the mouse location. Now try dragging the mouse. The MouseEvents generated are sent to the `mouseDragged()` method and the textfield method indicates this.

PopupMenuListener Interface

The JPopupMenu class is similar to the JInternalFrame class in that it has its own event, PopupMenuEvent, and its own listener interface, PopupMenuListener. This interface declares methods used to process PopupMenuEvent objects. These are generated when a JPopupMenu receives a command to become visible, when it receives a command to become invisible, or when the JPopupMenu is canceled. Although the PopupMenuListener interface declares more than one method, there is no corresponding adapter class.

Any class object can serve as a PopupMenuListener by implementing the PopupMenuListener interface. The syntax for doing this is

`public class MyClass implements PopupMenuListener`

Class MyClass would then provide an implementation of the methods declared in the PopupMenuListener interface.

For a PopupMenuListener to receive a PopupMenuEvent generated by a JPopupMenu, the JPopupMenu must register the PopupMenuListener. The JPopupMenu does this by adding the PopupMenuListener to its listener list using the `addPopupMenuListener()` method. To disconnect a PopupMenuListener from a JPopupMenu, the JPopupMenu must remove the PopupMenuListener from its listener list by invoking the `removePopupMenuListener()` method. The PopupMenuListener that was removed will no longer receive PopupMenuEvents generated by the JPopupMenu.

Syntax: public interface PopupMenuListener extends EventListener
Package: javax.swing.event
Interface hierarchy: EventListener—PopupMenuListener

The PopupMenuListener interface is part of the Swing event listener hierarchy.

Introduced: JDK 1.2

PopupMenuListener Interface Methods

```
public void popupMenuCanceled(PopupMenuEvent event)
```

```
public void popupMenuWillBecomeVisible(PopupMenuEvent event)
```

```
public void popupMenuWillBecomeInvisible(PopupMenuEvent event)
```

`popupMenuCanceled()` is called when the JPopupMenu is canceled or removed from the screen.

`popupMenuWillBecomeVisible()` is called just before the JPopupMenu is to become visible.

`popupMenuWillBecomeInvisible()` is called just before the JPopupMenu is to become invisible.

Listener Registration Methods

```
public void addPopupMenuListener(PopupMenuListener listener)
```

```
public void removePopupMenuListener(PopupMenuListener listener)
```

`addPopupMenuListener()` adds a PopupMenuListener to the invoking JPopupMenu's listener list. A PopupMenuEvent generated by the JPopupMenu will be sent to one of the three methods defined by the PopupMenuListener.

`removePopupMenuListener()` removes a PopupMenuListener from the invoking JPopupMenu component's listener list. The PopupMenuListener will no longer be notified when the component generates a PopupMenuEvent.

The `addPopupMenuListener()` and `removePopupMenuListener()` methods are defined in the JPopupMenu class.

EXAMPLE

See Chapter 6, Example 6.29 in the section "PopupMenuEvent Class," where a PopupMenuListener is used to detect changes in the state of a JPopupMenu object.

PropertyChangeListener Interface

The PropertyChangeListener interface declares one method, `propertyChange()`, that is used for processing PropertyChangeEvents that occur because a bound property of an object changes. Usually, this method is overridden to implement or respond to the property change. Because the PropertyChangeListener interface only declares one method, there is no corresponding adapter class.

Any class object can serve as a PropertyChangeListener by implementing the PropertyChangeListener interface. The syntax for doing this is

```
public class MyClass implements PropertyChangeListener
```

Class MyClass would then provide an implementation of the `propertyChange()` method declared in the PropertyChangeListener interface.

For a PropertyChangeListener to receive a PropertyChangeEvent generated by an event source, the source must register the PropertyChangeListener. The event source does this by adding the PropertyChangeListener to its listener list using the `addPropertyChangeListener()` method. To disconnect a PropertyChangeListener from an event source, the source must remove the PropertyChangeListener from its listener list by invoking the `removePropertyChangeListener()` method. The PropertyChangeListener that was removed will no longer receive PropertyChangeEvents generated by the event source.

Syntax:	public interface PropertyChangeListener extends EventListener
Package:	java.beans
Interface hierarchy:	EventListener—PropertyChangeListener
	Although the PropertyChangeListener interface is contained in the java.beans package, it is used with AWT and Swing components as well as Java Beans.
Introduced:	JDK 1.2

PropertyChangeListener Interface Methods

> **public void** `propertyChange(PropertyChangeEvent event)`

`propertyChange()` is called whenever a bound property is changed. The method is usually overridden to implement the property change.

Listener Registration Methods

> **public void** `addPropertyChangeListener(PropertyChangeListener listener)`
>
> **public void** `addPropertyChangeListener(String property, PropertyChangeListener listener)`
>
> **public void** `removePropertyChangeListener(PropertyChangeListener listener)`
>
> **public void** `removePropertyChangeListener(String property, PropertyChangeListener listener)`

`addPropertyChangeListener()` adds a PropertyChangeListener to the invoking object's listener list. A PropertyChangeEvent due to a change in a bound property generated by the object will be sent to the `propertyChange()` method of the PropertyChangeListener.

`removePropertyChangeListener()` removes a PropertyChangeListener from the invoking object's listener list. The PropertyChangeListener will no longer be notified when the object generates a PropertyChangeEvent.

The `addPropertyChangeListener()` and `removePropertyChangeListener()` methods are defined in the following classes and interfaces:

- Component class
- PropertyEditor interface
- PropertyChangeSupport class
- Customizer interface
- PropertyEditorSupport class
- JComponent class
- Action interface

- AbstractAction class
- PropertyChangeSupport class
- TableColumn class
- DefaultTreeSelectionModel class
- TreeSelectionModel interface
- Toolkit
- BeanContextChild interface
- BeanContextChildSupport class

EXAMPLE

See Chapter 6, Example 6.30 in the section "PropertyChangeEvent Class," where a property change listener is used to update the text color of a label.

TableColumnModelListener Interface

The TableColumnModelListener interface declares methods for processing events that are generated when some aspect of a TableColumnModel changes. Possible changes are that a column has been added, removed, moved, has had its margin changed, or has had its selection model changed. One or more of the methods declared in this interface is usually overridden to respond to changes in a table column model. Although the TableColumnModelListener interface declares more than one method, there is no corresponding adapter class.

Any class object can serve as a TableColumnModelListener by implementing the TableColumnModelListener interface. The syntax for doing this is

```
public class MyClass implements TableColumnModelListener
```

Class MyClass would then provide an implementation of the methods declared in the TableColumnModelListener interface.

For a TableColumnModelListener to receive a TableColumnModelEvent, ChangeEvent, or ListSelectionEvent generated by a TableColumnModel, the TableColumnModel must register the TableColumnModelListener. The TableColumnModel does this by adding the TableColumnModelListener to its listener list using the `addColumnModelListener()` method. To disconnect a TableColumnModelListener from a TableColumnModel, the TableColumnModel must remove the TableColumnModelListener from its listener list by invoking the `removeColumnModelListener()` method. The

TableColumnModelListener that was removed will no longer receive a TableColumnModelEvent, ChangeEvent, or ListSelectionEvent generated by the TableColumnModel.

Syntax: public interface TableColumnModelListener extends EventListener

Package: javax.swing.event

Interface hierarchy: EventListener—TableColumnModelListener

The TableColumnModelListener interface is part of the Swing event listener hierarchy.

Introduced: JDK 1.2

TableColumnModelListener Interface Methods

```
public void columnAdded(TableColumnModelEvent event)
public void columnMarginChanged(ChangeEvent event)
public void columnMoved(TableColumnModelEvent event)
public void columnRemoved(TableColumnModelEvent event)
public void columnSelectionChanged(ListSelectionEvent event)
```

`columnAdded()` is called when a TableColumnModelEvent is generated due to a column being added to the column model.

`columnMarginChanged()` is called when a column is moved due to a margin change. Note that this method takes a ChangeEvent as an argument.

`columnMoved()` is called when the TableColumnModelEvent is due to a column having moved.

`columnRemoved()` is called when the event is generated because a column was removed from the column model.

`columnSelectionChanged()` is called is the selection model of the TableColumnModel has been changed. Note that this method takes a ListSelectionEvent as an argument.

Listener Registration Methods

```
public void addColumnModelListener(TableColumnModelListener listener)
public void removeColumnModelListener(TableColumnModelListener listener)
```

addColumnModelListener() adds a TableColumnModelListener to the invoking TableColumnModel object's listener list. A TableColumnModelEvent, ListSelectionEvent, or ChangeEvent generated by the TableColumnModel will be sent to one of the five methods defined by the TableColumnModelListener.

removeColumnModelListener() removes a TableColumnModelListener from the invoking TableColumnModel object's listener list. The TableColumnModelListener will no longer be notified when the TableColumnModel generates a TableColumnModelEvent.

Note that these methods are named "addColumnModelListener" and "removeColumnModelListener" instead of "addTableColumnModelListener" and "removeTableColumnModelListener." Apparently, the full names were deemed to be too long.

The `addColumnModelListener()` and `removeColumnModelListener()` methods are defined in the DefaultTableColumnModel class and the TableColumnModel interface.

EXAMPLE

See Chapter 6, Example 6.33 in the section "TableColumnModelEvent Class," where a TableColumnModelListener is used to monitor changes to a table column model.

TableModelListener Interface

The TableModelListener interface declares one method, `tableChanged()`, that is used for processing TableModelEvent objects. These occur whenever a change is made to a TableModel. Possible changes include the addition or removal of rows or columns from the model or a change to the data contained inside the table. The TableModelListener interface declares only one method, so there is no corresponding adapter class.

Any class object can serve as a TableModelListener by implementing the TableModelListener interface. The syntax for doing this is

```
public class MyClass implements TableModelListener
```

Class MyClass would then provide an implementation of the method declared in the TableModelListener interface.

For a TableModelListener to receive a TableModelEvent generated by a TableModel, the TableModel must register the TableModelListener. The TableModel does this by adding the TableModelListener to its listener list using the `addTableModelListener()` method. To disconnect a TableModelListener from a TableModel, the source must remove the TableModelListener from its listener list by invoking the `removeTableModelListener()` method. The TableModelListener that was removed will no longer receive TableModelEvents generated by the TableModel.

An interesting note is that the JTable class uses a built-in TableModelListener to update the table display when changes are made to the table model.

Syntax:	public interface TableModelListener extends EventListener
Package:	javax.swing.event
Interface hierarchy:	EventListener—TableModelListener
	The TableModelListener interface is part of the Swing event listener hierarchy.
Introduced:	JDK 1.2

TableModelListener Interface Methods

```
public void tableChanged(TableModelEvent event)
```

`tableChanged()` is called when a TableModelEvent is generated by the table model. The TableModelEvent object contains detailed information about the nature of the event.

Listener Registration Methods

```
public void addTableModelListener(TableModelListener listener)
```

```
public void removeTableModelListener(TableModelListener listener)
```

`addTableModelListener()` adds a TableModelListener to the invoking TableModel object's listener list. A TableModelEvent generated by the TableModel will be sent to the `tableChanged()` method of the TableModelListener.

`removeTableModelListener()` removes a TableModelListener from the invoking TableModel object's listener list. The TableModelListener will no longer be notified when the TableModel generates a TableModelEvent.

The `addTableModelListener()` and `removeTableModel-Listener()` methods are defined in the TableModel interface and the AbstractTableModel Class.

EXAMPLE

See Chapter 6, Example 6.34 in the section "TableModel Event Class," where a TableModelListener is used to detect changes to the data contained inside a JTable.

TextListener Interface

The TextListener interface declares methods for processing TextEvent objects. These occur when the text inside a TextField or TextArea component is changed. The interface declares one method, `textValueChanged()`, that is called whenever a TextEvent is generated from an event source that has registered the TextListener. Because the TextListener interface has only one method, it does not have a corresponding adapter class.

Any class object can serve as a TextListener by implementing the TextListener interface. The syntax for doing this is

```
public class MyClass implements TextListener
```

Class MyClass would then provide an implementation of the `textValueChanged()` method.

For a TextListener to receive a TextEvent generated by an AWT text component, the component must register the TextListener. The AWT text component does this by adding the TextListener to its listener list using the `addTextListener()` method. To disconnect a TextListener from an AWT text component, the component must remove the TextListener from its listener list by invoking the `removeTextListener()` method. The TextListener that was removed will no longer receive TextEvents generated by the component.

Syntax:	public interface TextListener extends EventListener
Package:	java.awt.event
Interface hierarchy:	EventListener—TextListener
	The TextListener interface is part of the AWT event listener hierarchy.
Introduced:	JDK 1.1

TextListener Interface Methods

```
public void textValueChanged(TextEvent event)
```

The `textValueChanged()` method is called when a TextEvent object is generated by an event source that has registered the TextListener. The method is passed a reference to the TextEvent object that was generated.

Listener Registration Methods

```
public void addTextListener(TextListener listener)
public void removeTextListener(TextListener listener)
```

`addTextListener()` adds a TextListener to the invoking component's listener list. A TextEvent generated by the component will be sent to the `textChanged()` method of the TextListener.

`removeTextListener()` removes a TextListener from the invoking component's listener list. The TextListener will no longer be notified when the component generates a TextEvent.

The `addTextListener()` and `removeTextListener()` methods are defined in the TextComponent class. Keep in mind that only AWT text components will generate TextEvents and register TextListeners. Swing text components generate UndoableEditEvents and/or DocumentEvents when the text inside them is changed.

EXAMPLE

See Chapter 6, Example 6.35 in the section "TextEvent Class," where a TextListener is used to monitor changes to the text contained in a TextField object.

TreeExpansionListener Interface

The TreeExpansionListener interface is one of two interfaces (the other being the TreeWillExpandListener interface) that declare methods for processing TreeExpansionEvents. In this case, the methods process TreeExpansionEvents due to a node of a Tree object having expanded or collapsed. Although the TreeExpansionListener interface declares more than one method, there is no corresponding adapter class.

Any class object can serve as a TreeExpansionListener by implementing the TreeExpansionListener interface. The syntax for doing this is

```
public class MyClass implements TreeExpansionListener
```

Class MyClass would then provide an implementation of the methods declared in the TreeExpansionListener interface.

For a TreeExpansionListener to receive a TreeExpansionEvent generated by a JTree, the JTree must register the TreeExpansionListener. The JTree does this by adding the TreeExpansionListener to its listener list using the `addTreeExpansionListener()` method. To disconnect a TreeExpansionListener from a JTree, the JTree must remove the TreeExpansionListener from its listener list by invoking the `removeTreeExpansionListener()` method. The TreeExpansionListener that was removed will no longer receive TreeExpansionEvents generated by the JTree.

Syntax:	public interface TreeExpansionListener extends EventListener
Package:	javax.swing.event
Interface hierarchy:	EventListener—TreeExpansionListener
	The TreeExpansionListener interface is part of the Swing event listener hierarchy.
Introduced:	JDK 1.2

TreeExpansionListener Interface Methods

```
public void treeCollapsed(TreeExpansionEvent event)
public void treeExpanded(TreeExpansionEvent event)
```

`treeCollapsed()` is called when a node in the JTree object has been collapsed.

`treeExpanded()` is invoked when a node in the JTree object has been expanded.

Listener Registration Methods

```
public void addTreeExpansionListener(TreeExpansionListener listener)
public void removeTreeExpansionListener(TreeExpansionListener listener)
```

addTreeExpansionListener() adds a TreeExpansionListener to the invoking JTree component's listener list. A TreeExpansionEvent generated by the JTree will be sent to either the `treeCollapsed()` or `treeExpanded()` method of the TreeExpansionListener.

removeTreeExpansionListener() removes a TreeExpansionListener from the invoking JTree component's listener list. The TreeExpansionListener will no longer be notified when the component generates a TreeExpansionEvent.

The `addTreeExpansionListener()` and `removeTreeExpansionListener()` methods are defined in the JTree class.

EXAMPLE

In Example 8.10, a TreeExpansionListener is used to monitor changes in the expanded or collapsed state of the nodes of a JTree object. A JTree is created and placed on a JFrame. The JTree registers a TreeExpansionListener. Whenever the user expands or collapses a node, a TreeExpansionEvent is generated and sent to either the `treeCollapsed()` or `treeExpanded()` methods. These methods update a JTextField with the identity of the node that was expanded or collapsed.

EXAMPLE 8.10 TREEEXPANSIONLISTENER INTERFACE

```java
import javax.swing.*;
import javax.swing.tree.*;
import javax.swing.event.*;
import java.awt.*;
import java.awt.event.*;

public class TreeExpansionDemo2 extends JFrame
{
   private JTree tree;
   private JTextField jtf;

   public TreeExpansionDemo2()
   {
/*   A Collection of DefaultMutableTreeNode objects are created that   */
/*   will form the components of a tree.                               */

      DefaultMutableTreeNode league =
            new DefaultMutableTreeNode("Soccer League");
```

```
        DefaultMutableTreeNode north =
                new DefaultMutableTreeNode("North Division");
        DefaultMutableTreeNode south =
                new DefaultMutableTreeNode("South Division");

        DefaultMutableTreeNode jets =
                    new DefaultMutableTreeNode("Jets");
        DefaultMutableTreeNode raiders =
                    new DefaultMutableTreeNode("Raiders");
        DefaultMutableTreeNode fins =
                    new DefaultMutableTreeNode("Fins");
        DefaultMutableTreeNode shooters =
                    new DefaultMutableTreeNode("Shooters");
        DefaultMutableTreeNode lions =
                    new DefaultMutableTreeNode("Lions");
        DefaultMutableTreeNode tigers =
                    new DefaultMutableTreeNode("Tigers");

/* The node hierarchy is loaded into a DefaultTreeModel object.   */

        DefaultTreeModel dtm = new DefaultTreeModel(league);
        dtm.insertNodeInto(north, league, 0);
        dtm.insertNodeInto(south, league, 1);
        dtm.insertNodeInto(jets, north, 0);
        dtm.insertNodeInto(raiders, north, 1);
        dtm.insertNodeInto(fins, north, 2);
        dtm.insertNodeInto(shooters, south, 0);
        dtm.insertNodeInto(lions, south, 1);
        dtm.insertNodeInto(tigers, south, 2);

/* A JTree object is created using the previously created tree model. */
/* The JTree registers a TreeExpansionListener.                       */

        tree = new JTree(dtm);
        tree.setShowsRootHandles(true);
        tree.addTreeExpansionListener(new TreeExpansionHandler());

        jtf = new JTextField(20);
        jtf.setEditable(false);

        getContentPane().add( new JScrollPane(tree), BorderLayout.CENTER );
        getContentPane().add( jtf, BorderLayout.SOUTH );

        setDefaultCloseOperation(JFrame.EXIT_ON_CLOSE);
        setBounds(100, 100, 300, 300);
        setVisible(true);
    }

/* The TreeExpansionListener is implemented as an inner class.           */
/* When the user expands or collapses a node, a TreeExpansionEvent       */
/* is generated and sent to either the treeCollapsed() or                */
```

```
/*   treeExpanded() methods.  The identity of the node that caused    */
/*   the event is listed in a JTextField.                             */

   class TreeExpansionHandler implements TreeExpansionListener
   {
      public void treeCollapsed(TreeExpansionEvent event)
      {
         TreePath path = event.getPath();
         jtf.setText(""+path.getLastPathComponent()+" node collapsed");
      }

      public void treeExpanded(TreeExpansionEvent event)
      {
         TreePath path = event.getPath();
         jtf.setText(""+path.getLastPathComponent()+" node expanded");
      }
   }

   public static void main(String args[])
   {
      TreeExpansionDemo2 demo = new TreeExpansionDemo2();
   }
}
```

When you run this program, a JTree appears on the screen. Try expanding and collapsing some of the nodes. The identity of the node appears in the textfield.

TreeModelListener Interface

The TreeModelListener interface declares methods for processing TreeModelEvents. These occur when some aspect of a tree model is changed. Possible changes are that nodes have been inserted, removed, or changed in some other way. One or more methods declared in this interface are usually overridden to respond to a change in the tree model of a tree. Although the TreeModelListener interface declares more than one method, there is no corresponding adapter class.

Any class object can serve as a TreeModelListener by implementing the TreeModelListener interface. The syntax for doing this is

```
public class MyClass implements TreeModelListener
```

Class MyClass would then provide an implementation of the methods declared in the TreeModelListener interface.

For a TreeModelListener to receive a TreeModelEvent generated by a TreeModel, the TreeModel must register the TreeModelListener. The TreeModel does this by adding the TreeModelListener to its listener list using the `addTreeModelListener()` method. To disconnect a TreeModelListener from a TreeModel, the TreeModel must remove the TreeModelListener from its listener list by invoking the `removeTreeModelListener()` method. The TreeModelListener that was removed will no longer receive TreeModelEvents generated by the TreeModel.

Syntax:	public interface TreeModelListener extends EventListener
Package:	javax.swing.event
Interface hierarchy:	EventListener—TreeModelListener
	The TreeModelListener interface is part of the Swing event listener hierarchy.
Introduced:	JDK 1.2

TreeModelListener Interface Methods

```
public void treeNodesChanged(TreeModelEvent event)
public void treeNodesInserted(TreeModelEvent event)
public void treeNodesRemoved(TreeModelEvent event)
public void treeStructureChanged(TreeModelEvent event)
```

`treeNodesChanged()` is called when the TreeModelEvent is generated due to a change in an existing node or nodes.

`treeNodesInserted()` is invoked if one or more nodes have been inserted into the tree.

`treeNodesRemoved()` is called if one or more nodes were removed from the tree.

`treeStructureChanged()` is called if the change to the tree structure was drastic and the resulting TreeModelEvent cannot be properly assigned to one of the other three methods.

Listener Registration Methods

> public void addTreeModelListener(TreeModelListener listener)
>
> public void removeTreeModelListener(TreeModelListener listener)

addTreeModelListener() adds a TreeModelListener to the invoking TreeModel object's listener list. A TreeModelEvent generated by the TreeModel will be sent to one of the four methods defined by the TreeModelListener.

removeTreeModelListener() removes a TreeModelListener from the invoking TreeModel object's listener list. The TreeModelListener will no longer be notified when the TreeModel generates a TreeModelEvent.

The addTreeModelListener() and removeTreeModelListener() methods are defined in the TreeModel interface and the DefaultTreeModel class.

EXAMPLE

See Chapter 6, Example 6.37 in the section "TreeModelEvent Class," where a TreeModelListener is used to confirm the removal of a tree node.

TreeSelectionListener Interface

The TreeSelectionListener interface declares one method, valueChanged(), that is used for processing TreeSelectionEvents. These occur when the selection in a TreeSelectionModel changes—in other words, when the currently selected node of a tree changes. The valueChanged() method is usually overridden to respond to a node selection change. Because the TreeModelListener interface declares only one method, there is no corresponding adapter class.

Any class object can serve as a TreeSelectionListener by implementing the TreeSelectionListener interface. The syntax for doing this is

```
public class MyClass implements TreeSelectionListener
```

Class MyClass would then provide an implementation of the method declared in the TreeSelectionListener interface.

For a TreeSelectionListener to receive a TreeSelectionEvent generated by an event source, the source must register the TreeSelectionListener. The event source does this by adding the TreeSelectionListener to its listener list using the `addTreeSelectionListener()` method. For JTree objects, the TreeSelectionModel associated with the JTree can register the TreeSelectionListener or the JTree object itself can register the listener. To disconnect a TreeSelectionListener from an event source, the source must remove the TreeSelectionListener from its listener list by invoking the `removeTreeSelectionListener()` method. The TreeSelectionListener that was removed will no longer receive TreeSelectionEvents generated by the event source.

Syntax:	public interface TreeSelectionListener extends EventListener
Package:	javax.swing.event
Interface hierarchy:	EventListener—TreeSelectionListener
	The TreeSelectionListener interface is part of the Swing event listener hierarchy.
Introduced:	JDK 1.2

TreeSelectionListener Interface Methods

```
public void valueChanged(TreeSelectionEvent event)
```

`valueChanged()` is called whenever a TreeSelectionEvent is generated by the TreeSelectionModel.

Listener Registration Methods

```
public void addTreeSelectionListener(TreeSelectionListener listener)
public void removeTreeSelectionListener(TreeSelectionListener listener)
```

`addTreeSelectionListener()` adds a TreeSelectionListener to the invoking object's listener list. A TreeSelectionEvent generated by the object will be sent to the `valueChanged()` method of the TreeSelectionListener.

`removeTreeSelectionListener()` removes a TreeSelectionListener from the invoking object's listener list. The TreeSelectionListener will no longer be notified when the object generates a TreeSelectionEvent.

The `addTreeSelectionListener()` and `removeTreeSelectionListener()` methods are defined in the following classes and interfaces:

- DefaultTreeSelectionModel class
- JTree class
- TreeSelectionModel interface

EXAMPLE

See Chapter 6, Example 6.38 in the section "TreeSelectionEvent Class," where a TreeSelectionListener is used to monitor changes in the selected node of a JTree.

TreeWillExpandListener Interface

The TreeWillExpandListener interface is one of two interfaces (the other being the TreeExpansionListener interface) that declares methods for processing TreeExpansionEvents. As with the TreeExpansionListener interface, the methods declared in the TreeWillExpandListener interface are intended to process TreeExpansionEvents that result from a node of a tree object being expanded or collapsed. The difference is that TreeWillExpandListener methods are called before the expansion or collapse occurs. Although the TreeWillExpandListener interface declares more than one method, there is no corresponding adapter class.

TreeWillExpandListeners are useful for getting confirmation or system permission before allowing a node to be expanded or collapsed. This allows the program to prevent users who don't have permission from expanding or collapsing a tree node. It also gives users the chance to confirm a node expansion action before it takes place.

Any class object can serve as a TreeWillExpandListener by implementing the TreeWillExpandListener interface. The syntax for doing this is

```
public class MyClass implements TreeWillExpandListener
```

Class MyClass would then provide an implementation of the methods declared in the TreeWillExpandListener interface.

For a TreeWillExpandListener to receive a TreeExpansionEvent generated by a JTree, the JTree must register the TreeWillExpandListener. The JTree does this by adding the TreeWillExpandListener to its listener list using the `addTreeWillExpandListener()` method. To disconnect a TreeWill-ExpandListener from a JTree, the JTree must remove the TreeWillExpand-

Listener from its listener list by invoking the `removeTreeWillExpandListener()` method. The TreeWillExpand-Listener that was removed will no longer receive TreeExpansionEvents generated by the JTree.

Syntax: public interface TreeWillExpandListener extends EventListener

Package: javax.swing.event

Interface hierarchy: EventListener—TreeWillExpandListener

The TreeWillExpandListener interface is part of the Swing event listener hierarchy.

Introduced: JDK 1.2

TreeWillExpandListener Interface Methods

```
public void treeWillCollapse(TreeExpansionEvent event)
public void treeWillExpand(TreeExpansionEvent event)
```

`treeWillCollapse()` is called when a node from the JTree object is about to be collapsed.

`treeWillExpand()` is invoked when a node from the JTree object is about to be expanded.

Listener Registration Methods

```
public void addTreeWillExpandListener(TreeWillExpandListener listener)
public void removeTreeWillExpandListener(TreeWillExpandListener listener)
```

`addTreeWillExpandListener()` adds a TreeWillExpandListener to the invoking JTree component's listener list. A TreeExpansionEvent generated by the JTree will be sent to either the `treeWillCollapse()` or `treeWillExpand()` method of the TreeWillExpandListener.

`removeTreeWillExpandListener()` removes a TreeWillExpandListener from the invoking JTree component's listener list. The TreeWillExpandListener will no longer be notified before the component generates a TreeExpansionEvent.

The `addTreeWillExpandListener()` and `removeTreeWillExpandListener()` methods are defined in the JTree class.

EXAMPLE

See Chapter 6, Example 6.36 in the section "TreeExpansionEvent Class," where a TreeWillExpandListener is used to determine if a user has permission to expand a node of a JTree.

UndoableEditListener Interface

The UndoableEditListener interface is used to process UndoableEditEvent objects. This interface declares one method, `undoableEditHappened()`, that is used for processing UndoableEditEvents. These are generated whenever an edit that can be undone occurs. The `undoableEditHappened()` method is usually overridden to enable the undo-redo functionality. Because the UndoableEditListener interface declares only one method, there is no corresponding adapter class.

Any class object can serve as a UndoableEditListener by implementing the UndoableEditListener interface. The syntax for doing this is

```
public class MyClass implements UndoableEditListener
```

Class MyClass would then provide an implementation of the method declared in the UndoableEditListener interface.

For an UndoableEditListener to receive an UndoableEditEvent generated by an event source, the source must register the UndoableEditListener. The event source does this by adding the UndoableEditListener to its listener list using the `addUndoableEditListener()` method. To disconnect an UndoableEditListener from an event source, the source must remove the UndoableEditListener from its listener list by invoking the `removeUndoableEditListener()` method. The UndoableEditListener that was removed will no longer receive UndoableEditEvents generated by the event source.

Syntax:	public interface UndoableEditListener extends EventListener
Package:	javax.swing.event
Interface hierarchy:	EventListener—UndoableEditListener
	The UndoableEditListener interface is part of the Swing event listener hierarchy.
Introduced:	JDK 1.2

UndoableEditListener Interface Methods

```
public void undoableEditHappened(UndoableEditEvent event)
```

undoableEditHappened() is called whenever an UndoableEditEvent is generated from an event source that has registered the UndoableEditListener.

Listener Registration Methods

```
public void addUndoableEditListener(UndoableEditListener listener)
public void removeUndoableEditListener(UndoableEditListener listener)
```

addUndoableEditListener() adds an UndoableEditListener to the invoking object's listener list. An UndoableEditEvent generated by the object will be sent to the undoableEditHappened() method of the UndoableEditListener.

removeUndoableEditListener() removes an UndoableEditListener from the invoking object's listener list. The UndoableEditListener will no longer be notified when the object generates an UndoableEditEvent.

The addUndoableEditListener() and removeUndoableEditListener() methods are defined in the following classes and interfaces:

- AbstractDocument class
- Document interface
- UndoableEditSupport class.

EXAMPLE

See Chapter 6, Example 6.39 in the section "UndoableEditEvent Class," where an UndoableEditListener is used to provide the undo-redo functionality for a JTextArea.

VetoableChangeListener Interface

The VetoableChangeListener interface declares one method, vetoableChange(), that is used for processing PropertyChangeEvents that occur because an attempt is made to change a constrained property. This method is usually overridden to determine if the proposed property change is acceptable. Because the VetoableChangeListener interface only declares one method, there is no corresponding adapter class.

Any class object can serve as a VetoableChangeListener by implementing the VetoableChangeListener interface. The syntax for doing this is

```
public class MyClass implements VetoableChangeListener
```

Class MyClass would then provide an implementation of the `vetoableChange()` method declared in the VetoableChangeListener interface.

For an VetoableChangeListener to receive a PropertyChangeEvent generated by an event source, the source must register the VetoableChangeListener. The event source does this by adding the VetoableChangeListener to its listener list using the `addVetoableChangeListener()` method. To disconnect a VetoableChangeListener from an event source, the source must remove the VetoableChangeListener from its listener list by invoking the `removeVetoableChangeListener()` method. The VetoableChangeListener that was removed will no longer receive PropertyChangeEvents generated by the event source.

Syntax:	public interface VetoableChangeListener extends EventListener
Package:	java.beans
Interface hierarchy:	EventListener—VetoableChangeListener
	Although the VetoableChangeListener interface is contained in the java.beans package, it is used with Swing components as well as Java Beans.
Introduced:	JDK 1.2

VetoableChangeListener Interface Methods

```
public void vetoableChange(PropertyChangeEvent event)
```

`vetoableChange()` is called whenever an attempt is made to change a constrained property. This method is usually written to evaluate the change. If the change is unacceptable, a PropertyVetoException is thrown.

Listener Registration Methods

```
public void addVetoableChangeListener(VetoableChangeListener listener)
```

```
public void addVetoableChangeListener(String property,
VetoableChangeListener listener)
public void removeVetoableChangeListener(VetoableChangeListener
listener)
public void removeVetoableChangeListener(String property,
VetoableChangeListener listener)
```

`addVetoableChangeListener()` adds a VetoableChangeListener to the invoking object's listener list. A PropertyChangeEvent due to a change in a constrained property generated by the object will be sent to the `vetoableChange()` method of the VetoableChangeListener.

`removeVetoableChangeListener()` removes a VetoableChangeListener from the invoking object's listener list. The VetoableChangeListener will no longer be notified when the object generates a PropertyChangeEvent due to a change in a constrained property.

The `addVetoableChangeListener()` and `removeVetoableChangeListener()` methods are defined in the following classes and interfaces.

- JComponent
- VetoableChangeSupport class
- BeanContextChild interface
- BeanContextChildSupport class

EXAMPLE

See Chapter 7, "Event Support Classes," Example 7.5 in the section "VetoableChangeSupport Class," where a VetoableChangeListener is used to evaluate the acceptability of a proposed change to a constrained property.

WindowListener Interface

The WindowListener interface declares methods for processing WindowEvent objects. These occur whenever a window is opened, closed, closing, activated, deactivated, iconified, or deiconified. The interface defines seven methods, one of which will be called whenever a WindowEvent is generated from a window that has registered the WindowListener. The WindowListener interface has a corresponding adapter class.

One of the common uses of WindowListeners when used with AWT windows is to specify what is to happen when a window is closed. This might be to insure that the program terminates upon window closure, but can be any other operation as well.

Any class object can serve as a WindowListener by implementing the WindowListener interface. The syntax for doing this is

```
public class MyClass implements WindowListener
```

Class MyClass would then provide an implementation of the methods declared in the WindowListener interface. A WindowListener could also be created by extending the WindowAdapter class.

For an WindowListener to receive a WindowEvent generated by a container, the container must register the WindowListener. The container does this by adding the WindowListener to its listener list using the `addWindowListener()` method. To disconnect a WindowListener from a container, the container must remove the WindowListener from its listener list by invoking the `removeWindowListener()` method. The WindowListener that was removed will no longer receive WindowEvents generated by the container.

Syntax: public interface WindowListener extends EventListener

Package: java.awt.event

Interface hierarchy: EventListener—WindowListener

The WindowListener interface is part of the AWT event listener hierarchy.

Introduced: JDK 1.1

WindowListener Interface Methods

public void windowActivated(WindowEvent event)
public void windowClosed(WindowEvent event)
public void windowClosing(WindowEvent event)
public void windowDeactivated(WindowEvent event)
public void windowDeiconified(WindowEvent event)
public void windowIconified(WindowEvent event)
public void windowOpened(WindowEvent event)

These methods are used to process the various types of WindowEvents. They are implemented by the WindowListener to contain whatever code is necessary to process the event.

`windowActivated()` is called when a WindowEvent is generated due to a window becoming the user's active window. An activated window is one that has been brought to the front of the window hierarchy. Child components of the active window can attain keyboard focus.

`windowClosed()` is called when a WindowEvent is generated after a window has been closed.

`windowClosing()` is called when a WindowEvent is generated because a user is attempting to close a window.

`windowDeactivated()` is called when a WindowEvent is generated due to a window no longer serving as the user's active window. A deactivated window is one that is no longer at the front of the window hierarchy.

`windowDeiconified()` is called when a WindowEvent is generated due to a window changing from an iconified to normal state.

`windowIconified()` is called when a WindowEvent is generated due to a window becoming iconified. An iconified window will normally appear as a small icon on the screen.

`windowOpened()` is called when a WindowEvent is generated due to a window becoming visible for the first time.

Listener Registration Methods

```
public void addWindowListener(WindowListener listener)
public void removeWindowListener(WindowListener listener)
```

`addWindowListener()` adds a WindowListener to the invoking component's listener list. A WindowEvent generated by the component will be sent to one of the seven methods defined by the WindowListener.

`removeWindowListener()` removes a WindowListener from the invoking component's listener list. The WindowListener will no longer be notified when the component generates a WindowEvent.

The `addWindowListener()` and `removeWindowListener()` methods are defined in the Window class.

EXAMPLE

In Example 8.11, a WindowListener is used to track the status of a JFrame. A JFrame is created and registers a WindowListener. Whenever the JFrame is opened, closed, closing, activated, deactivated, iconified, or deiconified, a WindowEvent is generated and sent to the appropriate method of the WindowListener. The WindowListener updates a JTextField placed on another JFrame with the status of the first frame.

EXAMPLE 8.11 WINDOWLISTENER INTERFACE

```
import java.awt.*;
import java.awt.event.*;
import javax.swing.*;

public class WindowListenerDemo extends JFrame
                                implements WindowListener
{
   private JFrame frame1, frame2;
   private JTextField jtf;

   public WindowListenerDemo()
   {
/* A secondary JFrame is created and made visible.  The frame   */
/*   registers a WindowListener.                                */

      frame1 = new JFrame("Child Window");
      frame1.setBounds(400, 150, 200, 100);
      frame1.setVisible(true);
      frame1.addWindowListener(this);

      jtf = new JTextField(20);
      jtf.setEditable(false);

      getContentPane().add(jtf, BorderLayout.SOUTH);

      setDefaultCloseOperation(JFrame.EXIT_ON_CLOSE);
      setBounds(100, 100, 300, 200);
      setVisible(true);
   }

/* The WindowListenerDemo class serves as the WindowListener so   */
/*   it must provide implementation of the methods declared in the */
/*   WindowListener interface.  These methods are written to      */
/*   indicate the status of the child frame.                      */

   public void windowActivated(WindowEvent event)
   {
      jtf.setText("Child window now active");
   }
```

```java
    public void windowClosed(WindowEvent event)
    {
        jtf.setText("Child window closed");
    }

    public void windowClosing(WindowEvent event)
    {
        jtf.setText("Child window closing");
    }

    public void windowDeactivated(WindowEvent event)
    {
        jtf.setText("Child window no longer active");
    }

    public void windowDeiconified(WindowEvent event)
    {
        jtf.setText("Child window deiconified");
    }

    public void windowIconified(WindowEvent event)
    {
        jtf.setText("Child window iconified");
    }

    public void windowOpened(WindowEvent event)
    {
        jtf.setText("Child window opened");
    }

    public static void main(String args[])
    {
        WindowListenerDemo demo = new WindowListenerDemo();
    }
}
```

When you run this code, you will notice two frames appear on your screen. The one titled "Child Window" registers the WindowListener. Try manipulating the Child Window frame. Iconify it, deiconify it, make it active, inactive, and so on. All of these operations generate WindowEvents that update the JTextField contained by the other JFrame.

Other Listener Interfaces in the J2SE

The following is a brief description of other event listener interfaces contained in the J2SE that are not described in detail by this book. These listener interfaces are for events generated by a BeanContext, by a drag-and-drop operation, by a change to a namespace or naming and directory service, or as part of the Java sound API.

java.beans.beancontext.BeanContextMembershipListener – declares two methods that are called when a BeanContextMembershipEvent is generated due to a child or list of children being added to a BeanContext.

java.beans.beancontext.BeanContextServiceRevokedListener – declares one method that is called when a BeanContextServiceRevokedEvent is generated. These occur when a particular service is no longer available to a BeanContext.

java.beans.beancontext.BeanContextServicesListener – declares one method that is called when a BeanContextServiceAvailableEvent is generated. These occur when a service is registered with a BeanContext.

javax.sound.midi.ControllerEventListener – declares one method that is called when a Sequencer has encountered and processed a control-change event of interest to this listener.

java.awt.dnd.DragGestureListener – declares one method that is called to process a DragGestureEvent.

java.awt.dnd.DragSourceListener – declares five methods for processing events that are generated during drag-and-drop operations.

java.awt.dnd.DropTargetListener – declares five methods for processing events that are generated during drag-and-drop operations that involve a DropTarget object.

javax.sound.sampled.LineListener – declares one method that is called to process LineEvents. These occur when a line's status changes.

javax.sound.midi.MetaEventListener – declares one method that is called when a Sequencer has encountered and processed a MetaMessage in the sequence it is processing.

java.naming.event.NamespaceChangeListener – declares three methods that are used to process NamingEvents. These occur when a change is made to a namespace.

javax.naming.event.NamingListener – is the parent interface of the NamespaceListener, ObjectChangeListener, and UnsolicitedNotificationListener interfaces.

javax.naming.event.ObjectChangeListener – declares one method that is called to process a NamingEvent that results from an object in a namespace or naming and directory service being modified or replaced.

javax.naming.ldap.UnsolicitedNotificationListener – declares one method that is called to process an UnsolicitedNotificationEvent. These occur when an unsolicited notification is sent to a client.

LISTENER ADAPTER CLASSES

L istener adapter classes are provided as a convenience to the programmer. When you create an event listener directly by implementing the listener interface, you must provide implementations of every method in the interface whether you need to use them or not. Oftentimes, the unnecessary methods are simply implemented as stubs (methods with no bodies). The listener adapter classes provide the stub methods for you. They implement the corresponding interface and provide stubs for every method declared in the interface. To create an event listener using an adapter class, simply write a subclass of the adapter class and override the implementation of the listener methods that you need.

Generally speaking, any AWT listener interface that declares more than one method will have a corresponding adapter class. The multiple-method Swing listener interfaces oftentimes do not have a corresponding adapter class. The adapter classes are declared abstract. You don't use the adapter classes directly, but instead write subclasses of them.

COMPONENTADAPTER CLASS

The ComponentAdapter class implements the ComponentListener interface and provides stubs for the methods declared in that interface. To create a

ComponentListener using the ComponentAdapter class, simply write a subclass of ComponentAdapter and override the desired methods.

Syntax: public abstract class ComponentAdapter extends Object implements ComponentListener

Package: java.awt.event

Class hierarchy: Object—ComponentAdapter

Introduced: JDK 1.1

Constructors

public `ComponentAdapter()`

ComponentAdapter is an abstract class, but it provides one public constructor for use by subclasses of ComponentAdapter.

Fields and Constants

The ComponentAdapter class does not define or inherit any fields or constants.

ComponentAdapter Class Methods

public void `componentHidden(ComponentEvent event)`

public void `componentMoved(ComponentEvent event)`

public void `componentResized(ComponentEvent event)`

public void `componentShown(ComponentEvent event)`

The ComponentAdapter class provides stub implementations of the methods declared in the ComponentListener interface. These are empty methods. A subclass of ComponentAdapter would override one or more of these methods to provide the desired functionality.

`componentHidden()` is called when a ComponentEvent object is generated as a result of a component becoming invisible.

`componentMoved()` is called when a ComponentEvent object is generated as a result of a component being moved.

`componentResized()` is called when a ComponentEvent object is generated as a result of a component changing its size.

`componentShown()` is called when a ComponentEvent object is generated as a result of a component becoming visible.

Listener Registration Methods

<pre>
public void addComponentListener(ComponentListener listener)
public void removeComponentListener(ComponentListener listener)
</pre>

Remember that a ComponentAdapter is also a ComponentListener. The same `add()` and `remove()` methods are used to register or disconnect a ComponentAdapter.

`addComponentListener()` adds a ComponentListener to the invoking component's listener list. A ComponentEvent generated by the component will be sent to one of the four methods defined by the ComponentListener.

`removeComponentListener()` removes a ComponentListener from the invoking component's listener list. The ComponentListener will no longer be notified when the component generates a ComponentEvent.

The `addComponentListener()` and `removeComponentListener()` methods are defined in the Component class.

EXAMPLE

See Chapter 6, "Event Classes and Interfaces," Example 6.10 in the section "ComponentEvent Class," where a ComponentAdapter is used to limit the minimum allowable size of a JFrame.

CONTAINERADAPTER CLASS

The ContainerAdapter class implements the ContainerListener interface and provides stubs for the methods declared in that interface. To create a ContainerListener using the ContainerAdapter class, simply write a subclass of ContainerAdapter and override the desired methods.

Syntax: public abstract class ContainerAdapter extends Object implements ContainerListener

Package: java.awt.event

Class Hierarchy: Object—ContainerAdapter

Introduced: JDK 1.1

Constructors

```
public ContainerAdapter()
```

ContainerAdapter is an abstract class, but it provides one public constructor for use by subclasses of ContainerAdapter.

Fields and Constants

The ContainerAdapter class does not define or inherit any fields or constants.

ContainerAdapter Class Methods

```
public void componentAdded(ContainerEvent event)
public void componentRemoved(ContainerEvent event)
```

The ContainerAdapter class provides stub implementations of the methods declared in the ContainerListener interface. These are empty methods. A subclass of ContainerAdapter would override one or more of these methods to provide the desired functionality.

`componentAdded()` is called when a ContainerEvent object is generated as a result of a component being added to a container.

`componentRemoved()` is called when a ContainerEvent object is generated as a result of a component being removed from a container.

Listener Registration Methods

```
public void addContainerListener(ContainerListener listener)
public void removeContainerListener(ContainerListener listener)
```

Remember that a ContainerAdapter is also a ContainerListener. The same `add()` and `remove()` methods are used to register or disconnect a ContainerAdapter.

`addContainerListener()` adds a ContainerListener to the invoking container's listener list. A ContainerEvent generated by the container will be sent to either the `componentAdded()` or `componentRemoved()` method of the ContainerListener.

`removeContainerListener()` removes a ContainerListener from the invoking container's listener list. The ContainerListener will no longer be notified when the container generates a ContainerEvent.

The `addContainerListener()` and `removeContainerListener()` methods are defined in the Container class.

EXAMPLE

Example 9.1 is a revised version of Example 6.11 in the section "ContainerEvent Class" in Chapter 6, except that in this case the ContainerListener is implemented as an inner class that extends the ContainerAdapter class. As in Example 6.11, an "add" button on a JFrame is used to add JButtons to the center panel of the frame. Whenever a button is added, a ContainerEvent is generated and sent to the `componentAdded()` method of the ContainerListener. The textfield is updated to indicate the name of the JButton that was added.

The `componentRemoved()` method from the ContainerListener interface is not needed for this example. If a ContainerListener is used that implements the ContainerListener interface directly, a stub implementation of this method would still have to be provided. Using a ContainerAdapter avoids this step and simplifies the coding somewhat.

EXAMPLE 9.1 CONTAINERADAPTER CLASS

```
import javax.swing.*;
import java.awt.*;
import java.awt.event.*;

public class ContainerAdapterDemo extends JFrame
                                  implements ActionListener
{
   private JButton addButton;
   private JTextField jtf;
   private JPanel southPanel, centerPanel;
   private int count;

   public ContainerAdapterDemo()
   {
      count = 0;
```

```
/* A JButton and a JTextField are added to a JPanel.       */
/* The JPanel is placed in the South quadrant of the frame. */

    addButton = new JButton("add");
    addButton.addActionListener(this);

    jtf = new JTextField(20);
    jtf.setEditable(false);

    southPanel = new JPanel();
    southPanel.add(addButton);
    southPanel.add(jtf);

/* The centerPanel registers a ContainerListener.  */

    centerPanel = new JPanel();
    centerPanel.addContainerListener(new ContainerHandler());

    getContentPane().add(southPanel, BorderLayout.SOUTH);
    getContentPane().add(centerPanel, BorderLayout.CENTER);

    setDefaultCloseOperation(JFrame.EXIT_ON_CLOSE);
    setBounds(100, 100, 500, 200);
    setVisible(true);
  }

/* When the "add" button is pressed, a new JButton is placed       */
/* on the centerPanel.  This action generates a ContainerEvent     */
/* which is sent to the componentAdded() method. The revalidate()  */
/* method is used to update the display when a button is added.    */

  public void actionPerformed(ActionEvent event)
  {
     centerPanel.add(new JButton("Button "+count));
     centerPanel.revalidate();
     ++count;
  }

/* The ContainerListener is implemented as an inner class that    */
/* extends the ContainerAdapter class.  Only the componentAdded() */
/* is overridden.  This method obtains a reference to the JButton */
/* that was added to the centerPanel and updates the JTextField   */
/* to indicate which button was added.                            */

  class ContainerHandler extends ContainerAdapter
  {
     public void componentAdded(ContainerEvent event)
     {
        JButton button = (JButton)event.getChild();
```

```
                jtf.setText(button.getText()+" was added");
            }
        }

        public static void main(String args[])
        {
            ContainerAdapterDemo demo = new ContainerAdapterDemo();
        }
    }
```

Initially, when this example is run, the center panel and textfield are blank. Start pressing the "add" button to add buttons to the center panel. The resulting ContainerEvent objects are used to update the text inside the textfield.

FocusAdapter Class

The FocusAdapter class implements the FocusListener interface and provides stubs for the methods declared in that interface. To create a FocusListener using the FocusAdapter class, simply write a subclass of FocusAdapter and override the desired methods.

Syntax:	public abstract class FocusAdapter extends Object implements FocusListener
Package:	java.awt.event
Class Hierarchy:	Object—FocusAdapter
Introduced:	JDK 1.1

Constructors

```
public FocusAdapter()
```

FocusAdapter is an abstract class, but it provides one public constructor for use by subclasses of FocusAdapter.

Fields and Constants

The FocusAdapter class does not define or inherit any fields or constants.

FocusAdapter Class Methods

```
public void focusGained(FocusEvent event)
```
```
public void focusLost(FocusEvent event)
```

The FocusAdapter class provides stub implementations of the methods declared in the FocusListener interface. These are empty methods. A subclass of FocusAdapter would override one or more of these methods to provide the desired functionality.

`focusGained()` is called when a FocusEvent object is generated as a result of a component gaining focus.

`focusLost()` is called when a FocusEvent object is generated as a result of a component losing focus.

Listener Registration Methods

```
public void addFocusListener(FocusListener listener)
```
```
public void removeFocusListener(FocusListener listener)
```

Remember that a FocusAdapter is also a FocusListener. The same `add()` and `remove()` methods are used to register or disconnect a FocusAdapter.

`addFocusListener()` adds a FocusListener to the invoking component's listener list. A FocusEvent generated by the component will be sent to either the `focusGained()` or `focusLost()` method of the FocusListener.

`removeFocusListener()` removes a FocusListener from the invoking component's listener list. The FocusListener will no longer be notified when the component generates a FocusEvent.

The `addFocusListener()` and `removeFocusListener()` methods are defined in the Component class.

EXAMPLE

In Example 9.2, two JTextField objects are placed in the center panel of a JFrame. The textfields register a FocusListener. The FocusListener is implemented as an inner class that extends the FocusAdapter class. When one of the JTextFields gains focus, a FocusEvent is generated and sent to the focusGained() method. A third JTextField at the bottom of the frame indicates which JTextField has focus.

EXAMPLE 9.2 FOCUSADAPTER CLASS

```
import javax.swing.*;
import java.awt.*;
import java.awt.event.*;

public class FocusAdapterDemo extends JFrame
{
   private JTextField jtf1, jtf2, jtf3;
   private JLabel label1, label2;

   public FocusAdapterDemo()
   {
/*   Two JLabels and three JTextFields are created.    */
/*   Two of the textfields register a FocusListener    */

       jtf1 = new JTextField(20);
       jtf1.setBorder(BorderFactory.createLineBorder(Color.black));
       jtf1.setName("TextField 1");
       jtf1.addFocusListener(new FocusHandler());

       jtf2 = new JTextField(20);
       jtf2.setBorder(BorderFactory.createLineBorder(Color.black));
       jtf2.setName("TextField 2");
       jtf2.addFocusListener(new FocusHandler());

       jtf3 = new JTextField(20);
       jtf3.setEditable(false);

       label1 = new JLabel("Line 1");
       label1.setForeground(Color.black);

       label2 = new JLabel("Line 2");
       label2.setForeground(Color.black);

/*   The components are placed on the JFrame */

       JPanel p1 = new JPanel();
       p1.add(label1);
       p1.add(jtf1);

       JPanel p2 = new JPanel();
       p2.add(label2);
       p2.add(jtf2);
```

```java
            JPanel panel = new JPanel();
      panel.setLayout(new BoxLayout(panel, BoxLayout.Y_AXIS));
      panel.add(p1);
      panel.add(p2);

      getContentPane().add(panel, BorderLayout.CENTER);
      getContentPane().add(jtf3, BorderLayout.SOUTH);

      setDefaultCloseOperation(JFrame.EXIT_ON_CLOSE);
      setBounds(100, 100, 400, 200);
      setVisible(true);
   }

/* The FocusListener is implemented as an inner class that extends    */
/* the FocusAdapter class.  Whenever one of the JTextField objects    */
/* gains keyboard focus, a FocusEvent is generated and sent to the    */
/* focusGained() method.  The JTextField  at the bottom of the        */
/* JFrame is used to indicate which component has focus.              */

   class FocusHandler extends FocusAdapter
   {
      public void focusGained(FocusEvent event)
      {
         JTextField tf = (JTextField)event.getComponent();
         jtf3.setText(tf.getName()+" has focus");
      }

   }

   public static void main(String args[])
   {
      FocusAdapterDemo demo = new FocusAdapterDemo();
   }
}
```

When this application initially starts up, neither of the upper JTextField objects has keyboard focus. Click inside one or the other JTextFields causing it to gain focus. The bottom textfield will indicate which of the upper JTextField objects has focus.

HierarchyBoundsAdapter Class

The HierarchyBoundsAdapter class implements the HierarchyBoundsListener interface and provides stubs for the methods declared in that interface. To create a HierarchyBoundsListener using the HierarchyBoundsAdapter class, simply write a subclass of HierarchyBoundsAdapter and override the desired methods.

Syntax: public abstract class HierarchyBoundsAdapter extends Object implements HierarchyBoundsListener

Package: java.awt.event

Class Hierarchy: Object—HierarchyBoundsAdapter

Introduced: JDK 1.3

Constructors

```
public HierarchyBoundsAdapter()
```

HierarchyBoundsAdapter is an abstract class but it provides one public constructor for use by subclasses of HierarchyBoundsAdapter.

Fields and Constants

The HierarchyBoundsAdapter class does not define or inherit any fields or constants.

HierarchyBoundsAdapter Class Methods

```
public void ancestorMoved(HierarchyEvent event)
```
```
public void ancestorResized(HierarchyEvent event)
```

The HierarchyBoundsAdapter class provides stub implementations of the methods declared in the HierarchyBoundsListener interface. These are empty methods. A subclass of HierarchyBoundsAdapter would override one or more of these methods to provide the desired functionality.

`ancestorMoved()` is called when a HierarchyEvent object is generated as a result of an ancestor of the source component being moved.

`ancestorResized()` is called when a HierarchyEvent object is generated as a result of an ancestor of the source component being resized.

Listener Registration Methods

> public void addHierarchyBoundsListener(HierarchyBoundsListener listener)
>
> public void removeHierarchyBoundsListener(HierarchyBoundsListener listener)

Remember that a HierarchyBoundsAdapter is also a HierarchyBoundsListener. The same `add()` and `remove()` methods are used to register or disconnect a HierarchyBoundsAdapter.

`addHierarchyBoundsListener()` adds a HierarchyBoundsListener to the invoking component's listener list. A bounds-type HierarchyEvent generated by the component will be sent to either the `ancestorMoved()` or `ancestorResized()` method of the HierarchyBoundsListener.

`removeHierarchyBoundsListener()` removes a HierarchyBoundsListener from the invoking component's listener list. The HierarchyBoundsListener will no longer be notified when the component generates a hierarchy bounds event.

The `addHierarchyBoundsListener()` and `removeHierarchyBoundsListener()` methods are defined in the Component class.

EXAMPLE

See Chapter 6, Example 6.14 in the section "HierarchyEvent Class," where a HierarchyBoundsAdapter is used to maintain the proportional size of a JButton relative to its parent JFrame.

INTERNALFRAMEADAPTER CLASS

The InternalFrameAdapter class implements the InternalFrameListener interface and provides stubs for the methods declared in that interface. To create an InternalFrameListener using the InternalFrameAdapter class, simply write a subclass of InternalFrameAdapter and override the desired methods.

InternalFrameAdapter Class

Syntax: public abstract class InternalFrameAdapter extends Object implements InternalFrameListener

Package: javax.swing.event

Class Hierarchy: Object—InternalFrameAdapter

Introduced: JDK 1.2

Constructors

```
public InternalFrameAdapter()
```

InternalFrameAdapter is an abstract class, but it provides one public constructor for use by subclasses of InternalFrameAdapter.

InternalFrameAdapter Class Methods

```
public void internalFrameActivated(InternalFrameEvent event)
public void internalFrameClosed(InternalFrameEvent event)
public void internalFrameClosing(InternalFrameEvent event)
public void internalFrameDeactivated(InternalFrameEvent event)
public void internalFrameDeiconified(InternalFrameEvent event)
public void internalFrameIconified(InternalFrameEvent event)
public void internalFrameOpened(InternalFrameEvent event)
```

The InternalFrameAdapter class provides stub implementations of the methods declared in the InternalFrameListener interface. These are empty methods. A subclass of InternalFrameAdapter would override one or more of these methods to provide the desired functionality.

`internalFrameActivated()` is called when an InternalFrameEvent is generated due to an internal frame becoming active. An active internal frame is one that has been brought to the front of the window hierarchy. A child component of an active internal frame can acquire keyboard focus.

`internalFrameClosed()` is called when an InternalFrameEvent is generated after an internal frame has been closed.

`internalFrameClosing()` is called when an InternalFrameEvent is generated because a user is attempting to close an internal frame.

`internalFrameDeactivated()` is called when an InternalFrameEvent is generated due to an internal frame being deactivated. A deactivated internal frame is one that is no longer at the front of the window hierarchy.

`internalFrameDeiconified()` is called when an InternalFrameEvent is generated due to an internal frame changing from an iconified to normal state.

`internalFrameIconified()` is called when an InternalFrameEvent is generated due to an internal frame becoming iconified. An iconified internal frame will normally appear as a small icon on the screen.

`internalFrameOpened()` is called when an InternalFrameEvent is generated due to an internal frame becoming visible for the first time.

Listener Registration Methods

```
public void addInternalFrameListener(InternalFrameListener listener)
public void removeInternalFrameListener(InternalFrameListener listener)
```

Remember that an InternalFrameAdapter is also an InternalFrameListener. The same `add()` and `remove()` methods are used to register or disconnect an InternalFrameAdapter.

`addInternalFrameListener()` adds an InternalFrameListener to the invoking JInternalFrame component's listener list. An InternalFrameEvent generated by the JInternalFrame will be sent to one of the seven methods defined by the InternalFrameListener.

`removeInternalFrameListener()` removes an InternalFrameListener from the invoking JInternalFrame component's listener list. The InternalFrameListener will no longer be notified when the component generates an InternalFrameEvent.

The `addInternalFrameListener()` and `removeInternalFrameListener()` methods are defined in the JInternalFrame class.

EXAMPLE

Example 9.3 is a revised version of Example 6.19 in the section "InternalFrameEvent Class" in Chapter 6, except that in this version, the InternalFrameListener is created by extending the InternalFrameAdapter class.

As in Example 6.19, InternalFrameEvents are used to keep track of the iconified state of a JInternalFrame. A JInternalFrame is placed on a JFrame and registers an InternalFrameListener. Whenever the JInternalFrame is iconified or de-iconified, an InternalFrameEvent is generated and sent to either the `internalFrameIconified()` or `internalFrameDeiconified()` methods. The current iconified state of the JInternalFrame is listed inside a JTextField placed at the bottom of the frame.

The code listing for this example is given below. Note that this example uses an image file that is placed inside the internal frame. You can substitute any image file on your system to run this example.

EXAMPLE 9.3 INTERNALFRAMEADAPTER CLASS

```java
import javax.swing.*;
import javax.swing.event.*;
import java.awt.*;
import java.awt.event.*;

public class IntFrameAdaptDemo extends JFrame implements ActionListener
{
   private JInternalFrame jif;
   private JTextField jtf;
   private JButton button;

   public IntFrameAdaptDemo()
   {
/*   A JInternalFrame object is created and placed on a JFrame.      */
/*   The JInternalFrame registers an InternalFrameListener.          */

      jif = new JInternalFrame("Bailey", true, true, true, true);
      jif.getContentPane().add(new JLabel(new ImageIcon("Bailey.jpg")));
      jif.setSize(200, 100);
      jif.setDefaultCloseOperation(WindowConstants.HIDE_ON_CLOSE);
      jif.addInternalFrameListener(new InternalFrameHandler());

      button = new JButton("show");
      button.setBorder(BorderFactory.createRaisedBevelBorder());
      button.addActionListener(this);

      jtf = new JTextField(20);
      jtf.setEditable(false);

      JPanel centerPanel = new JPanel();
      centerPanel.add(jif);
```

```java
         JPanel southPanel = new JPanel();
         southPanel.add(jtf);
         southPanel.add(button);

         getContentPane().add(centerPanel, BorderLayout.CENTER);
         getContentPane().add(southPanel, BorderLayout.SOUTH);

         setDefaultCloseOperation(JFrame.EXIT_ON_CLOSE);
         setBounds(100, 100, 300, 300);
         setVisible(true);
      }

      /* The InternalFrameListener is implemented as an inner class that   */
      /* extends the InternalFrameAdapter class. If the JInternalFrame     */
      /* is iconified or deiconified, an InternalFrameEvent is             */
      /* generated and sent to the appropriate method where the iconified */
      /* state of the JInternalFrame is displayed in a JTextField.         */
      /* Because the InternalFrameAdapter class is used, implementations   */
      /* don't have to be provided for the methods declared in the         */
      /* InternalFrameListener interface that aren't needed for this       */
      /* example.                                                          */

      class InternalFrameHandler extends InternalFrameAdapter
      {
         public void internalFrameDeiconified(InternalFrameEvent event)
         {
            jtf.setText("internal frame deiconified");
            invalidate();
            validate();
         }

         public void internalFrameIconified(InternalFrameEvent event)
         {
            jtf.setText("internal frame iconified");
            invalidate();
            validate();
         }
      }

      /* When the "show" button is pressed, the JInternalFrame is made     */
      /* visible.                                                          */

      public void actionPerformed(ActionEvent event)
      {
         jif.show();
      }

      public static void main(String args[])
      {
```

```
        IntFrameAdaptDemo demo = new IntFrameAdaptDemo();
   }
}
```

When you first run this code, the JInternalFrame is not visible. Press the "show" button and the JInternalFrame appears. Press the "iconify" symbol at the top of the internal frame. The frame is iconified and the textfield displays this fact at the bottom of the JFrame. Clicking on the icon deiconifies the JInternalFrame, and an InternalFrameEvent object is used to update the textfield.

KeyAdapter Class

The KeyAdapter class implements the KeyListener interface and provides stubs for the methods declared in that interface. To create a KeyListener using the KeyAdapter class, simply write a subclass of KeyAdapter and override the desired methods.

Syntax:	public abstract class KeyAdapter extends Object implements KeyListener
Package:	java.awt.event
Class Hierarchy:	Object—KeyAdapter
Introduced:	JDK 1.1

Constructors

public `KeyAdapter()`

KeyAdapter is an abstract class, but it provides one public constructor for use by subclasses of KeyAdapter.

Fields and Constants

The KeyAdapter class does not define or inherit any fields or constants.

KeyAdapter Class Methods

> public void `keyPressed(KeyEvent event)`
>
> public void `keyReleased(KeyEvent event)`
>
> public void `keyTyped(KeyEvent event)`

The KeyAdapter class provides stub implementations of the methods declared in the KeyListener interface. These are empty methods. A subclass of KeyAdapter would override one or more of these methods to provide the desired functionality.

`keyPressed()` is called when a KeyEvent object is generated as a result of a user pressing a key over the bounding area of a component.

`keyReleased()` is called when a KeyEvent object is generated as a result of a user releasing a key over the bounding area of a component.

`keyTyped()` is called when a KeyEvent object is generated as a result of a user pressing and releasing a key over the bounding area of a component.

Listener Registration Methods

> public void `addKeyListener(KeyListener listener)`
>
> public void `removeKeyListener(KeyListener listener)`

Remember that a KeyAdapter is also a KeyListener. The same `add()` and `remove()` methods are used to register or disconnect a KeyAdapter.

`addKeyListener()` adds a KeyListener to the invoking component's listener list. A KeyEvent generated by the component will be sent to one of the three methods defined by the KeyListener.

`removeKeyListener()` removes a KeyListener from the invoking component's listener list. The KeyListener will no longer be notified when the component generates a KeyEvent.

The `addKeyListener()` and `removeKeyListener()` methods are defined in the Component class.

EXAMPLE

See Chapter 6, Example 6.22 in the section "KeyEvent Class," where a KeyAdapter is used add some keyboard-triggered functionality to a JFrame.

MouseAdapter Class

The MouseAdapter class implements the MouseListener interface and provides stubs for the methods declared in that interface. To create a MouseListener using the MouseAdapter class, simply write a subclass of MouseAdapter and override the desired methods.

Syntax:	public abstract class MouseAdapter extends Object implements MouseListener
Package:	java.awt.event
Class Hierarchy:	Object—MouseAdapter
Introduced:	JDK 1.1

Constructors

```
public MouseAdapter()
```

MouseAdapter is an abstract class, but it provides one public constructor for use by subclasses of MouseAdapter.

Fields and Constants

The MouseAdapter class does not define or inherit any fields or constants.

MouseAdapter Class Methods

```
public void mouseClicked(MouseEvent event)
```
```
public void mouseEntered(MouseEvent event)
```
```
public void mouseExited(MouseEvent event)
```
```
public void mousePressed(MouseEvent event)
```
```
public void mouseReleased(MouseEvent event)
```

The MouseAdapter class provides stub implementations of the methods declared in the MouseListener interface. These are empty methods. A subclass of MouseAdapter would override one or more of these methods to provide the desired functionality.

`mouseClicked()` is called when a MouseEvent is generated due to the mouse being clicked (pressed and released) over the bounding area of the event source.

`mouseEntered()` is called when a MouseEvent is generated due to the mouse entering the bounding area of the event source.

`mouseExited()` is called when a MouseEvent is generated due to the mouse leaving the bounding area of the event source.

`mousePressed()` is called when a MouseEvent is generated due to the mouse being pressed over the bounding area of the event source.

`mouseReleased()` is called when a MouseEvent is generated due to the mouse being released over the bounding area of the event source.

Listener Registration Methods

public void `addMouseListener(MouseListener listener)`

public void `removeMouseListener(MouseListener listener)`

Remember that a MouseAdapter is also a MouseListener. The same `add()` and `remove()` methods are used to register or disconnect a MouseAdapter.

`addMouseListener()` adds a MouseListener to the invoking component's listener list. A non-motion-oriented MouseEvent generated by the component will be sent to one of the five methods defined by the MouseListener.

`removeMouseListener()` removes a MouseListener from the invoking component's listener list. The MouseListener will no longer be notified when the component generates a non-motion-oriented MouseEvent.

The `addMouseListener()` and `removeMouseListener()` methods are defined in the Component class.

EXAMPLE

See Chapter 6, Example 6.28 in the section "MouseEvent Class," where a MouseAdapter is used to create a Java doodle pad.

MouseInputAdapter Class

The MouseInputAdapter class implements the MouseInputListener interface and provides stubs for the methods declared in that interface. The MouseInputListener interface contains all of the mouse listener methods in one place, and is essentially a combination of the MouseListener and MouseMotionListener interfaces. To create a MouseInputListener using the MouseInputAdapter class, simply write a subclass of MouseInputAdapter and override the desired methods.

Syntax:	public abstract class MouseInputAdapter extends Object implements MouseInputListener
Package:	javax.swing.event
Class hierarchy:	Object—MouseInputAdapter
Introduced:	JDK 1.2

Constructors

```
public MouseInputAdapter()
```

MouseInputAdapter is an abstract class, but it provides one public constructor for use by subclasses of MouseInputAdapter.

Fields and Constants

The MouseAdapter class does not define or inherit any fields or constants.

MouseInputAdapter Class Methods

```
public void mouseClicked(MouseEvent event)
```
```
public void mouseDragged(MouseEvent event)
```
```
public void mouseEntered(MouseEvent event)
```
```
public void mouseExited(MouseEvent event)
```

```
public void mouseMoved(MouseEvent event)
public void mousePressed(MouseEvent event)
public void mouseReleased(MouseEvent event)
```

The MouseInputAdapter class provides stub implementations of the methods declared in the MouseInputListener interface. These are empty methods. A subclass of MouseInputAdapter would override one or more of these methods to provide the desired functionality.

`mouseClicked()` is called when a MouseEvent is generated due to the mouse being clicked (pressed and released) over the bounding area of the event source.

`mouseDragged()` is called when a MouseEvent is generated due to the mouse being dragged (moved with one or more mouse buttons pressed) inside the bounding area of the event source.

`mouseEntered()` is called when a MouseEvent is generated due to the mouse entering the bounding area of the event source.

`mouseExited()` is called when a MouseEvent is generated due to the mouse leaving the bounding area of the event source.

`mouseMoved()` is called when a MouseEvent is generated due to the mouse moving inside the bounding area of the event source.

`mousePressed()` is called when a MouseEvent is generated due to the mouse being pressed over the bounding area of the event source.

`mouseReleased()` is called when a MouseEvent is generated due to the mouse being released over the bounding area of the event source.

Listener Registration Methods

```
public void addMouseListener(MouseInputListener listener)
public void addMouseMotionListener(MouseInputListener listener)
public void removeMouseListener(MouseInputListener listener)
public void removeMouseMotionListener(MouseInputListener listener)
```

For some reason, the Java API does not define `addMouseInput-Listener()` and `removeMouseInputListener()` methods. However, a MouseInputListener is also a MouseListener and a MouseMotionListener. To register a MouseInputAdapter to a GUI component, use either the `addMouseListener()` or `addMouseMotionListener()` methods and pass the method a reference to MouseInputAdapter (which is also a MouseInputListener).

One note of caution: If you use the `addMouseListener()` method to register the MouseInputAdapter, the listener will receive only non-motion-oriented mouse events. Similarly, if you use `addMouseMotionListener()`, the MouseInputAdapter will receive only motion-oriented mouse events. If you want the MouseInputAdapter to receive all types of events, you have to use both `add()` methods. The syntax for doing that would go something like this:

```
MyMouseInputAdapter listener = new MyMouseInputAdapter();
addMouseListener(listener);
addMouseMotionListener(listener);
```

The `removeMouseListener()` and `removeMouseMotionListener()` methods can be used to disconnect the invoking component from the MouseInputListener. The MouseInputListener will no longer be notified when the component generates a MouseEvent.

EXAMPLE

Example 9.4 is a revised version of Example 8.7 in the section "MouseInputListener Interface" in Chapter 8, "Event Listener Interfaces," where a MouseInputListener is used to create a doodle pad. In this example, the MouseInputListener is implemented by extending the MouseInputAdapter class.

As in Example 8.7, a doodle pad is created using a MouseInputListener to receive and process the mouse events. A JPanel is placed on a JFrame and registers a MouseInputListener. Whenever the user drags a line across the panel, MouseEvents are generated and sent to the `mousePressed()` and `mouseDragged()` methods. These methods draw a line following the path of the mouse.

EXAMPLE 9.4 MOUSEINPUTADAPTER CLASS

```
import java.awt.*;
import java.awt.event.*;
import javax.swing.*;
import javax.swing.event.*;

public class MouseInpAdaptDemo extends JFrame
{
    private JPanel panel;
```

```
      private int startX, startY, endX, endY;

      public MouseInpAdaptDemo()
      {

/*    A JPanel object is placed on a Frame and registers a         */
/*    MouseInputListener to receive both motion-oriented and       */
/*    non-motion-oriented MouseEvents.                             */

         panel = new JPanel();
         MouseInputHandler listener = new MouseInputHandler();
         panel.addMouseListener(listener);
         panel.addMouseMotionListener(listener);

         getContentPane().add(panel);

         setDefaultCloseOperation(JFrame.EXIT_ON_CLOSE);
         setBounds(100, 100, 300, 200);
         setVisible(true);
      }

/*    The MouseInputListener is implemented as an inner class that    */
/*    extends the MouseInputAdapter class.  When the user presses the */
/*    mouse inside the bounding area of the panel, a MouseEvent is    */
/*    generated and sent to the mousePressed() method.  This method   */
/*    sets the starting point for the line.  When the mouse is dragged */
/*    inside the panel, MouseEvents are generated and sent to the     */
/*    mouseDragged() method which draws a line according to the       */
/*    position of the mouse.  Because the MouseInputAdapter class is  */
/*    used, implementations do not have to be provided for the methods */
/*    declared in the MouseListener and MouseMotionListener interfaces */
/*    that aren't needed for this example.                            */

      class MouseInputHandler extends MouseInputAdapter
      {
         public void mousePressed(MouseEvent event)
         {
            startX = event.getX();
            startY = event.getY();
            endX = startX;
            endY = startY;
         }

         public void mouseDragged(MouseEvent event)
         {
            startX = endX;
            startY = endY;
            endX = event.getX();
            endY = event.getY();
            panel.getGraphics().drawLine(startX, startY, endX, endY);
```

```
            }
        }
        public static void main(String args[])
        {
            MouseInpAdaptDemo demo = new MouseInpAdaptDemo();
        }
    }
```

When you start this application, a blank frame appears on your screen. Press the mouse and drag it across the frame. A line is drawn. Practice writing your name. Draw a picture. Express any long-suppressed artistic talents.

MouseMotionAdapter Class

The MouseMotionAdapter class implements the MouseMotionListener interface and provides stubs for the methods declared in that interface. To create a MouseMotionListener using the MouseMotionAdapter class, simply write a subclass of MouseMotionAdapter and override the desired methods.

Syntax: public abstract class MouseMotionAdapter extends Object implements MouseMotionListener

Package: java.awt.event

Class Hierarchy: Object—MouseMotionAdapter

Introduced: JDK 1.1

Constructors

public MouseMotionAdapter()

MouseMotionAdapter is an abstract class, but it provides one public constructor for use by subclasses of MouseMotionAdapter.

Fields and Constants

The MouseMotionAdapter class does not define or inherit any fields or constants.

MouseMotionAdapter Class Methods

```
public void mouseDragged(MouseEvent event)
public void mouseMoved(MouseEvent event)
```

The MouseMotionAdapter class provides stub implementations of the methods declared in the MouseMotionListener interface. These are empty methods. A subclass of MouseMotionAdapter would override one or more of these methods to provide the desired functionality.

`mouseDragged()` is called when a MouseEvent is generated due to the mouse being dragged (moved with one or more mouse buttons pressed) inside the bounding area of the event source.

`mouseMoved()` is called when a MouseEvent is generated due to the mouse moving inside the bounding area of the event source.

Listener Registration Methods

```
public void addMouseMotionListener(MouseMotionListener listener)
public void removeMouseMotionListener(MouseMotionListener listener)
```

Remember that a MouseMotionAdapter is also a MouseMotionListener. The same `add()` and `remove()` methods are used to register or disconnect a MouseMotionAdapter.

`addMouseMotionListener()` adds a MouseMotionListener to the invoking component's listener list. A motion-oriented MouseEvent generated by the component will be sent to either the `mouseDragged()` or `mouseMoved()` method of the MouseMotionListener.

`removeMouseMotionListener()` removes a MouseMotionListener from the invoking component's listener list. The MouseMotionListener will no longer be notified when the component generates a motion-oriented MouseEvent.

The `addMouseMotionListener()` and `removeMouseMotionListener()` methods are defined in the Component class.

EXAMPLE

See Chapter 6, Example 6.28 in the section "MouseEvent Class," where a MouseMotionAdapter is used to create a Java doodle-pad.

WindowAdapter Class

The WindowAdapter class implements the WindowListener interface and provides stubs for the methods declared in that interface. To create a WindowListener using the WindowAdapter class, simply write a subclass of WindowAdapter and override the desired methods.

Syntax: public abstract class WindowAdapter extends Object implements WindowListener

Package: java.awt.event

Class Hierarchy: Object—WindowAdapter

Introduced: JDK 1.1

Constructors

```
public WindowAdapter()
```

WindowAdapter is an abstract class, but it provides one public constructor for use by subclasses of WindowAdapter.

Fields and Constants

The WindowAdapter class does not define or inherit any fields or constants.

WindowAdapter Class Methods

```
public void windowActivated(WindowEvent event)
public void windowClosed(WindowEvent event)
public void windowClosing(WindowEvent event)
public void windowDeactivated(WindowEvent event)
public void windowDeiconified(WindowEvent event)
```

```
public void windowIconified(WindowEvent event)
```
```
public void windowOpened(WindowEvent event)
```

The WindowAdapter class provides stub implementations of the methods declared in the WindowListener interface. These are empty methods. A subclass of WindowAdapter would override one or more of these methods to provide the desired functionality.

`windowActivated()` is called when a WindowEvent is generated due to a window becoming the user's active window. An activated window is one that has been brought to the front of the window hierarchy. A child component of an active window can attain keyboard focus.

`windowClosed()` is called when a WindowEvent is generated after a window has been closed.

`windowClosing()` is called when a WindowEvent is generated because a user is attempting to close a window.

`windowDeactivated()` is called when a WindowEvent is generated due to a window no longer serving as the user's active window. A deactivated window is one that is no longer at the front of the window hierarchy.

`windowDeiconified()` is called when a WindowEvent is generated due to a window changing from an iconified to a normal state.

`windowIconified()` is called when a WindowEvent is generated due to a window becoming iconified. An iconified window will normally appear as a small icon on the screen.

`windowOpened()` is called when a WindowEvent is generated due to a window becoming visible for the first time.

Listener Registration Methods

```
public void addWindowListener(WindowListener listener)
```
```
public void removeWindowListener(WindowListener listener)
```

Remember that a WindowAdapter is also a WindowListener. The same `add()` and `remove()` methods are used to register or disconnect a WindowAdapter.

`addWindowListener()` adds a WindowListener to the invoking component's listener list. A WindowEvent generated by the component will be sent to one of the seven methods defined by the WindowListener.

`removeWindowListener()` removes a WindowListener from the invoking component's listener list. The WindowListener will no longer be notified when the component generates a WindowEvent.

The `addWindowListener()` and `removeWindowListener()` methods are defined in the Window class.

EXAMPLE

See Chapter 6, Example 6.40 in the section "WindowEvent Class," where a WindowAdapter is used to ensure that a program terminates if the main window is closed.

10

EVENT LIFE CYCLE METHODS

The event life cycle methods are used to dispatch, coalesce, fire, and process event objects. The system will normally handle the actions represented by these methods automatically. Most of these methods have protected access, which means that only an object that is an instance of the class that defines the method or a subclass of that class can access them. The most common way a developer will use these methods is to modify or augment the event characteristics of an existing component or to provide event-generating capabilities to a user-defined component.

Just as the GUI component classes have an inheritance hierarchy, so do the event life cycle methods. The Component class defines the basic life cycle methods of enabling, disabling, coalescing, dispatching, and processing an AWTEvent. The Component class also defines the specific processing methods for the low-level events contained in the java.awt.event package.

Component subclasses contain event processing methods for the high-level events that the component is able to generate. Some of these classes will also provide an overridden version of the `processEvent()` method that is specific to the individual component. These methods can also be useful for determining what types of high-level events are generated by a given component. If a component class defines a `processActionEvent()` method, this tells you that the component can generate ActionEvents.

AWT menu components are not subclasses of the Component class and do not have access to the life cycle methods defined in that class. They have their own set of life cycle methods, starting with the `processEvent()` method in the MenuComponent class. The MenuComponent class is the parent class of all AWT menu components. Subclasses of MenuComponent define methods to process high-level events. They also contain overridden versions of the `processEvent()` method to handle their specific event needs.

This chapter lists all of the event life cycle methods defined in the java.awt, javax.swing, and java.beans packages. The listing is done alphabetically by class, from AbstractAction to Window.

AbstractAction Class Methods

> **protected void** `firePropertyChange(String propertyName, Object oldValue, Object newValue)`

`firePropertyChange()` is used to fire a PropertyChangeEvent representing a change in the value of a bound property. The event is sent to any registered PropertyChangeListeners in the invoking AbstractAction subclass component's listener list.

AbstractButton Class Methods

> **protected void** `fireActionPerformed(ActionEvent event)`
> **protected void** `fireItemStateChanged(ItemEvent event)`
> **protected void** `fireStateChanged()`

`fireActionPerformed()` sends the specified ActionEvent object to every ActionListener in the invoking component's listener list.

`fireItemStateChanged()` sends the specified ItemEvent object to every ItemListener in the invoking component's listener list.

`fireStateChanged()` sends a ChangeEvent object to every ChangeListener in the invoking component's listener list.

AbstractCellEditor Class Methods

> protected void fireEditingCanceled ()
>
> protected void fireEditingStopped ()

fireEditingCanceled() sends a ChangeEvent to the editingCanceled() method of every CellEditorListener in the invoking component's listener list.

fireEditingStopped() sends a ChangeEvent to the editingStopped() method of every CellEditorListener in the invoking component's listener list.

AbstractListModel Class Methods

> protected void fireContentsChanged(Object source, int indexStart, int indexEnd)
>
> protected void fireIntervalAdded(Object source, int indexStart, int indexEnd)
>
> protected void fireIntervalRemoved(Object source, int indexStart, int indexEnd)

fireContentsChanged() sends a ListDataEvent to the contentsChanged() method of every ListDataListener in the invoking component's listener list.

fireItemStateChanged() sends a ListDataEvent to the intervalAdded() method of every ListDataListener in the invoking component's listener list.

fireStateChanged() sends a ListDataEvent to the intervalRemoved() method of every ListDataListener in the invoking component's listener list.

Button Class Methods

> protected void processActionEvent(ActionEvent event)
>
> protected void processEvent(AWTEvent event)

`processActionEvent()` is used to process action events occurring on the button. This method will dispatch the event to any registered ActionListeners or to any components that are enabled to receive the event.

`processEvent()` is an overridden version of the method defined in the Component class and is used to process events generated by a Button. If the event is an ActionEvent, this method calls the `processActionEvent()` method. Otherwise, the Component class `processEvent()` method is called.

Checkbox Class Methods

protected void `processEvent(AWTEvent event)`
protected void `processItemEvent(ItemEvent event)`

`processEvent()` is an overridden version of the method defined in the Component class and is used to process events generated by a Checkbox component. If the event is an ItemEvent, this method calls the `processItemEvent()` method. Otherwise, the Component class `processEvent()` method is called.

`processItemEvent()` is used to process ItemEvents occurring on the Checkbox. This method will dispatch the event to any registered ItemListeners or to any components that are enabled to receive the event.

CheckboxMenuItem Class Methods

protected void `processEvent(AWTEvent event)`
protected void `processItemEvent(ItemEvent event)`

`processEvent()` is an overridden version of the method defined in the MenuItem class and is used to process events generated by a CheckboxMenuItem. If the event is an ItemEvent, this method calls the `processItemEvent()` method. Otherwise, the MenuItem class `processEvent()` method is called.

`processItemEvent()` is used to process ItemEvents occurring on the CheckboxMenuItem. This method will dispatch the event to any registered ItemListeners or to any components that are enabled to receive the event.

Choice Class Methods

> protected void processEvent(AWTEvent event)

> protected void processItemEvent(ItemEvent event)

`processEvent()` is an overridden version of the method defined in the Component class and is used to process events generated by a Choice component. If the event is an ItemEvent, this method calls the `processItemEvent()` method. Otherwise, the Component class `processEvent()` method is called.

`processItemEvent()` is used to process ItemEvents occurring on the Choice component. This method will dispatch the event to any registered ItemListeners or to any components that are enabled to receive the event.

Component Class Methods

The Component class defines the basic life cycle methods of enabling, disabling, coalescing, dispatching, and processing an AWTEvent. The Component class also defines the specific processing methods for the low-level events contained in the java.awt.event package.

Event Firing Methods

> protected void firePropertyChange(String propertyName, Object oldValue, Object newValue)

`firePropertyChange()` is used to fire a PropertyChangeEvent representing a change in the value of a bound property. The event is sent to any registered PropertyChangeListeners in the invoking component's listener list.

Event Processing Methods

> protected void processEvent(AWTEvent event)

> protected void processComponentEvent(ComponentEvent event)

> protected void processFocusEvent(FocusEvent event)

> protected void processHierarchyBoundsEvent(HierarchyEvent event)

protected void processHierarchyEvent(HierarchyEvent event)
protected void processInputMethodEvent(InputMethodEvent event)
protected void processKeyEvent(KeyEvent event)
protected void processMouseEvent(MouseEvent event)
protected void processMouseMotionEvent(MouseMotionEvent event)

`processEvent()` is called by the `dispatchEvent()` method. It determines what type of event has been passed to it and calls the specific process method to deal with the event. If a user-defined event is being used, this method would be overridden to provide access to the process method for the user-defined event. See the section "User-Defined Events" in Chapter 3, "Event Classes," for more details.

`processComponentEvent()` is called when the `processEvent()` method is passed a ComponentEvent object as an argument. It dispatches the event to any registered ComponentListener objects or to any components that have been enabled to receive ComponentEvents.

`processFocusEvent()` is called when the `processEvent()` method is passed a FocusEvent object as an argument. It dispatches the event to any registered FocusListener objects or to any components that have been enabled to receive FocusEvents.

`processHierarchyBoundsEvent()` is called when the `processEvent()` method is passed a hierarchy bounds-type HierarchyEvent object as an argument. It dispatches the event to any registered HierarchyBoundsListener objects or to any components that have been enabled to receive HierarchyEvents.

`processHierarchyEvent()` is called when the `processEvent()` method is passed a HierarchyEvent object as an argument. It dispatches the event to any registered HierarchyListener objects or to any components that have been enabled to receive HierarchyEvents.

`processInputMethodEvent()` is called when the `processEvent()` method is passed an InputMethodEvent object as an argument. It dispatches the event to any registered InputMethodListener objects or to any components that have been enabled to receive InputMethodEvents.

`processKeyEvent()` is called when the `processEvent()` method is passed a KeyEvent object as an argument. It dispatches the event to any registered KeyListener objects or to any components that have been enabled to receive KeyEvents.

`processMouseEvent()` is called when the `processEvent()` method is passed a non-motion-oriented MouseEvent object as an argument. It dispatches the event to any registered MouseListener objects or to any components that have been enabled to receive non-motion-oriented MouseEvents.

`processMouseMotionEvent()` is called when the `processEvent()` method is passed a motion-oriented MouseEvent object as an argument. It dispatches the event to any registered MouseMotionListener objects or to any components that have been enabled to receive motion-oriented MouseEvents.

Methods to Transmit, Receive, and Modify Events

protected AWTEvent `coalesceEvents(AWTEvent oldEvent, AWTEvent newEvent)`
protected final void `disableEvents(long eventMask)`
public final void `dispatchEvent(AWTEvent event)`
protected final void `enableEvents(long eventMask)`

`coalesceEvents()` attempts to combine an existing event on the event queue with a new event. The method either returns the coalesced event or returns null if the combination was not possible. This method is generally called by the system only and is used primarily to combine a series of sequential mouse or paint events into a single event.

`disableEvents()` prevents the event types corresponding to the specified event mask from being delivered to the invoking component. The event mask is a number identifying the event type.

`dispatchEvent()` dispatches the specified event by calling the invoking component's `processEvent()` method. This method is called automatically by the system and is sometimes used when creating user-defined components that generate events.

`enableEvents()` allows event types corresponding to the specified event mask to be delivered to the `processEvent()` method of the event source. Normally, events of a given type will be automatically enabled by the system when a listener for that event type is registered with the component. This method can be used to have events delivered to the invoking component's `processEvent()` method, whether or not a listener has been registered.

Deprecated Methods from the Component Class

```
public void deliverEvent(Event event)
public boolean handleEvent(Event event)
public boolean postEvent(Event event)
```

`deliverEvent()` is used in the Java 1.0.2 event model, is deprecated as of Java 1.1 and should not be used for new code. It has been replaced by the `dispatchEvent()` method.

`handleEvent()` is used in the Java 1.0.2 event model, is deprecated as of Java 1.1 and should not be used for new code. It has been replaced by the `processEvent()` method.

`postEvent()` is used in the Java 1.0.2 event model, is deprecated as of Java 1.1 and should not be used for new code. It has been replaced by the `dispatchEvent()` method.

EXAMPLE

In Example 10.1, a user-defined JButton is given some additional functionality by overriding the `processMouseEvent()` method. When the user presses the button, a MouseEvent is generated and sent to the `processMouseEvent()` method. This method checks to see if the event was due to the button being pressed. If this is true, the label color of the button is changed to red. When the button is released, the label color is reset to black. After the label color change, the `processMouseEvent()` method from the Component class is called, using the "super" keyword to perform the normal MouseEvent processing.

EXAMPLE 10.1 OVERRIDING AN EVENT PROCESSING METHOD

```
import javax.swing.*;
import javax.swing.event.*;
import java.awt.*;
import java.awt.event.*;

public class LifeCycleDemo extends JFrame
{
   MyButton button;

   public LifeCycleDemo()
   {
```

```
/*   A user-defined JButton is created and placed on a JFrame.   */

      button = new MyButton("help");

      JPanel centerPanel = new JPanel();
      centerPanel.add(button);

      getContentPane().add(centerPanel, BorderLayout.CENTER);

      setDefaultCloseOperation(JFrame.EXIT_ON_CLOSE);
      setBounds(100, 100, 300, 200);
      setVisible(true);
   }

   public static void main(String args[])
   {
      LifeCycleDemo demo = new LifeCycleDemo();
   }
}

/*   The MyButton class is a JButton that is given some added     */
/*   functionality by overriding the processMouseEvent() method   */

class MyButton extends JButton
{
   public MyButton(String label)
   {
      super(label);
      setForeground(Color.black);
      setBorder(BorderFactory.createCompoundBorder(
                BorderFactory.createRaisedBevelBorder(),
                BorderFactory.createEmptyBorder(10,10,10,10)));
      setFont(new Font("Serif", Font.BOLD, 12));
   }

/*   The processMouseEvent() method is overridden to change the color  */
/*   of the button label when the user presses it.  When the button is */
/*   released, the label color is re-set to be black.  This change     */
/*   happens regardless of whether the MouseEvent is sent to a         */
/*   listener or not.  After the label color change, the               */
/*   processMouseEvent() method from the Component class is called to  */
/*   perform the normal MouseEvent processing.                         */

   protected void processMouseEvent(MouseEvent event)
   {
      if ( event.getID() == MouseEvent.MOUSE_PRESSED )
      {
         setForeground(Color.red);
      }
      if ( event.getID() == MouseEvent.MOUSE_RELEASED )
      {
         setForeground(Color.black);
      }
```

```
        super.processMouseEvent(event);
    }
}
```

When you run this example, a Help button appears on the frame. Press the button with the mouse. Notice that the label color turns red. When you release the button, the label color turns black Note that the color change will take place whether or not this event is being listened to by any registered event listener because the change happens earlier in the event life cycle process.

Also see Chapter 6, Example 6.30 in the section "PropertyChangeEvent Class," where a PropertyChangeSupport object uses the `fireProperty-Change()` method to indicate a change in a bound property.

Container Class Methods

protected void processContainerEvent(ContainerEvent event)

protected void processEvent(AWTEvent event)

`processContainerEvent()` is used to process ContainerEvents occurring on the Container object. This method will dispatch the event to any registered ContainerListeners or to any components that are enabled to receive the event.

`processEvent()` is an overridden version of the method defined in the Component class and is used to process events generated by a Container. If the event is a ContainerEvent, this method calls the `process-Container-Event()` method. Otherwise, the Component class `processEvent()` method is called.

DefaultBoundedRangeModel Class Methods

protected void fireStateChanged()

fireStateChanged() sends a ChangeEvent to the stateChanged() method of every ChangeListener in the invoking component's listener list.

DEFAULTBUTTONMODEL CLASS METHODS

protected void fireActionPerformed(ActionEvent event)
protected void fireItemStateChanged(ItemEvent event)
protected void fireStateChanged()

fireActionPerformed() sends the specified ActionEvent to the actionPerformed() method of every ActionListener in the invoking component's listener list.

fireItemStateChanged() sends the specified ItemEvent object to the itemStateChanged() method of every ItemListener in the invoking component's listener list.

fireStateChanged() sends a ChangeEvent object to the stateChanged() method of every ChangeListener in the invoking component's listener list.

DEFAULTLISTCELLRENDERER CLASS METHODS

public void firePropertyChange(String propertyName, boolean oldValue, boolean newValue)
public void firePropertyChange(String propertyName, byte oldValue, byte newValue)
public void firePropertyChange(String propertyName, char oldValue, char newValue)
public void firePropertyChange(String propertyName, double oldValue, double newValue)
public void firePropertyChange(String propertyName, float oldValue, float newValue)

```
public void firePropertyChange(String propertyName, int
oldValue, int newValue)
public void firePropertyChange(String propertyName, long
oldValue, long newValue)
protected void firePropertyChange(String propertyName,
Object oldValue, Object newValue)
public void firePropertyChange(String propertyName, short
oldValue, short newValue)
```

`firePropertyChange()` is used to fire a PropertyChangeEvent representing a change in the value of a bound property. The event is sent to any registered PropertyChangeListeners in the invoking component's listener list. Note that the versions that take primitive variables have public access. The version that takes Object arguments has protected access.

DefaultListSelectionModel Class Methods

```
protected void fireValueChanged(boolean isAdjusting)
protected void fireValueChanged(int indexStart, int indexEnd)
protected void fireValueChanged(int indexStart, int indexEnd,
boolean isAdjusting)
```

`fireValueChanged()` sends a ListSelectionEvent to the `valueChanged()` method of every ListSelectionListener in the invoking component's listener list.

DefaultSingleSelectionModel Class Methods

```
protected void fireStateChanged()
```

`fireStateChanged()` sends a ChangeEvent to the `stateChanged()` method of every ChangeListener in the invoking component's listener list.

JApplet Class Methods

> protected void processKeyEvent(KeyEvent event)

processKeyEvent() is used to process KeyEvents occurring on a JApplet object. This method will dispatch the event to any registered KeyListeners or to any components that are enabled to receive the event.

JComboBox Class Methods

> protected void fireActionEvent()
>
> protected void fireItemStateChanged(ItemEvent event)
>
> protected void processKeyEvent(KeyEvent event)

fireActionEvent() sends an ActionEvent to the actionPerformed() method of every ActionListener in the invoking component's listener list.

fireItemStateChanged() sends an ItemEvent to the itemStateChanged() method of every ItemListener in the invoking component's listener list.

processKeyEvent() is used to process KeyEvents occurring on a JComboBox. Specifically, this method waits for the Tab key. If the Tab key is associated with the event, the popup window of the JComboBox is closed.

JComponent Class Methods

Event Firing Methods

> public void firePropertyChange(String propertyName, boolean oldValue, boolean newValue)
>
> public void firePropertyChange(String propertyName, byte oldValue, byte newValue)

public void firePropertyChange(String propertyName, char oldValue, char newValue)
public void firePropertyChange(String propertyName, double oldValue, double newValue)
public void firePropertyChange(String propertyName, float oldValue, float newValue)
public void firePropertyChange(String propertyName, int oldValue, int newValue)
public void firePropertyChange(String propertyName, long oldValue, long newValue)
protected void firePropertyChange(String propertyName, Object oldValue, Object newValue)
public void firePropertyChange(String propertyName, short oldValue, short newValue)
protected void fireVetoableChange(String propertyName, Object oldValue, Object newValue)

firePropertyChange() is used to fire a PropertyChangeEvent representing a change in the value of a bound property. The event is sent to any registered PropertyChangeListeners in the invoking component's listener list. Note that the versions that take primitive variables have public access. The version that takes Object arguments has protected access.

fireVetoableChange() is used to fire a PropertyChangeEvent representing a change in the value of a constrained property. The event is sent to any registered VetoableChangeListeners in the invoking component's listener list.

Event Processing Methods

protected void processComponentKeyEvent(KeyEvent event)
protected void processFocusEvent(FocusEvent event)
protected void processKeyEvent(KeyEvent event)
protected void processMouseMotionEvent(MouseEvent event)

The JComponent class defines methods for processing key, focus, and mouse-motion events. These methods are available to any subclasses of JComponent. The JComponent subclasses will sometimes override these methods for their own specific needs.

`processComponentKeyEvent()` is a specialized method that is intended to process a KeyEvent that has not been consumed by any listener object. The default implementation of this method does nothing. It is meant to be overridden to suit the particular needs of a given application.

`processFocusEvent()` is an overridden version of the method defined in the Component class and is used to process FocusEvents generated by a Swing GUI component. This method will dispatch the event to any registered FocusListeners or to any components that are enabled to receive the event.

`processKeyEvent()` is an overridden version of the method defined in the Component class and is used to process KeyEvents generated by a Swing GUI component. This method will dispatch the event to any registered KeyListeners or to any components that are enabled to receive the event.

`processMouseMotionEvent()` is an overridden version of the method defined in the Component class and is used to process motion-oriented MouseEvents generated by a Swing GUI component. This method will dispatch the event to any registered MouseMotionListeners or to any components that are enabled to receive the event.

JDialog Class Methods

protected void `processKeyEvent(KeyEvent event)`
protected void `processWindowEvent(WindowEvent event)`

`processKeyEvent()` overrides the method defined in the Component class and is used to process KeyEvents occurring on a JDialog object. This method will pass the KeyEvent along to any appropriate components contained in the dialog.

`processWindowEvent()` overrides the method defined in the Window class and is used to process WindowEvents occurring on a JDialog object. This method processes the WindowEvent according to the `defaultCloseOperation` property for the dialog.

JEditorPane Class Methods

> public void fireHyperlinkEvent(HyperlinkEvent event)
>
> protected void processComponentKeyEvent(KeyEvent event)
>
> protected void processComponentKeyEvent(KeyEvent event)
>
> protected void processKeyEvent(KeyEvent event)

fireHyperlinkEvent() sends a HyperlinkEvent to the hyperlinkUpdate() method of every HyperlinkListener in the invoking component's listener list.

processComponentKeyEvent() is an overridden version of the method defined in the JComponent class. This method insures that a non-editable JEditorPane will not receive keyboard focus. This method waits for a Tab or Shift-Tab keyboard sequence, which would request focus for the JEditorPane. If it detects this and the editor pane is non-editable, the FocusManager shifts focus to the next available component.

processKeyEvent() is an overridden version of the method defined in the JComponent class. This method consumes Tab and Shift-Tab keyboard events so the AWT doesn't attempt focus traversal if the user types a Tab character inside the JEditorPane.

JFrame Class Methods

> protected void processKeyEvent(KeyEvent event)
>
> protected void processWindowEvent(WindowEvent event)

processKeyEvent() overrides the method defined in the Component class and is used to process KeyEvents occurring on a JFrame object. This method will pass the KeyEvent along to any appropriate components contained in the frame.

processWindowEvent() overrides the method defined in the Window class and is used to process WindowEvents occurring on a JFrame object. This method processes the WindowEvent according to the defaultCloseOperation property for the frame.

JInternalFrame Class Methods

> protected void fireInternalFrameEvent(int eventID)

`fireInternalFrameEvent()` sends an InternalFrameEvent to every InternalFrameListener in the invoking component's listener list.

JList Class Methods

> protected void fireValueChanged(int indexStart, int indexEnd, boolean isAdjusting)

`fireValueChanged()` sends a ListSelectionEvent to the `valueChanged()` method of every ListSelectionListener in the invoking component's listener list.

JMenu Class Methods

> protected void fireMenuCanceled()
>
> protected void fireMenuDeselected()
>
> protected void fireMenuSelected()
>
> protected void processKeyEvent(KeyEvent event)

`fireMenuCanceled()` sends a MenuEvent to the `menuCanceled()` method of every MenuListener in the invoking component's listener list.

`fireMenuDeselected()` sends a MenuEvent to the `menuDeselected()` method of every MenuListener in the invoking component's listener list.

`fireMenuSelected()` sends a MenuEvent to the `menuSelected()` method of every MenuListener in the invoking component's listener list.

`processKeyEvent()` is used to process KeyEvents occurring on a JMenu. Specifically, this method looks for keystrokes representing mnemonics and accelerators for the menu items contained in the menu.

JMenuBar Class Methods

public void processKeyEvent(KeyEvent event, MenuElement[] path, MenuSelectionManager manager)

public void processMouseEvent(MouseEvent event, MenuElement[] path, MenuSelectionManager manager)

processKeyEvent() is used to process a KeyEvent that occurs along the specified MenuElement path. The default implementation of this method does nothing. It is intended to be overridden to provide whatever functionality is desired.

processMouseEvent() is used to process a MouseEvent that occurs along the specified MenuElement path. The default implementation of this method does nothing. It is intended to be overridden to provide whatever functionality is desired.

JMenuItem Class Methods

Event Firing Methods

protected void fireMenuDragMouseDragged(MenuDragMouseEvent event)

protected void fireMenuDragMouseEntered(MenuDragMouseEvent event)

protected void fireMenuDragMouseExited(MenuDragMouseEvent event)

protected void fireMenuDragMouseReleased(MenuDragMouseEvent event)

protected void fireMenuKeyPressed(MenuKeyEvent event)

protected void fireMenuKeyReleased(MenuKeyEvent event)

protected void fireMenuKeyTyped(MenuKeyEvent event)

fireMenuDragMouseDragged() sends a MenuDragMouseEvent to the menuDragMouseDragged() method of every MenuDragMouseListener in the invoking component's listener list.

fireMenuDragMouseEntered() sends a MenuDragMouseEvent to the menuDragMouseEntered() method of every MenuDragMouseListener in the invoking component's listener list.

`fireMenuDragMouseExited()` sends a MenuDragMouseEvent to the `menuDragMouseExited()` method of every MenuDragMouseListener in the invoking component's listener list.

`fireMenuDragMouseReleased()` sends a MenuDragMouseEvent to the `menuDragMouseReleased()` method of every MenuDragMouseListener in the invoking component's listener list.

`fireMenuKeyPressed()` sends a MenuKeyEvent to the `menuKeyPressed()` method of every MenuKeyListener in the invoking component's listener list.

`fireMenuKeyReleased()` sends a MenuKeyEvent to the `menuKeyReleased()` method of every MenuKeyListener in the invoking component's listener list.

`fireMenuKeyTyped()` sends a MenuKeyEvent to the `menuKeyTyped()` method of every MenuKeyListener in the invoking component's listener list.

Event Processing Methods

public void processKeyEvent(KeyEvent event, MenuElement[] path, MenuSelectionManager manager)
public void processMenuDragMouseEvent(MenuDragMouseEvent event)
public void processMenuKeyEvent(MenuKeyEvent event)
public void processMouseEvent(MouseEvent event, MenuElement[] path, MenuSelectionManager manager)

`processKeyEvent()` is used to process a KeyEvent that was forwarded from the specified MenuSelectionManager. This method is usually overridden to provide whatever functionality is desired.

`processMenuDragMouseEvent()` processes events caused by dragging the mouse across the display area of a menu.

`processMenuKeyEvent()` processes events caused by typing a keystroke when a menu popup display is visible.

`processMouseEvent()` is used to process a MouseEvent that was forwarded from the specified MenuSelectionManager. This method is usually overridden to provide whatever functionality is desired.

JPopupMenu Class Methods

Event Firing Methods

> protected void firePopupMenuCanceled()
>
> protected void firePopupMenuWillBecomeVisible()
>
> protected void firePopupMenuWillBecomeInvisible()

firePopupMenuCanceled() sends a PopupMenuEvent to the popupMenuCanceled() method of every PopupMenuListener in the invoking component's listener list.

firePopupMenuWillBecomVisible() sends a PopupMenuEvent to the popupMenuWillBecomeVisible() method of every PopupMenuListener in the invoking component's listener list.

firePopupMenuWillBecomeInvisible() sends a PopupMenuEvent to the popupMenuWillBecomeInvisible() method of every PopupMenuListener in the invoking component's listener list.

Event Processing Methods

> public void processKeyEvent(KeyEvent event, MenuElement[] path, MenuSelectionManager manager)
>
> public void processMouseEvent(MouseEvent event, MenuElement[] path, MenuSelectionManager manager)

processKeyEvent() is used to process a KeyEvent that occurs along the specified MenuElement path of a JPopupMenu. The default implementation of this method does nothing. It is intended to be overridden to provide whatever functionality is desired.

processMouseEvent() is used to process a MouseEvent that occurs along the specified MenuElement path of a JPopupMenu. The default implementation of this method does nothing. It is intended to be overridden to provide whatever functionality is desired.

JProgressBar Class Methods

protected void fireStateChanged()

fireStateChanged() sends a ChangeEvent to the stateChanged() method of every ChangeListener in the invoking component's listener list.

JScrollBar Class Methods

protected void fireAdjustmentValueChanged(int id, int type, int value)

fireAdjustmentValueChanged() sends an AdjustmentEvent to the adjustmentValueChanged() method of every AdjustmentListener in the invoking component's listener list.

JSlider Class Methods

protected void fireStateChanged()

fireStateChanged() sends a ChangeEvent to the stateChanged() method of every ChangeListener in the invoking component's listener list.

JTabbedPane Class Methods

protected void fireStateChanged()

fireStateChanged() sends a ChangeEvent to the stateChanged() method of every ChangeListener in the invoking component's listener list.

JTextArea Class Methods

> protected void processKeyEvent(KeyEvent event)

processKeyEvent() is an overridden version of the method defined in the JComponent class. This method consumes Tab and Shift-Tab keyboard events so the AWT doesn't attempt focus traversal if the user types a Tab inside the text area.

JTextField Class Methods

> protected void fireActionPerformed()
>
> public void postActionEvent()

fireActionPerformed() sends an ActionEvent to the actionPerformed() method of every ActionListener in the invoking component's listener list.

postActionEvent() sends an ActionEvent to the actionPerformed() method of every ActionListener in the invoking component's listener list. This method is normally called by the controller registered with the textfield.

JTree Class Methods

> public void fireTreeCollapsed(TreePath path)
>
> public void fireTreeExpanded(TreePath path)
>
> public void fireTreeWillCollapse(TreePath path)
>
> public void fireTreeWillExpand(TreePath path)
>
> protected void fireValueChanged(TreeSelection Event event)

fireTreeCollapsed() sends a TreeExpansionEvent to the treeCollapsed() method of every TreeExpansionListener in the invoking component's listener list.

List Class Methods

fireTreeExpanded() sends a TreeExpansionEvent to the treeExpanded() method of every TreeExpansionListener in the invoking component's listener list.

fireTreeWillCollapse() sends a TreeExpansionEvent to the treeWillCollapse() method of every TreeWillExpandListener in the invoking component's listener list.

fireTreeWillExpand() sends a TreeExpansionEvent to the treeWillExpand() method of every TreeWillExpandListener in the invoking component's listener list.

fireValueChanged() sends a TreeSelectionEvent to the valueChanged() method of every TreeSelctionListener in the invoking component's listener list.

JViewport Class Methods

protected void firePropertyChange(String propertyName, Object oldValue, Object newValue)

protected void fireStateChanged()

firePropertyChange() is used to fire a PropertyChangeEvent representing a change in the value of a bound property. The event is sent to any registered PropertyChangeListeners in the invoking component's listener list.

fireStateChanged() sends a ChangeEvent to the stateChanged() method of every ChangeListener in the invoking component's listener list.

List Class Methods

protected void processActionEvent(ActionEvent event)

protected void processEvent(AWTEvent event)

protected void processItemEvent(ItemEvent event)

processActionEvent() is used to process ActionEvents occurring on a List component. This method will dispatch the event to any registered ActionListeners or to any components that are enabled to receive the event.

`processEvent()` is an overridden version of the method defined in the Component class and is used to process events generated by a List component. If the event is an ActionEvent, this method calls the `processActionEvent()` method. If the event is an ItemEvent, this method calls the `processItemEvent()` method. Otherwise, the Component class `processEvent()` method is called.

`processItemEvent()` is used to process ItemEvents occurring on a List component. This method will dispatch the event to any registered ItemListeners or to any components that are enabled to receive the event.

MenuComponent Class Methods

AWT menu components are not subclasses of the Component class and do not have access to the life cycle methods defined in that class. They have their own set of life cycle methods, starting with the `processEvent()` method in the MenuComponent class. The MenuComponent class is the parent class of all AWT menu components.

> protected void `processEvent(AWTEvent event)`

This version of `processEvent()` method can be accessed by all AWT menu components. The `processEvent()` method is called by the `dispatchEvent()` method. It determines what type of event has been passed to it and calls the specific process method to deal with the event.

MenuItem Class Methods

> protected final void `disableEvents(long eventMask)`
> protected final void `enableEvents(long eventMask)`
> protected void `processActionEvent(ActionEvent event)`
> protected void `processEvent(AWTEvent event)`

`disableEvents()` prevents the event types corresponding to the specified event mask from being delivered to the invoking MenuItem. The event mask is a number identifying the event type.

`enableEvents()` allows event types corresponding to the specified event mask to be delivered to the `processEvent()` method of the invoking MenuItem. Normally, events of a given type will be automatically enabled by the system when a listener for that event type is registered with the component. This method can be used to have events delivered to the invoking component's `processEvent()` method, whether or not a listener has been registered.

`processActionEvent()` is used to process action events occurring on the MenuItem. This method will dispatch the event to any registered ActionListeners or to any components that are enabled to receive the event.

`processEvent()` is an overridden version of the method defined in the MenuComponent class and is used to process events generated by a MenuItem. If the event is an ActionEvent, this method calls the `processActionEvent()` method.

PropertyChangeSupport Class Methods

```
public void firePropertyChange(PropertyChangeEvent event)
```

```
public void firePropertyChange(String propertyName, boolean oldValue, boolean newValue)
```

```
public void firePropertyChange(String propertyName, int oldValue, int newValue)
```

```
public void firePropertyChange(String propertyName, Object oldValue, Object newValue)
```

`firePropertyChange()` is used to fire a PropertyChangeEvent representing a change in the value of a bound property. The event is sent to any registered PropertyChangeListeners in the invoking component's listener list. Note that these methods have public access. For more information on the PropertyChangeSupport class, see Chapter 7, "Event Support Classes."

Scrollbar Class Methods

protected void processAdjustmentEvent(AdjustmentEvent event)

protected void processEvent(AWTEvent event)

processAdjustmentEvent() is used to process AdjustmentEvents occurring on a Scrollbar component. This method will dispatch the event to any registered AdjustmentListeners or to any components that are enabled to receive the event.

processEvent() is an overridden version of the method defined in the Component class and is used to process events generated by a Scrollbar component. If the event is an AdjustmentEvent, this method calls the processAdjustmentEvent() method. Otherwise, the Component class processEvent() method is called.

SwingPropertyChangeSupport Class Methods

public void firePropertyChange(PropertyChangeEvent event)

public void firePropertyChange(String propertyName, Object oldValue, Object newValue)

firePropertyChange() is used to fire a PropertyChangeEvent representing a change in the value of a bound property. The event is sent to any registered PropertyChangeListeners in the invoking component's listener list. Note that these methods have public access. For more information on the SwingPropertyChangeSupport class, see Chapter 7.

TextComponent Class Methods

protected void processEvent(AWTEvent event)

protected void processTextEvent(TextEvent event)

processEvent() is an overridden version of the method defined in the Component class and is used to process events generated by an AWT text component. If the event is a TextEvent, this method calls the `processTextEvent()` method. Otherwise, the Component class `processEvent()` method is called.

`processTextEvent()` is used to process TextEvents occurring on the text component. This method will dispatch the event to any registered TextListeners or to any components that are enabled to receive the event.

TextField Class Methods

> protected void `processActionEvent(ActionEvent event)`
>
> protected void `processEvent(AWTEvent event)`

`processActionEvent()` is used to process action events occurring on the TextField. This method will dispatch the event to any registered ActionListeners or to any components that are enabled to receive the event.

`processEvent()` is an overridden version of the method defined in the Component class and is used to process events generated by a TextField. If the event is an ActionEvent, this method calls the `processActionEvent()` method. Otherwise, the Component class `processEvent()` method is called.

Timer Class Methods

> protected void `fireActionPerformed(ActionEvent event)`

`fireActionPerformed()` sends an ActionEvent to the `actionPerformed()` method of every ActionListener in the invoking component's listener list.

VetoableChangeSupport Class Methods

> public void `fireVetoableChange(PropertyChangeEvent event)`
>
> public void `fireVetoableChange(String propertyName, boolean oldValue, boolean newValue)`

```
public void fireVetoableChange(String propertyName, int
oldValue, int newValue)
```
```
public void fireVetoableChange(String propertyName, Object
oldValue, Object newValue)
```

`fireVetoableChange()` is used to fire a PropertyChangeEvent representing a change in the value of a constrained property. The event is sent to any registered VetoableChangeListeners in the invoking component's listener list. Note that these methods have public access. For more information on the VetoableChangeSupport class, see Chapter 7.

Window Class Methods

```
protected void processEvent(AWTEvent event)
```
```
protected void processWindowEvent(WindowEvent event)
```

`processEvent()` is an overridden version of the method defined in the Component class and is used to process events generated by a window. If the event is a WindowEvent, this method calls the `processWindowEvent()` method. Otherwise, the Component class `processEvent()` method is called.

`processWindowEvent()` is used to process WindowEvents occurring on a window. This method will dispatch the event to any registered WindowListeners or to any components that are enabled to receive the event.

PART III

ADVANCED TOPICS

Parts 1 and 2 of this book discussed the Java event handling topics that you will use and apply in most of your programming work. In Part 1, we introduced the concept of a Java event, including the difference between a local event and a remote event. We discussed the Java event model. Part 1 introduced the event classes, event listener interfaces, and the support classes and interfaces provided by the Java API as well as topics such as event consumption and the event dispatching thread. Part 2 of this book provided a complete technical reference of the local event classes, interfaces, and support methods contained in the J2SE.

In Part 3 of this book, we provide details on some more advanced event handling topics. These are things you might not need to use often, but they offer a lot of power and versatility—and can be a lot of fun to work with. We also demonstrate how everything we've learned so far can be put together to create useful, GUI-based, event-driven applications.

Previously in this book, we introduced the concept of an event listener list that is maintained by every event-generating object. In Chapter 11, "Event Listener Manager Classes," we describe in detail two classes that are used to manage this listener list. These classes define methods to add a listener to or remove a listener from the listener list, and can be used to send events to any registered listeners. These operations are normally handled by the system, but you can use these event-listener list manager classes to manipulate the listener list or to create new event-generating objects.

The Java API provides a multitude of built-in event classes and listener interfaces that cover almost every conceivable event-generating and handling need. You may, however, come across a situation where it would be advantageous to create a user-defined event. Java provides you with all of the building blocks to do this. The process of creating a user-defined event class, event listener, and event-generating component is discussed in Chapter 12, "User-Defined Event Classes and Event Listeners."

The code examples in Parts 1 and 2 have been relatively short, simple examples intended to focus on one or two topics in Java event handling. In Chapter 13, "Putting It All Together," we develop two real-world applications that demonstrate how events can be used to bring more complex programs to life. These applications create GUI front ends that use many different components that generate several types of events. We must make design decisions about how the event listeners will be implemented.

Finally in Chapter 14, "Distributed Events," we take a brief look at remote event handling. This book has focused on local event handling, the generation and processing of events generated by an application running on a single platform using a single JVM. Distributed or Web-based applications might run on multiple platforms using multiple JVMs. Java provides a framework for the generation, transmission, and processing of events generated by a remote source. A general discussion of the requirements of a remote event model is presented as are the remote event classes and interfaces defined in the Jini specification.

Event Listener Manager Classes

Java uses two classes to manage the event listener list associated with a given component. These are the AWTEventMulticaster and EventListenerList classes. These classes serve as event coordinators, if you pardon the expression. They maintain a list of the event listeners registered with a given component. They are also capable of sending an event generated by the component to the appropriate listeners in the component's listener list.

The system uses these classes internally as part of the event handling process. They are also available to the user and can be used to modify the event capabilities of existing components or to make new event-generating components. This chapter describes the event listener manager classes AWTEventMulticaster and EventListenerList.

AWTEventMulticaster Class

The AWTEventMulticaster class is used by the AWT to manage the list of AWT event listeners registered to a given component. It does this by maintaining a linked list of event listeners associated with the component. Every time an event source updates its listener list by calling the `add()` or `remove()` listener method, a new AWTEventMulticaster object containing the updated list is created.

The AWTEventMulticaster class is also responsible for dispatching an event to the appropriate listeners when the event is generated. The AWTEventMulticaster object has access to the methods defined in the event listeners. Whenever an event is generated, the AWTEventMulticaster sends the event to the appropriate method for every listener in the linked list. For example, if an ActionEvent object is generated, the multicaster will call the `actionPerformed()` method of every ActionListener in its linked list.

These operations usually go on in the background and are of no concern to the programmer. However, the AWTEventMulticaster class can be used to create new types of components that fire AWT events. It can also be used to extend the event capabilities of existing GUI components. For instance, a JLabel class can be defined such that the label can be selected, or a JButton class can be created that generates KeyEvents.

An AWTEventMulticaster only deals with the event types defined in the java.awt.event package. When working with Swing event types, the EventListenerList class can be used.

Syntax: public class AWTEventMulticaster extends Object implements ActionListener, AdjustmentListener, ComponentListener, ContainerListener, FocusListener, InputMethodListener, HierarchyListener, HierarchyBoundsListener, ItemListener, KeyListener, MouseListener, MouseMotionListener, TextListener, WindowListener

Package: java.awt

Class hierarchy: Object — AWTEventMulticaster

Introduced: JDK 1.1

Constructors

protected `AWTEventMulticaster(EventListener a, EventListener b)`

The AWTEventMulticaster class provides one protected constructor. The constructor creates an AWTEventMulticaster that chains EventListener `a` and EventListener `b` into a linked list. The system will automatically create an AWTEventMulticaster instance if the `add()` or `remove()` methods are invoked.

Fields

protected final EventListener a
protected final EventListener b

These fields are event listeners that represent either a single listener or a chain of listeners. They are used in conjunction with the AWTEventMulticaster constructor.

Methods to Add a Listener to a Listener List

public static ActionListener add(`ActionListener a, ActionListener b`)
public static AdjustmentListener add(`AdjustmentListener a, Adjustment Listener b`)
public static ComponentListener add(`ComponentListener a, ComponentListener b`)
public static ContainerListener add(`ContainerListener a, ContainerListener b`)
public static FocusListener add(`FocusListener a, FocusListener b`)
public static HierarchyBoundsListener add(`HierarchyBoundsListener a, HierarchyBoundsListener b`)
public static HierarchyListener add(`HierarchyListener a, HierarchyListener b`)
public static InputMethodListener add(`InputMethodListener a, InputMethod Listener b`)
public static ItemListener add(`ItemListener a, ItemListener b`)
public static KeyListener add(`KeyListener a, KeyListener b`)
public static MouseListener add(`MouseListener a, MouseListener b`)
public static MouseMotionListener add(`MouseMotionListener a, MouseMotionListener b`)
public static TextListener add(`TextListener a, TextListener b`)
public static WindowListener add(`WindowListener a, WindowListener b`)

These methods create an AWTEventMulticaster object that contains a linked list of EventListeners a and b. The arguments a and b can be a single event listener or a list of event listeners (another multicaster for instance). The

AWTEventMulticaster class implements all of the event listeners in the java.awt.event class, so an AWTEventMulticaster object is also an ActionListener, AdjustmentListener, ComponentListener, and so on. The return object for these methods is an event multicaster containing a linked list of the listeners of the specified type.

Listener Interface Methods

public void actionPerformed(ActionEvent event)
public void adjustmentValueChanged(AdjustmentEvent event)
public void ancestorMoved(HierarchyEvent event)
public void ancestorResized(HierarchyEvent event)
public void caretPositionChanged(InputMethodEvent event)
public void componentAdded(ContainerEvent event)
public void componentHidden(ComponentEvent event)
public void componentMoved(ComponentEvent event)
public void componentRemoved(Container Event event)
public void componentShown(ComponentEvent event)
public void focusGained(FocusEvent event)
public void focusLost(FocusEvent event)
public void hierarchyChanged(HierarchyEvent event)
public void inputMethodTextChanged(InputMethodEvent event)
public void itemStateChanged(ItemEvent event)
public void keyPressed(KeyEvent event)
public void keyReleased(KeyEvent event)
public void keyTyped(KeyEvent event)
public void mouseClicked(MouseEvent event)
public void mouseDragged(MouseEvent event)
public void mouseEntered(MouseEvent event)
public void mouseExited(MouseEvent event)
public void mouseMoved(MouseEvent event)

public void mousePressed(MouseEvent event)
public void mouseReleased(MouseEvent event)
public void textValueChanged(TextEvent event)
public void windowActivated(WindowEvent event)
public void windowClosed(WindowEvent event)
public void windowClosing(WindowEvent event)
public void windowDeactivated(WindowEvent event)
public void windowDeiconified(WindowEvent event)
public void windowIconified(WindowEvent event)
public void windowOpened(WindowEvent event)

The AWTEventMulticaster class implements all of the event listener interfaces in the java.awt.event package and must therefore provide implementation of all of the methods declared in those interfaces. These methods are used to broadcast an event to the corresponding method in all listeners of the same type contained in the listener list. For instance, if the AWTEventMulticaster object calls the actionPerformed() method, passing it an ActionEvent object as an argument, that ActionEvent will be sent to the actionPerformed() method of every ActionListener contained in the linked list managed by the AWTEventMulticaster.

Methods to Remove a Listener from a Listener List

public static ActionListener remove(ActionListener list, ActionListener b)
public static AdjustmentListener remove(AdjustmentListener list, AdjustmentListener b)
public static ComponentListener remove(ComponentListener list, ComponentListener b)
public static ContainerListener remove(ContainerListener list, ContainerListener b)
public static FocusListener remove(FocusListener list, FocusListener b)
public static HierarchyBoundsListener remove(HierarchyBoundsListener list, HierarchyBoundsListener b)

```
public static HierarchyListener remove(HierarchyListener list,
HierarchyListener b)
public static InputMethodListener remove(InputMethodListener list,
InputMethodListener b)
public static ItemListener remove(ItemListener list, ItemListener b)
public static KeyListener remove(KeyListener list, KeyListener b)
public static MouseListener remove(MouseListener list, MouseListener b)
public static MouseMotionListener remove(MouseMotionListener list,
MouseMotionListener b)
public static TextListener remove(TextListener list, TextListener b)
public static WindowListener remove(WindowListener list, WindowListener b)
```

These methods remove an event listener from an event listener list and return an AWTEventMulticaster containing the modified listener list. The `list` parameter is the current listener list. The `b` parameter is the event listener to be removed from the list.

Support Methods

```
protected static EventListener addInternal(EventListener a, EventListener b)
protected static EventListener remove(EventListener a)
protected static EventListener removeInternal(EventListener list, Event-
Listener b)
protected static void save(ObjectOutputStream stream, String string,
EventListener listener) throws IOException
protected void saveInternal(ObjectOutputStream stream, String string)
throws IOException
```

These methods provide support for the other methods defined in the AWTEventMulticaster class. They are generally not called by the user.

`addInternal()` is a support method for the `addListener()` methods defined in this class. It returns a listener list that combines listener sets a and b.

`remove()` is a support method for the `removeInternal()` method. It removes the specified EventListener from the invoking event multicaster and returns a multicaster containing the modified listener list.

`removeInternal()` is a support method for the `removeListener()` methods defined in the AWTEventMulticaster class. It removes listener b from the listener list `list` and returns a modified listener list.

`save()` is a support method for the `saveInternal()` method. The method writes the specified EventListener to the designated ObjectOutputStream.

`saveInternal()` is a support method used for AWTEventMulticaster class serialization. This method allows for the persistent storage of AWTEventMulticaster objects.

Methods Inherited from the java.lang.Object Class

> public final Class `getClass()`

`getClass()` returns a Class object representing the runtime class of the invoking object. In this case, it would return an object representing the java.awt.AWTEventMulticaster class.

The other methods inherited from the Object class, `clone()`, `equals()`, `hashCode()`, `notify()`, `notifyAll()`, and `wait()` are generally not used in conjunction with AWTEventMulticaster objects.

EXAMPLE

One difference between a JTextField and a JTextArea is that an ActionEvent is generated when a newline is entered in a JTextField, whereas a JTextArea treats a newline like any other valid text entry. JTextArea objects do not generate ActionEvents, but it might be useful to have them do so. For instance, the ActionEvent could indicate that the text entry into the JTextArea was complete and it was time to process the text inside the JTextArea. In Example 11.1, an AWTEventMulticaster object is used to allow JTextArea objects to generate an ActionEvent.

The NewTextArea class is created. This class is a subclass of JTextArea. When the mouse is pressed over a NewTextArea object while the CTRL and ALT keys are held down, an ActionEvent is generated.

EXAMPLE 11.1 USING AN AWTEVENTMULTICASTER

```java
import javax.swing.*;
import java.awt.event.*;
import java.awt.*;

public class NewTextArea extends JTextArea
{
/* The NewTextArea class adds an ActionListener to the JTextArea class   */
/* definition.  The ActionListener will later be used as an event        */
/* multicaster that will store a linked list of ActionListeners.         */

   ActionListener actionListenerList = null;

/* The NewTextArea constructor calls the corresponding JTextArea         */
/* constructor. To simplify this example a bit, only one NewTextArea     */
/* constructor is provided.                                              */

   public NewTextArea(int rows, int columns)
   {
      super(rows, columns);
   }

/* The processEvent() method is overridden to implement the ActionEvent  */
/* generating capability of the NewTextArea.  If the mouse is clicked    */
/* over the NewTextArea while the CTRL and ALT keys are held down, an    */
/* ActionEvent is created and sent to the actionPerformed() method of    */
/* every ActionListener contained in the listener list.                  */

   public void processEvent(AWTEvent event)
   {
      super.processEvent(event);
      if ( event.getID() == MouseEvent.MOUSE_CLICKED )
      {
         if ( actionListenerList != null )
         {
            if ( ((MouseEvent)event).isControlDown() &&
                 ((MouseEvent)event).isAltDown() )
            {
               ActionEvent ae =
                  new ActionEvent(this, ActionEvent.ACTION_PERFORMED,
                                  "CTRL-ENTER", ActionEvent.CTRL_MASK);
               actionListenerList.actionPerformed(ae);
            }
         }
      }
   }

/* These methods are provided so a NewTextArea object can register       */
/* and deregister an ActionListener.  The ActionListener object          */
```

```
/*   passed to these methods as an argument is added or removed from   */
/*   the linked list maintained by the multicaster. The return value   */
/*   from these methods is an event multicaster containing the         */
/*   current ActionListener list.                                      */

   public void addActionListener(ActionListener al)
   {
      actionListenerList = AWTEventMulticaster.add(actionListenerList, al);
   }

   public void removeActionListener(ActionListener al)
   {
      actionListenerList =
            AWTEventMulticaster.remove(actionListenerList, al);
   }
}
```

Let's take a look at each section of this class. The NewTextArea class declares an ActionListener. This ActionListener will later be "converted" into an AWTEventMulticaster that will maintain the list of registered ActionListeners for the NewTextArea object. The NewTextArea constructor simply calls the corresponding JTextArea constructor.

The `processEvent()` method is then overridden to generate an ActionEvent if the mouse is clicked over the NewTextArea while the CTRL and ALT keys are held down. We don't want to override any built-in event processing activity, so we first call the JTextArea class `processEvent()` method. We then check to see if the event being processed is a MouseEvent due to the mouse having been clicked. If it is, the method checks to see if there are any ActionListeners in the listener list. If there are, the method checks to see if the CTRL and ALT keys were held down when the mouse was clicked. If they were, an ActionEvent is generated and sent to every ActionListener in the listener list.

The NewTextArea class must also define the methods `add-ActionListener()` and `removeActionListener()` to add or remove an ActionListener from the listener list. An AWTEventMulticaster is used for this purpose. Look at the syntax:

```
actionListenerList = AWTEventMulticaster.add(actionListenerList, al);
```

Initially, the `actionListenerList` parameter is declared as an ActionListener. The return value of the `addActionListener()` method from the AWTEventMulticaster class is an event multicaster containing a list of ActionListeners. There is no conflict in assigning the `action-`

ListenerList parameter as the return value of the addActionListener() method because the AWTEventMulticaster class implements the ActionListener interface. Therefore, an AWTEventMulticaster is also an ActionListener. The actionListenerList parameter is initially set to be null. The first time the addActionListener() method is called, the actionListenerList parameter becomes an event multicaster that contains a list of ActionListener objects.

The driver class for this example is called MulticasterDemo. A NewTextArea is placed on a JFrame. The NewTextArea will look like any ordinary JTextArea. The NewTextArea registers an ActionListener. The MultiCasterDemo class serves as the ActionListener for this example and provides an implementation of the actionPerformed() method. This method determines which NewTextArea generated the ActionEvent and lists the number of lines of text contained in the NewTextArea in a JTextField located at the bottom of the JFrame. The code listing for the MultiCasterDemo class is shown in Example 11.2.

EXAMPLE 11.2 MULTICASTERDEMO CLASS

```
import javax.swing.*;
import java.awt.event.*;
import java.awt.*;

public class MulticasterDemo extends JFrame implements ActionListener
{
   NewTextArea textArea;
   JTextField jtf;

   public MulticasterDemo()
   {
/*  A NewTextArea object is created and placed on a JFrame.  */
/*  The NewTextArea registers an ActionListener.             */

      textArea = new NewTextArea(5,10);
      textArea.addActionListener(this);

      jtf = new JTextField(30);
      jtf.setEditable(false);

      JPanel centerPanel = new JPanel();
      centerPanel.add(new JScrollPane(textArea));

      getContentPane().add(centerPanel, BorderLayout.CENTER);
      getContentPane().add(jtf, BorderLayout.SOUTH);
```

EventListenerList Class

```
        setDefaultCloseOperation(JFrame.EXIT_ON_CLOSE);
        setBounds(100, 100, 250, 300);
        setVisible(true);
    }

/*  The MulticasterDemo class serves as the ActionListener and provides  */
/*  an implementation of the actionPerformed() method.  Whenever the     */
/*  mouse is clicked over the NewTextArea with the CTRL and ALT keys     */
/*  pressed down, an ActionEvent is generated and sent to the            */
/*  actionPerformed() method.  The number of lines currently in the      */
/*  NewTextArea is shown in the JTextField at the bottom of the frame.   */

    public void actionPerformed(ActionEvent event)
    {
        NewTextArea nta = (NewTextArea)event.getSource();
        jtf.setText("text area contains "+nta.getLineCount()+" lines");
    }

    public static void main(String args[])
    {
        MulticasterDemo mc = new MulticasterDemo();
    }
}
```

When you run this program, a text area appears on your screen. Type some text into the text area using more than one line. Now click the mouse on the NewTextArea while holding down the CTRL and ALT keys. The JTextField at the bottom of the frame displays the number of lines contained inside the NewTextArea.

EventListenerList Class

The EventListenerList class is similar in nature to the AWTEventMulticaster class in that it facilitates the addition and removal of event listeners. It also maintains a list of all registered event listeners that can be accessed when events need to be fired to them. While the AWTEventMulticaster can only deal with the event types defined in the java.awt.event package, the EventListenerList class can be used for any event type.

Another difference between the EventListenerList class and the AWTEventMulticaster class is the EventListenerList class does not implement any of the event listener interfaces. Therefore, the EventListenerList class does not contain methods for dispatching events to the appropriate methods of the listeners contained in the listener list. The user must provide the means for calling the appropriate listener method. See Example 11.3 for how this can be done.

The listener list maintained by an EventListenerList object is really a series of Class object/EventListener object pairs. The Class object can be used to identify the type of event listener. The EventListener object provides a reference to the listener itself.

Like the AWTEventMulticaster class, the EventListenerList class can be used to create new GUI components or to extend the event-generating capabilities of existing components. The EventListenerList class is also useful when working with user-defined events and event listeners. The JComponent class defines an EventListenerList object named `listenerList` as a protected field. This means that any subclass of JComponent has access to an EventListenerList that can be used to register event listeners to that component.

Syntax:	public class EventListenerList extends Object
Package:	javax.swing.event
Class hierarchy:	Object — EventListenerList
Introduced:	JDK 1.2

Constructors

public `EventListenerList()`

The EventListenerList class provides one public, no-argument constructor for creating EventListenerList objects.

EventListenerList Class Methods

public void `add(Class class, EventListener listener)`
public int `getListenerCount()`
public int `getListenerCount(Class class)`
public `Object[] getListenerList()`
public `EventListener[] getListeners(Class class)`
public void `remove(Class class, EventListener listener)`
public String `toString()`

`add()` is used to add the specified `listener` of type `class` to the listener list. Note that for listener classes contained in the Java API, the class argument would be something like *ActionListener.class*.

`getListenerCount()` returns the number of listeners contained in the list. If no class type is provided, the return value will be all of the listeners in the list. If a class type is specified, the return value will be the number of listeners of that type.

`getListenerList()` returns the array listener list as an array of listener type/listener object pairs. For instance, the first entry of the list would be a listener type, the second entry a listener object, the third entry a listener type, and so on.

`getListeners()` returns an array containing all of the listeners of a given type contained in the listener list. These will be the listener objects themselves and not the class type.

`remove()` is used to remove the specified `listener` of type `class` from the listener list.

`toString()` returns a String representation of the EventListenerList object.

Methods Inherited from the java.lang.Object Class

> public final Class `getClass()`

`getClass()` returns a Class object representing the runtime class of the invoking object. In this case it would return an object representing the javax.swing.event.EventListenerList class.

The other methods inherited from the Object class `clone()`, `equals()`, `hashCode()`, `notify()`, `notifyAll()`, and `wait()` are generally not used in conjunction with EventListenerList objects.

EXAMPLE

In Example 11.3, an EventListenerList object is used to create a class called NewLabel2. A NewLabel2 object is a label that is selected when the mouse enters its bounding area. The NewLabel2 is deselected when the mouse leaves its bounding area. When the selected state of the NewLabel2 object changes, it generates a ChangeEvent that is sent to any registered ChangeListeners. First, let's look at the NewLabel2 class.

EXAMPLE 11.3 NEWLABEL2 CLASS

```
import javax.swing.*;
import javax.swing.event.*;
import java.awt.event.*;
import java.awt.*;

public class NewLabel2 extends JLabel
{
/* The NewLabel2 class has a boolean instance variable that stores   */
/* the selected state of the NewLabel2.                              */

   boolean selected;

/* The NewLabel2 constructor calls the JLabel constructor.  It then  */
/* sets the initial selected state of the NewLabel2 and has the      */
/* NewLabel2 register a MouseListener.                               */

   public NewLabel2(String str)
   {
      super(str);
      selected = false;
      setFont(new Font("Serif", Font.PLAIN, 14));
      setForeground(Color.black);
      addMouseListener(new MouseHandler());
   }

   public boolean isSelected()
   {
      return selected;
   }

/* These methods are provided so a NewLabel2 object can register and */
/* deregister a ChangeListener object.  The add() and remove()       */
/* methods use the EventListenerList inherited from the JComponent   */
/* class which is named listenerList.  The listenerList object calls */
/* its own add() and remove() methods to add or remove listeners from*/
/* its listener list.                                                */

   public void addChangeListener(ChangeListener listener)
   {
      listenerList.add(ChangeListener.class, listener);
   }

   public void removeItemListener(ChangeListener listener)
   {
      listenerList.remove(ChangeListener.class, listener);
   }

/* A NewLabel2 object is selected when the mouse moves over its      */
```

```
/* bounding area and deselected when the mouse leaves the bounding   */
/* area. When the mouse enters the bounding area of the NewLabel2,   */
/* a MouseEvent is sent to the mouseEntered() method. This method    */
/* sets the selected state of the NewLabel2 to be true and calls the */
/* fireChangeEvent() method.  When the mouse leaves the bounding     */
/* area of the NewLabel2, a MouseEvent is sent to the mouseExited()  */
/* method which changes the selected state to be false and calls     */
/* the fireChangeEvent() method.                                     */

   class MouseHandler extends MouseAdapter
   {
      public void mouseEntered(MouseEvent event)
      {
         selected = true;
         fireChangeEvent();
      }

      public void mouseExited(MouseEvent event)
      {
         selected = false;
         fireChangeEvent();
      }
   }

/* The fireChangeEvent() method sends a ChangeEvent to every         */
/* ChangeListener in the listener list managed by the EventListenerList */
/* object.  The getListeners() method is used to return all of the   */
/* registered ChangeListeners.                                       */

   protected void fireChangeEvent()
   {
      ChangeEvent event = new ChangeEvent(this);
      ChangeListener[] cl =
(ChangeListener[])(listenerList.getListeners(ChangeListener.class));

      for(int i=0; i<cl.length; ++i)
      {
         cl[i].stateChanged(event);
      }
   }
}
```

The NewLabel2 class is a JLabel with some enhanced capability, so the NewLabel2 class extends the JLabel class. It defines a boolean instance variable named `selected`, which maintains the selected state of the NewLabel2.

The NewLabel2 constructor first invokes the JLabel constructor using the "super" keyword. It sets the selected state of the NewLabel2 to be false. The NewLabel2 object then registers a MouseListener. When the mouse enters the bounding area of the NewLabel2, the label is considered to be selected. When the mouse leaves the bounding area of the NewLabel2, the label is considered to be deselected. These MouseEvents must be received and processed by the MouseListener for this functionality to occur.

Because the NewLabel2 generates ChangeEvents, it must provide methods to add or remove ChangeListeners to or from its listener list. The NewLabel2 class is a subclass of JLabel, which itself is a subclass of JComponent, so the NewLabel2 class has access to the EventListenerList object that is declared as a field in the JComponent class. This EventListenerList object, named `listenerList`, is used to maintain the list of ChangeListeners registered to the NewLabel2.

When the mouse enters the bounding area of a NewLabel2 object, a MouseEvent is generated and sent to the `mouseEntered()` method. The selected state of the label is set to true and the `fireChangeEvent()` method is called. When the mouse leaves the bounding area of a NewLabel2 object, a MouseEvent is generated and sent to the `mouseExited()` method. The selected state of the label is set to false and the `fireChangeEvent()` method is called.

The `fireChangeEvent()` method uses the EventListenerList to retrieve the list of ChangeListeners registered to the NewLabel2 object. A ChangeEvent is sent to the `stateChanged()` method of each of the ChangeListeners.

Now let's take a look at the driver class for Example 11.4, the ListenerListDemo class.

EXAMPLE 11.4 LISTENERLISTDEMO CLASS

```
import javax.swing.*;
import javax.swing.event.*;
import java.awt.event.*;
import java.awt.*;

public class ListenerListDemo extends JFrame implements ChangeListener
{
    NewLabel2 lbl1, lbl2;
    JWindow window;
```

```
    JTextArea jta;
    String jacksonText, zacharyText;

    public ListenerListDemo()
    {
/*  Two NewLabel2 objects are created and placed on a JFrame.      */
/*  A NewLabel2 is a JLabel that can be selected and generate      */
/*  ChangeEvents.  The NewLabel2 objects register a ChangeListener */

        lbl1 = new NewLabel2("Jackson");
        lbl1.setBorder(BorderFactory.createEmptyBorder(10,10,10,10));
        lbl1.addChangeListener(this);

        lbl2 = new NewLabel2("Zachary");
        lbl2.setBorder(BorderFactory.createEmptyBorder(10,10,10,10));
        lbl2.addChangeListener(this);

        Box box = Box.createVerticalBox();
        box.add(lbl1);
        box.add(lbl2);

        getContentPane().add(box, BorderLayout.WEST);

/*  A JWindow object is created. The JWindow contains a JTextArea.  */
/*  The JWindow becomes visible whenever a NewLabel2 is selected    */
/*  and displays some information about the selected NewLabel2.     */

        jta = new JTextArea(10,10);
        jta.setEditable(false);
        jta.setLineWrap(true);
        jta.setWrapStyleWord(true);

        jacksonText = "Jackson likes to go to Zoo camp ";
        jacksonText = jacksonText.concat("where he learns about animals.");

        zacharyText = "Zachary loves to play with cars. ";
        zacharyText = zacharyText.concat(" He takes them everywhere he goes.");

        window = new JWindow();
        window.getContentPane().add(new JScrollPane(jta));
        window.setBounds(200, 100, 200, 200);
        window.setVisible(false);

        setDefaultCloseOperation(JFrame.EXIT_ON_CLOSE);
        setBounds(100, 100, 250, 200);
        setVisible(true);
    }

/*  The ListenerListDemo class serves as the ChangeListener for this  */
/*  example and provides an implementation of the stateChanged() method.*/
```

```
/* This method obtains a reference to the NewLabel2 object that      */
/* generated the ChangeEvent.  If the NewLabel2 was selected, the    */
/* JTextArea is updated to contain the text corresponding to the     */
/* event source and the JWindow is made visible.  If the event was   */
/* due to a NewLabel2 being deselected, the JWindow is made invisible */

    public void stateChanged(ChangeEvent event)
    {
       NewLabel2 nl2 = (NewLabel2)event.getSource();
       if ( nl2.isSelected() )
       {
          nl2.setForeground(Color.red);
          if ( nl2.getText().equals("Jackson") )
          {
             jta.setText(jacksonText);
          }
          if ( nl2.getText().equals("Zachary") )
          {
             jta.setText(zacharyText);
          }
          window.setVisible(true);
       }
       else
       {
          nl2.setForeground(Color.black);
          window.setVisible(false);
       }
    }

    public static void main(String args[])
    {
       ListenerListDemo demo = new ListenerListDemo();
    }
}
```

The ListenerListDemo class places two NewLabel2 objects on a JFrame. The NewLabel2 objects register a ChangeListener. When one of the NewLabel2 objects is selected, a JWindow containing a description of that label is made visible. When the NewLabel2 object is deselected, the JWindow is made invisible. A JTextArea object is used to display the information.

The ListenerListDemo class serves as the ChangeListener for this application and provides an implementation of the stateChange() method. This method obtains a reference to the NewLabel2 that generated the event. If the NewLabel2 was selected, the label color is changed to red, the appropriate text is placed in the JTextArea, and the JWindow is made visible. If the NewLabel2 is deselected, the label color is changed to black and the JWindow is made invisible.

When you run this example, initially the two labels appear on the screen. Move the mouse over one of them. The JWindow appears with a description of the label. Now move the mouse off of the label. The JWindow disappears. This occurs because an EventListenerList object has created a label that can generate ChangeEvents.

12

USER-DEFINED EVENT CLASSES AND EVENT LISTENERS

The Java API provides a large selection of event classes and listeners. It also provides the basic building blocks that permit you to create your own event classes and event listeners. You can define a new event class either from scratch, using the high-level event superclasses, EventObject and AWTEvent, or you can write a subclass of an EventObject or AWTEvent subclass such as the ComponentEvent or ActionEvent class.

All event listeners are subinterfaces of the EventListener interface. When writing your own listener interface, you can either extend EventListener directly or extend one of EventListener's subinterfaces. You simply declare whatever methods you want implemented inside your user-defined interface.

Now that you have a user-defined event class and a corresponding event listener, you need an object that can generate and fire the event. The simplest way of doing this is to write a subclass of an existing GUI component, adding the extra functionality that is required to generate your user-defined event.

You must also provide the means for this component to add or remove the user-defined event listener from its listener list. Java provides two event listener manager classes, AWTEventMulticaster and EventListenerList, for this purpose. These classes are described in detail in Chapter 11, "Event Listener Manager Classes."

The best way to illustrate the entire process is by way of example. In our example, a new event type, the ColorEvent class, is defined. A ColorEvent object represents a change in either the foreground or background color property of a component. The ColorEvent will contain information about the event source, the type of ColorEvent, and the new foreground or background color of the component.

A new GUI component that supports ColorEvents, the NewButton class, is also created. A NewButton is a JButton that generates ColorEvents when its foreground or background color is changed. The NewButton class must define methods to register or deregister a ColorListener. It must also provide the mechanism for firing ColorEvents when they are generated.

Finally, a ColorListener interface must be defined. This interface declares the methods that must be implemented by a ColorListener

This example is really intended to demonstrate the process of creating user-defined events and event listeners. Don't worry too much over whether a ColorEvent would be useful. We will now look at each of the previously mentioned steps in detail.

CREATING A USER-DEFINED EVENTLISTENER

Writing an event listener interface is a straightforward process. The user-defined event listener interface will either extend the EventListener interface or one of the EventListener subinterfaces. The user-defined listener interface declares one or more methods that will be implemented by listener objects of that type.

In our example, we will define the ColorListener interface. It defines one method that is called when a ColorEvent, our user-defined event type, is generated from a registered source.

EXAMPLE

Example 12.1 is the ColorListener interface. It extends the EventListener interface. Recall that the EventListener interface declares no methods, but is used as a marker to indicate that a subinterface of EventListener is a listener interface. The ColorListener interface declares one method, `colorChanged()`, that is called when a ColorEvent is generated by a registered source. Here is the code listing of the ColorListener interface.

EXAMPLE 12.1 COLORLISTENER INTERFACE

```
import java.util.EventListener;

public interface ColorListener extends EventListener
{
/*   The ColorListener interface declares one method    */

    public void colorChanged(ColorEvent event);
}
```

CREATING A USER-DEFINED EVENT CLASS

As with the listener interfaces, creating a user-defined event class is not all that difficult because the Java language provides all the necessary building blocks. User-defined event classes should be subclasses of EventObject, AWTEvent, or one of the EventObject or AWTEvent subclasses (ComponentEvent, ContainerEvent, etc.). The user-defined event class has access to all of the fields and methods of its super-classes, and simply adds whatever additional information or methods are required.

Getting back to our example, we define the ColorEvent class to represent a change in the foreground or background color of a component.

EXAMPLE

The ColorEvent class is written as a subclass of EventObject. A ColorEvent object therefore has access to the `source` field and `getSource()` method defined in the EventObject class. A ColorEvent object also contains the `id` and `color` fields. These fields store the identification constant associated with the ColorEvent and the new foreground or background color. The ColorEvent class defines the `getID()` and `getColor()` methods to return the current value of the `id` and `color` fields. The ColorEvent class code listing is shown in Example 12.2.

EXAMPLE 12.2 COLOREVENT CLASS

```
import java.util.EventObject;
import java.awt.Color;

public class ColorEvent extends EventObject
{
```

```
/* The ColorEvent class defines two static constants for   */
/* identifying the type of ColorEvent.                     */

   public static final int FOREGROUND_CHANGED = 0;
   public static final int BACKGROUND_CHANGED = 1;

/* The id and color fields are part of the information contained */
/* by a ColorEvent object.                                       */

   private int id;
   private Color color;

/* The ColorEvent constructor calls the EventObject constructor to */
/* initialize the source field.  It then initializes the id and    */
/* color fields.                                                   */

   public ColorEvent(Object source, int type, Color c)
   {
      super(source);
      id = type;
      color = c;
   }

/* The getID() method returns the identification constant associated */
/* with the ColorEvent.                                              */

   public int getID()
   {
      return id;
   }

/* The getColor() method returns the Color associated with the        */
/* ColorEvent.  This Color is the new foreground or background color. */

   public Color getColor()
   {
      return color;
   }
}
```

Let's look at this listing. Two identification constants, FOREGROUND_CHANGED and BACKGROUND_CHANGED, are defined. These constants identify the type of ColorEvent. One of these constants will be stored in the `id` field. A `color` field is also defined. This field contains the new foreground or background color.

The ColorEvent constructor first calls the EventObject constructor, passing it the source of the event. The ColorEvent constructor then initializes the `id` and `color` fields. Two other methods are defined in the ColorEvent class. The getID() method returns the identification constant of the event. This will be either the `FOREGROUND_CHANGED` or `BACKGROUND_CHANGED` constant. The `getColor()` method returns the new foreground or background color.

DEFINING A COMPONENT THAT SUPPORTS A USER-DEFINED EVENT

A user-defined event by its nature is unknown to the Java API. None of the existing GUI components will support it. We must therefore modify one or more GUI components to generate and process our user-defined event.

The easiest way to do this is to write a subclass of an existing GUI component. The subclass must provide methods to add or remove the event listener corresponding to the user-defined event. The subclass must also provide the means for generating the user-defined event and for sending the event to any registered listeners.

EXAMPLE

In Example 12.3, we will create a component that extends the JButton class and supports our user-defined ColorEvent. A NewButton class is written as a button that generates ColorEvents when its foreground or background color is changed. The NewButton class provides the additional functionality needed to support ColorEvents.

EXAMPLE 12.3 NEWBUTTON CLASS

```
import javax.swing.*;
import javax.swing.event.*;
import java.awt.event.*;
import java.awt.*;

public class NewButton extends JButton
{
/* The NewButton constructor simply calls the JButton class   */
/* constructor using the super keyword.                        */

   public NewButton(String str)
   {
      super(str);
   }

/* These methods are provided so a NewButton object can register and  */
```

```
/* deregister a ColorListener.  The add() and remove() methods use    */
/* the EventListenerList inherited from the JComponent class which is */
/* named listenerList.  The listenerList object calls its own add()   */
/* and remove() methods to add or remove listeners from its listener  */
/* list.                                                              */

   public void addColorListener(ColorListener listener)
   {
      listenerList.add(ColorListener.class, listener);
   }

   public void removeColorListener(ColorListener listener)
   {
      listenerList.remove(ColorListener.class, listener);
   }

/* The setForeground() and setBackground() methods are overridden to  */
/* provide the means for firing the ColorEvent.  The JButton class    */
/* version of the method is called first.  Then the fireColorEvent()  */
/* is called to generate and fire the event.                          */

   public void setForeground(Color color)
   {
      super.setForeground(color);
      fireColorEvent(ColorEvent.FOREGROUND_CHANGED, color);
   }

   public void setBackground(Color color)
   {
      super.setBackground(color);
      fireColorEvent(ColorEvent.BACKGROUND_CHANGED, color);
   }

/* The fireColorEvent() method generates a ColorEvent object based    */
/* on the identification constant and Color object passed to the      */
/* method.  The NewButton object that calls this method is            */
/* designated as the source of the event.  The fireColorEvent()       */
/* then uses the EventListenerList object listenerList to send        */
/* the ColorEvent to any registered ColorListeners.                   */

   protected void fireColorEvent(int id, Color color)
   {
      ColorEvent event = new ColorEvent(this, id, color);

      ColorListener[] cl =
(ColorListener[])(listenerList.getListeners(ColorListener.class));

      for(int i=0; i<cl.length; ++i)
      {
         cl[i].colorChanged(event);
```

            }
         }
      }

Let's go through this code listing step by step. The NewButton constructor simply calls the JButton constructor using the "super" keyword. The NewButton class then provides methods to register or deregister a ColorListener. Because JComponent is a superclass of NewButton, a NewButton object has access to the EventListenerList object named `listenerList` defined as a field in the JComponent class. Recall that an EventListenerList object can be used to maintain a list of event listeners. The `addColorListener()` and `removeColorListener()` methods use the EventListenerList object to add or remove ColorListeners from the ColorListener list.

Now a means must be implemented to generate a ColorEvent when the foreground or background color of the NewButton is changed. This is done by overriding the `setForeground()` and `setBackground()` methods. These methods initially call the JButton class versions using the "super" keyword. The JButton class methods take care of the details of changing the color. After this is done, the `fireColorEvent()` method is called with the appropriate identification constant and the updated color provided as parameters.

The `fireColorEvent()` method creates a ColorEvent object. It uses the listener list managed by the EventListenerList object to send the ColorEvent object to any registered ColorListeners. The `getListeners()` method is used to retrieve an array containing all (or any) ColorListeners in the listener list. The ColorEvent is sent to the `colorChanged()` method of these objects.

PUTTING IT ALL TOGETHER

Now that we have defined an event class, an event listener, and a GUI component that supports the event class and listener, we can apply these elements to an application. The ColorEventDemo class creates a NewButton object and places it on a JFrame. The NewButton registers a ColorListener. Menus are provided to change the foreground or background color of the NewButton.

When the user selects a color in the foreground color menu, an ActionEvent is generated and the `actionPerformed()` method of the ForegroundHandler class (an ActionListener) is called. This method determines which color was selected and has the NewButton object call its `setForeground()` method. A similar process occurs when the user selects a color in the background color menu.

When the foreground or background color of the NewButton is changed, a ColorEvent is generated and sent to the `colorChanged()` method defined in the ColorEventDemo class. This method extracts the identification constant and color associated with the event and prints this information inside a textfield at the bottom of the frame. The code listing for the ColorEventDemo class is shown in Example 12.4.

EXAMPLE 12.4 COLOREVENTDEMO CLASS

```java
import javax.swing.*;
import java.awt.event.*;
import java.awt.*;

public class ColorEventDemo extends JFrame implements ColorListener
{
    NewButton button;
    JTextField jtf;
    JMenu colorMenu, foregroundMenu, backgroundMenu;
    JMenuItem black, blue, red, cyan, yellow, lightGray;
    JMenuBar menuBar;

    public ColorEventDemo()
    {
/* A NewButton object is created and registers a ColorListener   */

        button = new NewButton("Button");
        button.setBorder(BorderFactory.createRaisedBevelBorder());
        button.addColorListener(this);

        jtf = new JTextField(30);
        jtf.setEditable(false);

/* Create two menus, a foreground color menu and a background color */
/* menu.  The menu items register an ActionListener.                */

        ForegroundHandler foreground = new ForegroundHandler();
        BackgroundHandler background = new BackgroundHandler();

        black = new JMenuItem("black");
        black.addActionListener(foreground);

        blue = new JMenuItem("blue");
        blue.addActionListener(foreground);

        red = new JMenuItem("red");
        red.addActionListener(foreground);
```

```
            cyan = new JMenuItem("cyan");
            cyan.addActionListener(background);

            yellow = new JMenuItem("yellow");
            yellow.addActionListener(background);

            lightGray = new JMenuItem("lightGray");
            lightGray.addActionListener(background);

            foregroundMenu = new JMenu("Foreground");
            foregroundMenu.add(black);
            foregroundMenu.add(blue);
            foregroundMenu.add(red);

            backgroundMenu = new JMenu("Background");
            backgroundMenu.add(cyan);
            backgroundMenu.add(yellow);
            backgroundMenu.add(lightGray);

            colorMenu = new JMenu("Color");
            colorMenu.add(foregroundMenu);
            colorMenu.add(backgroundMenu);

            menuBar = new JMenuBar();
            menuBar.add(colorMenu);

   /*  Place everything on the content pane of the JFrame.     */

            JPanel centerPanel = new JPanel();
            centerPanel.setLayout(new FlowLayout(FlowLayout.CENTER, 10, 10));
            centerPanel.add(button);

            getContentPane().add(menuBar, BorderLayout.NORTH);
            getContentPane().add(centerPanel, BorderLayout.CENTER);
            getContentPane().add(jtf, BorderLayout.SOUTH);

            setDefaultCloseOperation(JFrame.EXIT_ON_CLOSE);
            setBounds(100, 100, 250, 200);
            setVisible(true);
       }

   /*  The ColorEventDemo class serves as the ChangeListener for this  */
   /*  example and provides an implementation of the colorChanged()    */
   /*  method.  This method retrieves the identification constant for  */
   /*  the ColorEvent and the updated color and prints the information */
   /*  in a textfield.                                                 */

       public void colorChanged(ColorEvent event)
       {
          String str = "";
          if ( event.getID() == ColorEvent.FOREGROUND_CHANGED )
          {
```

```
         str = "Foreground ";
      }
      if ( event.getID() == ColorEvent.BACKGROUND_CHANGED )
      {
         str = "Background ";
      }

      String str2 = "";
      if ( event.getColor().equals(Color.black) ) str2 = "black";
      if ( event.getColor().equals(Color.red) ) str2 = "red";
      if ( event.getColor().equals(Color.blue) ) str2 = "blue";
      if ( event.getColor().equals(Color.cyan) ) str2 = "cyan";
      if ( event.getColor().equals(Color.yellow) ) str2 = "yellow";
      if ( event.getColor().equals(Color.lightGray) ) str2 = "light gray";

      jtf.setText(str+"color changed to "+str2);
   }

/* The ForegroundHandler class is an ActionListener that responds    */
/* to selections in the foreground color menu.  The actionPerformed() */
/* determines what color was selected and calls the setForeground()   */
/* method.                                                            */

   class ForegroundHandler implements ActionListener
   {
      public void actionPerformed(ActionEvent event)
      {
         if ( event.getActionCommand().equals("black")  )
         {
            button.setForeground(Color.black);
         }
         if ( event.getActionCommand().equals("blue")  )
         {
            button.setForeground(Color.blue);
         }
         if ( event.getActionCommand().equals("red")  )
         {
            button.setForeground(Color.red);
         }
      }
   }

/* The BackgroundHandler class is an ActionListener that responds    */
/* to selections in the background color menu.  The actionPerformed() */
/* determines what color was selected and calls the setBackground()   */
/* method.                                                            */

   class BackgroundHandler implements ActionListener
   {
      public void actionPerformed(ActionEvent event)
      {
         if ( event.getActionCommand().equals("cyan")  )
         {
```

```
            button.setBackground(Color.cyan);
        }
        if ( event.getActionCommand().equals("yellow")  )
        {
            button.setBackground(Color.yellow);
        }
        if ( event.getActionCommand().equals("lightGray")  )
        {
            button.setBackground(Color.lightGray);
        }
     }
  }

  public static void main(String args[])
  {
     ColorEventDemo demo = new ColorEventDemo();
  }
}
```

When you run this example, a button appears on the frame. Make a selection in the foreground color menu. The color of the button label changes and a message indicating what the change was appears in the textfield. Now make a selection in the background color menu. The background color changes and a message indicating what the change was appears in the textfield.

13

Putting It All Together

Up to this point, the examples shown in this book have been fairly short and simple. They are intended to demonstrate one or two elements of event handling without a lot of extra code to clutter up the main point of the example. In this chapter, we apply the things we have learned about Java event handling to more real-world applications. These programs use multiple components that generate several types of events. We must make decisions about how to implement the event listeners, how to respond to the events, and so on.

Stagnation Point Heating Rate Program

The first real-world example we will look at is a scientific application that computes the stagnation point heating of a sphere or cylinder entering a planetary atmosphere at high speeds. The user must supply a number of input parameters. This is accomplished using a GUI with a number of different types of components. The events generated by the GUI components are used to update the values of the input parameters.

Let's talk a little bit about what we are trying to compute with this application. When a spacecraft enters a planetary atmosphere at high speeds, the atmospheric gas compresses around the vehicle and forms a shockwave. As the gas travels through a shockwave, it experiences a sharp rise in pressure, temperature, and density. This layer of hot gas surrounding the spacecraft transfers energy to the vehicle surface causing the surface temperature to increase.

Usually, when a gas particle approaches a body in flight, it will change course and wrap around the body according to the contours of the body. At one point on the body, usually where the geometry is normal to the direction the body is traveling, the flow will not change course and wrap around, but instead will come to a complete stop. This is known as the stagnation point and is often the point of the body that experiences the highest heating rate. The program described in this section computes the stagnation point heating rate over a sphere or circular cylinder.

The stagnation point heating rate can be expressed as a function of the pre-shockwave temperature, density, and velocity; the surface temperature of the body; the geometry of the body; the nose radius of the body; and the atmosphere in which the body is traveling. The GUI front end to our stagnation point heating code must therefore accept inputs for these parameters. A display of the GUI is shown in Figure 13.1.

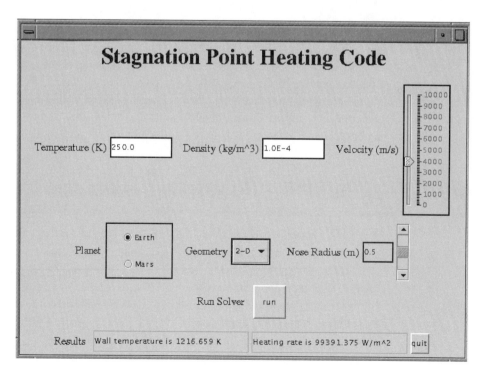

Figure 13.1 The Stagnation Point Heating Code GUI display.

The GUI intentionally uses many different types of components to accept user input. There are two JTextField objects for the input values of temperature and density. These will generate an ActionEvent when the JTextFields have focus and the Enter key is pressed. The velocity is determined using a JSlider. When the slider value is changed up or down, a ChangeEvent is generated. The type of planetary atmosphere is determined by JRadioButtons. There are two of them, representing Earth and Mars. The JRadioButtons are made mutually exclusive using a ButtonGroup. An ItemEvent is generated when the planet selection is changed.

The nose radius of the body is changed using a JScrollBar. When the value of the JScrollBar is changed, an AdjustmentEvent is generated. A non-editable textfield displays the current value of the nose radius. Two JButton objects are used to run the stagnation point heating rate solver and to quit the application. These will generate an ActionEvent when they are pressed. At the bottom of the GUI are two non-editable textfields that display the computed values of heating rate and surface temperature.

Once we have laid out all of our GUI components, we must decide how to implement the event listeners. The application won't do what we want unless we properly process the events that are generated when the user manipulates the components. Should we implement the listeners as inner classes, anonymous inner classes, separate classes, or should the application class itself implement the listeners? Should every component have its own event listener, or should one listener be shared among multiple components? One of the basic truths about event handling is that there is usually more than one way to do things. Sometimes it comes down to a matter of personal preference.

Let's look at the code listing in Example 13.1 to see how the event handling was performed.

EXAMPLE 13.1 STAGNATION POINT HEATING CODE

```
import javax.swing.*;
import java.awt.*;
import javax.swing.event.*;
import java.awt.event.*;

public class StagnationHeating extends JFrame implements ChangeListener,
                              AdjustmentListener,
                              ActionListener
{
   JLabel velocityLabel, temperatureLabel, densityLabel, titleLabel;
   JLabel noseLabel, planetLabel, geoLabel, runLabel, resultsLabel;
   JTextField temperatureTF, densityTF, noseTF, wallTempTF, heatingTF;
   JSlider velocitySlider;
```

```java
        JComboBox geoCB;
        JRadioButton earthRB, marsRB;
        ButtonGroup buttonGroup;
        JButton quitButton, runButton;
        JScrollBar noseScrollBar;

        double temperature, density, geometryFactor, emissivity, noseRadius;
        double molarMass, planetFactor, Cp;
        int velocity;
        String planet;
        double Tw = 300.0, heatingRate = 0.0;

        public StagnationHeating()
        {
    /* Give some initial values to the input parameters     */

            velocity = 4000;
            temperature = 250.0;
            density = 1.0e-4;
            geometryFactor = 0.7049;
            planet = "Earth";
            molarMass = 0.02885;
            planetFactor = 1.83e-4;
            Cp = 3.5;
            emissivity = 0.8;
            noseRadius = 0.5;

    /* Create a whole bunch of JLabels to label the various components    */

            velocityLabel = new JLabel("   Velocity (m/s)");
            velocityLabel.setForeground(Color.black);
            velocityLabel.setFont(new Font("Serif", Font.PLAIN, 12));

            temperatureLabel = new JLabel("Temperature (K)");
            temperatureLabel.setForeground(Color.black);
            temperatureLabel.setFont(new Font("Serif", Font.PLAIN, 12));

            densityLabel = new JLabel("   Density (kg/m^3)");
            densityLabel.setForeground(Color.black);
            densityLabel.setFont(new Font("Serif", Font.PLAIN, 12));

            noseLabel = new JLabel("    Nose Radius (m)");
            noseLabel.setForeground(Color.black);
            noseLabel.setFont(new Font("Serif", Font.PLAIN, 12));

            planetLabel = new JLabel("Planet");
            planetLabel.setForeground(Color.black);
            planetLabel.setFont(new Font("Serif", Font.PLAIN, 12));

            geoLabel = new JLabel("   Geometry");
            geoLabel.setForeground(Color.black);
            geoLabel.setFont(new Font("Serif", Font.PLAIN, 12));
```

```java
            runLabel = new JLabel("Run Solver   ");
            runLabel.setForeground(Color.black);
            runLabel.setFont(new Font("Serif", Font.PLAIN, 12));

            resultsLabel = new JLabel("Results   ");
            resultsLabel.setForeground(Color.black);
            resultsLabel.setFont(new Font("Serif", Font.PLAIN, 12));

            titleLabel = new JLabel("Stagnation Point Heating Code");
            titleLabel.setForeground(Color.black);
            titleLabel.setFont(new Font("Serif", Font.BOLD, 24));
            titleLabel.setHorizontalAlignment(SwingConstants.CENTER);

   /*  Start creating the GUI components. First, two JTextFields for    */
   /*  inputting the freestream (preshock) values of temperature        */
   /*  and density.  The textfields register an ActionListener.         */

            temperatureTF = new JTextField(8);

temperatureTF.setBorder(BorderFactory.createLineBorder(Color.black,2));
            temperatureTF.setText(""+temperature);
            temperatureTF.setName("temperature");
            temperatureTF.addActionListener(this);

            densityTF = new JTextField(8);
            densityTF.setBorder(BorderFactory.createLineBorder(Color.black,2));
            densityTF.setText(""+density);
            densityTF.setName("density");
            densityTF.addActionListener(this);

   /*  The freestream velocity is set using a JSlider.  The acceptable  */
   /*  range of velocity is specified to be between 0 and 10000 m/s.    */
   /*  The JSlider registers a ChangeListener to be notified when the   */
   /*  slider value is changed.                                         */

            velocitySlider = new JSlider(JSlider.VERTICAL, 0, 10000, velocity);
            velocitySlider.setMajorTickSpacing(1000);
            velocitySlider.setMinorTickSpacing(100);
            velocitySlider.setBorder(BorderFactory.createCompoundBorder(
                      BorderFactory.createEmptyBorder(2,2,2,2),
                      BorderFactory.createLineBorder(Color.black,2)));
            velocitySlider.setPaintTicks(true);
            velocitySlider.setPaintLabels(true);
            velocitySlider.setForeground(Color.black);
            velocitySlider.addChangeListener(this);

   /*  The program can handle both 2-D and 3-D geometries.  A JComboBox */
   /*  is used to switch between them.  The JComboBox registers an      */
   /*  ItemListener to update the geometry factor based on the geometry */
   /*  selection.                                                       */

            String[] options = { "2-D", "3-D" };
            geoCB = new JComboBox(options);
```

```
            geoCB.setBorder(BorderFactory.createLineBorder(Color.black,2));
            geoCB.addItemListener(new ComboBoxListener());

/*  The program can calculate stagnation point heating in both Earth   */
/*  and Mars atmospheres.  Two JRadioButtons that are associated       */
/*  (and made mutually exclusive) with a ButtonGroup are used to       */
/*  select the planet type.  The JRadioButtons register an ItemListener */

            earthRB = new JRadioButton("Earth");
            earthRB.setName("Earth");
            earthRB.setSelected(true);
            earthRB.setPreferredSize(new Dimension(100,40));
            earthRB.setHorizontalAlignment(SwingConstants.CENTER);

            marsRB = new JRadioButton("Mars");
            marsRB.setName("Mars");
            marsRB.setPreferredSize(new Dimension(100,40));
            marsRB.setHorizontalAlignment(SwingConstants.CENTER);

            RadioButtonListener listener = new RadioButtonListener();
            earthRB.addItemListener(listener);
            marsRB.addItemListener(listener);

            buttonGroup = new ButtonGroup();
            buttonGroup.add(earthRB);
            buttonGroup.add(marsRB);

            JPanel radioButtonPanel = new JPanel();
            radioButtonPanel.setLayout(new GridLayout(2,1));
            radioButtonPanel.setBorder(BorderFactory.createCompoundBorder(
                    BorderFactory.createEmptyBorder(2,2,2,2),
                    BorderFactory.createLineBorder(Color.black,2)));
            radioButtonPanel.add(earthRB);
            radioButtonPanel.add(marsRB);

/*  The nose radius of the body is input using a JScrollBar.           */
/*  The current value of the JScrollBar is displayed inside a          */
/*  JTextField.  The JScrollBar registers an AdjustmentListener        */
/*  that updates the noseRadius parameter when the value is changed.   */

            noseTF = new JTextField(4);
            noseTF.setBorder(BorderFactory.createLineBorder(Color.black,2));
            noseTF.setText(""+noseRadius);
            noseTF.setEditable(false);

            noseScrollBar = new JScrollBar(JScrollBar.VERTICAL,50,10,1,110);
            noseScrollBar.setPreferredSize(new Dimension(20,85));
            noseScrollBar.addAdjustmentListener(this);

/*  A JButton is created that will terminate the application when      */
/*  it is pressed.  It registers an ActionListener that is             */
/*  implemented as an anonymous inner class.                           */
```

```java
        quitButton = new JButton("quit");
        quitButton.setBorder(BorderFactory.createRaisedBevelBorder());
        quitButton.addActionListener(
                new ActionListener()
                {
                   public void actionPerformed(ActionEvent ae)
                   {
                      System.exit(0);
                   }
                });

/*   A JButton is created that will compute the surface heating rate   */
/*   It registers an ActionListener that is implemented as an          */
/*   anonymous inner class.                                            */

        runButton = new JButton("run");
        runButton.setPreferredSize(new Dimension(50,50));
        runButton.setBorder(BorderFactory.createRaisedBevelBorder());
        runButton.addActionListener(
                new ActionListener()
                {
                   public void actionPerformed(ActionEvent ae)
                   {
                      compute();
                   }
                });

/*   These textfields display the results */

        wallTempTF = new JTextField(20);
        wallTempTF.setEditable(false);

        heatingTF = new JTextField(20);
        heatingTF.setEditable(false);

/*   The various GUI components are placed on the JFrame   */

        JPanel northPanel = new JPanel();
        northPanel.add(temperatureLabel);
        northPanel.add(temperatureTF);
        northPanel.add(densityLabel);
        northPanel.add(densityTF);
        northPanel.add(velocityLabel);
        northPanel.add(velocitySlider);

        JPanel centerPanel = new JPanel();
        centerPanel.add(planetLabel);
        centerPanel.add(radioButtonPanel);
        centerPanel.add(geoLabel);
        centerPanel.add(geoCB);
        centerPanel.add(noseLabel);
        centerPanel.add(noseTF);
        centerPanel.add(noseScrollBar);
```

```
            JPanel southPanel = new JPanel();
            southPanel.add(runLabel);
            southPanel.add(runButton);

            JPanel southPanel2 = new JPanel();
            southPanel2.add(resultsLabel);
            southPanel2.add(wallTempTF);
            southPanel2.add(heatingTF);
            southPanel2.add(quitButton);

            JPanel middlePanel = new JPanel();
            middlePanel.setLayout(new BorderLayout());
            middlePanel.add(northPanel, BorderLayout.NORTH);
            middlePanel.add(centerPanel, BorderLayout.CENTER);
            middlePanel.add(southPanel, BorderLayout.SOUTH);

            Container c = getContentPane();
            c.setLayout(new BorderLayout(0,10));
            c.add(titleLabel, BorderLayout.NORTH);
            c.add(middlePanel, BorderLayout.CENTER);
            c.add(southPanel2, BorderLayout.SOUTH);

            setDefaultCloseOperation(JFrame.EXIT_ON_CLOSE);
            setBounds(100, 100, 700, 500);
            setVisible(true);
        }

    /* The compute() method calculates the stagnation point heating  */
    /* based on the input parameters by balancing the heat coming to */
    /* the surface from the shock layer with the heat radiating away */
    /* from the surface. The results are displayed in the textfields */
    /* at the bottom of the frame.                                   */

        protected void compute()
        {
            double a = 5.67e-8*emissivity;
            double b =
 geometryFactor*planetFactor*Math.sqrt(density/noseRadius)*
                    Math.pow(velocity,3.0);
            double c = 1.0/(temperature +
                    0.5*Math.pow(velocity,2.0)*molarMass/(Cp*8.3144));
            double delTw;

            for (int n=0; n<20; ++n)
            {
                delTw = -(a*Math.pow(Tw,4.0) + b*c*Tw - b)/
                        (4.0*a*Math.pow(Tw,3.0) + b*c);
                Tw += delTw;
            }

            heatingRate = 5.67e-8*emissivity*Math.pow(Tw,4.0);
```

```
         wallTempTF.setText("Wall temperature is "+(float)Tw+" K");
         heatingTF.setText("Heating rate is "+(float)heatingRate+" W/m^2");
      }

/*   The StagnationHeating class serves as the ActionListener for this  */
/*   program.  When one of the JTextFields has focus and the newline    */
/*   character is pressed, an ActionEvent is generated and sent to      */
/*   the actionPerformed() method.  This method converts the text       */
/*   inside the textfield to a double and assigns the temperature or    */
/*   density parameter to this value.                                   */

      public void actionPerformed(ActionEvent event)
      {
         JTextField jtf = (JTextField)event.getSource();
         if ( jtf.getName().equals("temperature") )
         {
            temperature = Double.valueOf(jtf.getText()).doubleValue();
         }
         if ( jtf.getName().equals("density") )
         {
            density = Double.valueOf(jtf.getText()).doubleValue();
         }
      }

/*   The StagnationHeating class serves as a ChangeListener and         */
/*   implements the stateChanged() method.  When the JSlider value      */
/*   is changed, a ChangeEvent is sent to this method.  The method      */
/*   updates the value of the velocity parameter to be the new          */
/*   value of the JSlider.                                              */

      public void stateChanged(ChangeEvent event)
      {
         JSlider slider = (JSlider)event.getSource();
         velocity = slider.getValue();
      }

/*   The StagnationHeating class serves as an AdjustmentListener and    */
/*   implements the adjustmentValueChanged() method.  When the JScrollBar */
/*   value is changed, an AdjustmentEvent is sent to this method.       */
/*   The JScrollBar defaults are that minimum value (1) is at the top   */
/*   and the maximum value that can be reached by moving the slider (100) */
/*   is at the bottom.  We want to make it appear as though the maximum */
/*   value of nose radius appears at the top of the JScrollBar. This is */
/*   done using the "101 - event.getValue();" syntax.  The noseRadius is */
/*   constrained between 0.01 and 1.0 meters.  This is accomplished by  */
/*   multiplying the modified JScrollBar value by 0.01.  The nose radius */
/*   is supposed to change in increments of 0.01, but sometimes round off */
/*   error will lead to a value such as 0.700000001.  This looks messy  */
/*   when displayed in the textfield.  The substring() method cleans    */
/*   this up if necessary.                                              */

      public void adjustmentValueChanged(AdjustmentEvent event)
      {
```

```
            int i = 101 - event.getValue();
            noseRadius = 0.01*i;
            String str = ""+noseRadius;
            if ( str.length() > 4 ) str = str.substring(0,4);
            noseTF.setText(str);
      }

/* Two separate ItemListeners are written, one for the JComboBox    */
/* and one for the JRadioButtons. This makes differentiating the    */
/* event source a bit easier.  The ComboBoxListener is notified     */
/* when the selection is changed in the JComboBox.  The getItem()   */
/* method is used to return the label of the selection and the      */
/* geometry scale factor is set accordingly.                        */

      class ComboBoxListener implements ItemListener
      {
        public void itemStateChanged(ItemEvent event)
        {
          if ( event.getItem().equals("2-D") )
          {
            geometryFactor = 0.7049;
          }
          if ( event.getItem().equals("3-D") )
          {
            geometryFactor = 1.0;
          }
        }
      }

/* The second ItemListener handles selections made to the           */
/* JRadioButtons.  The JRadioButtons are made mutually exclusive    */
/* by adding them to a ButtonGroup.  This means that two ItemEvents */
/* are generated when the selection is changed, one for the item    */
/* that was selected and one for the item that was deselected.      */
/* The getStateChanged() method is used to identify the event from  */
/* the element that was selected, and the planet String is updated. */

      class RadioButtonListener implements ItemListener
      {
        public void itemStateChanged(ItemEvent event)
        {
          if ( event.getStateChange() == ItemEvent.SELECTED )
          {
            planet = ((JRadioButton)event.getItemSelectable()).getName();
            if ( planet.equals("Earth") )
            {
              molarMass = 0.02885;
              planetFactor = 1.83e-4;
              Cp = 3.5;
            }
            if ( planet.equals("Mars") )
            {
              molarMass = 0.0435;
```

```
            planetFactor = 1.43e-4;
            Cp = 5.4;
        }
      }
    }
}

public static void main(String args[])
{
    StagnationHeating heat = new StagnationHeating();
}
}
```

This is quite a long code listing, so we will break down the event handling aspects one by one. You will notice that the StagnationHeating class implements some of the event listeners, other event listeners are implemented as inner classes, and still others are implemented as anonymous inner classes. Let's start with the JTextFields used for the temperature and density inputs. They register an ActionListener that is implemented by the StagnationHeating class. The `actionPerformed()` method is shown in Example 13.2.

EXAMPLE 13.2 HANDLING ACTIONEVENTS FROM THE JTEXTFIELDS

```
public void actionPerformed(ActionEvent event)
{
    JTextField jtf = (JTextField)event.getSource();
    if ( jtf.getName().equals("temperature") )
    {
        temperature = Double.valueOf(jtf.getText()).doubleValue();
    }
    if ( jtf.getName().equals("density") )
    {
        density = Double.valueOf(jtf.getText()).doubleValue();
    }
}
```

When one of the JTextFields has focus and the Enter key is pressed, an ActionEvent is generated and sent to this method. The `getSource()` method is used to return a reference to the JTextField that generated the event. If it was the temperature JTextField, the text inside the textfield is converted from a String to a primitive datatype (a double) and the `temperature` parameter is assigned this value. A similar operation occurs if the density JTextField generated the event.

The JSlider component used to specify the pre-shock velocity registers a ChangeListener that is also implemented by the StagnationHeating class. When the value of the slider is changed, a ChangeEvent is generated and sent to the `stateChanged()` method. This method is shown in Example 13.3.

EXAMPLE 13.3 HANDLING CHANGEEVENTS GENERATED BY THE JSLIDER

```
public void stateChanged(ChangeEvent event)
{
   JSlider slider = (JSlider)event.getSource();
   velocity = slider.getValue();
}
```

The `getSource()` method is used to return a reference to the event source. The `getValue()` method then returns the current value of the JSlider, and the velocity parameter is set to this value.

Several different components in this application can generate ItemEvents, in particular the JRadioButtons and the JComboBox. There are several ways we can implement the ItemListener for these components. We could register all of them to the same ItemListener and place logic in the `itemStateChanged()` method to determine which type of component generated the event. An easier way to do it is to define one ItemListener for the JRadioButtons and a second ItemListener for the JComboBox. This way, we don't have to worry about whether a JComboBox or JRadioButton generated the ItemEvent.

Let us start with the ItemListener for the JRadioButtons. It is implemented as an inner class. The code listing for this ItemListener is shown in Example 13.4.

EXAMPLE 13.4 HANDLING ITEMEVENTS GENERATED BY THE JRADIOBUTTONS

```
class RadioButtonListener implements ItemListener
{
   public void itemStateChanged(ItemEvent event)
   {
      if ( event.getStateChange() == ItemEvent.SELECTED )
      {
         planet = ((JRadioButton)event.getItemSelectable()).getName();
         if ( planet.equals("Earth") )
         {
            molarMass = 0.02885;
            planetFactor = 1.83e-4;
            Cp = 3.5;
         }
         if ( planet.equals("Mars") )
         {
```

```
            molarMass = 0.0435;
            planetFactor = 1.43e-4;
            Cp = 5.4;
         }
      }
   }
}
```

Because the JRadioButtons are associated with one another by a ButtonGroup, two ItemEvents are generated when the selection is changed, one for the item that was selected and one for the item that was deselected. The `itemStateChanged()` method of this ItemListener first identifies the ItemEvent generated by the JRadioButton that was selected. The method then sets some planet-specific data depending on which planet was selected. As a side note, the `molarMass` parameter represents the molecular weight of the atmospheric gas. The `planetFactor` is a constant that is used in the heat transfer correlation. The `Cp` parameter is the specific heat of the atmospheric gas.

The stagnation point heating rate is geometry-dependent. The application can compute the heat transfer to a sphere or to a cylinder, and a JComboBox is used to choose between these two. The JComboBox registers an ItemListener that is implemented as an inner class. The code listing for this ItemListener is shown in Example 13.5.

EXAMPLE 13.5 HANDLING ITEMEVENTS GENERATED BY THE JCOMBOBOX

```
class ComboBoxListener implements ItemListener
{
   public void itemStateChanged(ItemEvent event)
   {
      if ( event.getItem().equals("2-D") )
      {
         geometryFactor = 0.7049;
      }
      if ( event.getItem().equals("3-D") )
      {
         geometryFactor = 1.0;
      }
   }
}
```

The `itemStateChanged()` method uses the `getItem()` method to return the item that was selected. The return value of `getItem()` is component-specific. In the case of a JComboBox, the return value is a String, containing the label of the selected item. The geometry scaling factor is set depending on whether the 2-D or 3-D item was selected.

The final component for accepting user input, a JScrollBar, is used to change the nose radius of the body. An associated JTextField displays the current value of nose radius. The JScrollBar registers an AdjustmentListener that is implemented by the StagnationHeating class. The `adjustmentValueChanged()` method is listed in Example 13.6.

EXAMPLE 13.6 HANDLING ADJUSTMENTEVENTS GENERATED BY THE JSCROLLBAR

```
public void adjustmentValueChanged(AdjustmentEvent event)
{
   int i = 101 - event.getValue();
   noseRadius = 0.01*i;
   String str = ""+noseRadius;
   if ( str.length() > 4 ) str = str.substring(0,4);
   noseTF.setText(str);
}
```

When the value of the JScrollBar is changed, an AdjustmentEvent is generated and sent to the `adjustmentValueChanged()` method. The JScrollBar provides a range of integer values from 1 to 100, with the value 1 at the top of the JScrollBar. For this application, it was desired to have it appear as if the maximum value of the JScrollBar was at the top of the scrollbar. This is accomplished using the `101 - event.getValue();` syntax. The `noseRadius` parameter is intended to range from 0.01 to 1.0, so the adjusted value of the JScrollBar is multiplied by 0.01.

There are two other components in this example that generate events we wish to monitor. These are the JButtons labeled "run" and "quit". The run button calls the `compute()` method, which computes the stagnation heating and corresponding surface temperature based on the current value of the input parameters. The quit button terminates the application. Since both of these JButtons are intended to perform simple operations, they register ActionListeners that are implemented as anonymous inner classes. For instance, the run button uses the syntax shown in Example 13.7.

EXAMPLE 13.7 HANDLING THE RUN BUTTON

```
runButton.addActionListener(
         new ActionListener()
         {
            public void actionPerformed(ActionEvent ae)
```

```
                    {
                        compute();
                    }
                });
```

Note that the definition of the anonymous inner class is passed as the argument to the `addActionListener()` method. The quit button registers its ActionListener in a similar fashion.

Try running this application. Change the input parameters in various ways. This is a real-life application in that the methodology used will properly compute stagnation point heating. The only simplification made is that the specific heat (the `Cp` parameter) is constant. This is true for Earth's atmosphere at low temperatures, but it is not true for the carbon dioxide-dominated atmosphere of Mars. This program can show you how changing certain parameters affects the stagnation point heating rate experienced by a sphere or cylinder. For instance, if the nose radius is reduced, the heating and surface temperature increase.

A Java Document Editor

The second example in this chapter is an application that allows you to modify a DefaultStyledDocument object. These objects can be used to manage the content of Swing text components such as JTextAreas and JTextPanes. In this example, a JTextPane is used to display the contents of the DefaultStyledDocument. Changes in the way the DefaultStyledDocument appears in the JTextPane are made by changing a Style object associated with the DefaultStyledDocument. The application can also store a DefaultStyledDocument onto disk and can read in a previously stored DefaultStyledDocument.

All of the options for reading, writing, and manipulating a DefaultStyledDocument are implemented using menu items. The menu items generate events when they are selected. These events are processed using ActionListener, ItemListener, UndoableEditListener, and MenuDragMouseListener objects.

The appearance of the GUI for this example is shown in Figure 13.2.

The GUI itself is fairly simple. The content pane contains a JScrollPane, which itself contains a JTextPane. The JTextPane has an associated DefaultStyledDocument object. It is the DefaultStyledDocument that we wish

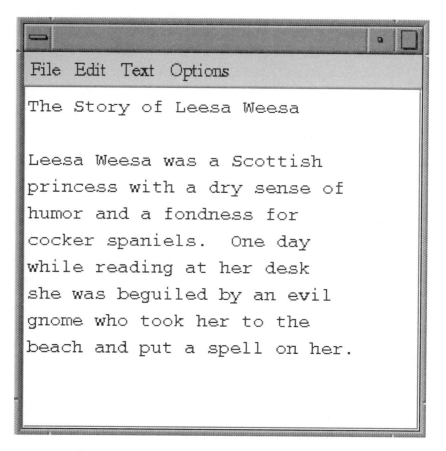

Figure 13.2 DocumentEditor GUI display.

to modify. Specifically, we will modify a Style object that describes how the content of the Document will look inside the JTextPane.

All of the other components of this application are contained inside the menu bar at the top of the frame. The menu bar contains four JMenu objects. The JMenus contain an assortment of JMenuItems, JRadioButtons, and JCheckBoxMenuItems. These menu items are used to read, write, and modify a DefaultStyledDocument.

All of the menu items register an event listener to process the events that they will generate. As with the stagnation point heating program, we must make decisions as to how these listeners will be implemented. Some of the listeners will be implemented by the DocumentEditor class. Others will be implemented as inner classes. Still others will be implemented as anonymous inner classes. Let's look at the code listing in Example 13.8.

EXAMPLE 13.8 DOCUMENTEDITOR PROGRAM

```java
import javax.swing.*;
import java.awt.*;
import java.awt.event.*;
import javax.swing.event.*;
import java.io.*;
import javax.swing.text.*;
import javax.swing.undo.*;

public class DocumentEditor extends JFrame implements ActionListener,
                                            UndoableEditListener,
                                                ItemListener,
                                        MenuDragMouseListener
{
   private JTextPane textPane;
   private JMenu fileMenu, editMenu, textMenu, sizeMenu, fontMenu,
            styleMenu, optionsMenu;
   private JMenuBar menuBar;
   private JMenuItem clearItem, openItem, saveItem, quitItem,
                cutItem, copyItem, pasteItem, undoItem, redoItem,
                font10, font12, font14;
   private JMenuItem monospaced, serif, helvetica, dialog;
   private JRadioButtonMenuItem plainItem, boldItem;
   private JCheckBoxMenuItem italicItem, dynamicItem;
   private JFileChooser jfc;
   private UndoManager undoManager;
   private ButtonGroup buttonGroup;
   private DefaultStyledDocument doc;
   private Style logicalStyle;

   public DocumentEditor()
   {
      undoManager = new UndoManager();

/* A DefaultStyledDocument is created.  A JTextPane is used to     */
/* display the DefaultStyledDocument.  The Style object associated */
/* with the first paragraph of the document is obtained.  The      */
/* DefaultStyledDocument registers an UndoableEditListener.        */

      doc = new DefaultStyledDocument();
      textPane = new JTextPane(doc);
      logicalStyle = doc.getLogicalStyle(0);
      doc.addUndoableEditListener(this);

/* A JFileChooser is used with the I/O menu options.   */

      jfc = new JFileChooser();
```

```
            jfc.setSize(400, 300);

/*  A lot of JMenuItem objects are created.  These provide the options  */
/*  for changing the DefaultStyledDocument.  The JMenuItems register    */
/*  ActionListeners to receive the events generated when they are      */
/*  selected.  The JMenuItem objects are added to JMenu objects which   */
/*  in turn are added to the JMenuBar of the JFrame.                    */

            openItem = new JMenuItem("open");
            openItem.setAccelerator(
               KeyStroke.getKeyStroke('O',InputEvent.CTRL_MASK,false));
            openItem.addActionListener(this);

            clearItem = new JMenuItem("clear");
            clearItem.setAccelerator(
               KeyStroke.getKeyStroke('N',InputEvent.CTRL_MASK,false));
            clearItem.addActionListener(this);

            saveItem = new JMenuItem("save");
            saveItem.setAccelerator(
               KeyStroke.getKeyStroke('S',InputEvent.CTRL_MASK,false));
            saveItem.addActionListener(this);

/*  The "quit" JMenuItem registers an ActionListener that is implemented */
/*  as an anonymous inner class.  When the "quit" menu item is selected, */
/*  the program terminates.                                              */

            quitItem = new JMenuItem("quit");
            quitItem.setAccelerator(
               KeyStroke.getKeyStroke('Q',InputEvent.CTRL_MASK,false));
            quitItem.addActionListener(
                       new ActionListener()
                       {
                          public void actionPerformed(ActionEvent ae)
                          {
                             System.exit(0);
                          }
                       });

            fileMenu = new JMenu("File");
            fileMenu.setFont(new Font("Serif", Font.PLAIN, 12));
            fileMenu.add(openItem);
            fileMenu.add(clearItem);
            fileMenu.add(saveItem);
            fileMenu.add(quitItem);

            cutItem = new JMenuItem("cut");
            cutItem.setAccelerator(
               KeyStroke.getKeyStroke('X',InputEvent.CTRL_MASK,false));
            cutItem.addActionListener(this);

             copyItem = new JMenuItem("copy");
             copyItem.setAccelerator(
```

```java
      KeyStroke.getKeyStroke('C',InputEvent.CTRL_MASK,false));
copyItem.addActionListener(this);

pasteItem = new JMenuItem("paste");
pasteItem.setAccelerator(
   KeyStroke.getKeyStroke('V',InputEvent.CTRL_MASK,false));
pasteItem.addActionListener(this);

undoItem = new JMenuItem("undo");
undoItem.setAccelerator(
   KeyStroke.getKeyStroke('U',InputEvent.CTRL_MASK,false));
undoItem.setEnabled(false);
undoItem.addActionListener(this);

redoItem = new JMenuItem("redo");
redoItem.setAccelerator(
   KeyStroke.getKeyStroke('R',InputEvent.CTRL_MASK,false));
redoItem.setEnabled(false);
redoItem.addActionListener(this);

editMenu = new JMenu("Edit");
editMenu.setFont(new Font("Serif", Font.PLAIN, 12));
editMenu.add(cutItem);
editMenu.add(copyItem);
editMenu.add(pasteItem);
editMenu.add(undoItem);
editMenu.add(redoItem);

font10 = new JMenuItem("10");
font12 = new JMenuItem("12");
font14 = new JMenuItem("14");

SizeHandler handler = new SizeHandler();
font10.addActionListener(handler);
font12.addActionListener(handler);
font14.addActionListener(handler);

sizeMenu = new JMenu("Size");
sizeMenu.add(font10);
sizeMenu.add(font12);
sizeMenu.add(font14);

dialog = new JMenuItem("Dialog");
serif = new JMenuItem("Serif");
monospaced = new JMenuItem("Monospaced");
helvetica = new JMenuItem("Helvetica");

FontHandler fonter = new FontHandler();
dialog.addActionListener(fonter);
serif.addActionListener(fonter);
monospaced.addActionListener(fonter);
helvetica.addActionListener(fonter);
```

```
            fontMenu = new JMenu("Font");
            fontMenu.add(dialog);
            fontMenu.add(serif);
            fontMenu.add(monospaced);
            fontMenu.add(helvetica);

  /*  The options to switch from plain to bold text are implemented     */
  /*  as JRadioButtonMenuItems.  These components are made mutually     */
  /*  exclusive using a ButtonGroup.  They register an ItemListener.    */

            plainItem = new JRadioButtonMenuItem("Plain");
            plainItem.setSelected(true);
            plainItem.addItemListener(this);

            boldItem = new JRadioButtonMenuItem("Bold");
            boldItem.addItemListener(this);

            buttonGroup = new ButtonGroup();
            buttonGroup.add(plainItem);
            buttonGroup.add(boldItem);

  /*  The italic style option is implemented using a JCheckBoxMenuItem. */
  /*  This object registers an ItemListener that is implemented as an   */
  /*  inner class.                                                      */

            italicItem = new JCheckBoxMenuItem("Italic");
            italicItem.addItemListener(new ItalicHandler());

            styleMenu = new JMenu("Style");
            styleMenu.add(plainItem);
            styleMenu.add(boldItem);
            styleMenu.add(italicItem);

            textMenu = new JMenu("Text");
            textMenu.setFont(new Font("Serif", Font.PLAIN, 12));
            textMenu.add(fontMenu);
            textMenu.add(styleMenu);
            textMenu.add(sizeMenu);

  /*  A "Dynamic Font Update" JCheckBoxMenuItem is created.  It registers */
  /*  an ItemListener that is implemented as an inner class.              */

            dynamicItem = new JCheckBoxMenuItem("Dynamic Font Update");
            dynamicItem.addItemListener(new DynamicHandler());

            optionsMenu = new JMenu("Options");
            optionsMenu.setFont(new Font("Serif", Font.PLAIN, 12));
            optionsMenu.add(dynamicItem);

            menuBar = new JMenuBar();
            menuBar.add(fileMenu);
            menuBar.add(editMenu);
            menuBar.add(textMenu);
```

```java
            menuBar.add(optionsMenu);

            setJMenuBar(menuBar);
            getContentPane().add(new JScrollPane(textPane));

            setDefaultCloseOperation(JFrame.EXIT_ON_CLOSE);
            setBounds(100, 100, 500, 500);
            setVisible(true);
        }

/*  Most of the JMenuItems register an ActionListener that is      */
/*  implemented by the DocumentEditor class.  The actionCommand    */
/*  associated with the ActionEvent is used to determine the       */
/*  event source.                                                  */

        public void actionPerformed(ActionEvent event)
        {

/*  When the "open" menu item is selected, a JFileChooser is used  */
/*  to show a file dialog.  The user makes a selection of a file   */
/*  representing a DefaultStyledDocument that was previously stored */
/*  to disk.  This file is read and the Document of the JTextPane  */
/*  is set to the associated DefaultStyledDocument object.         */

            if ( event.getActionCommand().equals("open") )
            {
               int choice = jfc.showOpenDialog(this);

               if (choice == JFileChooser.APPROVE_OPTION)
               {
                  String filename = jfc.getSelectedFile().getAbsolutePath();

                  try
                  {
                     ObjectInputStream ois =
                       new ObjectInputStream(new FileInputStream(filename));
                     doc = (DefaultStyledDocument)ois.readObject();
                     textPane.setDocument(doc);
                     logicalStyle = doc.getLogicalStyle(0);
                     doc.addUndoableEditListener(this);
                     ois.close();
                  }
                  catch (Exception e){};
               }
            }

/*  If the "clear" menu item is selected, the text contained by the */
/*  document is removed.                                            */

            if ( event.getActionCommand().equals("clear") )
            {
               textPane.setText("");
            }
```

```
/* The "save" menu item causes the DefaultStyledDocument object    */
/* associated with the JTextPane to be written to disk.  The       */
/* DefaultStyledDocument removes any event listeners from its      */
/* listener list before it is written to disk.                     */

      if ( event.getActionCommand().equals("save") )
      {
         int choice = jfc.showSaveDialog(this);

         if (choice == JFileChooser.APPROVE_OPTION)
         {
            String filename = jfc.getSelectedFile().getAbsolutePath();

            try
            {
               ObjectOutputStream oos =
                 new ObjectOutputStream(new FileOutputStream(filename));
               doc.removeUndoableEditListener(this);
               oos.writeObject(doc);
               doc.addUndoableEditListener(this);
               oos.close();
            }
            catch (IOException ioe){};
         }
      }

/* The "cut", "copy", and "paste" menu items implement the cut, copy, */
/* and paste functions.                                               */

      if ( event.getActionCommand().equals("cut") )
      {
        textPane.cut();
      }
      if ( event.getActionCommand().equals("copy") )
      {
        textPane.copy();
      }
      if ( event.getActionCommand().equals("paste") )
      {
        textPane.paste();
      }

/* The "undo" and "redo" menu items cause an undoable edit to be   */
/* undone or redone.  The "undo" menu item is only enabled if      */
/* there is an undoable edit that can be undone.  The "redo" menu  */
/* item is only enabled if there is an undoable edit that can be   */
/* redone.                                                         */

      if ( event.getActionCommand().equals("undo") )
      {
         try
         {
```

```java
            undoManager.undo();
            redoItem.setEnabled(undoManager.canRedo());
            undoItem.setEnabled(undoManager.canUndo());
         }
         catch (CannotUndoException cue) {}
      }
      if ( event.getActionCommand().equals("redo") )
      {
         try
         {
            undoManager.redo();
            redoItem.setEnabled(undoManager.canRedo());
            undoItem.setEnabled(undoManager.canUndo());
         }
         catch (CannotRedoException cre) {}
      }
   }

/* This itemStateChanged() method handles events generated by the    */
/* "Plain" and "Bold" JRadioButtonMenuItem objects. The bold         */
/* attribute of the logical style associated with the                */
/* DefaultStyledDocument is set according to which button is selected. */

   public void itemStateChanged(ItemEvent event)
   {
      if ( plainItem.isSelected() )
      {
         StyleConstants.setBold(logicalStyle, false);
      }
      if ( boldItem.isSelected() )
      {
         StyleConstants.setBold(logicalStyle, true);
      }

   }

/* The UndoableEditDemo class serves as the UndoableEditListener,    */
/* so it provides an implementation of the undoableEditHappened()    */
/* method.  When the user executes an undoable edit in the text      */
/* area, an UndoableEditEvent is generated and sent to this method.  */
/* The method adds the edit to the list managed by the UndoManager.  */
/* The "undo" and "redo" menu items are enabled or disabled depending */
/* on whether subsequent undo and redo operations are possible.      */

   public void undoableEditHappened(UndoableEditEvent event)
   {
      undoManager.addEdit(event.getEdit());
      redoItem.setEnabled(undoManager.canRedo());
      undoItem.setEnabled(undoManager.canUndo());
   }

/* If the "Dynamic Font Update" JCheckBoxMenuItem is selected and the */
/* user drags the mouse through the "Font" menu MenuDragMouseEvents   */
```

```
/* are generated.  The menuDragMouseEntered() method is implemented   */
/* such that the font property of the logical style associated with the */
/* DefaultStyledDocument is dynamically updated depending on which    */
/* "Font" menu item is currently active.  The other methods declared   */
/* in the MenuDragMouseListener interface are implemented as stubs.   */

   public void menuDragMouseEntered(MenuDragMouseEvent event)
   {
      JMenuItem item = (JMenuItem)event.getComponent();
      StyleConstants.setFontFamily(logicalStyle, item.getActionCommand());
   }

   public void menuDragMouseDragged(MenuDragMouseEvent event) {}
   public void menuDragMouseExited(MenuDragMouseEvent event) {}
   public void menuDragMouseReleased(MenuDragMouseEvent event) {}

/* This ActionListener is used with the font size menu items.     */
/* The actionPerformed() method determines what the current       */
/* font and style are then parses the selected menu item label    */
/* to determine what the font size should be.                     */

   class SizeHandler implements ActionListener
   {
      public void actionPerformed(ActionEvent event)
      {
         int size = Integer.parseInt(event.getActionCommand());
         StyleConstants.setFontSize(logicalStyle, size);
      }
   }

/* This ActionListener is used with the font type menu items.     */
/* The actionPerformed() method sets the fontFamily property of   */
/* logical style associated with the DefaultStyledDocument to be  */
/* whatever Font menu item was selected.                          */

   class FontHandler implements ActionListener
   {
      public void actionPerformed(ActionEvent event)
      {
         StyleConstants.setFontFamily(logicalStyle,event.getActionCommand());
      }
   }

/* This ItemListener is used to process events generated by the   */
/* "Italic" JCheckBoxMenuItem.  If the Italic box has been selected, */
/* the font style is changed to italic.  If the Italic box is     */
/* unchecked, the style is changed to plain.                      */

   class ItalicHandler implements ItemListener
   {
      public void itemStateChanged(ItemEvent event)
      {
```

```
                if ( event.getStateChange() == ItemEvent.SELECTED )
                {
                    StyleConstants.setItalic(logicalStyle, true);
                }
                else
                {
                    StyleConstants.setItalic(logicalStyle, false);
                }
            }
        }

    /*  This ItemListener is used to process events generated by the    */
    /*  "Dynamic Font Update" JCheckBoxMenuItem.  If the checkbox has   */
    /*  been selected, the Font menu items add a MenuDragMouseListener  */
    /*  to their listener list.  If the checkbox is deselected, the     */
    /*  Font menu items remove a MenuDragMouseListener from their       */
    /*  listener list.                                                  */

        class DynamicHandler implements ItemListener
        {
            public void itemStateChanged(ItemEvent event)
            {
                if ( event.getStateChange() == ItemEvent.SELECTED )
                {
                    dialog.addMenuDragMouseListener(DocumentEditor.this);
                    serif.addMenuDragMouseListener(DocumentEditor.this);
                    monospaced.addMenuDragMouseListener(DocumentEditor.this);
                    helvetica.addMenuDragMouseListener(DocumentEditor.this);
                }
                else
                {
                    dialog.removeMenuDragMouseListener(DocumentEditor.this);
                    serif.removeMenuDragMouseListener(DocumentEditor.this);
                    monospaced.removeMenuDragMouseListener(DocumentEditor.this);
                    helvetica.removeMenuDragMouseListener(DocumentEditor.this);
                }
            }
        }

        public static void main(String args[])
        {
            DocumentEditor je = new DocumentEditor();
        }
    }
```

This program looks really long, but most of it consists of creating and displaying the GUI components and implementing the event listeners. Let's go through it step-by-step.

The purpose of this program is to be able to read, write, and modify a DefaultStyledDocument object. The DocumentEditor constructor creates an initial DefaultStyledDocument object and wraps a JTextPane around it. A Style object corresponding to the logical style of the first paragraph of the DefaultStyledDocument is obtained. The attributes of this Style object will be changed to change the way the DefaultStyledDocument is displayed by the JTextPane.

The remainder of the constructor involves creating the menu components. The JMenuItem objects register an ActionListener to receive the events they will generate when selected. Many of the JMenuItems register the ActionListener implemented by the DocumentEditor class. The `actionPerformed()` method of this listener uses the `getAction-Command()` method to determine the source of the event. For instance, look at the code excerpt in Example 13.9.

EXAMPLE 13.9 PROCESSING ACTIONEVENTS

```
if ( event.getActionCommand().equals("open") )
{
   int choice = jfc.showOpenDialog(this);

   if (choice == JFileChooser.APPROVE_OPTION)
   {
      String filename = jfc.getSelectedFile().getAbsolutePath();

      try
      {
         ObjectInputStream ois =
           new ObjectInputStream(new FileInputStream(filename));
         doc = (DefaultStyledDocument)ois.readObject();
         textPane.setDocument(doc);
         logicalStyle = doc.getLogicalStyle(0);
         doc.addUndoableEditListener(this);
         ois.close();
      }
      catch (Exception e){};
   }
}
```

This section of code is executed if the "open" menu item is selected. When this happens, an ActionEvent is generated with "open" as its action command. This option is used to read in a previously stored DefaultStyledDocument object. A JFileChooser displays a dialog from which the user can enter a selection. An ObjectInputStream is then used to read in the file.

The "Size" and "Font" menu items register a separate ActionListener that is implemented as an inner class. This is because the action command from the events generated by these components can be used directly to respond to the event. Implementing the listener for these objects as a separate inner class avoids a number of `if( event.getActionCommand().equals() )` statements. For instance, the code listing for the "Size" menu item ActionListener is shown in Example 13.10.

EXAMPLE 13.10 IMPLEMENTING AN ACTIONLISTENER AS AN INNER CLASS

```
class SizeHandler implements ActionListener
{
   public void actionPerformed(ActionEvent event)
   {
      int size = Integer.parseInt(event.getActionCommand());
      StyleConstants.setFontSize(logicalStyle, size);
   }
}
```

The action command for these events contains a String representation of the desired font size. The action command is converted from a String to an int, and the font size attribute of the Style object is set to this value. In a similar fashion, the "Font" menu item ActionListener is written as in Example 13.11.

EXAMPLE 13.11 HANDLING EVENTS FROM THE FONT MENU ITEM

```
class FontHandler implements ActionListener
{
   public void actionPerformed(ActionEvent event)
   {
StyleConstants.setFontFamily(logicalStyle,event.getActionCommand());
   }
}
```

In this case, the action command is the new font name, so the font family attribute of the Style object can be set to the action command directly.

The JRadioButtonMenuItem and JCheckBoxMenuItem objects all generate ItemEvents when they are selected or deselected. Now we face an event listener design question. Should we tie a single ItemListener to all ItemEvent sources and write a block of code to determine the component that generated the event, or should we use multiple ItemListeners, perhaps even one for each ItemEvent-generating component?

It was decided to take a middle course between these two design options. To avoid having to determine what type of component generated a given

ItemEvent, the JRadioButtonMenuItem and JCheckBoxMenuItem objects register separate ItemListeners. The JRadioButtonMenuItems use an ItemListener that is implemented by the DocumentEditor class. The `itemStateChanged()` method for this listener looks like Example 13.12.

EXAMPLE 13.12 HANDLING ITEMEVENTS GENERATED BY THE JRADIOBUTTONMENUITEMS

```
public void itemStateChanged(ItemEvent event)
{
   if ( plainItem.isSelected() )
   {
      StyleConstants.setBold(logicalStyle, false);
   }
   if ( boldItem.isSelected() )
   {
      StyleConstants.setBold(logicalStyle, true);
   }
}
```

This method knows that the ItemEvent was generated by one of the two JRadioButtonMenuItem objects. It simply tests to see which one was selected and updates the bold attribute of the Style object accordingly.

The two JCheckBoxMenuItems register their own ItemListener that is implemented as an inner class. The ItemListener registered to the "Italic" JCheckBoxMenuItem tests to see if the "Italic" JCheckBoxMenuItem is selected or deselected. It then updates the italic attribute of the Style object according to the selected state.

The DocumentEditor application has a special menu option under the Options menu that causes the program to dynamically update the font of the DefaultStyledDocument as the mouse is dragged through the Font menu. This capability is toggled on and off using the "Dynamic Font Update" JCheckBoxMenuItem. This object registers the following ItemListener, shown in Example 13.13.

EXAMPLE 13.13 HANDLING ITEMEVENTS GENERATED BY THE JCHECKBOXMENUITEM

```
class DynamicHandler implements ItemListener
{
   public void itemStateChanged(ItemEvent event)
   {
      if ( event.getStateChange() == ItemEvent.SELECTED )
```

```
            {
                dialog.addMenuDragMouseListener(DocumentEditor.this);
                serif.addMenuDragMouseListener(DocumentEditor.this);
                monospaced.addMenuDragMouseListener(DocumentEditor.this);
                helvetica.addMenuDragMouseListener(DocumentEditor.this);
            }
            else
            {
                dialog.removeMenuDragMouseListener(DocumentEditor.this);
                serif.removeMenuDragMouseListener(DocumentEditor.this);
                monospaced.removeMenuDragMouseListener(DocumentEditor.this);
                helvetica.removeMenuDragMouseListener(DocumentEditor.this);
            }
        }
    }
```

If the "Dynamic Font Update" JCheckBoxMenuItem is selected, a MenuDragMouseListener is added to the listener list of all the menu items in the Font menu. If the JCheckBoxMenuItem is deselected, the Font menu items remove the MenuDragMouseListener from their listener list. If the Dynamic Font Update capability is activated, a MenuDragMouseEvent will be sent to the MenuDragMouseListener if the mouse is dragged through the Font menu. The MenuDragMouseListener is implemented by the DocumentEditor class and has the code listing shown in Example 13.14.

EXAMPLE 13.14 IMPLEMENTING A MENUDRAGMOUSELISTENER

```
public void menuDragMouseEntered(MenuDragMouseEvent event)
{
    JMenuItem item = (JMenuItem)event.getComponent();
    StyleConstants.setFontFamily(logicalStyle, item.getActionCommand());
}

public void menuDragMouseDragged(MenuDragMouseEvent event) {}
public void menuDragMouseExited(MenuDragMouseEvent event) {}
public void menuDragMouseReleased(MenuDragMouseEvent event) {}
```

We only really care about the event that occurs when the mouse enters the bounding area of a menu item, so we only provide a meaningful implementation to the `menuDragMouseEntered()` method. The MenuDragMouseListener interface has no corresponding adapter class, so we have to implement every method in some fashion. The other methods are implemented as stubs. The `menuDragMouseEntered()` method determines the JMenuItem that generated the event and sets the font family attribute of the Style object to be the action command (which is the label) of the event source.

The DocumentEditor class supports the ability to undo and/or redo an UndoableEdit object. The DefaultStyledDocument registers an UndoableEditListener that is implemented by the DocumentEditor class. The DocumentEditor class uses an UndoManager object to keep track of any undoable edits that occur. The code listing for the `undoableEditHappened()` method is shown in Example 13.15.

EXAMPLE 13.15 PROCESSING UNDOABLE EDITS

```
public void undoableEditHappened(UndoableEditEvent event)
{
   undoManager.addEdit(event.getEdit());
   redoItem.setEnabled(undoManager.canRedo());
   undoItem.setEnabled(undoManager.canUndo());
}
```

If an UndoableEditEvent is generated, the corresponding UndoableEdit is added to the list of such edits maintained by the UndoManager. The UndoManager then sets the enabled state of the "undo" and "redo" menu items according to whether an "undo" or "redo" operation can now be performed.

When you start this application, you will see an empty JTextPane. Type something into the text area. Play around with the editing functions. Change the type, size, and style of the font. Activate the "Dynamic Font Update" capability and see what happens. Now save the DefaultStyledDocument object to disk. Clear the JTextPane and try to read in the file you just saved. Your previous creation, including your font type, size, and style choices, should appear in the JTextPane.

14

DISTRIBUTED EVENTS

Up to this point in the book, we have discussed events generated by an application running on a single machine using a single JVM. This is the local, or Java Bean, component event model. A network-based or Web-based application running on different platforms or under different JVMs, or both, cannot use the local event model to process events because there is no way to process events generated from a remote source. Fortunately, there are distributed event model frameworks for dealing with remote events. For example, the Jini specification provides such a framework.

One caveat before we begin a discussion of the distributed event model is that this is not a book on Jini or JavaSpaces. An adequate description of these topics would (and does) take up an entire book on its own. This chapter is intended to provide a high-level view of distributed event handling and the distributed event model. Consult a Jini or JavaSpaces reference, such as *Core Jini, Second Edition* by W. Keith Edwards, for complete details on the Jini and JavaSpaces technologies.

Distributed Event Model

Local events are handled by Java in a structured, systematic manner. Events are generated, placed on the event queue, and processed according to the Java 1.0 or 1.1 event model. The Java API provides all of the tools to generate and process events. The system takes care of most of the dirty work for you. All you generally need to do is register one or more event listeners to the desired components and override the appropriate event listener methods.

Distributed events also use a systematic, structured approach, but distributed events pose some additional problems. Events can be generated from any number of remote sources and may not arrive at the event listener in the order in which they were generated. Network problems might indefinitely delay a remote event or even prevent it from ever being delivered to its desired target. There also has to be some mechanism for transferring the remote event from its source to the event listener that has registered an interest in receiving the event.

At first glance, the distributed event model is similar to the local event model. An object that is interested in the remote event registers its interest with the remote object that will generate the event. When an event is generated by the remote source, it is sent to a remote event listener. This listener may be the same object that registered interest in the event, or it may be another object. The destination of the event can be specified in the interest registration process.

A distributed event model, whether it's the Jini model we are describing here or some other model, will have two things in common. The first is that the remote events will have to be serialized; that is to say, the events will have to be stored on a remote machine and then restored when they reach their target destination. Any remote event class therefore will have to implement the java.io.Serializable interface.

Remote events are subclasses of the RemoteEvent class that is defined in the net.jini.core.event package. A RemoteEvent object contains an identifier constant for the type of event it represents. Because remote events may not be delivered to their destination in the order they were generated, a RemoteEvent object is also given a sequence number. This sequence number is an increasing value relative to an earlier event of the same type. This can provide information about when the event occurred. The RemoteEvent contains a java.rmi.MarshalledObject that is returned to the event source upon delivery of the event to its destination. A RemoteEvent object also contains a reference to the event source.

The second common element among any distributed event model is that the listener classes have to be written such that they can receive event notification via some sort of network connection rather than by the direct method invocation used in the local event model. The listener class, at the very least, will have to implement the Remote interface. Any implementation of a remote event listener will also likely be a subclass of java.rmi.server.UnicastRemoteObject to allow event listener's methods to be called from a lookup service running on a separate address space.

The RemoteEventListener interface, defined in the net.jini.core.event package, serves as the listener interface for all remote event listeners. This interface declares one method, `notify()`, that is called when an event is received from a registered remote event source. The `notify()` method takes a RemoteEvent object as an argument. This RemoteEvent will in all probability be one of the RemoteEvent subclasses. The `instanceof` operator can be used to identify the type of RemoteEvent.

One thing that is not provided by the distributed event model is an interface or method to register interest in a remote event. This is because a remote event can represent a wide variety of event types, and objects may want to register interest in a particular event type in a particular (and specialized) manner. However, a user-defined registration interface will have to follow certain design parameters. It will probably define a registration method that will pass information between the remote event listener and the event source. This method will supply the event source with the identification constant of interest, a reference to the object that will be returned upon event notification, some information about the duration of the event registration period, and a reference to the remote event listener. The registration method might return an EventRegistration object that contains information about the event registration.

The distributed event model provides for a third-party object that is placed between the event source and the object that will receive notification of the remote event. The third-party can be used to manage the event notification process. It can, for instance, be used to enact some form of event guarantee procedure. It can store event notifications until they are needed by the destination. The third-party can also be used to filter or reroute event notifications. The exact form of a third-party object is left up to the needs of the application and the developer's imagination, but, ultimately, all third-party objects will invoke the `notify()` method of the destination event listener object.

This description is really only the Jini implementation of a distributed event model. There are other possibilities for what a distributed event model would look like. For instance, an alternative distributed event model might define different event listener interfaces for the different types of distributed events. The alternative model might not provide sequence numbers and might instead implement some mechanism for the sequential delivery of distributed events.

Remote Event Classes

The Jini API provides a number of remote event classes. The superclass of all remote events is the RemoteEvent class from the net.jini.core.event package. The ServiceEvent class denotes an event that is generated when a lookup service experiences a change in state. The RemoteDiscoveryEvent class represents an event generated by a lookup discovery service when it discovers or discards a lookup service matching a certain criteria. The RenewalFailureEvent class encapsulates an event that is generated by a lease renewal set when a client lease cannot be renewed before the expiration of the lease.

You may have already noticed some "Jini-jargon" in the above paragraph. You will see a lot more of it in the following description of the remote event classes. Some of the terminology is explained in detail, and some is not. If there is any confusion over the terminology used in this section, consult a Jini reference for edification.

RemoteEvent Class

The RemoteEvent class is the parent class of all remote event classes. A RemoteEvent object contains information about its event identifier, the event source, the event sequence number, and the MarshalledObject that will be returned to the event source when event notification occurs. The sequence number is an increasing value that can indicate the time the event occurred relative to another event of the source. This is relevant because remote events are not guaranteed to be delivered in the order that they were generated.

Syntax:	public class RemoteEvent extends EventObject
Package:	net.jini.core.event.RemoteEvent
Class hierarchy:	Object—EventObject—RemoteEvent
	The RemoteEvent class is a subclass of EventObject and, as such, a RemoteEvent object has access to the methods defined in the EventObject and Object classes.
Introduced:	Jini 1.0

Constructors

```
public RemoteEvent(Object source, long eventID, long
seqNum, MarshalledObject handback)
```

The RemoteEvent class provides one public constructor for creating RemoteEvent objects. The `source` is the object that generated the event. The `eventID` parameter is a number that identifies the event. This identification will be relative to the object that generated the event. The `seqNum` parameter is the sequence number and is used to specify when the event occurred relative to other events from the same event source. The `handback` parameter is a MarshalledObject object that was passed as part of the original event registration. This object is returned to the event source when event notification occurs. The MarshalledObject class is defined in the java.rmi package and represents a byte stream containing a serialized representation of an object. A MarshalledObject is used to pass objects between remote destinations.

Fields

protected long `eventID`
protected MarshalledObject `handback`
protected long `seqNum`
protected Object `source`

`eventID` is the event identification constant.

`handback` is an object returned to the event source upon event notification.

`seqNum` is the sequence number for the event relative to other events generated by the same source.

`source` is a reference to the object that generated the event.

RemoteEvent Class Methods

public long `getID()`
public MarshalledObject `getRegistrationObject()`
public long `getSequenceNumber()`

These methods return the value of the fields associated with the RemoteEvent object.

`getID()` returns the identification constant for the invoking RemoteEvent object.

`getRegistrationObject()` returns the MarshalledObject that was passed as part of the event registration. This object will be returned to the event source upon event notification.

`getSequenceNumber()` returns the sequence number for this event.

Methods Inherited from the java.util.EventObject Class

public Object `getSource()`
public String `toString()`

`getSource()` returns a reference to the object that generated the RemoteEvent.

`toString()` returns a String representation of the invoking RemoteEvent.

Methods Inherited from the java.lang.Object Class

public final Class `getClass()`

`getClass()` returns a Class object representing the runtime class of the invoking object. In this case, it would return an object representing the net.jini.core.event.RemoteEvent class.

The other methods inherited from the Object class, `clone()`, `equals()`, `hashCode()`, `notify()`, `notifyAll()`, and `wait()` are generally not used in conjunction with RemoteEvent objects.

RemoteDiscoveryEvent Class

A RemoteDiscoveryEvent object is generated by a lookup discovery service when it discovers or discards a lookup service matching a certain criteria. The lookup discovery service would send the RemoteDiscoveryEvent to any RemoteEventListener that is implemented by the client and registered with the lookup service.

A RemoteDiscoveryEvent object contains information about its event identifier, the event source, the event sequence number, a MarshalledObject that will be returned to the event source when event notification occurs, and whether the event was due to a lookup service being discovered or discarded. The sequence number is an increasing value that can indicate the time the event occurred relative to another event of the source. This is relevant because remote events are not guaranteed to be delivered in the order that they were generated.

Syntax:	public class RemoteDiscoveryEvent extends RemoteEvent
Package:	net.jini.discovery.RemoteDiscoveryEvent
Class hierarchy:	Object—EventObject—RemoteEvent—RemoteDiscoveryEvent
	The RemoteDiscoveryEvent class is a subclass of RemoteEvent and, as such, a RemoteDiscoveryEvent object has access to the methods defined in the RemoteEvent, Event Object, and Object classes.
Introduced:	Jini 1.0

Constructors

```
public RemoteDiscoveryEvent(Object source, long eventID,
long seqNum, MarshalledObject handback, boolean
discarded, Map groups) throws IOException
```

The RemoteDiscoveryEvent class provides one public constructor for creating RemoteDiscoveryEvent objects. The `source` is the object that generated the event. The `eventID` parameter is a number that identifies the event. This identification will be relative to the object that generated the event. The `seqNum` parameter is the sequence number and is used to specify when the event occurred relative to other events from the same event source. The `handback` parameter is a MarshalledObject object that was passed as part of the original event registration. This object is returned to the event source when event notification occurs. The `discarded` parameter is true if the event was due to a lookup service having been discarded and false if the event was due to a lookup service discovery. The `groups` parameter provides a mapping of the service ID of every discovered or discarded lookup service referenced by the event with the member groups to which those lookup services belong.

Fields

protected boolean `discarded`
protected java.util.Map `groups`
protected java.util.ArrayList `marshalledRegs`
protected `ServiceRegistrar[] regs`

`discarded` indicates whether the event was due to a lookup service being discarded (true) or discovered (false).

`groups` is a Map object containing a mapping of the service IDs of every discovered or discarded lookup service referenced by the event with the member groups to which those lookup services belong.

`MarshalledRegs` is a list of the marshalled ServiceRegistrar proxy objects corresponding to a recently discovered or discarded lookup service.

`regs` is an array containing a subset of the proxy objects of the lookup service or services to which this event is associated.

In addition to these fields, a RemoteDiscoveryEvent object has access to the `eventID`, `handback`, `seqNum`, and `source` fields from the RemoteEvent class.

RemoteDiscoveryEvent Class Methods

public Map `getGroups()`
public `ServiceRegistrar() getRegistrars()` throws LookupUnmarshalException
public boolean `isDiscarded()`

`getGroups()` returns a mapping of the service ID of every discovered or discarded lookup service referenced by the event (the keys) with the member groups to which those lookup services belong (the values).

`getRegistrars()` returns an array of proxies to the discovered or discarded lookup services that caused the RemoteDiscoveryEvent to be generated.

`isDiscarded()` returns true if the invoking RemoteDiscoveryEvent was due to a lookup service being discarded, and false if it was due to a lookup service being discovered.

Methods Inherited from the net.jini.core.event.RemoteEvent Class

public long `getID()`
public MarshalledObject `getRegistrationObject()`
public long `getSequenceNumber()`

`getID()` returns the identification constant for the invoking RemoteDiscoveryEvent object.

`getRegistrationObject()` returns the MarshalledObject that was passed as part of the event registration. This object will be returned to the event source upon event notification.

`getSequenceNumber()` returns the sequence number for this event.

Methods Inherited from the java.util.EventObject Class

public Object `getSource()`
public String `toString()`

`getSource()` returns a reference to the object that generated the RemoteDiscoveryEvent.

`toString()` returns a String representation of the invoking RemoteDiscoveryEvent.

Methods Inherited from the java.lang.Object Class

public final Class `getClass()`

`getClass()` returns a Class object representing the runtime class of the invoking object. In this case, it would return an object representing the net.jini.discovery.RemoteDiscoveryEvent class.

The other methods inherited from the Object class, `clone()`, `equals()`, `hashCode()`, `notify()`, `notifyAll()`, and `wait()` are generally not used in conjunction with RemoteDiscoveryEvent objects.

RenewalFailureEvent Class

A RenewalFailureEvent object is generated by a lease renewal set when a client lease cannot be renewed before the expiration of the lease. The RenewalFailureEvent class is abstract, meaning that a RenewalFailureEvent object is never created directly, but rather, subclasses of RenewalFailureEvent are defined and used.

A RenewalFailureEvent object contains information about the event source, the event sequence number, and a MarshalledObject that will be returned to the event source when event notification occurs.

Syntax: public abstract class RenewalFailureEvent Event extends RemoteEvent

Package: net.jini.lease. RenewalFailureEvent

Class hierarchy: Object—EventObject—RemoteEvent—RenewalFailureEvent

The RenewalFailureEvent class is a subclass of RemoteEvent and, as such, a RenewalFailureEvent object has access to the methods defined in the RemoteEvent, EventObject, and Object classes.

Introduced: Jini 1.0

Constructors

```
public RenewalFailureEvent(LeaseRenewalSet source, long
seqNum, MarshalledObject handback)
```

The RenewalFailureEvent class provides one public constructor for use by RenewalFailureEvent subclass objects. The `source` is the LeaseRenewalSet object that generated the event. The `seqNum` parameter is the sequence number and is used to specify when the event occurred relative to other events from the same event source. The `handback` parameter is a MarshalledObject object that was passed as part of the original event registration. This object is returned to the event source when event notification occurs. The event ID for all RenewalFailureEvents is `LeaseRenewalSet.RENEWAL_FAILURE_EVENT_ID`.

Fields

The RenewalFailureEvent class defines no new fields, but a RenewalFailureEvent object has access to the `eventID`, `handback`, `seqNum`, and `source` fields from the RemoteEvent class.

RenewalFailureEvent Class Methods

```
public abstract Lease getLease() throws IOException, ClassNotFoundException
public Throwable getThrowable() throws IOException, ClassNotFoundException
```

`getLease()` returns a reference to the Lease object that could not be renewed.

`getThrowable()` returns a reference to the Throwable object, if any, that was thrown by the last renewal attempt. The return value will be null if the last lease renewal attempt was successful or if there was no attempt to renew the lease before the lease expired.

Methods Inherited from the net.jini.core.event.RemoteEvent Class

public long `getID()`
public MarshalledObject `getRegistrationObject()`
public long `getSequenceNumber()`

`getID()` returns the identification constant for the invoking RenewalFailureEvent object.

`getRegistrationObject()` returns the MarshalledObject that was passed as part of the event registration. This object will be returned to the event source upon event notification.

`getSequenceNumber()` returns the sequence number for this event.

Methods Inherited from the java.util.EventObject Class

public Object `getSource()`
public String `toString()`

`getSource()` returns a reference to the object that generated the RenewalFailureEvent.

`toString()` returns a String representation of the invoking RenewalFailureEvent.

Methods Inherited from the java.lang.Object Class

public final Class `getClass()`

`getClass()` returns a Class object representing the runtime class of the invoking object. In this case, it would return an object representing the net.jini.lease.RenewalFailureEvent class.

The other methods inherited from the Object class, `clone()`, `equals()`, `hashCode()`, `notify()`, `notifyAll()`, and `wait()` are generally not used in conjunction with RenewalFailureEvent objects.

ServiceEvent Class

A ServiceEvent object is generated when a lookup service experiences a change in state. This state change may involve the lookup service being registered, a lease cancellation, a lease expiration, or some other attribute change operation.

A ServiceEvent object contains information about its event identifier, the event source, the event sequence number, a MarshalledObject that will be returned to the event source when event notification occurs, and whether the event was due to a lookup service being discovered or discarded. The sequence number is an increasing value that can indicate the time the event occurred relative to another event of the source. This is relevant because remote events are not guaranteed to be delivered in the order that they were generated.

Syntax: public abstract class ServiceEvent extends RemoteEvent

Package: net.jini.core.lookup.ServiceEvent

Class hierarchy: Object—EventObject—RemoteEvent—ServiceEvent

The ServiceEvent class is a subclass of RemoteEvent and, as such, a ServiceEvent object has access to the methods defined in the RemoteEvent, EventObject, and Object classes.

Introduced: Jini 1.0

Constructors

```
public ServiceEvent(Object source, long eventID, long seqNum, MarshalledObject handback, ServiceID serviceID, int transition)
```

The ServiceEvent class provides one public constructor for creating ServiceEvent objects. The `source` is the object that generated the event. The `eventID` parameter is a number that identifies the event. This identification will be relative to the object that generated the event. The `seqNum` parameter is the sequence number and is used to specify when the event occurred relative to other events from the same event source. The `handback` parameter is a MarshalledObject object that was passed as part of the original event registration. This object is returned to the event source when event notification occurs. The `serviceID` parameter is the ServiceID object of the item that caused the event. The `transition` is a constant that defines the state change that triggered the event.

Fields

protected ServiceID `serviceID`

protected int `transition`

serviceID is the ServiceID of the object that triggered the event.

transition is an int detailing the nature of the state change. Its value will be one of the TRANSITION constants defined in the net.jini.core.lookup.ServiceRegistrar interface.

In addition to these fields, a ServiceEvent object has access to the eventID, handback, seqNum, and source fields from the RemoteEvent class.

ServiceEvent Class Methods

| public ServiceID getServiceID() |
| public int getTransition() |
| public abstract ServiceItem getServiceItem() |

getServiceID() returns the ServiceID of the object that triggered the event.

getTransition() returns an int representing the state change that was responsible for causing the event.

getServiceItem() returns the new state of the item that triggered the event or null if the item was deleted from the lookup service.

Methods Inherited from the net.jini.core.event.RemoteEvent Class

| public long getID() |
| public MarshalledObject getRegistrationObject() |
| public long getSequenceNumber() |

getID() returns the identification constant for the invoking ServiceEvent object.

getRegistrationObject() returns the MarshalledObject that was passed as part of the event registration. This object will be returned to the event source upon event notification.

getSequenceNumber() returns the sequence number for this event.

Methods Inherited from the java.util.EventObject Class

| public Object getSource() |
| public String toString() |

`getSource()` returns a reference to the object that generated the ServiceEvent.

`toString()` returns a String representation of the invoking ServiceEvent.

Methods Inherited from the java.lang.Object Class

> public final Class `getClass()`

`getClass()` returns a Class object representing the runtime class of the invoking object. In this case, it would return an object representing the net.jini.core.lookup.ServiceEvent class.

The other methods inherited from the Object class, `clone()`, `equals()`, `hashCode()`, `notify()`, `notifyAll()`, and `wait()` are generally not used in conjunction with ServiceEvent objects.

Remote Event Listener Interfaces

The Jini specification provides one interface as the basis for all remote event listeners, the RemoteEventListener interface. A description of this interface, as well as a description of the Remote interface from the java.rmi package, is provided in this section.

Remote Interface

The Remote interface declares no methods and defines no fields. It is used as a marker to indicate that an interface that extends the Remote interface declares methods that can be invoked from a remote virtual machine. The RemoteEventListener interface, the defining interface for remote event listeners, extends the Remote interface.

Syntax:	public interface Remote
Package:	java.rmi
Interface hierarchy:	Remote
	The Remote interface is at the top of its interface hierarchy. Notable subinterfaces include the RemoteEventListener interface.
Introduced:	JDK 1.1

Remote Interface Methods

The Remote interface declares no methods. This interface is used as a marker to indicate that a class that implements the interface is one that can be accessed from a remote virtual machine.

RemoteEventListener Interface

The RemoteEventListener interface declares one method, `notify()`, that is called when a RemoteEvent is generated by another object. The object that is to receive the RemoteEvent must implement this interface. The object that implements this interface and receives the RemoteEvent does not have to be the object that initially registered an interest in the occurrence of a RemoteEvent. The object that is intended to receive the event can be specified as such in the destination parameter of the registration call.

Syntax:	public interface RemoteEventListener extends Remote, EventListener
Package:	net.jini.core.event
Interface hierarchy:	EventListener—RemoteEventListener Remote
	The RemoteEventListener interface extends both the EventListener and Remote interfaces. The EventListener and Remote interfaces define no fields or methods, but are used as markers to indicate a certain functionality. The EventListener interface specifies that the RemoteEventListener interface defines an event listener. The Remote interface, which is defined in the java.rmi package, identifies the RemoteEventListener interface as one whose methods can be accessed from a remote virtual machine.
Introduced:	Jini 1.0

RemoteEventListener Interface Methods

> public void `notify(RemoteEvent event)` throws UnknownEventException, RemoteException

`notify()` is called whenever a RemoteEvent event is generated by a registered source. An UnknownEventException is thrown if the recipient of the event does not recognize the combination of the event identifier and event source as something in which it is interested. A RemoteException is thrown if a communication-related problem occurs during the event notification.

Remote Event Listener Support Classes

The net.jini.core.event package contains one class, the EventRegistration class, that can be used in the process of registering a remote event listener to an event source. An EventRegistration object can be used as a return value for event-interest registration methods.

EventRegistration Class

This is a utility class provided for use as a return value for remote event listener registration methods. It contains information about the event source, identification number, and sequence number. It also contains a Lease object that specifies the length and terms of the event registration

Syntax:	public class EventRegistration extends Object implements Serializable
Package:	net.jini.core.event.EventRegistration
Class hierarchy:	Object—Event Registration
	The EventRegistration class is a subclass of Object and has access to the methods defined in the Object class.
Introduced:	Jini 1.0

Constructors

```
public EventRegistration(long eventID, Object source,
Lease lease, long seqNum)
```

The EventRegistration class provides one public constructor for creating EventRegistration objects. The `eventID` parameter is a number that identifies the event. This identification will be relative to the object that generated the event. The `source` is the object that generated the event. The `lease` parameter is a Lease object containing information about the event registration lease. The `seqNum` parameter is the sequence number and is used to specify when the event occurred relative to other events from the same event source.

Fields

protected long `eventID`

protected Lease `lease`

protected long `seqNum`
protected Object `source`

`eventID` is the event identification constant.

`lease` is a Lease object containing information about the event registration lease.

`seqNum` is the sequence number for the event relative to other events generated by the same source.

`source` is a reference to the object that generated the event.

EventRegistration Class Methods

public long `getID()`
public Lease `getLease()`
public long `getSequenceNumber()`
public Object `getSource()`

`getID()` returns the identification constant that will be used for all RemoteEvents generated for this registration.

`getLease()` returns the Lease object for this event registration.

`getSequenceNumber()` returns the sequence number for the event type that was current when the registration took place. This allows for comparison with sequence numbers from future registrations.

`getSource()` returns a reference to the event source that will be used for all RemoteEvents generated for this registration.

Methods Inherited from the java.lang.Object Class

public final Class `getClass()`
public String `toString()`

`getClass()` returns a Class object representing the runtime class of the invoking object. In this case, it would return an object representing the net.jini.core.event.EventRegistration class.

`toString()` returns a String representation of the invoking EventRegistration object.

The other methods inherited from the Object class, `clone()`, `equals()`, `hashCode()`, `notify()`, `notifyAll()`, and `wait()` are generally not used in conjunction with EventRegistration objects.

EXAMPLE

As it turns out, a simple example of remote event handling involves significantly more code than a simple local event handling example does. The example provided here is taken from *Core Jini*, which is an excellent reference on Jini technology.

In Example 14.1, a ServiceInfoWatcher object is used to solicit remote events from a lookup service when a change occurs to the lookup service. This change might be, for instance, if a new service is added or if an existing service is removed. The ServiceInfoWatcher class also defines a RemoteEventListener that receives and processes the events when they are generated.

EXAMPLE 14.1 SERVICEINFOWATCHER CLASS

```
import net.jini.core.lookup.ServiceRegistrar;
import net.jini.core.lookup.ServiceEvent;
import net.jini.core.lookup.ServiceItem;
import net.jini.core.lookup.ServiceID;
import net.jini.core.event.RemoteEvent;
import net.jini.core.event.EventRegistration;
import net.jini.core.event.RemoteEventListener;
import net.jini.core.lease.Lease;
import net.jini.lease.LeaseRenewalManager;
import java.rmi.RemoteException;
import java.rmi.server.UnicastRemoteObject;
import java.util.HashMap;
import java.io.IOException;

public class ServiceInfoWatcher extends ServiceInfoSearcher {
    protected Listener listener;
    protected LeaseRenewalManager mgr;
    protected HashMap leases = new HashMap();
    protected int transitions =
        ServiceRegistrar.TRANSITION_MATCH_NOMATCH |
        ServiceRegistrar.TRANSITION_NOMATCH_MATCH |
        ServiceRegistrar.TRANSITION_MATCH_MATCH;

    class Listener extends UnicastRemoteObject
        implements RemoteEventListener {

        public Listener() throws RemoteException {
        }
```

```java
    public void notify(RemoteEvent ev)
        throws RemoteException {
        if (!(ev instanceof ServiceEvent)) {
            System.err.println("Unexpected event: " +
                               ev.getClass().getName());
            return;
        }

        ServiceEvent serviceEvent = (ServiceEvent) ev;

        switch (serviceEvent.getTransition()) {
        case ServiceRegistrar.TRANSITION_NOMATCH_MATCH:
            addService(serviceEvent.getServiceItem());
            break;
        case ServiceRegistrar.TRANSITION_MATCH_NOMATCH:
            removeService(serviceEvent.getServiceID());
            break;
        case ServiceRegistrar.TRANSITION_MATCH_MATCH:
            serviceChanged(serviceEvent.getServiceItem());
            break;
        }
    }
}

public ServiceInfoWatcher()
    throws IOException, RemoteException {
    mgr = new LeaseRenewalManager();
    listener = new Listener();
}

protected void removeService(ServiceID serviceID) {
    services.remove(serviceID);
    System.out.println("Service no longer available: "
                       + serviceID);
}

protected void serviceChanged(ServiceItem item) {
    services.put(item.serviceID, item);
    System.out.println("Service updated: " +
                       item.serviceID);
    printServiceInfo(item);
}

// override addRegistrar and removeRegistrar to have them
// ask for/terminate event solicitations whenever we find a
// lookup service.
protected void addRegistrar(ServiceRegistrar reg) {
    try {
        super.addRegistrar(reg);

        EventRegistration er = reg.notify(tmpl,
                                          transitions,
                                          listener,
```

```
                                            null,
                                            10 * 60 * 1000);
            // do something with lease
            leases.put(reg.getServiceID(), er.getLease());
            mgr.renewUntil(er.getLease(), Lease.ANY, null);
        } catch (RemoteException ex) {
            System.err.println("Can't solicit event: " +
                               ex.getMessage());
        }
    }
    protected void removeRegistrar(ServiceRegistrar reg) {
        try {
            super.removeRegistrar(reg);

            // terminate leases on this dude.
            Lease lease = (Lease)
                leases.get(reg.getServiceID());

            if (lease == null)
                return;

            leases.remove(reg.getServiceID());
            // May raise unknown lease exception or
            // remote exception. Should be ok to ignore
            // here...
            mgr.cancel(lease);
        } catch (Exception ex) {
        }
    }

    public static void main(String[] args) {
        try {
            ServiceInfoWatcher watcher = new ServiceInfoWatcher();
            new Thread(watcher).start();
        } catch (Exception ex) {
            System.err.println("Error starting watcher: " +
                               ex.getMessage());
        }
    }
}
```

This code looks a little hairy, but it's really not too hard to see what is going on. The first thing that must be done is that the ServiceInfoWatcher class must notify the lookup service that it wants to receive events. It does this by having a ServiceRegistrar object invoke its `notify()` method in the `addRegistrar()` method. This is shown in Example 14.2.

EXAMPLE 14.2 NOTIFYING THE LOOKUP SERVICE

```
protected void addRegistrar(ServiceRegistrar reg) {
    try {
        super.addRegistrar(reg);

        EventRegistration er = reg.notify(tmpl,
                                          transitions,
                                          listener,
                                            null,
                                          10 * 60 * 1000);
        // do something with lease
        leases.put(reg.getServiceID(), er.getLease());
        mgr.renewUntil(er.getLease(), Lease.ANY, null);
    } catch (RemoteException ex) {
        System.err.println("Can't solicit event: " +
                           ex.getMessage());
    }
}
```

The `tmpl` parameter is a ServiceTemplate object that contains information on the services that should be looked for. The `transitions` parameter is a flag containing the types of events that are desired. For instance, the ServiceInfoWatcher class may want to be notified of events due to a desired service being added to or removed from the lookup service. The `listener` parameter is the RemoteEventListener that will receive the events. The fourth argument is the MarshalledObject that will be returned to the event source upon event notification. In this case, the argument is set to null, meaning that no MarshalledObject will be returned. The final argument is the lease duration, which is set to be 10 minutes. The return argument of this `notify()` method is an EventRegistration object containing the lease for the registration.

The remote event listener is defined as an inner class that extends the java.rmi.server.UnicastRemoteObject class and implements the RemoteEventListener interface. The UnicastRemoteObject class is used as a superclass because the event listener's `notify()` method may have to be called from a lookup service running on a separate address space. The listener class definition is shown in Example 14.3.

EXAMPLE 14.3 LISTENER CLASS DEFINITION

```
class Listener extends UnicastRemoteObject
    implements RemoteEventListener {

    public Listener() throws RemoteException {
    }
```

```
            public void notify(RemoteEvent ev)
                throws RemoteException {
                if (!(ev instanceof ServiceEvent)) {
                    System.err.println("Unexpected event: " +
                                       ev.getClass().getName());
                    return;
                }

                ServiceEvent serviceEvent = (ServiceEvent) ev;

                switch (serviceEvent.getTransition()) {
                case ServiceRegistrar.TRANSITION_NOMATCH_MATCH:
                    addService(serviceEvent.getServiceItem());
                    break;
                case ServiceRegistrar.TRANSITION_MATCH_NOMATCH:
                    removeService(serviceEvent.getServiceID());
                    break;
                case ServiceRegistrar.TRANSITION_MATCH_MATCH:
                    serviceChanged(serviceEvent.getServiceItem());
                    break;
                }
            }
        }
```

When a remote event is generated by the lookup service, it is sent to the `notify()` method of the Listener class. This method tests to see if the event is a ServiceEvent, the event-type that interests us in this example. If the event is a ServiceEvent, the `getTransition()` method is used to determine the type of ServiceEvent. Based on the event type, one of three event processing methods is called.

That is really all there is to it in this example. You may have noticed that the ServiceInfoWatcher class extends another class called ServiceInfoSearcher. This is another example from *Core Jini*. Example 14.4 is the code listing for that class.

EXAMPLE 14.4 SERVICEINFOSEARCHER CLASS

```
import net.jini.discovery.LookupDiscoveryManager;
import net.jini.discovery.DiscoveryManagement;
import net.jini.discovery.DiscoveryEvent;
import net.jini.discovery.DiscoveryListener;
import net.jini.core.lookup.ServiceMatches;
import net.jini.core.lookup.ServiceItem;
import net.jini.core.lookup.ServiceTemplate;
import net.jini.core.lookup.ServiceRegistrar;
```

```java
import net.jini.lookup.entry.ServiceInfo;
import net.jini.core.entry.Entry;
import java.util.HashMap;
import java.rmi.RemoteException;
import java.rmi.RMISecurityManager;
import java.io.IOException;

public class ServiceInfoSearcher implements Runnable {
    protected HashMap registrars = new HashMap();
    protected HashMap services = new HashMap();
    protected ServiceTemplate tmpl;

    class Discoverer implements DiscoveryListener {
        public void discovered(DiscoveryEvent ev) {
            ServiceRegistrar[] newregs = ev.getRegistrars();
            for (int i=0 ; i<newregs.length ; i++) {
                addRegistrar(newregs[i]);
            }
        }
        public void discarded(DiscoveryEvent ev) {
            ServiceRegistrar[] newregs = ev.getRegistrars();
            for (int i=0 ; i<newregs.length ; i++) {
                removeRegistrar(newregs[i]);
            }
        }
    }

    public ServiceInfoSearcher() throws IOException {
        if (System.getSecurityManager() == null) {
            System.setSecurityManager(
                new RMISecurityManager());
        }

        // build our template
        Entry[] attrTemplates = new Entry[1];
        attrTemplates[0] =
            new ServiceInfo(null, null, null,
                        null, null, null);
        tmpl = new ServiceTemplate(null,
                            null,
                            attrTemplates);

        // set up for discovery
        LookupDiscoveryManager disco =
            new
 LookupDiscoveryManager(LookupDiscoveryManager.ALL_GROUPS,
                                null, new Discoverer());
    }

    protected synchronized void addRegistrar(ServiceRegistrar reg) {
        if (registrars.containsKey(reg.getServiceID()))
```

```java
            return;

        registrars.put(reg.getServiceID(), reg);
        findServices(reg);
    }
    protected synchronized void removeRegistrar(ServiceRegistrar reg)
{
        if (!registrars.containsKey(reg.getServiceID()))
            return;

        registrars.remove(reg.getServiceID());
    }

    void findServices(ServiceRegistrar reg) {
        try {
            ServiceMatches matches =
                reg.lookup(tmpl, Integer.MAX_VALUE);

            for (int i=0 ; i<matches.totalMatches ; i++) {
                if (services.containsKey(matches.items[i].serviceID))
                    continue;

                addService(matches.items[i]);
            }
        } catch (RemoteException ex) {
            System.err.println("Couldn't search: " +
                               ex.getMessage());
        }
    }

    protected void addService(ServiceItem item) {
        services.put(item.serviceID, item);
        System.out.println("New service found: " +
                           item.serviceID);
        printServiceInfo(item);
    }

    public static void printServiceInfo(ServiceItem item) {
        for (int i=0 ; i<item.attributeSets.length ; i++) {
            if (item.attributeSets[i] instanceof ServiceInfo) {
                ServiceInfo info =
                    (ServiceInfo) item.attributeSets[i];
                System.out.println("  Name = " +
                                   info.name);
                System.out.println("  Manufacturer = " +
                                   info.manufacturer);
                System.out.println("  Vendor = " +
                                   info.vendor);
                System.out.println("  Version = " +
                                   info.version);
                System.out.println("  Model = " +
                                   info.model);
```

Remote Event Listener Support Classes

```
                System.out.println("  Serial Number = " +
                                    info.serialNumber);

                System.out.println("  Proxy is " +
                                    item.service);
            }
        }
    }

    public void run() {
        while (true) {
            try {
                Thread.sleep(Long.MAX_VALUE);
            } catch (InterruptedException ex) {
            }
        }
    }

    public static void main(String args[]) {
        try {
            ServiceInfoSearcher searcher =
                new ServiceInfoSearcher();
            new Thread(searcher).start();
        } catch (Exception ex) {
            System.err.println("Error starting searcher: " +
                                ex.getMessage());
            ex.printStackTrace();
        }
    }
}
```

Running this example is not as straightforward as running the other examples. You will first have to download and install Jini on your machine. The Jini Network Technology Web site can be found *at www.sun.com/jini/*. Once you have Jini on your system, you will have to compile the code and generate RMI stubs for the RemoteEventListener implementation. The recommended process from *Core Jini,* is shown in Example 14.5.

EXAMPLE 14.5 COMPILING AND RUNNING THE REMOTE EVENT EXAMPLE

```
On Windows Machines:

javac -classpath C:\files;
                 C:\jini1.1\lib\jini-core.jar;
                 C:\jini1.1\lib\jini-ext.jar;
                 C:\jini1.1\lib\sun-util.jar;
                 C:\client
      -d C:\client
         C:\files\corejini\chapter9\ServiceInfoWatcher.java
```

```
rmic -classpath C:\files;
              C:\jini1.1\lib\jini-core.jar;
              C:\jini1.1\lib\jini-ext.jar;
              C:\jini1.1\lib\sun-util.jar;
              C:\client
     -d C:\client
         corejini.chapter9.ServiceInfoWatcher.Listener

mkdir C:\client_dl\corejini\chapter9
cd C:\client\corejini\chapter9
copy ServiceInfoWatcher$Listener_Stub.class
     C:\client-dl\corejini\chapter9
java -cp C:\jini1.1\lib\jini-core.jar;
         C:\jini1.1\lib\jini-ext.jar;
         C:\jini1.1\lib\sun-util.jar;
         C:\client
       -Djava.security.policy=C:\files\policy
       -Djava.rmi.server.codebase=http://myhost:8086/
corejini.chapter9.ServiceInfoWatcher


On UNIX Machines:

javac -classpath /files:
               /files/jini1_1/lib/jini-core.jar:
               /files/jini1_1/lib/jini-ext.jar:
               /files/jini1_1/lib/sun-util.jar:
               /files/client
     -d /files/client
         /files/corejini/chapter9/ServiceInfoWatcher.java

rmic -classpath /files:
               /files/jini1_1/lib/jini-core.jar:
               /files/jini1_1/lib/jini-ext.jar:
               /files/jini1_1/lib/sun-util.jar:
               /files/client
-d /files/client
     corejini.chapter9.ServiceInfoWatcher.Listener

mkdir /files/client_dl/corejini/chapter9
cd /files/client
cp ServiceInfoWatcher$Listener.class
     /files/client_dl/corejini/chapter9

java -cp /files/jini1_1/lib/jini-core.jar:
         /files/jini1_1/lib/jini-ext.jar:
         /files/jini1_1/lib/sun-util.jar:
         /files/client
-Djava.security.policy=/files/policy
      -Djava.rmi.server.codebase=http://myhost:8086/
corejini.chapter9.ServiceInfoWatcher
```

When the application starts, it searches for Jini services that have a ServiceInfo attribute on them and prints information about these services to standard output. The program then waits for ServiceEvents generated by a lookup service. Any time a service that has a ServiceInfo attribute is added or discarded, the program prints out information about it.

This whole process assumes that you have Jini services running in your network. If there aren't any, the application will just wait and display nothing. To find out more about how to install Jini services on your network, consult W. Keith Edwards' *Core Jini, Second Edition*.

APPENDIX

Java GUI Components and the Events They Generate

The following is a list of Java GUI components, the events they generate, and how they generate them. The listing contains every GUI component in the java.awt and javax.swing packages, as well as selected GUI component classes from the javax.swing.text, javax.swing.table, and javax.swing.tree packages. Each listing contains both low-level and high-level events and indicates how the event is generated. The list primarily contains the concrete GUI component classes, but also lists the event capability of the Component, MenuComponent, TextComponent, AbstractButton, and JComponent classes. These serve as superclasses for other GUI component classes.

One thing to notice is that the Swing components have a greater event generating capacity than their AWT counterparts. This is in part because the AWT components generally do not generate the events defined in the javax.swing.event package. Another reason is due to some structural changes in the Java language that occurred between the introduction of AWT and Swing. For instance, AWT menu components are subclasses of the MenuComponent class that itself is a subclass of the Object class. Therefore, AWT menu components do not have access to the low-level events that Component subclasses do. Swing menu components are subclasses of both the Component and JComponent classes and generate all of the low-level events corresponding to these classes.

Another thing to note is that the Swing high-level containers (JFrame, JInternalFrame, JDialog, JApplet, JWindow) do not generate Container events. This is because components are not placed directly onto the high-level window but instead are placed on one of the subpanes of the JRootPane associated with the high-level window.

This list can help point out some interesting differences between similar components. For instance, the JSlider and JScrollBar components look and act in a similar fashion, but their event capabilities are quite different. A JScrollBar generates AdjustmentEvents when its value is changed. The JSlider generates ChangeEvents when its value is changed. The JSlider can generate FocusEvents and KeyEvents. The JScrollBar does not.

javax.swing.AbstractButton

The AbstractButton class is the super-class of the JButton, JToggleButton, JCheckBox, JRadioButton, JMenuItem, JRadioButtonMenuItem, JMenu, and JCheckBoxMenuItem classes. It defines methods to add and remove ActionListener, ChangeListener, and ItemListener objects.

javax.swing.Action

ActionEvent	is sent to the `actionPerformed()` method implemented by the Action object when the button or menu item representing the Action is selected.

java.applet.Applet

ComponentEvent	when the Applet is shown, hidden, moved, or resized.
ContainerEvent	when a component is added or removed from the Applet.
FocusEvent	when the Applet gains or loses focus.
KeyEvent	when the Applet has focus and a key is pressed, released, or typed.
MouseEvent	when the mouse is moved in, is dragged across, enters, or exits the bounding area of the Applet. Also occurs when the mouse is pressed, released, or clicked within the bounding area.
PropertyChangeEvent	when any properties associated with the Applet are changed.

javax.swing.Box

ComponentEvent	when the Box is shown, hidden, moved, or resized.
ContainerEvent	when a component is added to removed from the Box.
FocusEvent	when the Box gains or loses focus.
HierarchyEvent	when the position, size, contents, or visibility of some element of the Box object's component hierarchy is changed.
MouseEvent	when the mouse is moved in, is dragged across, enters, or exits the bounding area of the Box. Also occurs when the mouse is pressed, released, or clicked within the bounding area.
PropertyChangeEvent	when any properties associated with the Box are changed.

java.awt.Button

ActionEvent	when the Button is pressed.
ComponentEvent	when the Button is shown, hidden, moved, or resized.
FocusEvent	when the Button gains or loses focus.
HierarchyEvent	when the position, size, contents, or visibility of some element of the Button object's component hierarchy is changed.
MouseEvent	when the mouse is moved in, is dragged across, enters, or exits the bounding area of the Button. Also occurs when the mouse is pressed, released, or clicked within the bounding area.
PropertyChangeEvent	when any properties associated with the Button are changed.

java.awt.Canvas

ComponentEvent	when the Canvas is shown, hidden, moved, or resized.
FocusEvent	when the Canvas gains or loses focus.
HierarchyEvent	when the position, size, contents, or visibility of some element of the Canvas object's component hierarchy is changed.

| MouseEvent | when the mouse is moved in, is dragged across, enters, or exits the bounding area of the Canvas. Also occurs when the mouse is pressed, released, or clicked within the bounding area. |
| PropertyChangeEvent | when any properties associated with the Canvas are changed. |

java.awt.Checkbox

ComponentEvent	when the Checkbox is shown, hidden, moved, or resized.
FocusEvent	when the Checkbox gains or loses focus.
HierarchyEvent	when the position, size, contents, or visibility of some element of the Checkbox object's component hierarchy is changed.
ItemEvent	when the Checkbox is checked or unchecked.
MouseEvent	when the mouse is moved in, is dragged across, enters, or exits the bounding area of the Checkbox. Also occurs when the mouse is pressed, released, or clicked within the bounding area.
PropertyChangeEvent	when any properties associated with the Checkbox are changed.

java.awt.CheckboxMenuItem

| ActionEvent | when the CheckboxMenuItem is selected. Selecting the CheckboxMenuItem will change its checked state. |
| ItemEvent | when the CheckboxMenuItem is checked or unchecked. |

java.awt.Choice

ComponentEvent	when the Choice is shown, hidden, moved, or resized.
FocusEvent	when the Choice gains or loses focus.
HierarchyEvent	when the position, size, contents, or visibility of some element of the Choice object's component hierarchy is changed.

ItemEvent	when the Choice is checked or unchecked.
MouseEvent	when the mouse is moved in, is dragged across, enters, or exits the bounding area of the Choice. Also occurs when the mouse is pressed, released, or clicked within the bounding area.
PropertyChangeEvent	when any properties associated with the Choice are changed.

java.awt.Component

The Component class is the parent of all Java GUI components. It defines methods to add and remove ComponentListener, FocusListener, HierarchyBoundsListener, HierarchyListener, InputMethodListener, KeyListener, MouseListener, MouseMotionListener, and PropertyChangeListener objects.

java.awt.Container

ComponentEvent	when the Container is shown, hidden, moved, or resized.
ContainerEvent	when a component is added or removed from the Container.
FocusEvent	when the Container gains or loses focus.
HierarchyEvent	when the position, size, contents, or visibility of some element of the Container object's component hierarchy is changed.
MouseEvent	when the mouse is moved in, is dragged across, enters, or exits the bounding area of the Container. Also occurs when the mouse is pressed, released, or clicked within the bounding area.
WindowEvent	when the Container window is activated, deactivated, opened, closed, closing, iconified, or deiconified.
PropertyChangeEvent	when any properties associated with the Container are changed.

java.awt.Dialog

ComponentEvent	when the Dialog is shown, hidden, moved, or resized.
ContainerEvent	when a component is added or removed from the Dialog.

FocusEvent	when the Dialog gains or loses focus.
MouseEvent	when the mouse is moved in, is dragged across, enters, or exits the bounding area of the Dialog. Also occurs when the mouse is pressed, released, or clicked within the bounding area.
WindowEvent	when the Dialog window is activated, deactivated, opened, closed, closing, iconified, or deiconified.
PropertyChangeEvent	when any properties associated with the Dialog are changed.

java.awt.FileDialog

ComponentEvent	when the FileDialog is shown, hidden, moved, or resized.
FocusEvent	when the FileDialog gains or loses focus.
HierarchyEvent	when the position, size, contents, or visibility of some element of the FileDialog object's component hierarchy is changed.
WindowEvent	when the FileDialog window is activated, deactivated, opened, closed, closing, iconified, or deiconified.
PropertyChangeEvent	when any properties associated with the FileDialog are changed.

java.awt.Frame

ComponentEvent	when the Frame is shown, hidden, moved, or resized.
ContainerEvent	when a component is added or removed from the Frame.
HierarchyEvent	when the position, size, contents, or visibility of some element of the Frame object's component hierarchy is changed.
MouseEvent	when the mouse is moved in, is dragged across, enters, or exits the bounding area of the Frame. Also occurs when the mouse is pressed, released, or clicked within the bounding area.
WindowEvent	when the Frame window is activated, deactivated, opened, closed, closing, iconified, or deiconified.

PropertyChangeEvent	when any properties associated with the Frame are changed.

javax.swing.JApplet

ComponentEvent	when the JApplet is shown, hidden, moved, or resized.
ContainerEvent	when a component is added or removed from the JApplet.
FocusEvent	when the JApplet gains or loses focus.
KeyEvent	when the JApplet has focus and a key is pressed, released, or typed.
MouseEvent	when the mouse is moved in, is dragged across, enters, or exits the bounding area of the JApplet. Also occurs when the mouse is pressed, released, or clicked within the bounding area.
PropertyChangeEvent	when any properties associated with the JApplet are changed.

javax.swing.JButton

ActionEvent	when the JButton is pressed.
AncestorEvent	when the JButton or one of its ancestor containers is moved or if an ancestor container is added to or removed from the JButton object's component hierarchy.
ChangeEvent	when a change is made to one of the properties of the button model associated with the JButton.
ComponentEvent	when the JButton is shown, hidden, moved, or resized.
FocusEvent	when the JButton gains or loses focus.
HierarchyEvent	when the position, size, contents, or visibility of some element of the JButton object's component hierarchy is changed.
KeyEvent	when the JButton has focus and a key is pressed, released, or typed.
MouseEvent	when the mouse is moved in, is dragged across, enters, or exits the bounding area of the JButton. Also occurs when the mouse is pressed, released, or clicked within the bounding area.

PropertyChangeEvent	when any properties associated with the JButton are changed.

javax.swing.JCheckBox

ActionEvent	when the mouse is clicked over the JCheckBox.
AncestorEvent	when the JCheckBox or one of its ancestor containers is moved or if an ancestor container is added to or removed from the JCheckBox object's component hierarchy.
ChangeEvent	when a change is made to one of the properties of the button model associated with the JCheckBox.
ComponentEvent	when the JCheckBox is shown, hidden, moved, or resized.
FocusEvent	when the JCheckBox gains or loses focus.
HierarchyEvent	when the position, size, contents, or visibility of some element of the JCheckBox object's component hierarchy is changed.
ItemEvent	when the JCheckBox is selected or deselected.
KeyEvent	when the JCheckBox has focus and a key is pressed, released, or typed.
MouseEvent	when the mouse is moved in, is dragged across, enters, or exits the bounding area of the JCheckBox. Also occurs when the mouse is pressed, released, or clicked within the bounding area.
PropertyChangeEvent	when any properties associated with the JCheckBox are changed.

javax.swing.JCheckBoxMenuItem

ActionEvent	when the mouse is released over the JCheckBoxMenuItem.
AncestorEvent	when the JCheckBoxMenuItem or one of its ancestor containers is moved or if an ancestor container is added to or removed from the JCheckBoxMenuItem object's component hierarchy.
ChangeEvent	when a change is made to one of the properties of the button model associated with the JCheckBoxMenuItem.

Java GUI Components and the Events They Generate

ComponentEvent	when the JCheckBoxMenuItem is moved or resized.
HierarchyEvent	when the position, size, contents, or visibility of some element of the JCheckBoxMenuItem object's component hierarchy is changed.
ItemEvent	when the JCheckBoxMenuItem is selected or deselected.
MenuDragMouseEvent	when the JCheckBoxMenuItem is selected and the mouse is dragged inside its bounding area.
MenuKeyEvent	when the JCheckBoxMenuItem is selected and a key is pressed, released, or typed.
MouseEvent	when the mouse is moved in, enters, or exits the bounding area of the JCheckBoxMenuItem. Also occurs when the mouse is pressed or released within the bounding area.
PropertyChangeEvent	when any properties associated with the JCheckBoxMenuItem are changed.

javax.swing.JColorChooser

AncestorEvent	when the JColorChooser or one of its ancestor containers is moved or if an ancestor container is added to or removed from the JColorChooser object's component hierarchy.
ComponentEvent	when the JColorChooser is shown, hidden, moved, or resized.
HierarchyEvent	when the position, size, contents, or visibility of some element of the JColorChooser object's component hierarchy is changed.
MouseEvent	when the mouse is moved in, is dragged across, enters, or exits the bounding area of the JColorChooser. Also occurs when the mouse is pressed, released, or clicked within the bounding area.
PropertyChangeEvent	when any properties associated with the JColorChooser are changed. javax.swing.JComboBox

javax.swing.JComboBox

ActionEvent	when the user explicitly selects one of the items in the JComboBox.
AncestorEvent	when the JComboBox or one of its ancestor containers is moved or if an ancestor container is added to or removed from the JComboBox object's component hierarchy.
ComponentEvent	when the JComboBox is moved or resized.
HierarchyEvent	when the position, size, contents, or visibility of some element of the JComboBox object's component hierarchy is changed.
ItemEvent	when selected item in the JComboBox changes for any reason.
PropertyChangeEvent	when any properties associated with the JComboBox are changed.

javax.swing.JComponent

The JComponent class is the parent class of all Swing GUI component classes, with the exception of the Timer and ProgressMonitor classes. The JComponent class defines the `add()` and `remove()` methods for AncestorListener, PropertyChangeListener, and VetoableChangeListener objects.

javax.swing.JDesktopPane

AncestorEvent	when the JDesktopPane or one of its ancestor containers is moved or if an ancestor container is added to or removed from the JDesktopPane object's component hierarchy.
ComponentEvent	when the JDesktopPane is shown, hidden, moved, or resized.
ContainerEvent	when a component is added to or removed from the JDesktopPane.
HierarchyEvent	when the position, size, contents, or visibility of some element of the JDesktopPane object's component hierarchy is changed.
MouseEvent	when the mouse is moved in, is dragged across, enters, or exits the bounding area of the JDesktopPane. Also occurs when the mouse is pressed, released, or clicked within the bounding area.

PropertyChangeEvent	when any properties associated with the JDesktopPane are changed.

javax.swing.JDialog

ComponentEvent	when the JDialog is shown, hidden, moved, or resized.
FocusEvent	when the JDialog gains or loses focus.
HierarchyEvent	when the position, size, contents, or visibility of some element of the JDialog object's component hierarchy is changed.
KeyEvent	when the JDialog has focus and a key is pressed, released, or typed.
MouseEvent	when the mouse is moved in, is dragged across, enters, or exits the bounding area of the JDialog. Also occurs when the mouse is pressed, released, or clicked within the bounding area.
PropertyChangeEvent	when any properties associated with the JDialog are changed.
WindowEvent	when the JDialog is activated, deactivated, opened, closed, closing, iconified, or deiconified.

javax.swing.JEditorPane

AncestorEvent	when the JEditorPane or one of its ancestor containers is moved or if an ancestor container is added to or removed from the JEditorPane object's component hierarchy.
CaretEvent	when the caret position of the JEditorPane is changed.
ComponentEvent	when the JEditorPane is shown, hidden, moved, or resized.
DocumentEvent	when text is inserted in or removed from the JEditorPane or if one or more attributes of the Document object associated with the JEditorPane are changed.
FocusEvent	when the JEditorPane gains or loses focus.
HierarchyEvent	when the position, size, contents, or visibility of some element of the JEditorPane object's component hierarchy is changed.

HyperlinkEvent	when a hyperlink is selected in the HTML page displayed by the JEditorPane. Also occurs when the mouse enters or exits the bounding area of the hyperlink.
HTMLFrameHyperlinkEvent	when a hyperlink is selected in the HTML frame displayed by the JEditorPane. Also occurs when the mouse enters or exits the bounding area of the hyperlink.
KeyEvent	when the JEditorPane has focus and a key is pressed, released, or typed.
MouseEvent	when the mouse is moved in, dragged across, enters, or exits the bounding area of the JEditorPane. Also occurs when the mouse is pressed, released, or clicked within the bounding area.
PropertyChangeEvent	when any properties associated with the JEditorPane are changed.
UndoableEditEvent	when an edit that can be undone is performed inside the JEditorPane.

javax.swing.JFileChooser

ActionEvent	when the user clicks on the Open, Save, or Cancel buttons.
AncestorEvent	when the JFileChooser or one of its ancestor containers is moved or if an ancestor container is added to or removed from the JFileChooser object's component hierarchy.
ComponentEvent	when the JFileChooser is shown, hidden, moved, or resized.
HierarchyEvent	when the position, size, contents, or visibility of some element of the JFileChooser object's component hierarchy is changed.
MouseEvent	when the mouse is moved in, dragged across, enters, or exits the bounding area of the JFileChooser. Also occurs when the mouse is pressed, released, or clicked within the bounding area.
PropertyChangeEvent	when any properties associated with the JFileChooser are changed.

javax.swing.JFrame

ComponentEvent	when the JFrame is shown, hidden, moved, or resized.
FocusEvent	when the JFrame gains or loses focus.
HierarchyEvent	when the position, size, contents, or visibility of some element of the JFrame object's component hierarchy is changed.
KeyEvent	when the JFrame has focus and a key is pressed, released, or typed.
MouseEvent	when the mouse is moved in, is dragged across, enters, or exits the bounding area of the JFrame. Also occurs when the mouse is pressed, released, or clicked within the bounding area.
PropertyChangeEvent	when any properties associated with the JFrame are changed.
WindowEvent	when the JFrame window is activated, deactivated, opened, closed, closing, iconified, or deiconified.

javax.swing.JInternalFrame

AncestorEvent	when the JInternalFrame or one of its ancestor containers is moved or if an ancestor container is added to or removed from the JInternalFrame object's component hierarchy.
ComponentEvent	when the JInternalFrame is shown, hidden, moved, or resized.
HierarchyEvent	when the position, size, contents, or visibility of some element of the JInternalFrame object's component hierarchy is changed.
InternalFrameEvent	when the JInternalFrame window is activated, deactivated, opened, closed, closing, iconified, or deiconified.
MouseEvent	when the mouse is moved in, is dragged across, enters, or exits the bounding area of the JInternalFrame. Also occurs when the mouse is pressed, released, or clicked within the bounding area.

PropertyChangeEvent	when any properties associated with the JInternalFrame are changed.

javax.swing.JLabel

AncestorEvent	when the JLabel or one of its ancestor containers is moved or if an ancestor container is added to or removed from the JLabel object's component hierarchy.
ComponentEvent	when the JLabel is shown, hidden, moved, or resized.
HierarchyEvent	when the position, size, contents, or visibility of some element of the JLabel object's component hierarchy is changed.
MouseEvent	when the mouse is moved in, dragged across, enters, or exits the bounding area of the JLabel. Also occurs when the mouse is pressed, released, or clicked within the bounding area.
PropertyChangeEvent	when any properties associated with the JLabel are changed.

javax.swing.JLayeredPane

AncestorEvent	when theJLayeredPane or one of its ancestor containers is moved or if an ancestor container is added to or removed from the object's component hierarchy.
ComponentEvent	when the JLayeredPane is shown, hidden, moved, or resized.
ContainerEvent	when a component is added or removed from the JLayeredPane.
HierarchyEvent	when the position, size, contents, or visibility of some element of the JLayeredPane object's component hierarchy is changed.
MouseEvent	when the mouse is moved in, is dragged across, enters, or exits the bounding area of the JLayeredPane. Also occurs when the mouse is pressed, released, or clicked within the bounding area.
PropertyChangeEvent	when any properties associated with the JLayeredPane are changed.

javax.swing.JList

AncestorEvent	when the JList or one of its ancestor containers is moved or if an ancestor container is added to or removed from the JList object's component hierarchy.
ComponentEvent	when the JList is shown, hidden, moved, or resized.
FocusEvent	when the JList gains or loses focus.
HierarchyEvent	when the position, size, contents, or visibility of some element of the JList object's component hierarchy is changed.
KeyEvent	when the JList has focus and a key is pressed, released, or typed.
ListDataEvent	when the contents of the ListModel associated with a JList are changed.
ListSelectionEvent	when a change is made to the selected item of a JList.
MouseEvent	when the mouse is moved in, dragged across, enters, or exits the bounding area of the JList. Also occurs when the mouse is pressed, released, or clicked within the bounding area.
PropertyChangeEvent	when any properties associated with the JList are changed.

javax.swing.JMenu

AncestorEvent	when the JMenu or one of its ancestor containers is moved or if an ancestor container is added to or removed from the JMenu object's component hierarchy.
ChangeEvent	when a change is made to one of the properties of the button model associated with the JMenu.
ComponentEvent	when the JMenu is hidden, moved or resized.
FocusEvent	when the JMenu gains or loses focus.
HierarchyEvent	when the position, size, contents, or visibility of some element of the JMenu object's component hierarchy is changed.
ItemEvent	when any element of the JMenu is selected.

KeyEvent	when the JMenu has focus and a key is pressed, released, or typed.
MenuDragMouseEvent	when the JMenu is selected and the mouse is dragged inside its bounding area.
MenuEvent	when the JMenu is selected or deselected.
MenuKeyEvent	when the JMenu is selected and a key is pressed, released, or typed.
MouseEvent	when the mouse is moved in, dragged down, enters, or exits the bounding area of the JMenu. Also occurs when the mouse is pressed or released within the bounding area.
PropertyChangeEvent	when any properties associated with the JMenu are changed.

javax.swing.JMenuBar

AncestorEvent	when the JMenuBar or one of its ancestor containers is moved or if an ancestor container is added to or removed from the JMenuBar object's component hierarchy.
ComponentEvent	when the JMenuBar is hidden, moved or resized.
ContainerEvent	when a menu is added to or removed from the JMenuBar.
HierarchyEvent	when the position, size, contents, or visibility of some element of the JMenuBar object's component hierarchy is changed.
MouseEvent	when the mouse is moved in, dragged across, enters, or exits the bounding area of the JMenuBar. Also occurs when the mouse is pressed, released, or clicked within the bounding area.
PropertyChangeEvent	when any properties associated with the JMenuBar are changed.

javax.swing.JMenuItem

ActionEvent	when the mouse is released over the JMenuItem.
AncestorEvent	when the JMenuItem or one of its ancestor containers is moved or if an ancestor container is added to or removed from the JMenuItem object's component hierarchy.

ChangeEvent	when a change is made to one of the properties of the button model associated with the JMenuItem.
ComponentEvent	when the JMenuItem is moved or resized.
HierarchyEvent	when the position, size, contents, or visibility of some element of the JMenuItem object's component hierarchy is changed.
MenuDragMouseEvent	when the JMenuItem is selected and the mouse is dragged inside its bounding area.
MenuKeyEvent	when the JMenuItem is selected and a key is pressed, released, or typed.
MouseEvent	when the mouse is moved in, enters, or exits the bounding area of the JMenuItem. Also occurs when the mouse is pressed or released within the bounding area.
PropertyChangeEvent	when any properties associated with the JMenuItem are changed.

javax.swing.JOptionPane

AncestorEvent	when the JOptionPane or one of its ancestor containers is moved or if an ancestor container is added to or removed from the JOptionPane object's component hierarchy.
ComponentEvent	when the JOptionPane is shown, hidden, moved, or resized.
ContainerEvent	when a component is added or removed from the JOptionPane.
HierarchyEvent	when the position, size, contents, or visibility of some element of the JOptionPane object's component hierarchy is changed.
MouseEvent	when the mouse is moved in, is dragged across, enters, or exits the bounding area of the JOptionPane. Also occurs when the mouse is pressed, released, or clicked within the bounding area.
PropertyChangeEvent	when any properties associated with the JOptionPane are changed.

javax.swing.JPanel

AncestorEvent	when the JPanel or one of its ancestor containers is moved or if an ancestor container is added to or removed from the JPanel object's component hierarchy.
ComponentEvent	when the JPanel is shown, hidden, moved, or resized.
ContainerEvent	when a component is added or removed from the JPanel.
HierarchyEvent	when the position, size, contents, or visibility of some element of the JPanel object's component hierarchy is changed.
MouseEvent	when the mouse is moved in, is dragged across, enters, or exits the bounding area of the JPanel. Also occurs when the mouse is pressed, released, or clicked within the bounding area.
PropertyChangeEvent	when any properties associated with the JPanel are changed.

javax.swing.JPasswordField

ActionEvent	when the JPasswordField has keyboard focus and the Return or Enter key is pressed.
AncestorEvent	when the JPasswordField or one of its ancestor containers is moved or if an ancestor container is added to or removed from the JPasswordField object's component hierarchy.
CaretEvent	when the caret position of the JPasswordField is changed.
ComponentEvent	when the JPasswordField is shown, hidden, moved, or resized.
DocumentEvent	when text is inserted in or removed from the JPasswordField or if one or more attributes of the Document object associated with the JPasswordField are changed.
FocusEvent	when the JPasswordField gains or loses focus.
HierarchyEvent	when the position, size, contents, or visibility of some element of the JPasswordField object's component hierarchy is changed.

KeyEvent	when the JPasswordField has focus and a key is pressed, released, or typed.
MouseEvent	when the mouse is moved in, dragged across, enters, or exits the bounding area of the JPasswordField. Also occurs when the mouse is pressed, released, or clicked within the bounding area.
PropertyChangeEvent	when any properties associated with the JPasswordField are changed.
UndoableEditEvent	when an edit that can be undone is performed inside the JPasswordField.

javax.swing.JPopupMenu

AncestorEvent	when the JPopupMenu or one of its ancestor containers is moved or if an ancestor container is added to or removed from the JPopupMenu object's component hierarchy.
ComponentEvent	when the JPopupMenu is shown, hidden, moved, or resized.
ContainerEvent	when a menu item is added or removed from the JPopupMenu. HierarchyEvent when the position, size, contents, or visibility of some element of the JPopupMenu object's component hierarchy is changed.
MouseEvent	when the mouse is moved in, is dragged across, enters, or exits the bounding area of the JPopupMenu. Also occurs when the mouse is pressed, released, or clicked within the bounding area.
PopupMenuEvent	when the JPopupMenu will become visible, will become invisible, or if the menu is canceled.
PropertyChangeEvent	when any properties associated with the JPopupMenu are changed.

javax.swing.JProgressBar

AncestorEvent	when the JProgressBar or one of its ancestor containers is moved or if an ancestor container is added to or removed from the JProgressBar object's component hierarchy.

ChangeEvent	when the value of the JProgressBar is changed.
ComponentEvent	when the JProgressBar is shown, hidden, moved, or resized.
HierarchyEvent	when the position, size, contents, or visibility of some element of the JProgressBar object's component hierarchy is changed.
MouseEvent	when the mouse is moved in, dragged across, enters, or exits the bounding area of the JProgressBar. Also occurs when the mouse is pressed, released, or clicked within the bounding area.
PropertyChangeEvent	when any properties associated with the JProgressBar are changed.

javax.swing.JRadioButton

ActionEvent	when the mouse is clicked over the JRadioButton.
AncestorEvent	when the JRadioButton or one of its ancestor containers is moved or if an ancestor container is added to or removed from the JRadioButton object's component hierarchy.
ChangeEvent	when a change is made to one of the properties of the button model associated with the JRadioButton.
ComponentEvent	when the JRadioButton is shown, hidden, moved, or resized.
FocusEvent	when the JRadioButton gains or loses focus.
HierarchyEvent	when the position, size, contents, or visibility of some element of the JRadioButton object's component hierarchy is changed.
ItemEvent	when the JRadioButton is selected or deselected.
KeyEvent	when the JRadioButton has focus and a key is pressed, released, or typed.
MouseEvent	when the mouse is moved in, dragged across, enters, or exits the bounding area of the JRadioButton. Also occurs when the mouse is pressed, released, or clicked within the bounding area.
PropertyChangeEvent	when any properties associated with the JRadioButton are changed.

javax.swing.JRadioButtonMenuItem

ActionEvent	when the mouse is released over the JRadioButtonMenuItem.
AncestorEvent	when the JRadioButtonMenuItem or one of its ancestor containers is moved or if an ancestor container is added to or removed from the JRadioButtonMenuItem object's component hierarchy.
ChangeEvent	when a change is made to one of the properties of the button model associated with the JRadioButtonMenuItem.
ComponentEvent	when the JRadioButtonMenuItem is moved or resized.
HierarchyEvent	when the position, size, contents, or visibility of some element of the JRadioButtonMenuItem object's component hierarchy is changed.
ItemEvent	when the JRadioButtonMenuItem is selected or deselected.
MenuDragMouseEvent	when the JRadioButtonMenuItem is selected and the mouse is dragged inside its bounding area.
MenuKeyEvent	when the JRadioButtonMenuItem is selected and a key is pressed, released, or typed.
MouseEvent	when the mouse is moved in, enters, or exits the bounding area of the JRadioButtonMenuItem. Also occurs when the mouse is pressed or released within the bounding area.
PropertyChangeEvent	when any properties associated with the JRadioButtonMenuItem are changed.

javax.swing.JRootPane

AncestorEvent	when the JRootPane or one of its ancestor containers is moved or if an ancestor container is added to or removed from the JRootPane object's component hierarchy.
ComponentEvent	when the JRootPane is shown, hidden, moved, or resized.
HierarchyEvent	when the position, size, contents, or visibility of some element of the JRootPane object's component hierarchy is changed.

MouseEvent	when the mouse is moved in, is dragged across, enters, or exits the bounding area of the JRootPane. Also occurs when the mouse is pressed, released, or clicked within the bounding area.
PropertyChangeEvent	when any properties associated with the JRootPane are changed.

javax.swing.JScrollBar

AdjustmentEvent	when the value of the JScrollBar is changed.
AncestorEvent	when the JScrollBar or one of its ancestor containers is moved or if an ancestor container is added to or removed from the JScrollBar object's component hierarchy.
ComponentEvent	when the JScrollBar is shown, hidden, moved, or resized.
HierarchyEvent	when the position, size, contents, or visibility of some element of the JScrollBar object's component hierarchy is changed.
MouseEvent	when the mouse is moved in, dragged across, enters, or exits the bounding area of the JScrollBar. Also occurs when the mouse is pressed, released, or clicked within the bounding area.
PropertyChangeEvent	when any properties associated with the JScrollBar are changed.

javax.swing.JScrollPane

AncestorEvent	when the JScrollPane or one of its ancestor containers is moved or if an ancestor container is added to or removed from the JScrollPane object's component hierarchy.
ComponentEvent	when the JScrollPane is shown, hidden, moved, or resized.
ContainerEvent	when a component is added to or removed from the JScrollPane.
HierarchyEvent	when the position, size, contents, or visibility of some element of the JScrollPane object's component hierarchy is changed.

MouseEvent	when the mouse is moved in, dragged across, enters, or exits the bounding area of the JScrollPane. Also occurs when the mouse is pressed, released, or clicked within the bounding area.
PropertyChangeEvent	when any properties associated with the JScrollPane are changed.

javax.swing.JSeparator

AncestorEvent	when the JSeparator or one of its ancestor containers is moved or if an ancestor container is added to or removed from the JSeparator object's component hierarchy.
ComponentEvent	when the JSeparator is shown, hidden, moved, or resized.
HierarchyEvent	when the position, size, contents, or visibility of some element of the JSeparator object's component hierarchy is changed.
MouseEvent	when the mouse is moved in, dragged across, enters, or exits the bounding area of the JSeparator. Also occurs when the mouse is pressed, released, or clicked within the bounding area.
PropertyChangeEvent	when any properties associated with the JSeparator are changed.

javax.swing.JSlider

AncestorEvent	when the JSlider or one of its ancestor containers is moved or if an ancestor container is added to or removed from the JSlider object's component hierarchy.
ChangeEvent	when the value of the JSlider is changed.
ComponentEvent	when the JSlider is shown, hidden, moved, or resized.
FocusEvent	when the JSlider gains or loses focus.
HierarchyEvent	when the position, size, contents, or visibility of some element of the JSlider object's component hierarchy is changed.
KeyEvent	when the JSlider has focus and a key is pressed, released, or typed.

MouseEvent	when the mouse is moved in, dragged across, enters, or exits the bounding area of the JSlider. Also occurs when the mouse is pressed, released, or clicked within the bounding area.
PropertyChangeEvent	when any properties associated with the JSlider are changed.

javax.swing.JSplitPane

AncestorEvent	when the JSplitPane or one of its ancestor containers is moved or if an ancestor container is added to or removed from the JSplitPane object's component hierarchy.
ComponentEvent	when the JSplitPane is shown, hidden, moved, or resized.
ContainerEvent	when a component is added to or removed from the JSplitPane.
HierarchyEvent	when the position, size, contents, or visibility of some element of the JSplitPane object's component hierarchy is changed.
MouseEvent	when the mouse is moved in, dragged across, enters, or exits the bounding area of the JSplitPane. Also occurs when the mouse is pressed, released, or clicked within the bounding area.
PropertyChangeEvent	when any properties associated with the JSplitPane are changed.

javax.swing.JTabbedPane

AncestorEvent	when the JTabbedPane or one of its ancestor containers is moved or if an ancestor container is added to or removed from the JTabbedPane object's component hierarchy.
ChangeEvent	when the selected tab of the JTabbedPane changes.
ComponentEvent	when the JTabbedPane is shown, hidden, moved, or resized.
ContainerEvent	when a component is added to or removed from the JTabbedPane.

HierarchyEvent	when the position, size, contents, or visibility of some element of the JTabbedPane object's component hierarchy is changed.
MouseEvent	when the mouse is moved in, dragged across, enters, or exits the bounding area of the JTabbedPane. Also occurs when the mouse is pressed, released, or clicked within the bounding area.
PropertyChangeEvent	when any properties associated with the JTabbedPane are changed.

javax.swing.table.JTable

AncestorEvent	when the JTable or one of its ancestor containers is moved or if an ancestor container is added to or removed from the JTable object's component hierarchy.
ChangeEvent	when the margin of one of the columns of the JTable changes or if the editing session of a JTable cell is canceled or stopped.
ComponentEvent	when the JTable is shown, hidden, moved, or resized.
ContainerEvent	when a component is added to or removed from the JTable. If one of the JTable entries is edited, a ContainerEvent is generated.
FocusEvent	when the JTable gains or loses focus.
HierarchyEvent	when the position, size, contents, or visibility of some element of the JTable object's component hierarchy is changed.
KeyEvent	when the JTable has focus and a key is pressed, released, or typed.
ListSelectionEvent	when the selected column of a JTable changes.
MouseEvent	when the mouse is moved in, dragged across, enters, or exits the bounding area of the JTable. Also occurs when the mouse is pressed, released, or clicked within the bounding area.
PropertyChangeEvent	when any properties associated with the JTable are changed.

TableColumnModelEvent	when the TableColumnModel associated with the JTable is changed by adding, removing, or moving a column in the model.
TableModelEvent	when a change is made to the TableModel associated with the JTable.

javax.swing.JTextArea

AncestorEvent	when the JTextArea or one of its ancestor containers is moved or if an ancestor container is added to or removed from the JTextArea object's component hierarchy.
CaretEvent	when the caret position of the JTextArea is changed.
ComponentEvent	when the JTextArea is shown, hidden, moved, or resized.
DocumentEvent	when text is inserted in or removed from the JTextArea or if one or more attributes of the Document object associated with the JTextArea are changed.
FocusEvent	when the JTextArea gains or loses focus.
HierarchyEvent	when the position, size, contents, or visibility of some element of the JTextArea object's component hierarchy is changed.
KeyEvent	when the JTextArea has focus and a key is pressed, released, or typed.
MouseEvent	when the mouse is moved in, dragged across, enters, or exits the bounding area of the JTextArea. Also occurs when the mouse is pressed, released, or clicked within the bounding area.
PropertyChangeEvent	when any properties associated with the JTextArea are changed.
UndoableEditEvent	when an edit that can be undone is performed inside the JTextArea.

javax.swing.text.JTextComponent

The JTextComponent class is the parent of the Swing text component classes JEditorPane, JTextArea, JTextField, and JPasswordField. The JTextComponent class defines the methods to add and remove CaretListener and InputMethodListener objects.

javax.swing.JTextField

ActionEvent	when the JTextField has keyboard focus and the Return or Enter key is pressed.
AncestorEvent	when the JTextField or one of its ancestor containers is moved or if an ancestor container is added to or removed from the JTextField object's component hierarchy.
CaretEvent	when the caret position of the JTextField is changed.
ComponentEvent	when the JTextField is shown, hidden, moved, or resized.
DocumentEvent	when text is inserted in or removed from the JTextField or if one or more attributes of the Document object associated with the JTextField are changed.
FocusEvent	when the JTextField gains or loses focus.
HierarchyEvent	when the position, size, contents, or visibility of some element of the JTextField object's component hierarchy is changed.
KeyEvent	when the JTextField has focus and a key is pressed, released, or typed.
MouseEvent	when the mouse is moved in, dragged across, enters, or exits the bounding area of the JTextField. Also occurs when the mouse is pressed, released, or clicked within the bounding area.
PropertyChangeEvent	when any properties associated with the JTextField are changed.
UndoableEditEvent	when an edit that can be undone is performed inside the JTextField.

javax.swing.JTextPane

AncestorEvent	when the JTextPane or one of its ancestor containers is moved or if an ancestor container is added to or removed from the JTextPane object's component hierarchy.
CaretEvent	when the caret position inside the JTextPane changes.

ComponentEvent	when the JTextPane is shown, hidden, moved, or resized.
DocumentEvent	when text is inserted in or removed from the JTextPane or if one or more attributes of the Document object associated with the JTextPane are changed.
FocusEvent	when the JTextPane gains or loses focus.
HierarchyEvent	when the position, size, contents, or visibility of some element of the JTextPane object's component hierarchy is changed.
KeyEvent	when the JTextPane has focus and a key is pressed, released, or typed.
MouseEvent	when the mouse is moved in, dragged across, enters, or exits the bounding area of the JTextPane. Also occurs when the mouse is pressed, released, or clicked within the bounding area.
PropertyChangeEvent	when any properties associated with the JTextPane are changed.
UndoableEditEvent	when an edit that can be undone is performed inside the JTextPane.

javax.swing.JToggleButton

ActionEvent	when the mouse is clicked over the JToggleButton.
AncestorEvent	when the JToggleButton or one of its ancestor containers is moved or if an ancestor container is added to or removed from the JToggleButton object's component hierarchy.
ChangeEvent	when a change is made to one of the properties of the button model associated with the JToggleButton.
ComponentEvent	when the JToggleButton is shown, hidden, moved, or resized.
FocusEvent	when the JToggleButton gains or loses focus.
HierarchyEvent	when the position, size, contents, or visibility of some element of the JToggleButton object's component hierarchy is changed.
ItemEvent	when the JToggleButton is selected or deselected.
KeyEvent	when the JToggleButton has focus and a key is pressed, released, or typed.

MouseEvent	when the mouse is moved in, dragged across, enters, or exits the bounding area of the JToggleButton. Also occurs when the mouse is pressed, released, or clicked within the bounding area.
PropertyChangeEvent	when any properties associated with the JToggleButton are changed.

javax.swing.JToolBar

AncestorEvent	when the JToolBar or one of its ancestor containers is moved or if an ancestor container is added to or removed from the JToolBar object's component hierarchy.
ComponentEvent	when the JToolBar is shown, hidden, moved, or resized.
ContainerEvent	when a component is added to removed from the JToolBar.
FocusEvent	when the JToolBar gains or loses focus.
HierarchyEvent	when the position, size, contents, or visibility of some element of the JToolBar object's component hierarchy is changed.
MouseEvent	when the mouse is moved in, is dragged across, enters, or exits the bounding area of the JToolBar. Also occurs when the mouse is pressed, released, or clicked within the bounding area.
PropertyChangeEvent	when any properties associated with the JToolBar are changed

javax.swing.tree.JTree

AncestorEvent	when the JTree or one of its ancestor containers is moved or if an ancestor container is added to or removed from the JTree object's component hierarchy.
ChangeEvent	when the editing session of a JTree node is canceled or stopped.
ComponentEvent	when the JTree is shown, hidden, moved, or resized.

ContainerEvent	when a component is added to or removed from the JTree. If one of the JTree nodes is edited, a ContainerEvent is generated.
FocusEvent	when the JTree gains or loses focus.
HierarchyEvent	when the position, size, contents, or visibility of some element of the JTree object's component hierarchy is changed.
KeyEvent	when the JTree has focus and a key is pressed, released, or typed.
MouseEvent	when the mouse is moved in, dragged across, enters, or exits the bounding area of the JTree. Also occurs when the mouse is pressed, released, or clicked within the bounding area.
PropertyChangeEvent	when any properties associated with the JTree are changed.
TreeExpansionEvent	when a node of the JTree is about to expand, has expanded, is about to collapse, or has collapsed.
TreeModelEvent	when a node is added or removed from the JTree or if the TreeModel associated with the JTree changes in some other way.
TreeSelectionEvent	when the selected node of the JTree changes.

javax.swing.JViewport

AncestorEvent	when the JViewport or one of its ancestor containers is moved or if an ancestor container is added to or removed from the JViewport object's component hierarchy.
ChangeEvent	when the JViewport changes its extent size, view size, or the area of the component that is displayed.
ComponentEvent	when the JViewport is shown, hidden, moved, or resized.
HierarchyEvent	when the position, size, contents, or visibility of some element of the JViewport object's component hierarchy is changed.
PropertyChangeEvent	when any properties associated with the JViewport are changed, except those that cause a ChangeEvent.

javax.swing.JWindow

ComponentEvent	when the JWindow is shown, hidden, moved, or resized.
FocusEvent	when the JWindow gains or loses focus.
HierarchyEvent	when the position, size, contents, or visibility of some element of the JWindow object's component hierarchy is changed.
KeyEvent	when the JWindow has focus and a key is pressed, released, or typed.
MouseEvent	when the mouse is moved in, is dragged across, enters, or exits the bounding area of the JWindow. Also occurs when the mouse is pressed, released, or clicked within the bounding area.
PropertyChangeEvent	when any properties associated with the JWindow are changed.
WindowEvent	when the JWindow is activated, deactivated, opened, closed, closing, iconified, or deiconified.

java.awt.Label

ComponentEvent	when the Label is shown, hidden, moved, or resized.
FocusEvent	when the Label gains or loses focus.
HierarchyEvent	when the position, size, contents, or visibility of some element of the Label object's component hierarchy is changed.
KeyEvent	when the Label has keyboard focus and a key is pressed, released, or typed.
MouseEvent	when the mouse is moved in, is dragged across, enters, or exits the bounding area of the Label. Also occurs when the mouse is pressed, released, or clicked within the bounding area.
PropertyChangeEvent	when any properties associated with the Label are changed.

java.awt.List

ActionEvent	when the mouse is double-clicked on a List element.

ComponentEvent	when the List is shown, hidden, moved, or resized.
FocusEvent	when the List gains or loses focus.
HierarchyEvent	when the position, size, contents, or visibility of some element of the List object's component hierarchy is changed.
ItemEvent	when the mouse is single-clicked on a List element.
KeyEvent	when the List has keyboard focus and a key is pressed, released, or typed.
MouseEvent	when the mouse is moved in, is dragged across, enters, or exits the bounding area of the List. Also occurs when the mouse is pressed, released, or clicked within the bounding area.
PropertyChangeEvent	when any properties associated with the List are changed.

java.awt.Menu

ActionEvent	when any element contained by the Menu is selected.

java.awt.MenuBar

Does not generate any events.

java.awt.MenuComponent

The MenuComponent class is the parent of all AWT menu components. It defines the `addActionListener()` and `removeActionListener()` methods.

java.awt.MenuItem

ActionEvent	when the MenuItem is selected.

java.awt.Panel

ComponentEvent	when the Panel is shown, hidden, moved, or resized.
ContainerEvent	when a component is added or removed from the Panel.

HierarchyEvent	when the position, size, contents, or visibility of some element of the Panel object's component hierarchy is changed.
MouseEvent	when the mouse is moved in, is dragged across, enters, or exits the bounding area of the Panel. Also occurs when the mouse is pressed, released, or clicked within the bounding area.
PropertyChangeEvent	when any properties associated with the Panel are changed.

java.awt.PopupMenu

ActionEvent	when any element contained in the PopupMenu is selected.

javax.swing.ProgressMonitor

Does not generate any events.

java.awt.Robot

The Robot class defines methods that simulate KeyEvents and MouseEvents.

java.awt.Scrollbar

AdjustmentEvent	when the value of the Scrollbar is changed.
ComponentEvent	when the Scrollbar is shown, hidden, moved, or resized.
HierarchyEvent	when the position, size, contents, or visibility of some element of the Scrollbar object's component hierarchy is changed.
MouseEvent	when the mouse is enters, exits, or is moved inside the bounding area of the Scrollbar.
PropertyChangeEvent	when any properties associated with the Scrollbar are changed.

java.awt.ScrollPane

ComponentEvent	when the ScrollPane is shown, hidden, moved, or resized.
ContainerEvent	when a component is added or removed from the ScrollPane.

HierarchyEvent	when the position, size, contents, or visibility of some element of the ScrollPane object's component hierarchy is changed.
MouseEvent	when the mouse is moved in, is dragged across, enters, or exits the bounding area of the ScrollPane. Also occurs when the mouse is pressed, released, or clicked within the bounding area.
PropertyChangeEvent	when any properties associated with the ScrollPane are changed.

java.awt.TextArea

ComponentEvent	when the TextArea is shown, hidden, moved, or resized.
FocusEvent	when the TextArea gains or loses focus.
HierarchyEvent	when the position, size, contents, or visibility of some element of the TextArea object's component hierarchy is changed.
KeyEvent	when the TextArea has keyboard focus and a key is pressed, released, or typed.
MouseEvent	when the mouse is moved in, is dragged across, enters, or exits the bounding area of the TextArea. Also occurs when the mouse is pressed, released, or clicked within the bounding area.
TextEvent	when the text inside the TextArea is changed
PropertyChangeEvent	when any properties associated with the TextArea are changed.

java.awt.TextComponent

The TextComponent class is the parent of the AWT text component classes TextArea and TextField. It defines the `addTextListener()` and `removeTextListener()` methods used by its subclasses.

java.awt.TextField

ActionEvent	when the TextField has focus and the Enter or Return key is pressed
ComponentEvent	when the TextField is shown, hidden, moved, or resized.

FocusEvent	when the TextField gains or loses focus.
HierarchyEvent	when the position, size, contents, or visibility of some element of the TextField object's component hierarchy is changed.
KeyEvent	when the TextField has keyboard focus and a key is pressed, released, or typed.
MouseEvent	when the mouse is moved in, is dragged across, enters, or exits the bounding area of the TextField. Also occurs when the mouse is pressed, released, or clicked within the bounding area.
TextEvent	when the text inside the TextField is changed
PropertyChangeEvent	when any properties associated with the TextField are changed.

javax.swing.Timer

ActionEvent	one or more times after a specified delay.

java.awt.Window

ComponentEvent	when the Window is shown, hidden, moved, or resized.
ContainerEvent	when a component is added or removed from the Window.
HierarchyEvent	when the position, size, contents, or visibility of some element of the Window object's component hierarchy is changed.
MouseEvent	when the mouse enters or exits the bounding area of the Window.
WindowEvent	when the Window is activated, deactivated, opened, closed, closing, iconified, or deiconified.
PropertyChangeEvent	when any properties associated with the Window are changed.

INDEX

A
_postEdit() method
  UndoableEditSupport class, 277
Abstract Window Toolkit, 2
action() method
  Event class, 8
ActionEvent class, 27, 80
  getActionCommand(), 82
  getModifiers() , 82
  paramString(), 82
ActiveEvent interface, 86
  dispatch(), 87
ActionListener interface, 39, 296
  actionPerformed(), 296
  addActionListener(), 297
  removeActionListener(), 297
actionPerformed() method
  ActionListener interface, 297
  AWTEventMulticaster class, 454
add() method
  AWTEventMulticaster class, 453
  EventListenerList class, 462
addActionListener() method, 297
addAdjustmentListener() method, 299
addAncestorListener() method, 301
addAWTEventListener() method, 302
addCaretListener() method, 305
addCellEditorListener() method, 307
addChangeListener() method, 311
addColumnModelListener() method, 368
addComponentListener() method, 314
addContainerListener() method, 318
addDocumentListener() method, 319
addFocusListener() method, 322
addHierarchyBoundsListener() method, 324
addHierarchyListener() method, 327
addHyperlinkListener() method, 332
addInputMethodListener() method, 334
addInternal() method
  AWTEventMulticaster class, 456
addInternalFrameListener() method, 336
addItemListener() method, 337
addKeyListener() method, 340
addListDataListener() method, 342
addListSelectionListener() method, 345
addMenuDragMouseListener() method, 347
addMenuKeyListener() method, 349
addMenuListener() method, 351
addMouseListener() method, 357
addMouseMotionListener() method, 361
addPopupMenuListener() method, 364
addPropertyChangeListener() method
  PropertyChangeSupport class, 271
  SwingPropertyChangeSupport class, 273
addTableModelListener() method, 370
addTextListener() method, 372
addTreeExpansionListener() method, 373
addTreeModelListener() method, 378
addTreeSelectionListener() method, 379
addTreeWillExpandListener() method, 381
addUndoableEditListener() method
  UndoableEditSupport class, 277
addVetoableChangeListener() method
  VetoableChangeSupport class, 285
addWindowListener() method, 387
AdjustmentEvent class, 27, 92
  getAdjustable(), 94
  getAdjustmentType(), 94
  getValue(), 95
  paramString(), 95
AdjustmentListener interface, 39, 298
  addAdjustmentListener(), 299
  adjustmentValueChanged(), 298
  removeAdjustmentListener(), 299
adjustmentValueChanged() method
  AdjustmentListener interface, 299

adjustmentValueChanged() method *(cont.)*
    AWTEventMulticaster class, 454
ancestorAdded() method
    AncestorListener interface, 300
AncestorEvent class, 28, 98
    getAncestor(), 100
    getAncestorParent(), 100
    getComponent(), 100
AncestorListener interface, 41, 299
    addAncestorListener(), 301
    ancestorAdded(), 300
    ancestorMoved(), 300
    ancestorRemoved(), 300
    removeAncestorListener(), 301
ancestorMoved() method
    AncestorListener interface, 300
    AWTEventMulticaster class, 454
    HierarchyBoundsAdapter class, 401
    HierarchyBoundsListener interface, 323
ancestorRemoved() method
    AncestorListener interface, 300
ancestorResized() method
    AWTEventMulticaster class, 454
    HierarchyBoundsAdapter class, 401
    HierarchyBoundsListener interface, 323
AWTEvent class, 26, 103
    consume(), 105
    finalize(), 105
    getID(), 105
    isConsumed(), 105
    paramString(), 105
    toString(), 105
AWTEventListener interface, 39, 301
    addAWTEventListener(), 302
    eventDispatched(), 302
    removeAWTEventListener(), 302
AWTEventMulticaster class, 60, 451

B
BeanContextEvent class, 268
BeanContextMembershipEvent class, 268
BeanContextMembershipListener interface, 390
BeanContextServiceAvailableEvent class, 268
BeanContextServiceRevokedEvent class, 268
BeanContextServiceRevokedListener interface, 390
BeanContextServicesListener interface, 390
beginUpdate() method
    UndoableEditSupport class, 277

C
CaretEvent class, 29, 106
    getDot(), 107
    getMark(), 107

CaretListener interface, 41, 304
    addCaretListener(), 305
    caretUpdate(), 305
    removeCaretListener(), 305
caretPositionChanged() method
    AWTEventMulticaster class, 454
    InputMethodListener interface, 333
caretUpdate() method
    CaretListener interface, 305
CellEditorListener interface, 41, 306
    addCellEditorListener(), 307
    editingCanceled(), 307
    editingStopped(), 307
    removeCellEditorListener(), 307
changedUpdate() method
    DocumentListener interface, 319
ChangeEvent class, 29, 110
ChangeListener interface, 41, 310
    addChangeListener(), 311
    removeChangeListener(), 311
    stateChanged(), 311
cloneWithSource() method
    TreeSelectionEvent class, 255
coalesceEvents() method
    Component class, 17, 427
columnAdded() method
    TableColumnModelListener interface, 368
columnMarginChanged() method
    TableColumnModelListener interface, 368
columnMoved() method
    TableColumnModelListener interface, 368
columnRemoved() method
    TableColumnModelListener interface, 368
columnSelectionChanged() method
    TableColumnModelListener interface, 368
ComponentAdapter class, 391
    componentHidden(), 392
    componentMoved(), 392
    componentResized(), 392
    componentShown(), 392
componentAdded() method
    AWTEventMulticaster class, 454
    ContainerAdapter class, 394
    ContainerListener interface, 317
ComponentEvent class, 26, 114
    getComponent(), 115
    paramString(), 115
componentHidden() method
    AWTEventMulticaster class, 454
    ComponentAdapter class, 392
    ComponentListener interface, 313
ComponentListener interface, 39, 312
    addComponentListener(), 314

INDEX

componentHidden(), 313
componentMoved(), 313
componentResized(), 313
componentShown(), 313
removeComponentListener(), 314
componentMoved() method
    AWTEventMulticaster class, 454
    ComponentAdapter class, 392
    ComponentListener interface, 313
componentRemoved() method
    AWTEventMulticaster class, 454
    ContainerAdapter class, 394
    ContainerListener interface, 317
componentResized() method
    ComponentAdapter class, 392
    ComponentListener interface, 313
componentShown() method
    AWTEventMulticaster class, 454
    ComponentAdapter class, 392
    ComponentListener interface, 313
consume() method
    AWTEvent class, 105
    InputEvent class, 157
    InputMethodEvent class, 161
ContainerAdapter class, 393
    componentAdded(), 394
    componentRemoved(), 394
ContainerEvent class, 26, 118
    getChild(), 120
    getContainer(), 120
    paramString(), 120
ContainerListener interface, 39, 316
    addContainerListener(), 318
    componentAdded(), 317
    componentRemoved(), 317
    removeContainerListener(), 318
contentsChanged() method
    ListDataListener interface, 343
ControllerEventListener interface, 390
createCompoundEdit() method
    UndoableEditSupport class, 277

D

DefaultStyledDocument class, 497
deliverEvent() method
    Component class, 20, 428
disableEvents() method
    Component class, 17, 427
    MenuItem class, 444
dispatch() method
    ActiveEvent interface, 87
    InvocationEvent class, 171

dispatchEvent() method
    Component class, 17, 427
    EventQueue class, 71
Distributed event model, 514
DocumentEvent interface, 31, 124
    getChange(), 125
    getDocument(), 125
    getLength(), 125
    getOffset(), 125
    getType(), 125
DocumentEvent.ElementChange interface, 127
    getChildrenAdded(), 128
    getChildrenRemoved(), 128
    getElement(), 128
    getIndex(), 128
DocumentEvent.EventType class, 128
DocumentListener interface, 41, 318
    addDocumentListener(), 319
    changedUpdate(), 319
    insertUpdate(), 319
    removeDocumentListener(), 319
    removeUpdate(), 319
DragGestureEvent class, 268
DragGestureListener interface, 390
DragSourceEvent class, 268
DragSourceDragEvent class, 268
DragSourceDropEvent class, 268
DragSourceListener interface, 390
DropTargetDragEvent class, 268
DropTargetDropEvent class, 268
DropTargetEvent class, 268
DropTargetListener interface, 390

E

editingCanceled() method
    CellEditorListener interface, 307
editingStopped() method
    CellEditorListener interface, 307
enableEvents() method
    Component class, 17, 427
    MenuItem class, 444
endUpdate() method
    UndoableEditSupport class, 277
Event consumption, 67
eventDispatched() method
    AWTEventListener interface, 302
event dispatching thread, 75
    running code from, 75
EventListener interface, 39, 320
EventListenerList class, 61, 461
Event listeners, 43
    connecting to an event source, 55
    creating, 44

Event listeners *(cont.)*
  disconnecting from an event source, 56
  user-defined, 54, 472
EventObject class, 25, 129
  getSource(), 130
  toString(), 130
Event queue, 70
EventQueue class, 71
  dispatchEvent(), 71
  getNextEvent(), 71
  invokeAndWait(), 71
  invokeLater(), 72
  isDispatchThread(), 72
  peekEvent(), 72
  pop(), 72
  postEvent(), 72
  push(), 72
EventRegistration class, 528
  getID(), 529
  getLease(), 529
  getSequenceNumber(), 529
  getSource(), 529
Events
  class hierarchy, 23
  definition of, 3
  determining source of, 63
  evolution of, 4
  life cycle, 15
  local vs. distributed, 4
  low-level vs. high-level, 25
  user-defined, 36, 473
  user-generated, 33

F
finalize() method
  AWTEvent class, 105
fireActionEvent() method
  JComboBox class, 433
fireActionPerformed() method
  AbstractButton class, 422
  DefaultButtonModel class, 431
  JTextField class, 442
  Timer class, 447
fireAdjustmentValueChanged() method
  JScrollBar class, 441
fireContentsChanged() method
  AbstractListModel class, 423
fireEditingCanceled() method
  AbstractCellEditor class, 423
fireEditingStopped() method
  AbstractCellEditor class, 423
fireHyperlinkEvent() method
  JEditorPane class, 436

fireInternalFrameEvent() method
  JInternalFrame class, 437
fireIntervalAdded() method
  AbstractListModel class, 423
fireIntervalRemoved() method
  AbstractListModel class, 423
fireItemStateChanged() method
  AbstractButton class, 422
  DefaultButtonModel class, 431
  JComboBox class, 433
fireMenuCanceled() method
  JMenu class, 437
fireMenuDeselected() method
  JMenu class, 437
fireMenuDragMouseDragged() method
  JMenuItem class, 438
fireMenuDragMouseEntered() method
  JMenuItem class, 438
fireMenuDragMouseExited() method
  JMenuItem class, 438
fireMenuDragMouseReleased() method
  JMenuItem class, 438
fireMenuKeyPressed() method
  JMenuItem class, 438
fireMenuKeyReleased() method
  JMenuItem class, 438
fireMenuKeyTyped() method
  JMenuItem class, 438
fireMenuSelected() method
  JMenu class, 437
firePopupMenuCanceled() method
  JPopupMenu class, 440
firePopupMenuWillBecomeInvisible() method
  JPopupMenu class, 440
firePopupMenuWillBecomeVisible() method
  JPopupMenu class, 440
firePropertyChange() method
  AbstractAction class, 422
  Component class, 20, 425
  DefaultListCellRenderer class, 431
  JComponent class, 433
  JViewport class, 443
  PropertyChangeSupport class, 271, 445
  SwingPropertyChangeSupport class, 273, 446
fireStateChanged() method
  AbstractButton class, 422
  DefaultBoundedRangeModel class, 430
  DefaultButtonModel class, 431
  DefaultSingleSelectionModel class, 432
  JProgressBar class, 441
  JSlider class, 441
  JTabbedPane class, 441
  JViewport class, 443

INDEX 581

fireTreeCollapsed() method
    JTree class, 442
fireTreeExpanded() method
    JTree class, 442
fireTreeWillCollapse() method
    JTree class, 442
fireTreeWillExpand() method
    JTree class, 442
fireValueChanged() method
    DefaultListSelectionModel class, 432
    JList class, 437
    JTree class, 442
fireVetoableChange() method
    JComponent class, 434
    VetoableChangeSupport class, 285, 447
FocusAdapter class, 397
    focusGained(), 398
    focusLost(), 398
FocusEvent class, 26, 131
    isTemporary(), 133
    paramString(), 133
focusGained() method
    AWTEventMulticaster class, 454
    FocusAdapter class, 398
    FocusListener interface, 321
FocusListener interface, 39, 320
    addFocusListener(), 322
    focusGained(), 321
    focusLost(), 321
    removeFocusListener(), 322
focusLost() method
    AWTEventMulticaster class, 454
    FocusAdapter class, 398
    FocusListener interface, 321

G

getActionCommand() method
    ActionEvent class, 82
getAdjustable() method
    AdjustmentEvent class, 94
getAdjustmentType() method
    AdjustmentEvent class, 94
getAncestor() method
    AncestorEvent class, 100
getAncestorParent() method
    AncestorEvent class, 100
getCaret() method
    InputMethodEvent class, 161
getChange() method
    DocumentEvent interface, 125
getChanged() method
    HierarchyEvent class, 139

getChangedParent() method
    HierarchyEvent class, 139
getChangeFlags() method
    HierarchyEvent class, 139
getChild() method
    ContainerEvent class, 120
getChildIndices() method
    TreeModelEvent class, 249
getChildren() method
    TreeModelEvent class, 249
getChildrenAdded() method
    DocumentEvent.ElementChange interface, 128
getChildrenRemoved() method
    DocumentEvent.ElementChange interface, 128
getClickCount() method
    MouseEvent class, 214
getColumn() method
    TableModelEvent class, 236
getCommittedCharacterCount() method
    InputMethodEvent class, 161
getComponent() method
    AncestorEvent class, 100
    ComponentEvent class, 115
    HierarchyEvent class, 139
getContainer() method
    ContainerEvent class, 120
getDescription() method
    HyperlinkEvent class, 151
getDocument() method
    DocumentEvent interface, 125
getDot() method
    CaretEvent class, 107
getEdit() method
    UndoableEditEvent class, 260
getElement() method
    DocumentEvent.EventChange interface, 128
getEventType() method
    HyperlinkEvent class, 151
getException() method
    InvocationEvent class, 171
getFirstIndex() method
    ListSelectionEvent class, 193
getFirstRow() method
    TableModelEvent class, 236
getFromIndex() method
    TableColumnModelEvent class, 231
getGroups() method
    RemoteDiscoveryEvent class, 520
getID() method
    AWTEvent class, 105
    EventRegistration class, 529
    RemoteEvent class, 517

getIndex() method
    DocumentEvent.EventChange
        interface, 128
getIndex0() method
    ListDataEvent class, 188
getIndex1() method
    ListDataEvent class, 188
getInternalFrame() method
    InternalFrameEvent class, 165
getItem() method
    ItemEvent class, 176
getItemSelectable() method
    ItemEvent class, 176
getKeyChar() method
    KeyEvent class, 182
getKeyCode() method
    KeyEvent class, 182
getKeyModifiersText() method
    KeyEvent class, 182
getKeyText() method
    KeyEvent class, 182
getLastIndex() method
    ListSelectionEvent class, 193
getLastRow() method
    TableModelEvent class, 236
getLease() method
    EventRegistration class, 529
    RenewalFailureEvent class, 522
getLength() method
    DocumentEvent interface, 125
getListenerCount() method
    EventListenerList class, 462
getListenerList() method
    EventListenerList class, 462
getListeners() method, 59
    EventListenerList class, 462
getMark() method
    CaretEvent class, 107
getMenuSelectionManager() method
    MenuDragMouseEvent class, 197
    MenuKeyMouseEvent class, 207
getModifiers() method,
    ActionEvent class, 82
    InputEvent class, 157
getNewLeadSelectionPath() method
    TreeSelectionEvent class, 255
getNewValue() method
    PropertyChangeEvent class, 224
getNextEvent() method
    EventQueue class, 71
getOffset() method
    DocumentEvent interface, 125

getOldLeadSelectionPath() method
    TreeSelectionEvent class, 255
getOldValue() method
    PropertyChangeEvent class, 224
getPath() method
    MenuDragMouseEvent class, 197
    MenuKeyMouseEvent class, 207
    TreeExpansionEvent class, 244
    TreeModelEvent class, 249
    TreeSelectionEvent class, 255
getPaths() method
    TreeSelectionEvent class, 255
getPoint() method
    MouseEvent class, 214
getPropagationID() method
    PropertyChangeEvent class, 224
getPropertyName() method
    PropertyChangeEvent class, 224
getRegistrars() method
    RemoteDiscoveryEvent class, 520
getRegistrationObject() method
    RemoteEvent class, 517
getSequenceNumber() method
    EventRegistration class, 529
    RemoteEvent class, 517
getServiceID() method
    ServiceEvent class, 525
getServiceItem() method
    ServiceEvent class, 525
getSource() method
    EventObject, 130
    EventRegistration class, 529
getSourceElement() method
    HTMLFrameHyperlinkEvent class, 144
getStateChange() method
    ItemEvent class, 176
getTarget() method
    HTMLFrameHyperlinkEvent class, 144
getText() method
    InputMethodEvent class, 161
getThrowable() method
    RenewalFailureEvent class, 522
getToIndex() method
    TableColumnModelEvent class, 231
getTransition() method
    ServiceEvent class, 525
getTreePath() method
    TreeModelEvent class, 249
getType() method
    DocumentEvent interface, 125
    ListDataEvent class, 188
    TableModelEvent class, 236

getUpdateLevel() method
   UndoableEditSupport class, 277
getURL() method
   HyperlinkEvent class, 151
getValue() method
   AdjustmentEvent class, 95
getValueIsAdjusting() method
   ListSelectionEvent class, 193
getVisiblePosition() method
   InputMethodEvent class, 161
getWhen() method
   InputEvent class, 157
getWindow() method
   WindowEvent class, 265
getX() method
   MouseEvent class, 214
getY() method
   MouseEvent class, 214
gotFocus() method
   Event class, 8

H

handleEvent() method
   Component class, 20, 428
hasListeners() method
   PropertyChangeSupport class, 271
   SwingPropertyChangeSupport class, 273
   VetoableChangeSupport class, 285
HierarchyBoundsAdapter class, 400
   ancestorMoved(), 401
   ancestorResized(), 401
HierarchyBoundsListener interface, 39, 322
   addHierarchyBoundsListener(), 324
   ancestorMoved(), 323
   ancestorResized(), 323
   removeHierarchyBoundsListener(), 324
hierarchyChanged() method
   AWTEventMulticaster class, 454
   HierarchyListener interface, 327
HierarchyEvent class, 26, 136
   getChanged(), 139
   getChangedParent(), 139
   getChangeFlags(), 139
   getComponent(), 139
   paramString(), 139
HierarchyListener interface, 39, 327
   addHierarchyListener(), 327
   hierarchyChanged(), 327
   removeHierarchyListener(), 327
HTMLFrameHyperlinkEvent class, 32, 142
   getSourceElement(), 144
   getTarget(), 144

HyperlinkEvent class, 29, 149
   getDescription(), 151
   getEventType(), 151
   getURL(), 151
HyperlinkEvent.EventType class, 155
HyperlinkListener interface, 41, 331
   addHyperlinkListener(), 332
   hyperlinkUpdate(), 331
   removeHyperlinkListener(), 332
hyperlinkUpdate() method
   HyperlinkListener interface, 331

I

InputEvent class, 156
   consume(), 157
   getModifiers(), 157
   getWhen(), 157
   isAltDown(), 157
   isAltGraphDown(), 157
   isConsumed(), 157
   isControlDown(), 158
   isMetaDown(), 158
   isShiftDown(), 158
InputMethodEvent class, 26, 159
   consume(), 161
   getCaret(), 161
   getCommittedCharacterCount(), 161
   getText(), 161
   getVisiblePosition(), 161
   isConsumed(), 161
   paramString(), 161
InputMethodListener interface, 39, 332
   addInputMethodListener(), 334
   caretPositionChanged(), 333
   inputMethodTextChanged(), 333
   removeInputMethodListener(), 334
inputMethodTextChanged() method
   AWTEventMulticaster class, 454
   InputMethodListener interface, 333
insertUpdate() method
   DocumentListener interface, 319
Interfaces, 38
internalFrameActivated() method
   InternalFrameAdapter class, 403
   InternalFrameListener interface, 335
InternalFrameAdapter class, 402
   internalFrameActivated(), 403
   internalFrameClosed(), 403
   internalFrameClosing(), 403
   internalFrameDeactivated(), 403
   internalFrameDeiconified(), 403
   internalFrameIconified(), 403
   internalFrameOpened(), 403

internalFrameClosed() method
    InternalFrameAdapter class, 403
    InternalFrameListener interface, 335
internalFrameClosing() method
    InternalFrameAdapter class, 403
    InternalFrameListener interface, 335
internalFrameDeactivated() method
    InternalFrameAdapter class, 403
    InternalFrameListener interface, 335
internalFrameDeiconified() method
    InternalFrameAdapter class, 403
    InternalFrameListener interface, 335
InternalFrameEvent class, 29, 163
    getInternalFrame(), 165
    paramString(), 165
internalFrameIconified() method
    InternalFrameAdapter class, 403
    InternalFrameListener interface, 335
InternalFrameListener interface, 41, 334
    addInternalFrameListener(), 336
    internalFrameActivated(), 335
    internalFrameClosed(), 335
    internalFrameClosing(), 335
    internalFrameDeactivated(), 335
    internalFrameDeiconified(), 335
    internalFrameIconified(), 335
    internalFrameOpened(), 335
    removeInternalFrameListener(), 336
internalFrameOpened() method
    InternalFrameAdapter class, 403
    InternalFrameListener interface, 335
intervalAdded() method
    ListDataListener interface, 343
intervalRemoved() method
    ListDataListener interface, 343
InvocationEvent class, 28, 168
    dispatch(), 171
    getException(), 171
    paramString(), 171
invokeAndWait() method
    EventQueue class, 71
invokeLater() method
    EventQueue class, 72
isActionKey() method
    KeyEvent class, 182
isAddedPath() method
    TreeSelectionEvent class, 255
isAltDown() method
    InputEvent class, 157
isAltGraphDown() method
    InputEvent class, 157
isConsumed() method
    AWTEvent class, 105

InputEvent class, 157
InputMethodEvent class, 161
isControlDown() method
    InputEvent class, 158
isDiscarded() method
    RemoteDiscoveryEvent class, 520
isDispatchThread() method
    EventQueue class, 72
isMetaDown() method
    InputEvent class, 158
isPopupTrigger() method
    MouseEvent class, 214
isShiftDown() method
    InputEvent class, 158
isTemporary() method
    FocusEvent class, 133
ItemEvent class, 27, 174
    getItem(), 176
    getItemSelectable(), 176
    getStateChange(), 176
    paramString(), 176
ItemListener interface, 39, 337
    addItemListener(), 338
    itemStateChanged(), 337
    removeItemListener(), 338
itemStateChanged() method
    AWTEventMulticaster class, 454
    ItemListener interface, 337

J
Java event model
    1.0 event model, 6
    1.1 event model, 9
JavaSpaces, 513
Java Virtual Machine, 4
Jini, 513

K
KeyAdapter class, 407
    keyPressed(), 408
    keyReleased(), 408
    keyTyped(), 408
keyDown() method
    Event class, 8
KeyEvent class, 26, 179
    getKeyChar(), 182
    getKeyCode(), 182
    getKeyModifiersText(), 182
    getKeyText(), 182
    isActionKey(), 182
    paramString(), 182
    setKeyChar(), 183
    setKeyCode(), 183

Index

setModifiers(), 183
setSource(), 183
KeyListener interface, 40, 339
   addKeyListener() , 340
   keyPressed(), 339
   keyReleased(), 339
   keyTyped(), 339
   removeKeyListener(), 340
keyPressed() method
   AWTEventMulticaster class, 454
   KeyListener interface, 339
keyReleased() method
   AWTEventMulticaster class, 454
   KeyListener interface, 339
keyTyped() method
   AWTEventMulticaster class, 454
   KeyListener interface, 339
keyUp() method
   Event class, 8

L

LineEvent class, 268
LineListener interface, 390
ListDataEvent Class, 29, 186
   getIndex0(), 188
   getIndex1(), 188
   getType(), 188
ListDataListener interface, 41, 342
   addListDataListener(), 343
   contentsChanged(), 343
   intervalAdded(), 343
   intervalRemoved(), 343
   removeListDataListener(), 343
listener adapter classes, 50
ListSelectionEvent class, 29, 192
   getFirstIndex(), 193
   getLastIndex(), 193
   getValueIsAdjusting(), 193
   toString(), 193
ListSelectionListener interface, 41, 344
   addListSelectionListener(), 345
   removeListSelectionListener(), 345
   valueChanged(), 345
lostFocus() method
   Event class, 9

M

menuCanceled() method
   MenuListener interface, 350
menuDeselected() method
   MenuListener interface, 350

menuDragMouseDragged() method
   MenuDragMouseListener interface, 347
menuDragMouseEntered() method
   MenuDragMouseListener interface, 347
MenuDragMouseEvent class, 29, 196
   getMenuSelectionManager(), 197
   getPath(), 197
menuDragMouseExited() method
   MenuDragMouseListener interface, 347
MenuDragMouseListener interface, 41, 346
   addMenuDragMouseListener(), 347
   menuDragMouseDragged(), 347
   menuDragMouseEntered(), 347
   menuDragMouseExited(), 347
   menuDragMouseReleased(), 347
   removeMenuDragMouseListener(), 347
menuDragMouseReleased() method
   MenuDragMouseListener interface, 347
MenuEvent class, 29, 202
MenuKeyEvent class, 29, 205
   getMenuSelectionManager(), 207
   getPath(), 207
MenuKeyListener interface, 41, 348
   addMenuKeyListener(), 349
   menuKeyPressed(), 349
   menuKeyReleased(), 349
   menuKeyTyped(), 349
   removeMenuKeyListener(), 349
menuKeyPressed() method
   MenuKeyListener interface, 349
menuKeyReleased() method
   MenuKeyListener interface, 349
menuKeyTyped() method
   MenuKeyListener interface, 349
MenuListener interface, 41, 349
   addMenuListener(), 351
   menuCanceled(), 350
   menuDeselected(), 350
   menuSelected(), 350
   removeMenuListener(), 351
menuSelected() method
   MenuListener interface, 350
MetaEventListener interface, 390
MouseAdapter class, 408
   mouseClicked(), 409
   mouseEntered(), 409
   mouseExited(), 409
   mousePressed(), 409
   mouseReleased(), 409
mouseClicked() method
   AWTEventMulticaster class, 454
   MouseAdapter class, 409
   MouseInputAdapter class, 411

mouseClicked() method *(cont.)*
    MouseListener interface, 357
mouseDown() method
    Event class, 9
mouseDrag() method
    Event class, 9
mouseDragged() method
    AWTEventMulticaster class, 454
    MouseInputAdapter class, 411
    MouseMotionAdapter class, 416
    MouseMotionListener interface, 361
mouseEnter() method
    Event class, 9
mouseEntered() method
    AWTEventMulticaster class, 454
    MouseAdapter class, 409
    MouseInputAdapter class, 411
    MouseListener interface, 357
MouseEvent class, 26, 212
    getClickCount(), 214
    getPoint(), 214
    getX(), 214
    getY(), 214
    isPopupTrigger(), 214
    paramString(), 214
    translatePoint(), 214
mouseExit() method
    Event class, 9
mouseExited() method
    AWTEventMulticaster class, 454
    MouseAdapter class, 409
    MouseInputAdapter class, 411
    MouseListener interface, 357
MouseInputAdapter class, 411
    mouseClicked(), 411
    mouseDragged(), 411
    mouseEntered(), 411
    mouseExited(), 411
    mouseMoved(), 412
    mousePressed(), 412
    mouseReleased(), 412
MouseInputListener interface, 41, 351
MouseListener interface, 40, 356
    addMouseListener(), 357
    mouseClicked(), 357
    mouseEntered(), 357
    mouseExited(), 357
    mousePressed(), 357
    mouseReleased(), 357
    removeMouseListener(), 357
MouseMotionAdapter class, 415
    mouseDragged(), 416
    mouseMoved(), 416

MouseMotionListener interface, 40, 360
    addMouseMotionListener(), 361
    mouseDragged(), 361
    mouseMoved(), 361
    removeMouseMotionListener(), 361
mouseMove() method
    Event class, 9
mouseMoved() method
    AWTEventMulticaster class, 454
    MouseInputAdapter class, 412
    MouseMotionAdapter class, 416
    MouseMotionListener interface, 361
mousePressed() method
    AWTEventMulticaster class, 455
    MouseAdapter class, 409
    MouseInputAdapter class, 412
    MouseListener interface, 357
mouseReleased() method
    AWTEventMulticaster class, 455
    MouseAdapter class, 409
    MouseInputAdapter class, 412
    MouseListener interface, 357
mouseUp() method
    Event class, 9

N
NamespaceChangeListener interface, 390
NamingEvent class, 268
NamingExceptionEvent class, 268
NamingListener interface, 390
notify() method
    RemoteEventListener interface, 527

O
ObjectChangeListener, 390

P
PaintEvent class, 218
paramString() method
    ActionEvent class, 82
    AdjustmentEvent class, 95
    AWTEvent class, 105
    ComponentEvent class, 115
    ContainerEvent class, 120
    FocusEvent class, 133
    HierarchyEvent class, 139
    InputMethodEvent class, 161
    InternalFrameEvent class, 165
    InvocationEvent class, 171
    ItemEvent class, 176
    KeyEvent class, 182
    MouseEvent class, 214
    TextEvent class, 240

INDEX

WindowEvent class, 265
peekEvent() method
    EventQueue class, 72
pop() method
    EventQueue class, 72
popupMenuCanceled() method
    PopupMenuListener interface, 364
PopupMenuEvent class, 29, 219
PopupMenuListener interface, 41, 363
    addPopupMenuListener(), 364
    popupMenuCanceled(), 364
    popupMenuWillBecomeInvisible(), 364
    popupMenuWillBecomeVisible(), 364
    removePopupMenuListener(), 364
popupMenuWillBecomeInvisible() method
    PopupMenuListener interface, 364
popupMenuWillBecomeVisible() method
    PopupMenuListener interface, 364
postActionEvent() method
    JTextField class, 442
postEdit() method
    UndoableEditSupport class, 277
postEvent() method
    Component class, 20, 428
    EventQueue class, 72
processActionEvent() method
    Button class, 21, 423
    List class, 443
    MenuItem class, 444
    TextField class, 447
processComponentEvent() method
    Component class, 18, 425
processComponentKeyEvent() method
    JComponent class, 434
    JEditorPane class, 436
processContainerEvent() method
    Container class, 430
processEvent() method
    Button class, 21, 423
    Checkbox class, 424
    CheckboxMenuItem class, 424
    Component class, 18, 425
    Container class, 430
    List class, 443
    MenuComponent class, 444
    MenuItem class, 444
    TextComponent class, 446
    TextField class, 447
    Window class, 448
processFocusEvent() method
    Component class, 18, 425
    JComponent class, 434

processHierarchyBoundsEvent() method
    Component class, 18, 425
process HierarchyEvent() method
    Component class, 18, 426
processInputMethodEvent() method
    Component class, 18, 426
processItemEvent() method
    Checkbox class, 424
    CheckboxMenuItem class, 424
    List class, 443
processKeyEvent() method
    Component class, 18, 426
    JApplet class, 433
    JComboBox class, 433
    JComponent class, 434
    JDialog class, 435
    JEditorPane class, 436
    JFrame class, 436
    JMenu class, 437
    JMenuBar class, 438
    JMenuItem class, 439
    JPopupMenu class, 440
    JTextArea class, 442
processMenuDragMouseEvent() method
    JMenuItem class, 439
processMenuKeyEvent() method
    JMenuItem class, 439
processMouseEvent() method
    Component class, 18, 426
    JMenuBar class, 438
    JMenuItem class, 439
    JPopupMenu class, 440
processMouseMotionEvent() method
    Component class, 18, 426
    JComponent class, 434
processTextEvent() method
    TextComponent class, 446
processWindowEvent() method
    JDialog class, 435
    JFrame class, 436
    Window class, 448
propertyChange() method
    PropertyChangeListener interface, 366
PropertyChangeEvent class, 32, 223
    getNewValue(), 224
    getOldValue(), 224
    getPropagationID(), 224
    getPropertyName(), 224
PropertyChangeListener interface, 42, 366
    addPropertyChangeListener(), 366
    propertyChange(), 366
    removePropertyChangeListener(), 366

PropertyChangeSupport class, 32, 270
    addPropertyChangeListener(), 271
    firePropertyChange(), 271
    hasListeners(), 271
    removePropertyChangeListener(), 271
push() method
    EventQueue class, 72

R

RemoteDiscoveryEvent class, 518
    getGroups(), 520
    getRegistrars(), 520
    isDiscarded(), 520
RemoteEvent class, 516
    getID(), 517
    getRegistrationObject(), 517
    getSequenceNumber(), 517
RemoteEventListener interface, 527
    notify(), 527
Remote interface, 526
remove() method
    AWTEventMulticaster class, 455
    EventListenerList class, 462
removeActionListener() method, 297
removeAdjustmentListener() method, 299
removeAncestorListener() method, 301
removeAWTEventListener() method, 302
removeCaretListener() method, 305
removeCellEditorListener() method, 307
removeChangeListener() method, 311
removeColumnModelListener() method, 368
removeComponentListener() method, 314
removeContainerListener() method, 318
removeDocumentListener() method, 319
removeFocusListener() method, 322
removeHierarchyBoundsListener() method, 324
removeHierarchyListener() method, 327
removeHyperlinkListener() method, 332
removeInputMethodListener() method, 334
removeInternal() method
    AWTEventMulticaster class, 456
removeInternalFrameListener() method, 336
removeItemListener() method, 338
removeKeyListener() method, 340
removeListDataListener() method, 343
removeListSelectionListener() method, 345
removeMenuDragMouseListener() method, 347
removeMenuKeyListener() method, 349
removeMenuListener() method, 351
removeMouseListener() method, 357
removeMouseMotionListener() method, 361
removePopupMenuListener() method, 364

removePropertyChangeListener() method
    PropertyChangeSupport class, 271
    SwingPropertyChangeSupport class, 273
removeTableModelListener() method, 370
removeTextListener() method, 372
removeTreeExpansionListener() method, 373
removeTreeModelListener() method, 378
removeTreeSelectionListener() method, 379
removeTreeWillExpandListener() method, 381
removeUndoableEditListener() method
    UndoableEditSupport class, 277
removeUpdate() method
    DocumentListener interface, 319
removeVetoableChangeListener() method
    VetoableChangeSupport class, 285
removeWindowListener() method, 387
RenewalFailureEvent class, 521
    getLease(), 522
    getThrowable(), 522

S

save() method
    AWTEventMulticaster class, 456
saveInternal() method
    AWTEventMulticaster class, 456
ServiceEvent class, 523
    getServiceID(), 525
    getServiceItem(), 525
    getTransition(), 525
setKeyChar() method
    KeyEvent class, 183
setKeyCode() method
    KeyEvent class, 183
setModifiers() method
    KeyEvent class, 183
setPropagationID() method
    PropertyChangeEvent class, 224
setSource() method
    KeyEvent class, 183
Stagnation point heating, 483
stateChanged() method
    ChangeListener interface, 311
Style interface, 497
SwingPropertyChangeSupport class, 31, 272
    addPropertyChangeListener(), 273
    firePropertyChange(), 273
    hasListeners(), 273
    removePropertyChangeListener() 273

T

tableChanged() method
    TableModelListener interface, 370

INDEX

TableColumnModelEvent class, 29, 230
   getFromIndex(), 231
   getToIndex(), 231
TableColumnModelListener interface, 41, 367
   addColumnModelListener(), 368
   columnAdded(), 368
   columnMarginChanged(), 368
   columnMoved(), 368
   columnRemoved(), 368
   columnSelectionChanged(), 368
   removeColumnModelListener() 368
TableModelEvent class, 29, 234
   getFirstRow(), 236
   getLastRow(), 236
   getColumn(), 236
   getType(), 236
TableModelListener interface, 41, 369
   addTableModelListener(), 370
   removeTableModelListener(), 370
   tableChanged(), 370
TextEvent class, 27, 239
   paramString() , 240
TextListener interface, 40, 371
   addTextListener(), 372
   removeTextListener(), 372
   textValueChanged(), 372
textValueChanged() method
   AWTEventMulticaster class, 455
   TextListener interface, 372
toString() method
   AWTEvent class, 105
   EventListenerList class, 462
   EventObject class, 130
   ListSelectionEvent class, 193
   TreeModelEvent class, 249
   UndoableEditSupport class, 277
translatePoint() method
   MouseEvent class, 214
treeCollapsed() method
   TreeExpansionListener interface, 373
treeExpanded() method
   TreeExpansionListener interface, 373
TreeExpansionEvent class, 29, 243
   getPath(), 244
TreeExpansionListener interface, 41, 372
   addTreeExpansionListener(), 373
   removeTreeExpansionListener(), 373
   treeCollapsed(), 373
   treeExpanded(), 373
TreeModelEvent class, 29, 248
   getChildIndices(), 249
   getChildren(), 249

   getPath(), 249
   getTreePath(), 249
   toString(), 249
TreeModelListener interface, 41, 376
   addTreeModelListener(), 378
   treeNodesChanged(), 377
   treeNodesInserted(), 377
   treeNodesRemoved(), 377
   treeStructureChanged(), 377
   removeTreeModelListener(), 378
treeNodesChanged() method
   TreeModelListener interface, 377
treeNodesInserted() method
   TreeModelListener interface, 377
treeNodesRemoved() method
   TreeModelListener interface, 377
TreeSelectionEvent class, 29, 253
   cloneWithSource(), 255
   getNewLeadSelectionPath(), 255
   getOldLeadSelectionPath(), 255
   getPath(), 255
   getPaths(), 255
   isAddedPath(), 255
TreeSelectionListener interface, 42, 378
   addTreeSelectionListener(), 379
   removeTreeSelectionListener(), 379
   valueChanged(), 379
treeStructureChanged() method
   TreeModelListener interface, 377
treeWillCollapse() method
   TreeWillExpandListener interface, 381
treeWillExpand() method
   TreeWillExpandListener interface, 381
TreeWillExpandListener interface, 42, 380
   addTreeWillExpandListener(), 381
   removeTreeWillExpandListener(), 381
   treeWillCollapse(), 381
   treeWillExpand(), 381

U
UndoableEditEvent class, 29, 258
   getEdit(), 259
undoableEditHappened() method
   UndoableEditListener interface, 383
UndoableEditListener interface, 42, 382
   addUndoableEditListener(), 383
   removeUndoableEditListener(), 383
   undoableEditHappened(), 383
UndoableEditSupport class, 32, 276
   _postEdit(), 277
   addUndoableEditListener(), 277
   beginUpdate(), 277

UndoableEditSupport class *(cont.)*
    createCompoundEdit(), 277
    endUpdate(), 277
    getUpdateLevel(), 277
    postEdit(), 277
    removeUndoableEditListener(), 277
    toString(), 277
UnsolicitedNotificationEvent class, 268
UnsolicitedNotificationListener interface, 390
User-defined event listeners, 54, 472
User-defined events, 36, 473
User-generated events, 33

V

valueChanged() method
    ListSelectionListener interface, 345
    TreeSelectionListener interface, 379
vetoableChange() method
    VetoableChangeListener interface, 384
VetoableChangeListener interface, 42, 383
    addVetoableChangeListener(), 384
    removeVetoableChangeListener(), 385
    vetoableChange(), 384
VetoableChangeSupport class, 32, 284
    addVetoableChangeListener(), 285
    fireVetoableChange(), 285
    hasListeners(), 285
    removeVetoableChangeListener(), 285

W

windowActivated() method
    AWTEventMulticaster class, 455
    WindowAdapter class, 417
    WindowListener interface, 386
WindowAdapter class, 417
    windowActivated(), 417
    windowClosed(), 417
    windowClosing(), 417
    windowDeactivated(), 417

windowDeiconified(), 417
windowIconified(), 418
windowOpened(), 418
windowClosed() method
    AWTEventMulticaster class, 455
    WindowAdapter class, 417
    WindowListener interface, 386
windowClosing() method
    AWTEventMulticaster class, 455
    WindowAdapter class, 417
    WindowListener interface, 386
windowDeactivated() method
    AWTEventMulticaster class, 455
    WindowAdapter class, 417
    WindowListener interface, 386
windowDeiconified() method
    AWTEventMulticaster class, 455
    WindowAdapter class, 417
    WindowListener interface, 386
WindowEvent class, 26, 263
    getWindow() , 265
    paramString(), 265
windowIconified() method
    AWTEventMulticaster class, 455
    WindowAdapter class, 418
    WindowListener interface, 386
WindowListener interface, 40, 385
    addWindowListener(), 387
    windowActivated(), 386
    windowClosed(), 386
    windowClosing(), 386
    windowDeactivated(), 386
    windowDeiconified(), 386
    windowIconified(), 386
    windowOpened(), 386
    removeWindowListener(), 387
windowOpened() method
    AWTEventMulticaster class, 455
    WindowAdapter class, 418
    WindowListener interface, 386

PRENTICE HALL
Professional Technical Reference
Tomorrow's Solutions for Today's Professionals.

Keep Up-to-Date with
PH PTR Online!

We strive to stay on the cutting edge of what's happening in professional computer science and engineering. Here's a bit of what you'll find when you stop by **www.phptr.com**:

- **Special interest areas** offering our latest books, book series, software, features of the month, related links and other useful information to help you get the job done.

- **Deals, deals, deals!** Come to our promotions section for the latest bargains offered to you exclusively from our retailers.

- **Need to find a bookstore?** Chances are, there's a bookseller near you that carries a broad selection of PTR titles. Locate a Magnet bookstore near you at www.phptr.com.

- **What's new at PH PTR?** We don't just publish books for the professional community, we're a part of it. Check out our convention schedule, join an author chat, get the latest reviews and press releases on topics of interest to you.

- **Subscribe today! Join PH PTR's monthly email newsletter!**

Want to be kept up-to-date on your area of interest? Choose a targeted category on our website, and we'll keep you informed of the latest PH PTR products, author events, reviews and conferences in your interest area.

Visit our mailroom to subscribe today! **http://www.phptr.com/mail_lists**

LICENSE AGREEMENT AND LIMITED WARRANTY

READ THE FOLLOWING TERMS AND CONDITIONS CAREFULLY BEFORE OPENING THIS CD PACKAGE. THIS LEGAL DOCUMENT IS AN AGREEMENT BETWEEN YOU AND PRENTICE-HALL, INC. (THE "COMPANY"). BY OPENING THIS SEALED CD PACKAGE, YOU ARE AGREEING TO BE BOUND BY THESE TERMS AND CONDITIONS. IF YOU DO NOT AGREE WITH THESE TERMS AND CONDITIONS, DO NOT OPEN THE CD PACKAGE. PROMPTLY RETURN THE UNOPENED CD PACKAGE AND ALL ACCOMPANYING ITEMS TO THE PLACE YOU OBTAINED THEM FOR A FULL REFUND OF ANY SUMS YOU HAVE PAID.

1. **GRANT OF LICENSE:** In consideration of your purchase of this book, and your agreement to abide by the terms and conditions of this Agreement, the Company grants to you a nonexclusive right to use and display the copy of the enclosed software program (hereinafter the "SOFTWARE") on a single computer (i.e., with a single CPU) at a single location so long as you comply with the terms of this Agreement. The Company reserves all rights not expressly granted to you under this Agreement.

2. **OWNERSHIP OF SOFTWARE:** You own only the magnetic or physical media (the enclosed CD) on which the SOFTWARE is recorded or fixed, but the Company and the software developers retain all the rights, title, and ownership to the SOFTWARE recorded on the original CD copy(ies) and all subsequent copies of the SOFTWARE, regardless of the form or media on which the original or other copies may exist. This license is not a sale of the original SOFTWARE or any copy to you.

3. **COPY RESTRICTIONS:** This SOFTWARE and the accompanying printed materials and user manual (the "Documentation") are the subject of copyright. The individual programs on the CD are copyrighted by the authors of each program. Some of the programs on the CD include separate licensing agreements. If you intend to use one of these programs, you must read and follow its accompanying license agreement. You may not copy the Documentation or the SOFTWARE, except that you may make a single copy of the SOFTWARE for backup or archival purposes only. You may be held legally responsible for any copying or copyright infringement which is caused or encouraged by your failure to abide by the terms of this restriction.

4. **USE RESTRICTIONS:** You may not network the SOFTWARE or otherwise use it on more than one computer or computer terminal at the same time. You may physically transfer the SOFTWARE from one computer to another provided that the SOFTWARE is used on only one computer at a time. You may not distribute copies of the SOFTWARE or Documentation to others. You may not reverse engineer, disassemble, decompile, modify, adapt, translate, or create derivative works based on the SOFTWARE or the Documentation without the prior written consent of the Company.

5. **TRANSFER RESTRICTIONS:** The enclosed SOFTWARE is licensed only to you and may not be transferred to any one else without the prior written consent of the Company. Any unauthorized transfer of the SOFTWARE shall result in the immediate termination of this Agreement.

6. **TERMINATION:** This license is effective until terminated. This license will terminate automatically without notice from the Company and become null and void if you fail to comply with any provisions or limitations of this license. Upon termination, you shall destroy the Documentation and all copies of the SOFTWARE. All provisions of this Agreement as to warranties, limitation of liability, remedies or damages, and our ownership rights shall survive termination.

7. **MISCELLANEOUS:** This Agreement shall be construed in accordance with the laws of the United States of America and the State of New York and shall benefit the Company, its affiliates, and assignees.

8. **LIMITED WARRANTY AND DISCLAIMER OF WARRANTY:** The Company warrants that the SOFTWARE, when properly used in accordance with the Documentation, will operate in substantial conformity with the description of the SOFTWARE set forth in the Documentation. The Company does not warrant that the SOFTWARE will meet your requirements or that the operation

of the SOFTWARE will be uninterrupted or error-free. The Company warrants that the media on which the SOFTWARE is delivered shall be free from defects in materials and workmanship under normal use for a period of thirty (30) days from the date of your purchase. Your only remedy and the Company's only obligation under these limited warranties is, at the Company's option, return of the warranted item for a refund of any amounts paid by you or replacement of the item. Any replacement of SOFTWARE or media under the warranties shall not extend the original warranty period. The limited warranty set forth above shall not apply to any SOFTWARE which the Company determines in good faith has been subject to misuse, neglect, improper installation, repair, alteration, or damage by you. EXCEPT FOR THE EXPRESSED WARRANTIES SET FORTH ABOVE, THE COMPANY DISCLAIMS ALL WARRANTIES, EXPRESS OR IMPLIED, INCLUDING WITHOUT LIMITATION, THE IMPLIED WARRANTIES OF MERCHANTABILITY AND FITNESS FOR A PARTICULAR PURPOSE. EXCEPT FOR THE EXPRESS WARRANTY SET FORTH ABOVE, THE COMPANY DOES NOT WARRANT, GUARANTEE, OR MAKE ANY REPRESENTATION REGARDING THE USE OR THE RESULTS OF THE USE OF THE SOFTWARE IN TERMS OF ITS CORRECTNESS, ACCURACY, RELIABILITY, CURRENTNESS, OR OTHERWISE.

IN NO EVENT, SHALL THE COMPANY OR ITS EMPLOYEES, AGENTS, SUPPLIERS, OR CONTRACTORS BE LIABLE FOR ANY INCIDENTAL, INDIRECT, SPECIAL, OR CONSEQUENTIAL DAMAGES ARISING OUT OF OR IN CONNECTION WITH THE LICENSE GRANTED UNDER THIS AGREEMENT, OR FOR LOSS OF USE, LOSS OF DATA, LOSS OF INCOME OR PROFIT, OR OTHER LOSSES, SUSTAINED AS A RESULT OF INJURY TO ANY PERSON, OR LOSS OF OR DAMAGE TO PROPERTY, OR CLAIMS OF THIRD PARTIES, EVEN IF THE COMPANY OR AN AUTHORIZED REPRESENTATIVE OF THE COMPANY HAS BEEN ADVISED OF THE POSSIBILITY OF SUCH DAMAGES. IN NO EVENT SHALL LIABILITY OF THE COMPANY FOR DAMAGES WITH RESPECT TO THE SOFTWARE EXCEED THE AMOUNTS ACTUALLY PAID BY YOU, IF ANY, FOR THE SOFTWARE.

SOME JURISDICTIONS DO NOT ALLOW THE LIMITATION OF IMPLIED WARRANTIES OR LIABILITY FOR INCIDENTAL, INDIRECT, SPECIAL, OR CONSEQUENTIAL DAMAGES, SO THE ABOVE LIMITATIONS MAY NOT ALWAYS APPLY. THE WARRANTIES IN THIS AGREEMENT GIVE YOU SPECIFIC LEGAL RIGHTS AND YOU MAY ALSO HAVE OTHER RIGHTS WHICH VARY IN ACCORDANCE WITH LOCAL LAW.

ACKNOWLEDGMENT

YOU ACKNOWLEDGE THAT YOU HAVE READ THIS AGREEMENT, UNDERSTAND IT, AND AGREE TO BE BOUND BY ITS TERMS AND CONDITIONS. YOU ALSO AGREE THAT THIS AGREEMENT IS THE COMPLETE AND EXCLUSIVE STATEMENT OF THE AGREEMENT BETWEEN YOU AND THE COMPANY AND SUPERSEDES ALL PROPOSALS OR PRIOR AGREEMENTS, ORAL, OR WRITTEN, AND ANY OTHER COMMUNICATIONS BETWEEN YOU AND THE COMPANY OR ANY REPRESENTATIVE OF THE COMPANY RELATING TO THE SUBJECT MATTER OF THIS AGREEMENT.

Should you have any questions concerning this Agreement or if you wish to contact the Company for any reason, please contact in writing at the address below.

Robin Short

Prentice Hall PTR

One Lake Street

Upper Saddle River, New Jersey 07458

About the CD-ROM

This CD-ROM contains all of the examples described in this book. It contains not only the Java source code but also the associated HTML and JPEG files used with some of the examples. To run the examples, you must have Java JDK 1.3 installed on your system. Many of the examples use language elements that were introduced in JDK 1.3. To upgrade your system to version 1.3, see the Sun Web site at *http://java.sun.com*.

Any Windows or UNIX system that has Java JDK 1.3 installed can run the example code contained on this CD. Apple currently does not support JDK 1.3, although you may be able to find an IDE that be can used to run the examples on a Mac.

Simply load the CD into your machine and copy any or all of the files to your system. The examples are all standalone programs and are compiled and run in a similar fashion. For instance, to create the byte code for the SimpleExample.java program you would type

```
javac SimpleExample.java
```

To run the example, you would then type

```
java SimpleExample
```

There is a README file at the top of the CD directory structure that provides more details about downloading and running the examples.

Some text editors, for example SimpleText on a Mac, may not properly interpret the line breaks in the code listings. They may appear as symbols. To correct this, you can open the file in Microsoft Word and save it as a text-only file.

Technical Support

Prentice Hall does not offer technical support for any of the programs on the CD-ROM. However, if the CD is damaged, you may obtain a replacement copy by sending an email describing the problem to *disc_exchange@phptr.com*.